"DID YOU HEAR WHAT EDDIE GEIN DONE?"

Written by

HAROLD SCHECHTER

and

ERIC POWELL

Illustrated by

ERIC POWELL

Designed by

PHIL BALSMAN

Edited by

TRACY MARSH

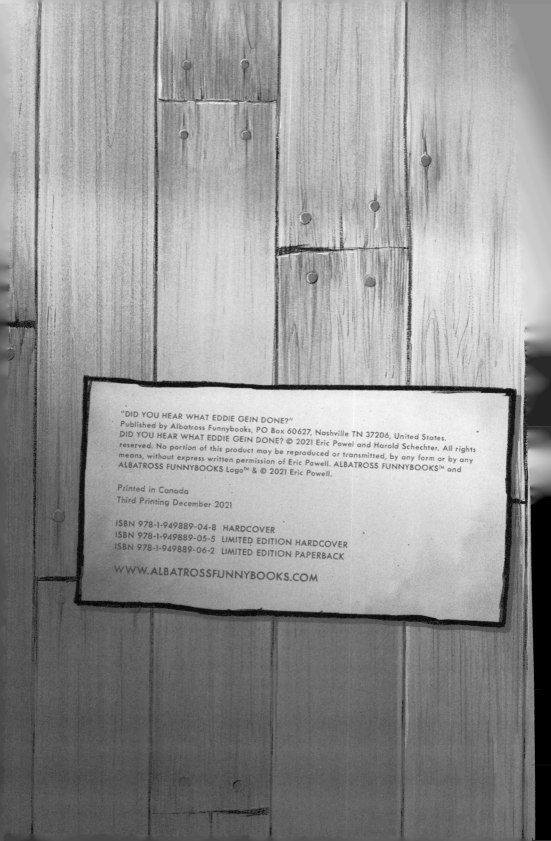

"DID YOU HEAR WHAT EDDIE GEIN DONE?"
Published by Albatross Funnybooks, PO Box 60627, Nashville TN 37206, United States.
DID YOU HEAR WHAT EDDIE GEIN DONE? © 2021 Eric Powel and Harold Schechter. All rights
reserved. No portion of this product may be reproduced or transmitted, by any form or by any
means, without express written permission of Eric Powell. ALBATROSS FUNNYBOOKS™ and
ALBATROSS FUNNYBOOKS Logo™ & © 2021 Eric Powell.

Printed in Canada
Third Printing December 2021

ISBN 978-1-949889-04-8 HARDCOVER
ISBN 978-1-949889-05-5 LIMITED EDITION HARDCOVER
ISBN 978-1-949889-06-2 LIMITED EDITION PAPERBACK

WWW.ALBATROSSFUNNYBOOKS.COM

TABLE OF CONTENTS

THANKS

Harold dedicates this book, with endless love, to the incomparable Kimiko Hahn.

Eric dedicates this book, with mild enthusiasm, to the kindest heart he knows, Andrea Smith.

Special thanks to David Fincher, John Carpenter, Sandy King, Scott Ian, Mike Mignola, Thierry Mornet, Denis Kitchen, William Stout and the home of cheese curds and the Green Bay Packers, the great state of Wisconsin.

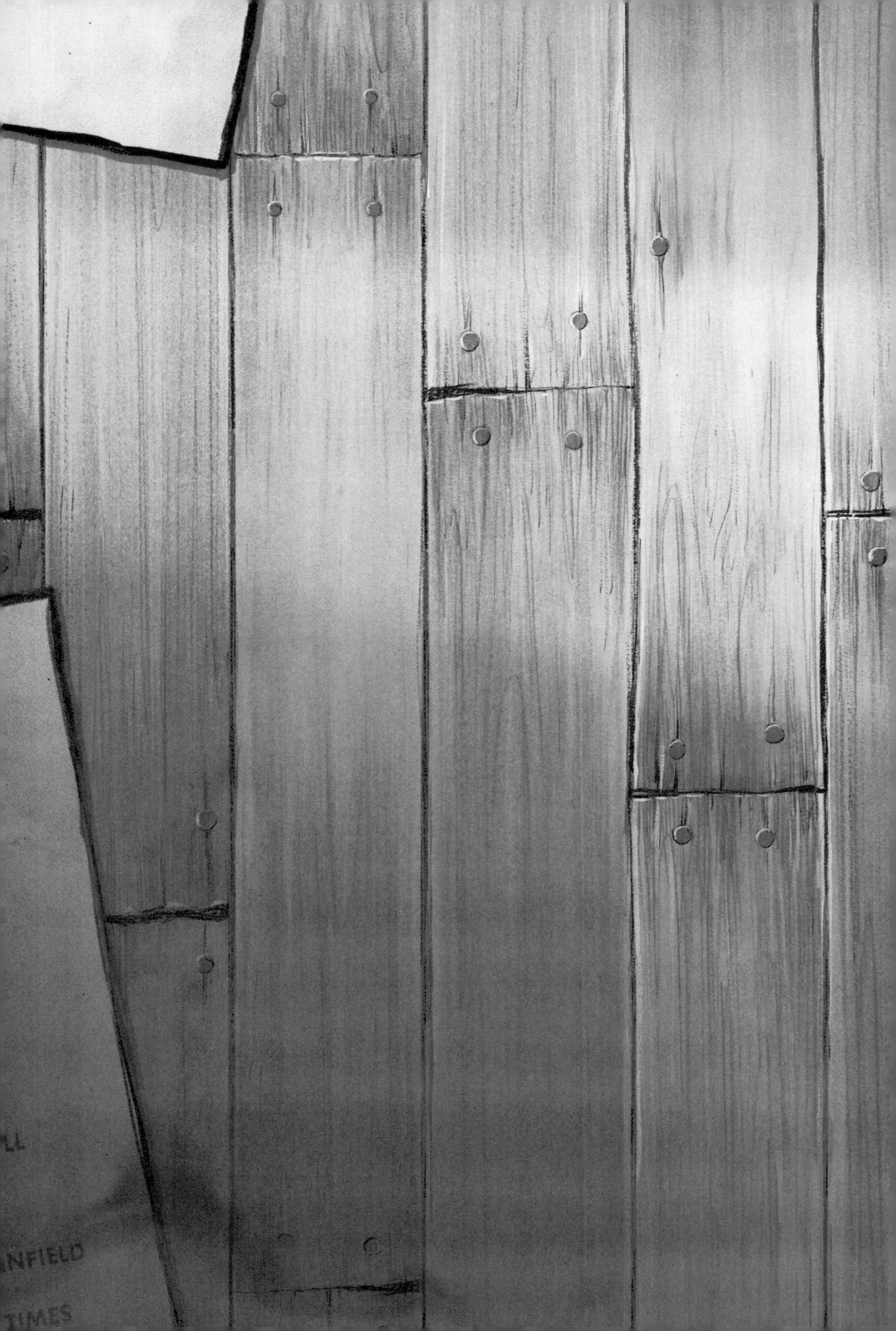
LL
NFIELD
TIMES

★ EXTRA ★   CHAPTER 1   ★ EXTRA ★

★★★ Tuesday, November 17th, 1957   10¢ ★★★

BASED ON A TRUE STORY

By Leland Bynquist
Lead reporter, Cita-Deal

Gein was in court again on Friday for a brief appearance before Circuit Judge Herbert A. Bunde. Dressed in baggy green work pants and a blue woolen jacket, Eddie, his stubbled face displaying no trace of emotion, was led into the large, high-ceilinged courtroom by Sheriff Schley. About eighty spectators, at least thirty of them newsmen, half filled the courtroom; the crowd was hushed as the fragile-looking "ghoul-slayer" was brought before the bench, though the stern photographers present were squirming with frustration. At Eddie's request, they had been barred by Judge Bunde, a stern, no-nonsense jurist, from taking pictures during the proceedings.

Throughout the week, rumors had continued to circulate that certain individuals in Plainfield were outraged at the notion that Gein, by pleading insanity, might evade punishment for his crimes. District Attorney Kileen had sought to reassure the public by stating categorically that "Gein would never walk the streets of Plainfield again." Still, there was a good deal of bitterness at the thought that Gein might end up in a mental hospital, which, as far as certain people were concerned, would be tantamount to his getting away with murder. Rumor, who had several years earlier been the first to notice

coming from the cemetery or noticed Gein's pickup truck parked there in the night and wondered what the strange little recluse was up to.

One person eminently qualified to comment on the situation was the sexton of the Plainfield cemetery, Pat Danna, who completely discounted Gein's story. Danna insisted that during the time he'd been caretaker, no graves had ever been molested. He was out at the cemetery all the time, mowing it once a week.

Still, of the few equally improbable alternatives, most Plainfield residents found it easier to conceive of Eddie Gein as a mass murderer than a ghoul. "The people here will have to be shown the dug-up graves before they'll believe it," Ed Mansilla told a reporter, summing up the sentiments of his fellow townspeople. And indeed, digging up some graves did seem to be the only way the matter would ever be definitively resolved.

At first, Kileen seemed strongly opposed to the idea of disinterment. As the district attorney of Waushara County, he was concerned only about the slaying of Mrs. Worden, to which Gein had already confessed. As for the other remains uncovered in Gein's charnel house, Kileen seemed willing to take the prisoner at his word. During a meeting with reporters on Wednesday, Kileen had announced that Waushara County was not about to

Handy Man Is Grilled by DA

Body of Missing Plainfield Woman Discovered at Farm Home of Ed Gein

By Kent Blake
Staff Reporter, Cita-Deal

Belter, who had announced several hours before that he intended to get an independent medical opinion on Gein's sanity from a Milwaukee psychiatrist, concurred with Kileen. He told the judge that Gein had admitted removing entire corpses and various body parts from graves. "Some mental aberration is involved," was Belter's assessment.

The entire arraignment lasted little more than five minutes. After listening to the recommendations of the prosecutor and the defense attorney,

counsel for the state and the counsel for the defendant," he said, "that expert determination be had whether he is now competent to stand trial," as well as whether he was sane at the time of Mrs. Worden's murder.

Then Bunde signed an order committing Eddie to the Central State Hospital for the Criminally Insane at Waupun for a thirty-day examination period and remanded him to the custody of Sheriff Schley, who led Eddie back to the jailhouse to await transportation to the

"You can't apply
morality to insane
persons."

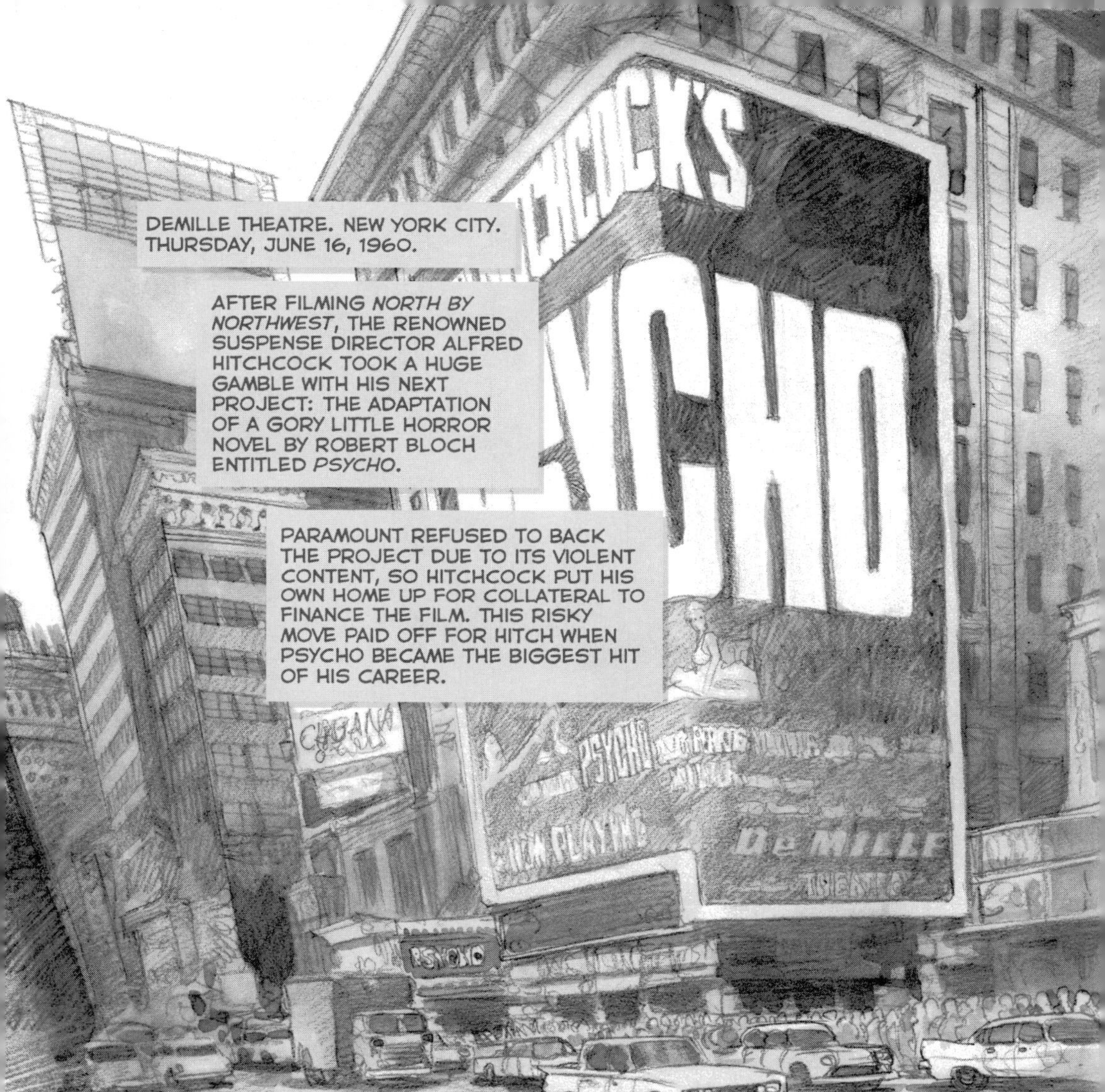
DEMILLE THEATRE. NEW YORK CITY.
THURSDAY, JUNE 16, 1960.
AFTER FILMING *NORTH BY NORTHWEST*, THE RENOWNED SUSPENSE DIRECTOR ALFRED HITCHCOCK TOOK A HUGE GAMBLE WITH HIS NEXT PROJECT: THE ADAPTATION OF A GORY LITTLE HORROR NOVEL BY ROBERT BLOCH ENTITLED *PSYCHO*.
PARAMOUNT REFUSED TO BACK THE PROJECT DUE TO ITS VIOLENT CONTENT, SO HITCHCOCK PUT HIS OWN HOME UP FOR COLLATERAL TO FINANCE THE FILM. THIS RISKY MOVE PAID OFF FOR HITCH WHEN PSYCHO BECAME THE BIGGEST HIT OF HIS CAREER.
PSYCHO
PSYCHO

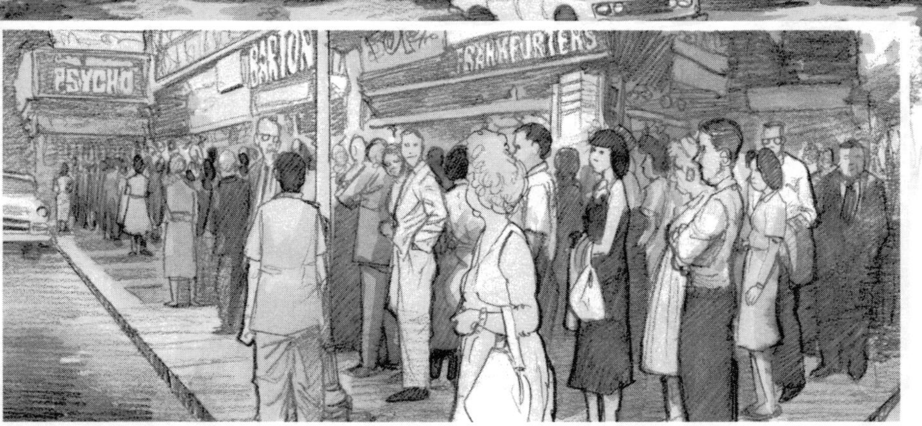
PSYCHO
FRANKFURTERS

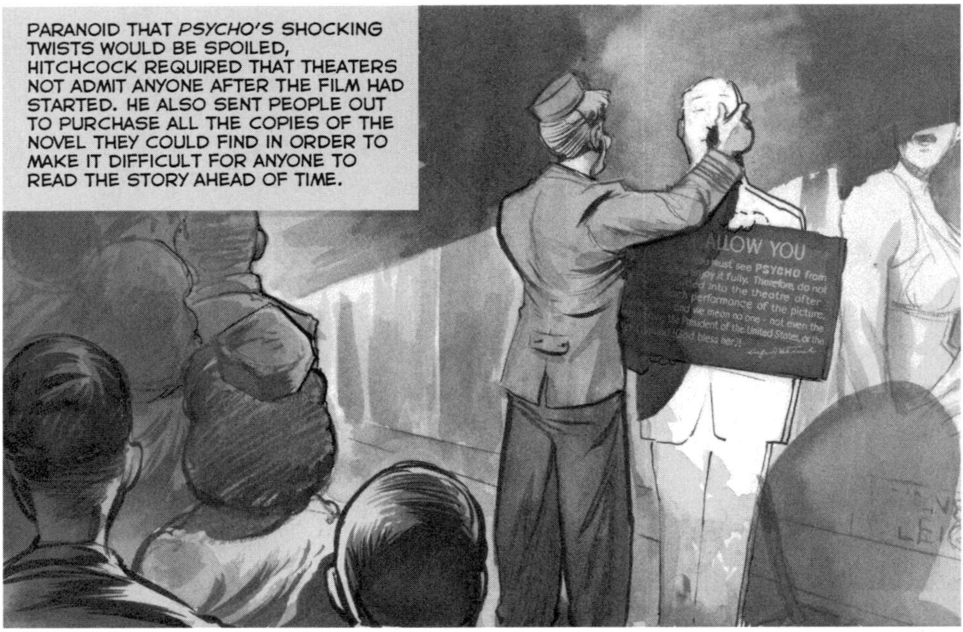
PARANOID THAT *PSYCHO*'S SHOCKING TWISTS WOULD BE SPOILED, HITCHCOCK REQUIRED THAT THEATERS NOT ADMIT ANYONE AFTER THE FILM HAD STARTED. HE ALSO SENT PEOPLE OUT TO PURCHASE ALL THE COPIES OF THE NOVEL THEY COULD FIND IN ORDER TO MAKE IT DIFFICULT FOR ANYONE TO READ THE STORY AHEAD OF TIME.

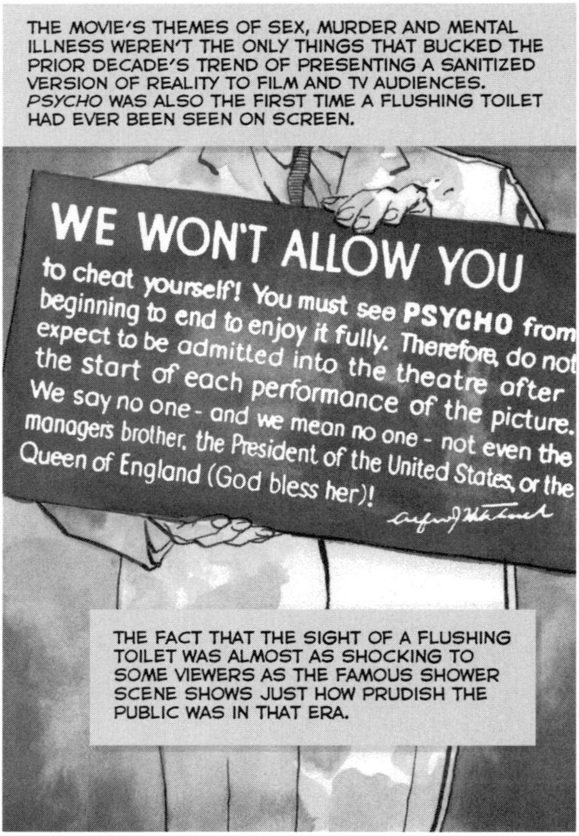
THE MOVIE'S THEMES OF SEX, MURDER AND MENTAL ILLNESS WEREN'T THE ONLY THINGS THAT BUCKED THE PRIOR DECADE'S TREND OF PRESENTING A SANITIZED VERSION OF REALITY TO FILM AND TV AUDIENCES. *PSYCHO* WAS ALSO THE FIRST TIME A FLUSHING TOILET HAD EVER BEEN SEEN ON SCREEN.
WE WON'T ALLOW YOU
to cheat yourself! You must see PSYCHO from
beginning to end to enjoy it fully. Therefore, do not
expect to be admitted into the theatre after
the start of each performance of the picture.
We say no one - and we mean no one - not even the
managers brother, the President of the United States, or the
Queen of England (God bless her)!
THE FACT THAT THE SIGHT OF A FLUSHING TOILET WAS ALMOST AS SHOCKING TO SOME VIEWERS AS THE FAMOUS SHOWER SCENE SHOWS JUST HOW PRUDISH THE PUBLIC WAS IN THAT ERA.

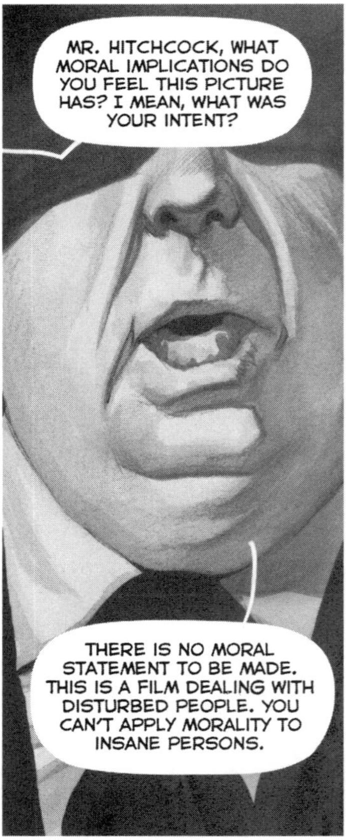
MR. HITCHCOCK, WHAT MORAL IMPLICATIONS DO YOU FEEL THIS PICTURE HAS? I MEAN, WHAT WAS YOUR INTENT?
THERE IS NO MORAL STATEMENT TO BE MADE. THIS IS A FILM DEALING WITH DISTURBED PEOPLE. YOU CAN'T APPLY MORALITY TO INSANE PERSONS.

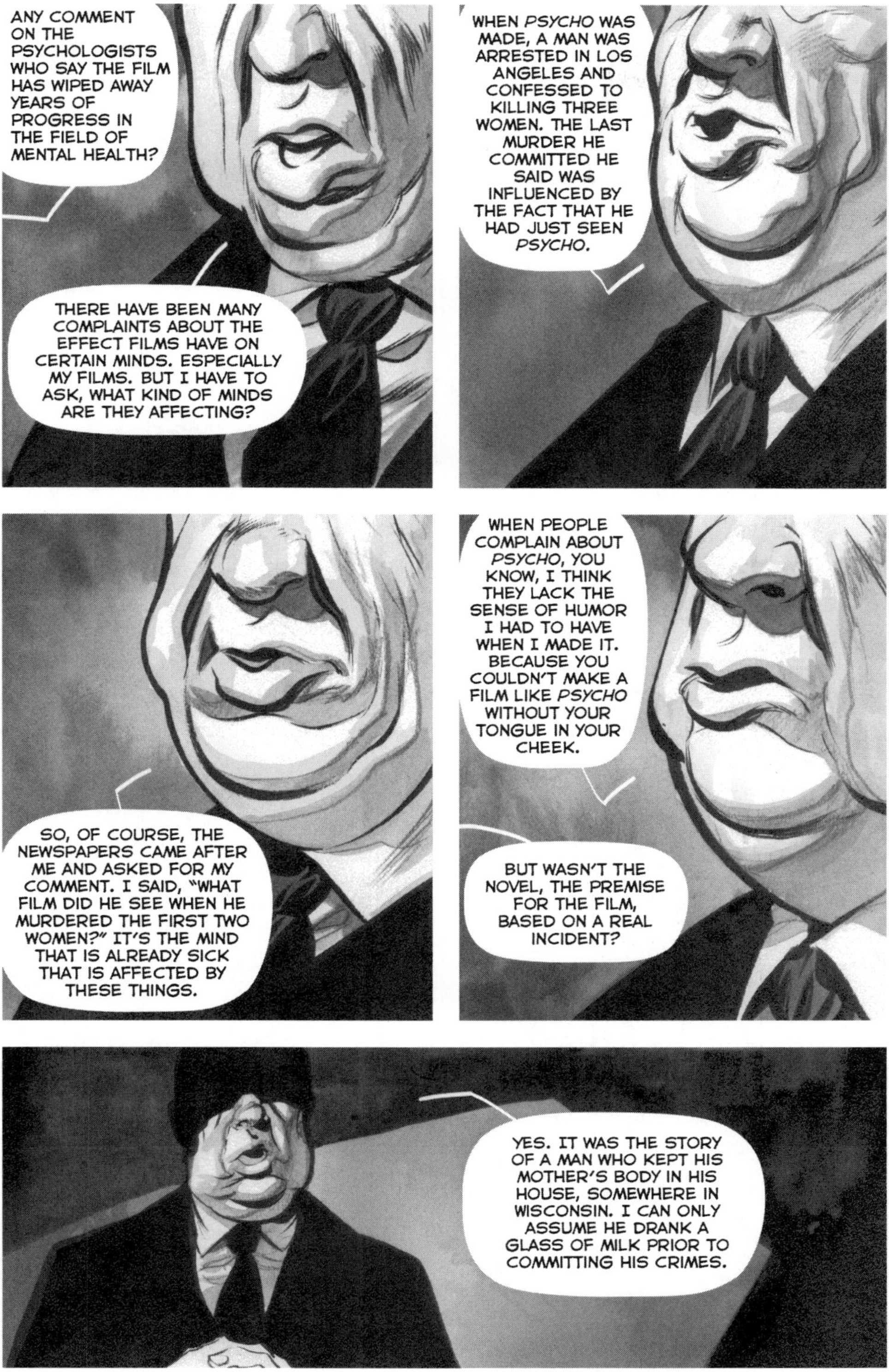
ANY COMMENT ON THE PSYCHOLOGISTS WHO SAY THE FILM HAS WIPED AWAY YEARS OF PROGRESS IN THE FIELD OF MENTAL HEALTH?
THERE HAVE BEEN MANY COMPLAINTS ABOUT THE EFFECT FILMS HAVE ON CERTAIN MINDS. ESPECIALLY MY FILMS. BUT I HAVE TO ASK, WHAT KIND OF MINDS ARE THEY AFFECTING?
WHEN *PSYCHO* WAS MADE, A MAN WAS ARRESTED IN LOS ANGELES AND CONFESSED TO KILLING THREE WOMEN. THE LAST MURDER HE COMMITTED HE SAID WAS INFLUENCED BY THE FACT THAT HE HAD JUST SEEN *PSYCHO*.
SO, OF COURSE, THE NEWSPAPERS CAME AFTER ME AND ASKED FOR MY COMMENT. I SAID, "WHAT FILM DID HE SEE WHEN HE MURDERED THE FIRST TWO WOMEN?" IT'S THE MIND THAT IS ALREADY SICK THAT IS AFFECTED BY THESE THINGS.
WHEN PEOPLE COMPLAIN ABOUT *PSYCHO*, YOU KNOW, I THINK THEY LACK THE SENSE OF HUMOR I HAD TO HAVE WHEN I MADE IT. BECAUSE YOU COULDN'T MAKE A FILM LIKE *PSYCHO* WITHOUT YOUR TONGUE IN YOUR CHEEK.
BUT WASN'T THE NOVEL, THE PREMISE FOR THE FILM, BASED ON A REAL INCIDENT?
YES. IT WAS THE STORY OF A MAN WHO KEPT HIS MOTHER'S BODY IN HIS HOUSE, SOMEWHERE IN WISCONSIN. I CAN ONLY ASSUME HE DRANK A GLASS OF MILK PRIOR TO COMMITTING HIS CRIMES.

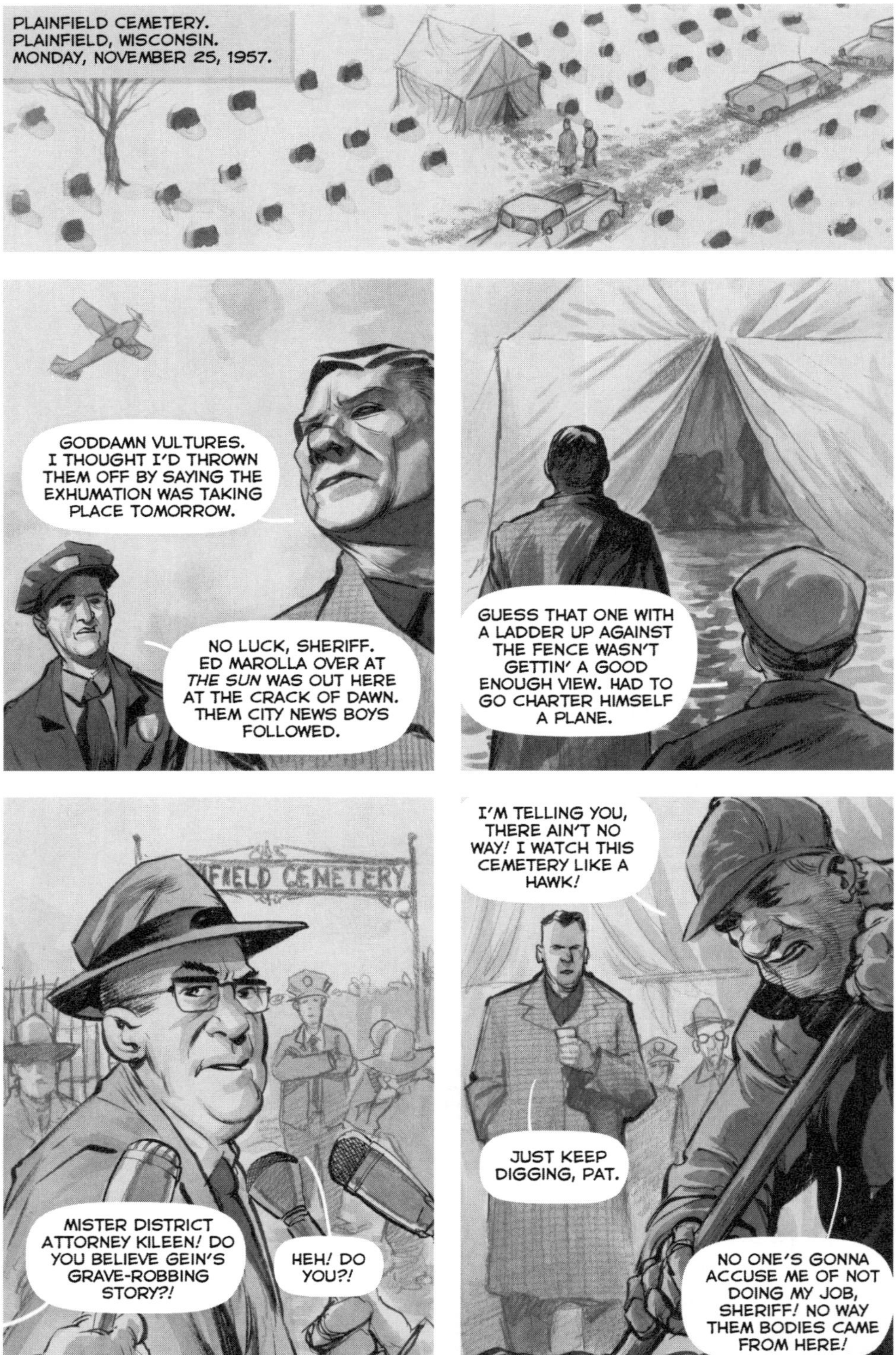
PLAINFIELD CEMETERY.
PLAINFIELD, WISCONSIN.
MONDAY, NOVEMBER 25, 1957.
GODDAMN VULTURES. I THOUGHT I'D THROWN THEM OFF BY SAYING THE EXHUMATION WAS TAKING PLACE TOMORROW.
NO LUCK, SHERIFF. ED MAROLLA OVER AT *THE SUN* WAS OUT HERE AT THE CRACK OF DAWN. THEM CITY NEWS BOYS FOLLOWED.
GUESS THAT ONE WITH A LADDER UP AGAINST THE FENCE WASN'T GETTIN' A GOOD ENOUGH VIEW. HAD TO GO CHARTER HIMSELF A PLANE.
FIELD CEMETERY
MISTER DISTRICT ATTORNEY KILEEN! DO YOU BELIEVE GEIN'S GRAVE-ROBBING STORY?!
HEH! DO YOU?!
I'M TELLING YOU, THERE AIN'T NO WAY! I WATCH THIS CEMETERY LIKE A HAWK!
JUST KEEP DIGGING, PAT.
NO ONE'S GONNA ACCUSE ME OF NOT DOING MY JOB, SHERIFF! NO WAY THEM BODIES CAME FROM HERE!

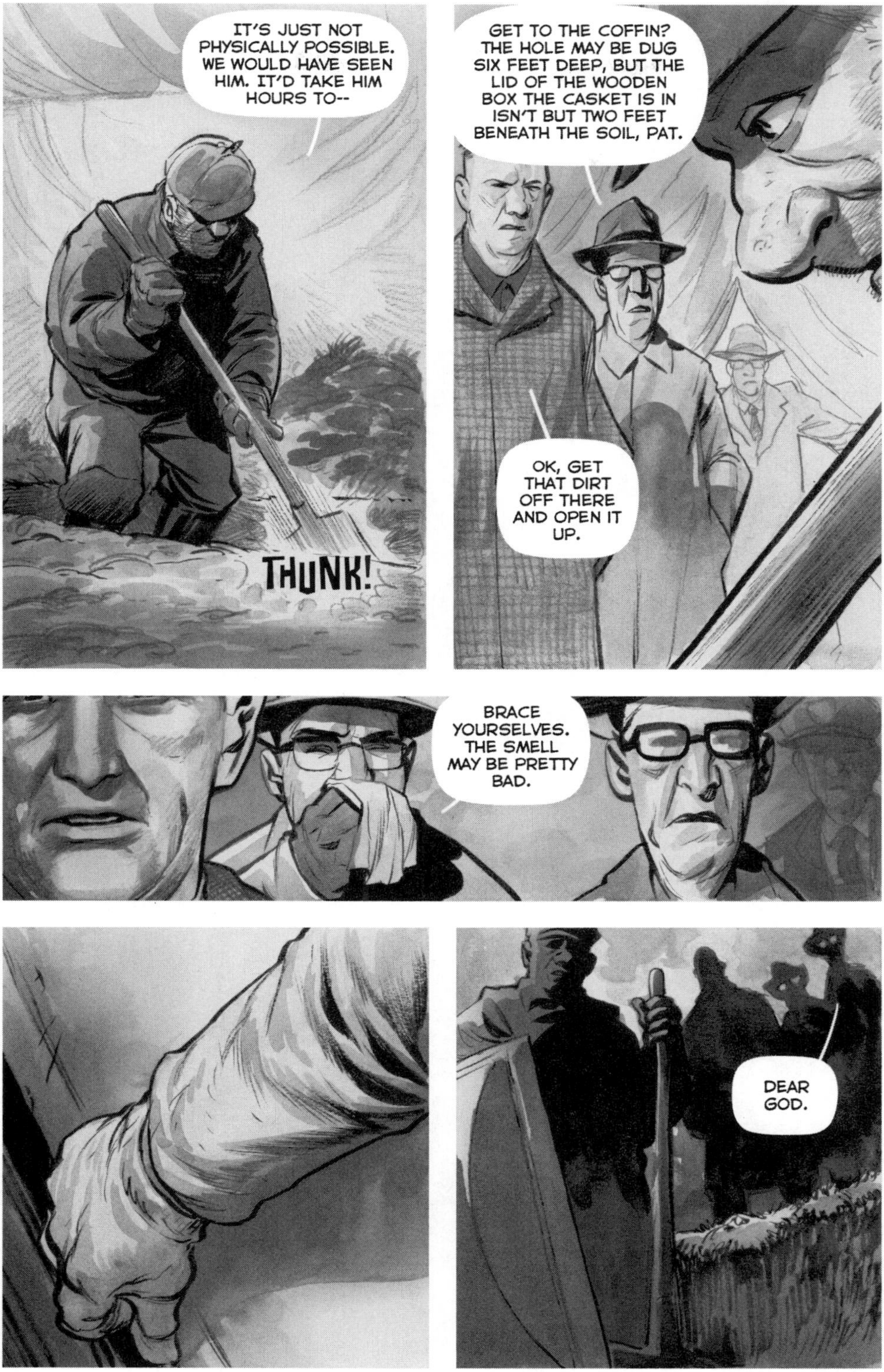
IT'S JUST NOT PHYSICALLY POSSIBLE. WE WOULD HAVE SEEN HIM. IT'D TAKE HIM HOURS TO--
THUNK!
GET TO THE COFFIN? THE HOLE MAY BE DUG SIX FEET DEEP, BUT THE LID OF THE WOODEN BOX THE CASKET IS IN ISN'T BUT TWO FEET BENEATH THE SOIL, PAT.
OK, GET THAT DIRT OFF THERE AND OPEN IT UP.
BRACE YOURSELVES. THE SMELL MAY BE PRETTY BAD.
DEAR GOD.

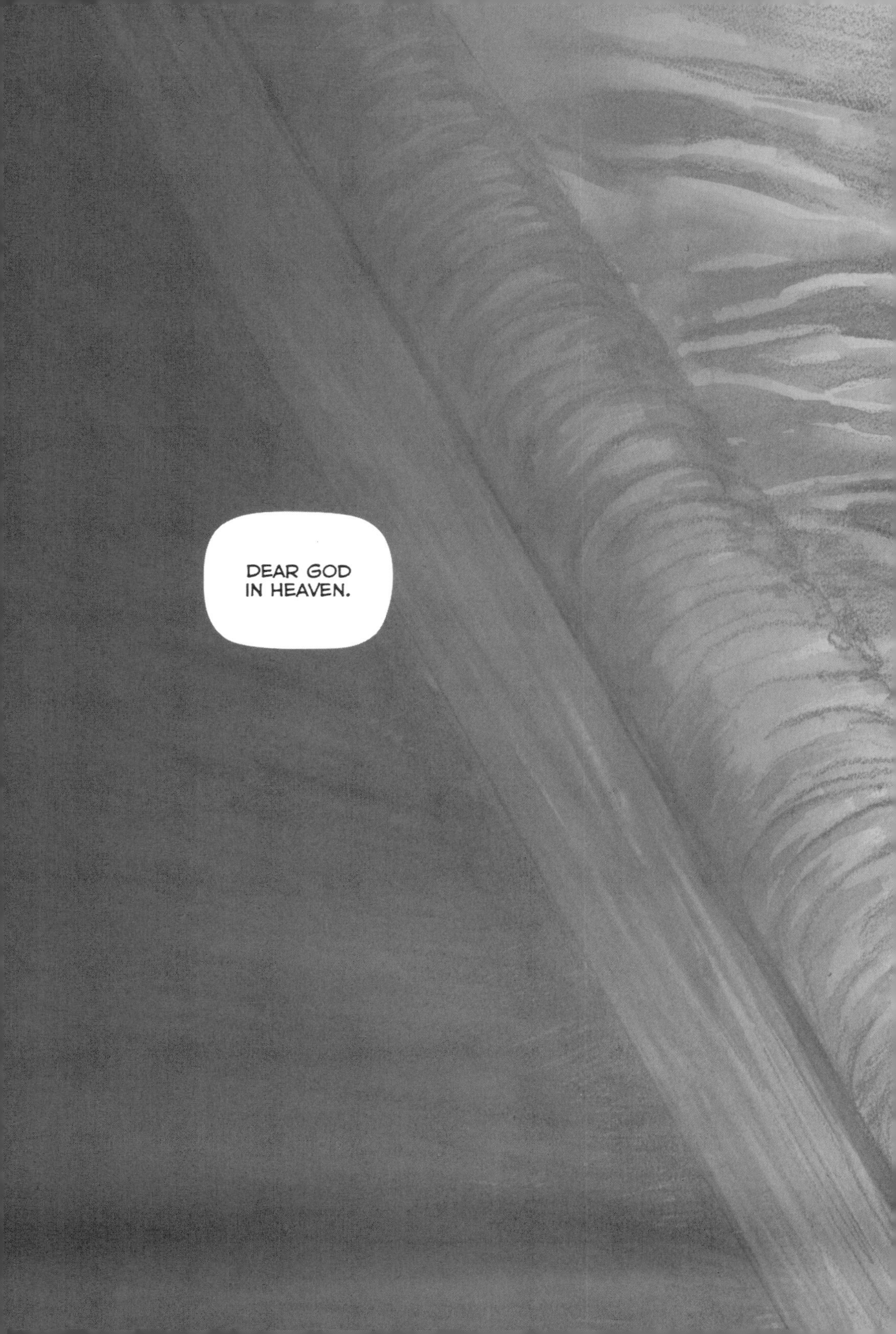
DEAR GOD
IN HEAVEN.

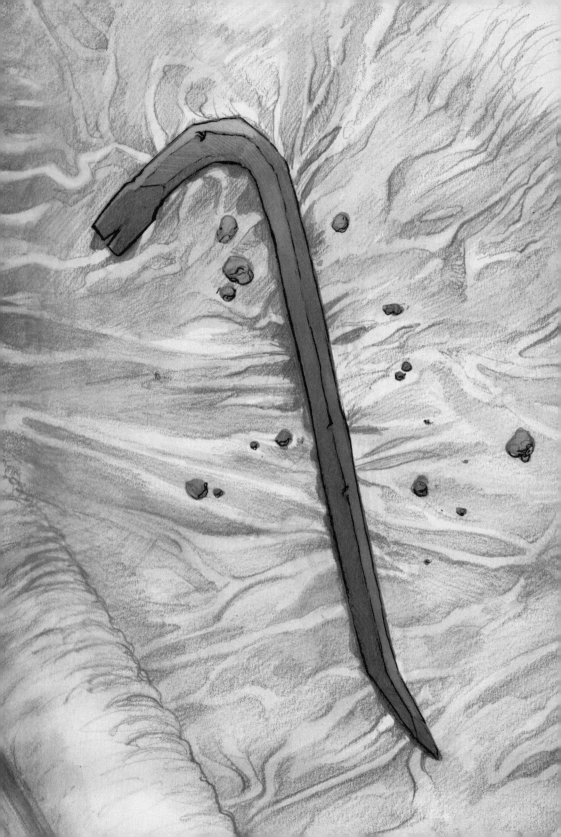

DAILY

CHAPTER 2

★ ★ ★ Thursday, November 19th, 1957

10¢ ★ ★ ★

BAD BEGINNINGS

By Dale Simons
Staff Reporter, City desk

Gein was in court again on Friday for a brief appearance before Circuit Judge Herbert A. Bunde. Dressed in baggy green work pants and a blue woolen jacket, Eddie, his stubbled face displaying no trace of emotion, was led into the large, high-ceilinged courtroom by Sheriff Schley.

About eighty spectators, at least thirty of them newsmen, half filled the courtroom. The crowd was hushed as the fragile-looking "ghoul-slayer" was brought before the bench, though the news photographers present were squirming with frustration. At Eddie's request, they had been barred by Judge Bunde, a stern, no-nonsense jurist, from taking pictures during the proceedings. Throughout the week, rumors had continued to circulate that certain individuals in Plainfield were outraged at the notion that Gein, by pleading insanity, might evade punishment for his crimes.

District Attorney Kileen had sought to reassure the public by stating categorically that "Gein would never walk the streets of Plainfield again." Still, there was a great deal of bitterness as the thought that Gein might end up in a mental hospital, which, as far as certain people were concerned, would be

determination he had whether he is now competent to stand trial," as well as whether he won one at the time of Mrs. Worden's murder.

Then Bunde signed an order committing Eddie to the Central State Hospital for the Criminally Insane at Waupun for a thirty-day examination period and remanded him to the custody of Sheriff Schley, to await transportation to the mental institution.

Though Gein was a wiry fellow, it seemed impossible that he could have had the strength to dig up a grave by himself, break open the casket, remove the corpse and perform its grisly operations on it, then rebury the coffin and smooth over the sandy soil so that no trace of his crime remained—all in the space of a few hours.

Moreover, the townspeople didn't see how such an activity could possibly have gone undetected, particularly over the course of several years. Gein, they argued, would have had to perform his nocturnal pillaging by lantern light, and even in an area as isolated and lonely as Plainfield, it is hardly conceivable that no one would have spotted a suspicious glow coming from the cemetery or noticed Gein's pickup truck parked there in the

dug-up graves before they'd believe it," Ed Marolla told a reporter, summing up the sentiments of his fellow townspeople. And indeed, digging up some of graves did seem to be the only way the matter would ever be definitively resolved.

At first, Kileen seemed strongly opposed to the idea of disinterment. As the district attorney of Waushara County, he was concerned only about the slaying of Mrs. Worden, in which Gein had already confessed. As the other remains were uncovered in Gein's charnel house, Kileen seemed willing to take the prisoner at his word.

During a meeting with reporters on Wednesday, Kileen had announced that Eddie, to the Central State Hospital for the Criminally Insane at Waupun for a thirty-day examination period and remanded him to the custody of Sheriff Schley, who had Eddie back to the jailhouse to await transportation to the mental institution.

Ed Gein Will Appear Before Judge Bunde

By Leeland Byngurst
Lead reporter, City desk

The arrest arrangement lasted little more than five minutes. After listening to the recommendations of the prosecutor and the defense attorney, Judge Bunde made a statement.

"It now seems advisable under the circumstances as related by both the counsel for the state and the counsel for the defendant," he said, "that expert determination be had whether he is now competent to stand trial," as well as whether he was sane at the time of Mrs. Worden's murder.

Then Bunde signed an order committing Eddie to the Central State Hospital for the Criminally Insane at Waupun for a thirty-day examination period and remanded him to the custody of Sheriff Schley, who had Eddie back to the jailhouse to await transportation to the mental institution.

no trace of his crime remained—all in the space of a few hours. Moreover, the townspeople didn't see how such an activity could possibly have gone undetected, particularly over the course of several years. Gein, they argued, would have had to perform his nocturnal pillaging by lantern light, and even in an area as isolated and lonely as Plainfield, it hardly seemed credible that no one would have to the recommendations of the prosecutor and the defense attorney. Judge Bunde made a statement.

"It now seems advisable under the circumstances as related by both the counsel for the state and the counsel for the defendant," he said, "that expert determination be had whether he is now competent to stand trial," as well as whether he was sane at the time of Mrs. Worden's murder.

Then Bunde signed an order committing Eddie to the Central State Hospital for the Criminally Insane at Waupun for a thirty-day

Discovered at Farm Home

By Ken Blake
Staff reporter, City desk

"Well, you won't grow up to be like the rest of them, God as my witness, I'll see to that."

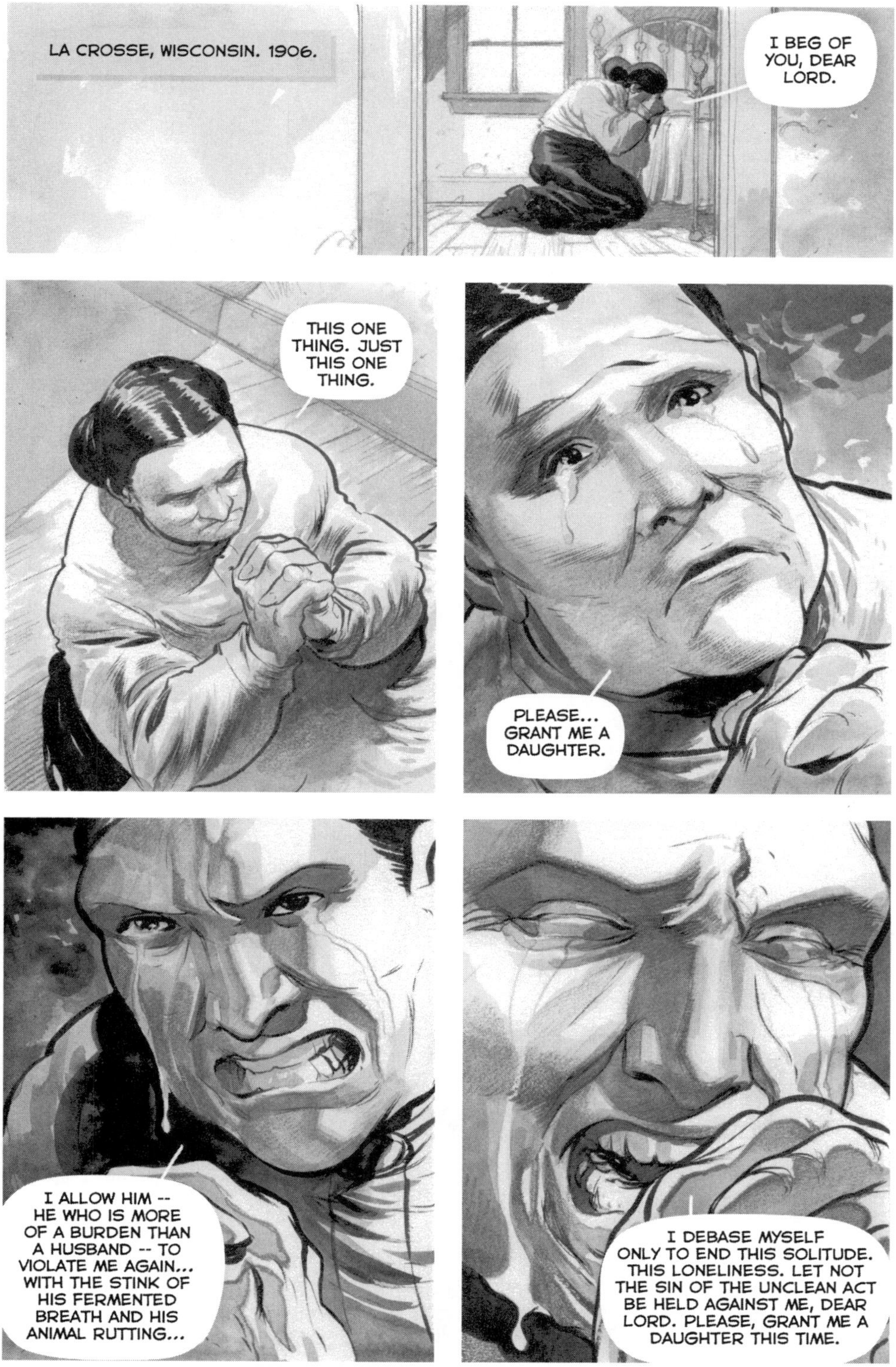
LA CROSSE, WISCONSIN. 1906.
I BEG OF YOU, DEAR LORD.
THIS ONE THING. JUST THIS ONE THING.
PLEASE... GRANT ME A DAUGHTER.
I ALLOW HIM -- HE WHO IS MORE OF A BURDEN THAN A HUSBAND -- TO VIOLATE ME AGAIN... WITH THE STINK OF HIS FERMENTED BREATH AND HIS ANIMAL RUTTING...
I DEBASE MYSELF ONLY TO END THIS SOLITUDE. THIS LONELINESS. LET NOT THE SIN OF THE UNCLEAN ACT BE HELD AGAINST ME, DEAR LORD. PLEASE, GRANT ME A DAUGHTER THIS TIME.

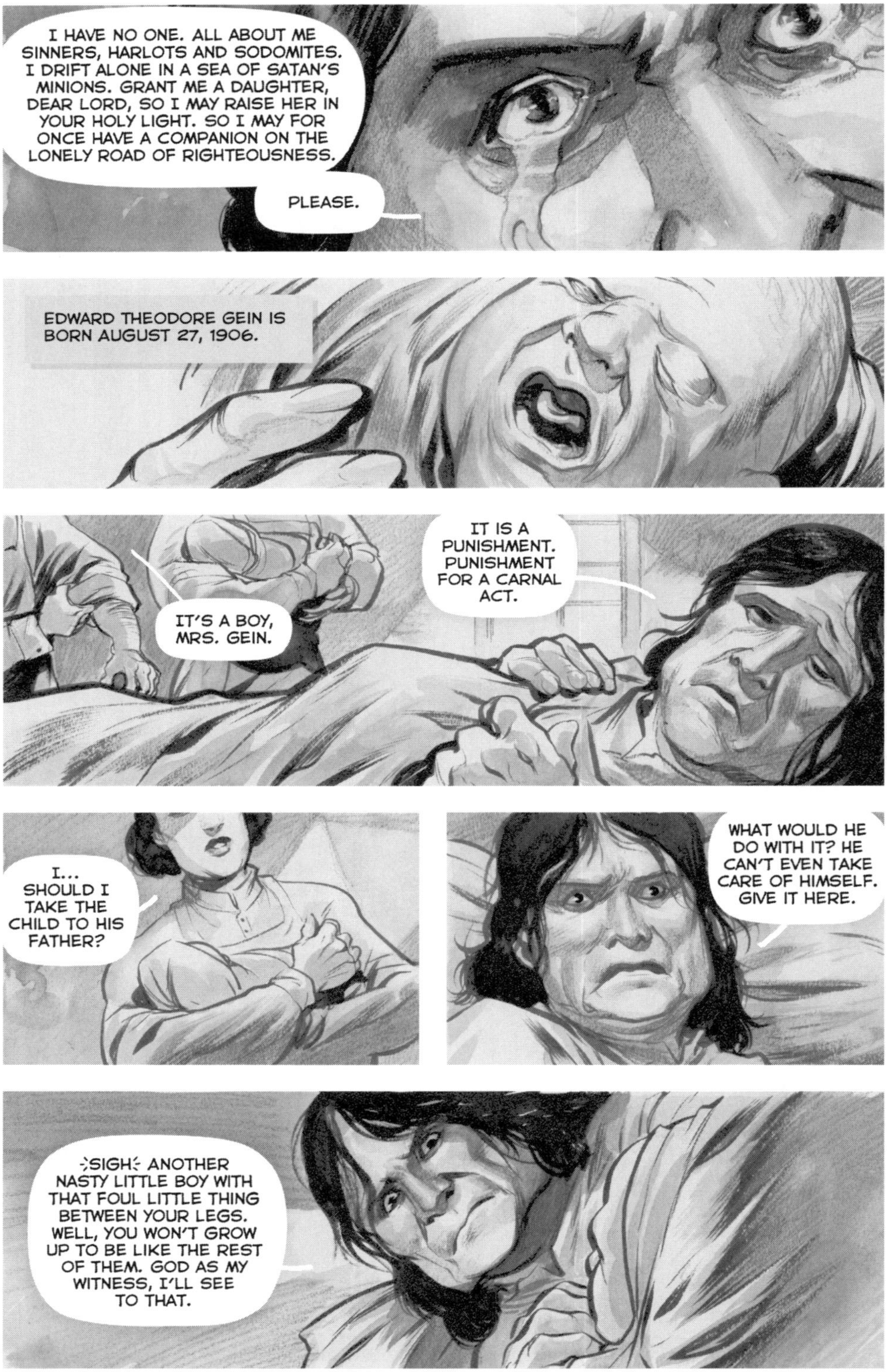
I HAVE NO ONE. ALL ABOUT ME SINNERS, HARLOTS AND SODOMITES. I DRIFT ALONE IN A SEA OF SATAN'S MINIONS. GRANT ME A DAUGHTER, DEAR LORD, SO I MAY RAISE HER IN YOUR HOLY LIGHT. SO I MAY FOR ONCE HAVE A COMPANION ON THE LONELY ROAD OF RIGHTEOUSNESS.
PLEASE.
EDWARD THEODORE GEIN IS BORN AUGUST 27, 1906.
IT'S A BOY, MRS. GEIN.
IT IS A PUNISHMENT. PUNISHMENT FOR A CARNAL ACT.
I... SHOULD I TAKE THE CHILD TO HIS FATHER?
WHAT WOULD HE DO WITH IT? HE CAN'T EVEN TAKE CARE OF HIMSELF. GIVE IT HERE.
SIGH ANOTHER NASTY LITTLE BOY WITH THAT FOUL LITTLE THING BETWEEN YOUR LEGS. WELL, YOU WON'T GROW UP TO BE LIKE THE REST OF THEM. GOD AS MY WITNESS, I'LL SEE TO THAT.

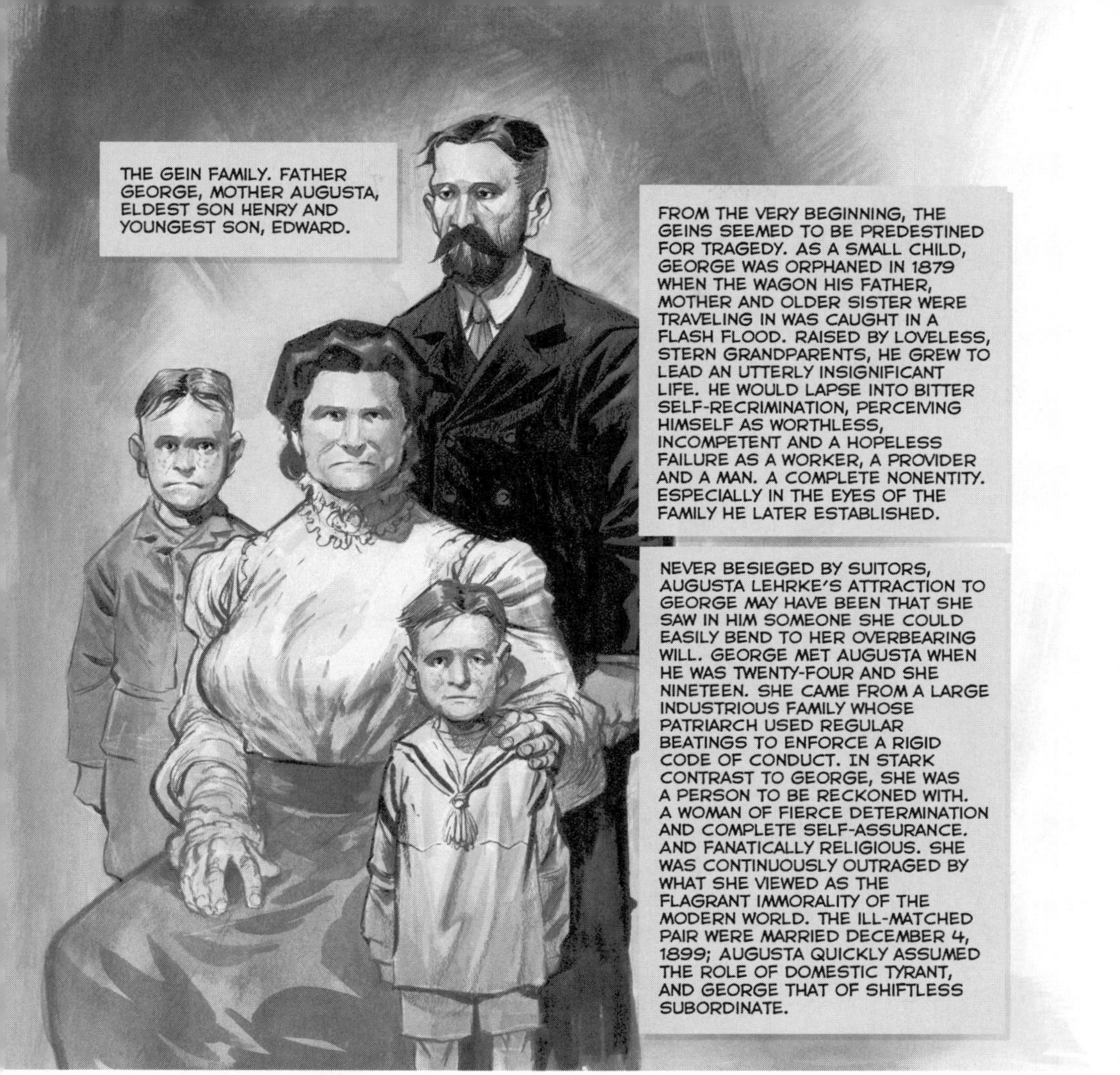
THE GEIN FAMILY. FATHER GEORGE, MOTHER AUGUSTA, ELDEST SON HENRY AND YOUNGEST SON, EDWARD.
FROM THE VERY BEGINNING, THE GEINS SEEMED TO BE PREDESTINED FOR TRAGEDY. AS A SMALL CHILD, GEORGE WAS ORPHANED IN 1879 WHEN THE WAGON HIS FATHER, MOTHER AND OLDER SISTER WERE TRAVELING IN WAS CAUGHT IN A FLASH FLOOD. RAISED BY LOVELESS, STERN GRANDPARENTS, HE GREW TO LEAD AN UTTERLY INSIGNIFICANT LIFE. HE WOULD LAPSE INTO BITTER SELF-RECRIMINATION, PERCEIVING HIMSELF AS WORTHLESS, INCOMPETENT AND A HOPELESS FAILURE AS A WORKER, A PROVIDER AND A MAN. A COMPLETE NONENTITY. ESPECIALLY IN THE EYES OF THE FAMILY HE LATER ESTABLISHED.
NEVER BESIEGED BY SUITORS, AUGUSTA LEHRKE'S ATTRACTION TO GEORGE MAY HAVE BEEN THAT SHE SAW IN HIM SOMEONE SHE COULD EASILY BEND TO HER OVERBEARING WILL. GEORGE MET AUGUSTA WHEN HE WAS TWENTY-FOUR AND SHE NINETEEN. SHE CAME FROM A LARGE INDUSTRIOUS FAMILY WHOSE PATRIARCH USED REGULAR BEATINGS TO ENFORCE A RIGID CODE OF CONDUCT. IN STARK CONTRAST TO GEORGE, SHE WAS A PERSON TO BE RECKONED WITH. A WOMAN OF FIERCE DETERMINATION AND COMPLETE SELF-ASSURANCE. AND FANATICALLY RELIGIOUS. SHE WAS CONTINUOUSLY OUTRAGED BY WHAT SHE VIEWED AS THE FLAGRANT IMMORALITY OF THE MODERN WORLD. THE ILL-MATCHED PAIR WERE MARRIED DECEMBER 4, 1899; AUGUSTA QUICKLY ASSUMED THE ROLE OF DOMESTIC TYRANT, AND GEORGE THAT OF SHIFTLESS SUBORDINATE.

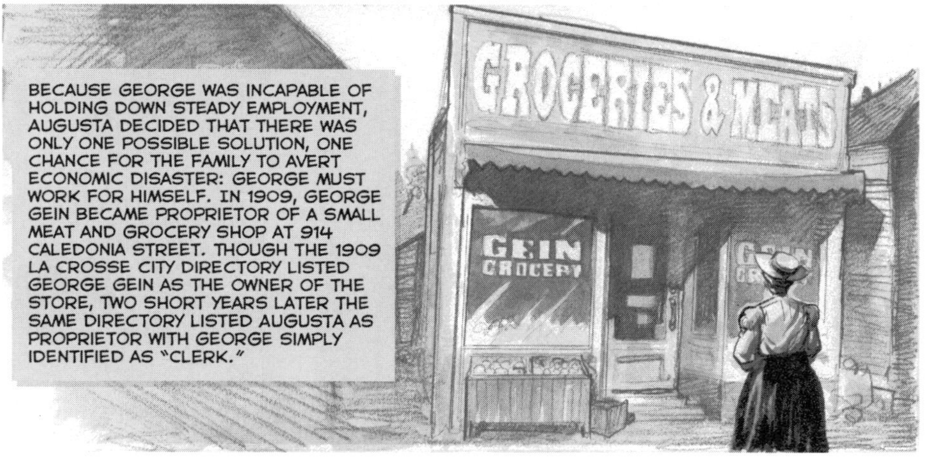
BECAUSE GEORGE WAS INCAPABLE OF HOLDING DOWN STEADY EMPLOYMENT, AUGUSTA DECIDED THAT THERE WAS ONLY ONE POSSIBLE SOLUTION, ONE CHANCE FOR THE FAMILY TO AVERT ECONOMIC DISASTER: GEORGE MUST WORK FOR HIMSELF. IN 1909, GEORGE GEIN BECAME PROPRIETOR OF A SMALL MEAT AND GROCERY SHOP AT 914 CALEDONIA STREET. THOUGH THE 1909 LA CROSSE CITY DIRECTORY LISTED GEORGE GEIN AS THE OWNER OF THE STORE, TWO SHORT YEARS LATER THE SAME DIRECTORY LISTED AUGUSTA AS PROPRIETOR WITH GEORGE SIMPLY IDENTIFIED AS "CLERK."
GROCERIES & MEATS
GEIN
GROCERY

LA CROSSE, WISCONSIN. 1912.

HENRY, MAKE SURE THOSE LABELS ARE POINTED OUT.

YES, MA'AM.

WHAT A BRIGHT LITTLE BOY. ALREADY READING. WHAT IS IT? ADVENTURE STORIES? PIRATES?

IT'S--

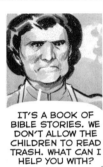

IT'S A BOOK OF BIBLE STORIES. WE DON'T ALLOW THE CHILDREN TO READ TRASH. WHAT CAN I HELP YOU WITH?

OH, WELL, I SAW IN THE PAPER THAT YOU WERE PARTICIPATING IN THE PALMOLIVE GIVEAWAY?

ANOTHER BEGGAR.

HERE YOU ARE. ONE BAR PER CUSTOMER. WHAT ELSE CAN I GET FOR YOU?

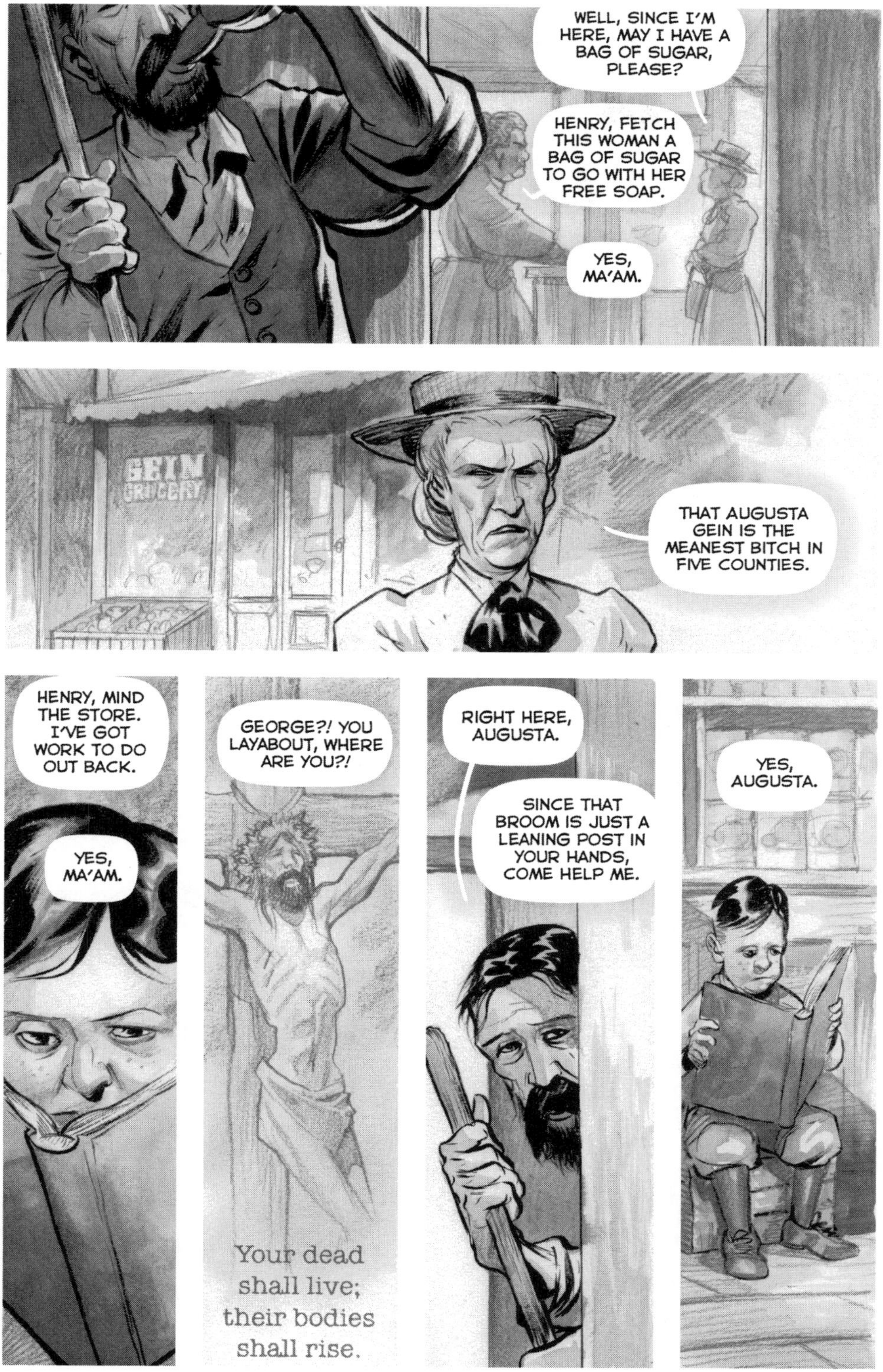

WELL, SINCE I'M HERE, MAY I HAVE A BAG OF SUGAR, PLEASE?
HENRY, FETCH THIS WOMAN A BAG OF SUGAR TO GO WITH HER FREE SOAP.
YES, MA'AM.
GEIN GROCERY
THAT AUGUSTA GEIN IS THE MEANEST BITCH IN FIVE COUNTIES.
HENRY, MIND THE STORE. I'VE GOT WORK TO DO OUT BACK.
YES, MA'AM.
GEORGE?! YOU LAYABOUT, WHERE ARE YOU?!
Your dead shall live; their bodies shall rise.
RIGHT HERE, AUGUSTA.
SINCE THAT BROOM IS JUST A LEANING POST IN YOUR HANDS, COME HELP ME.
YES, AUGUSTA.

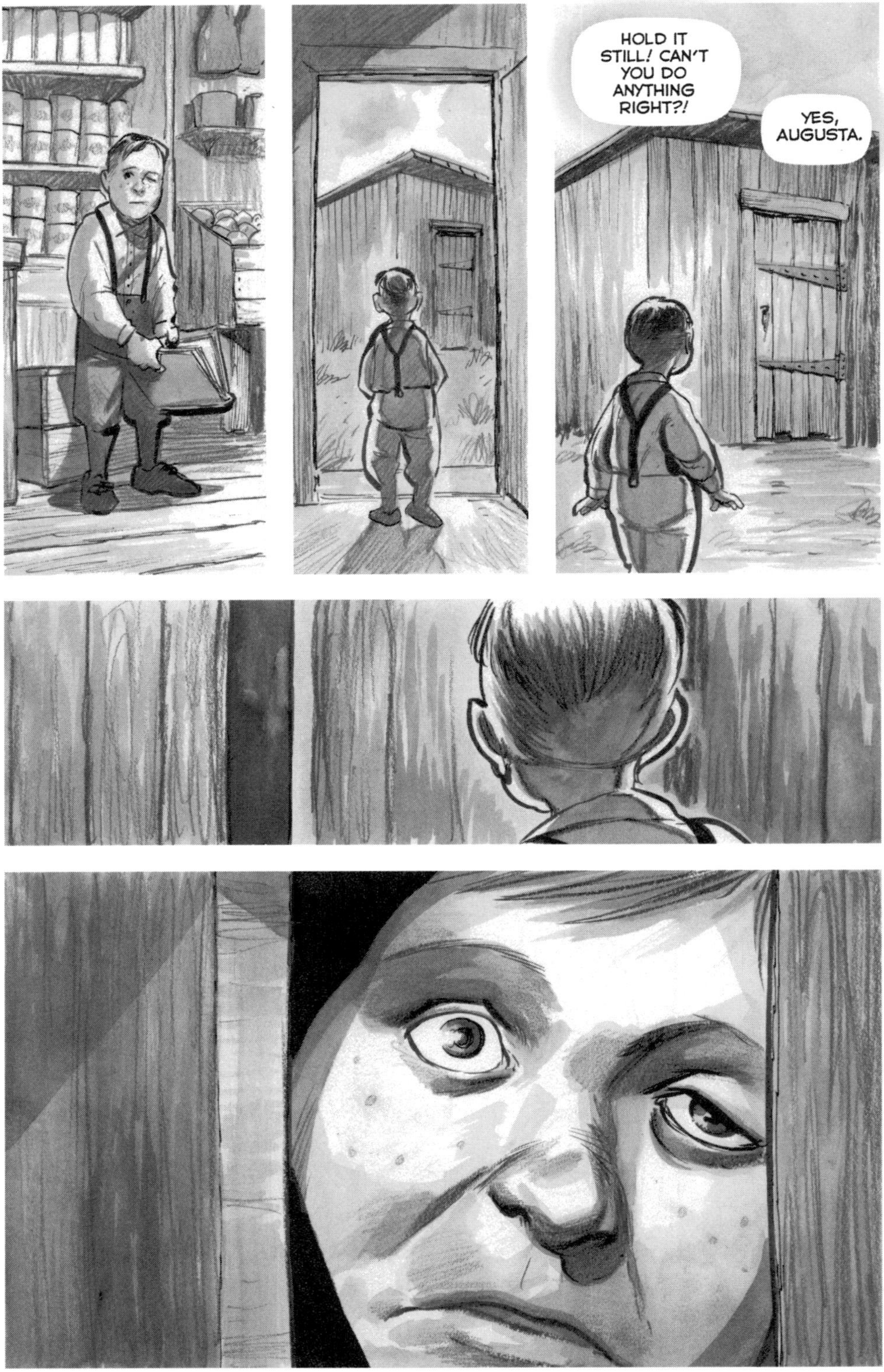
HOLD IT STILL! CAN'T YOU DO ANYTHING RIGHT?!
YES, AUGUSTA.

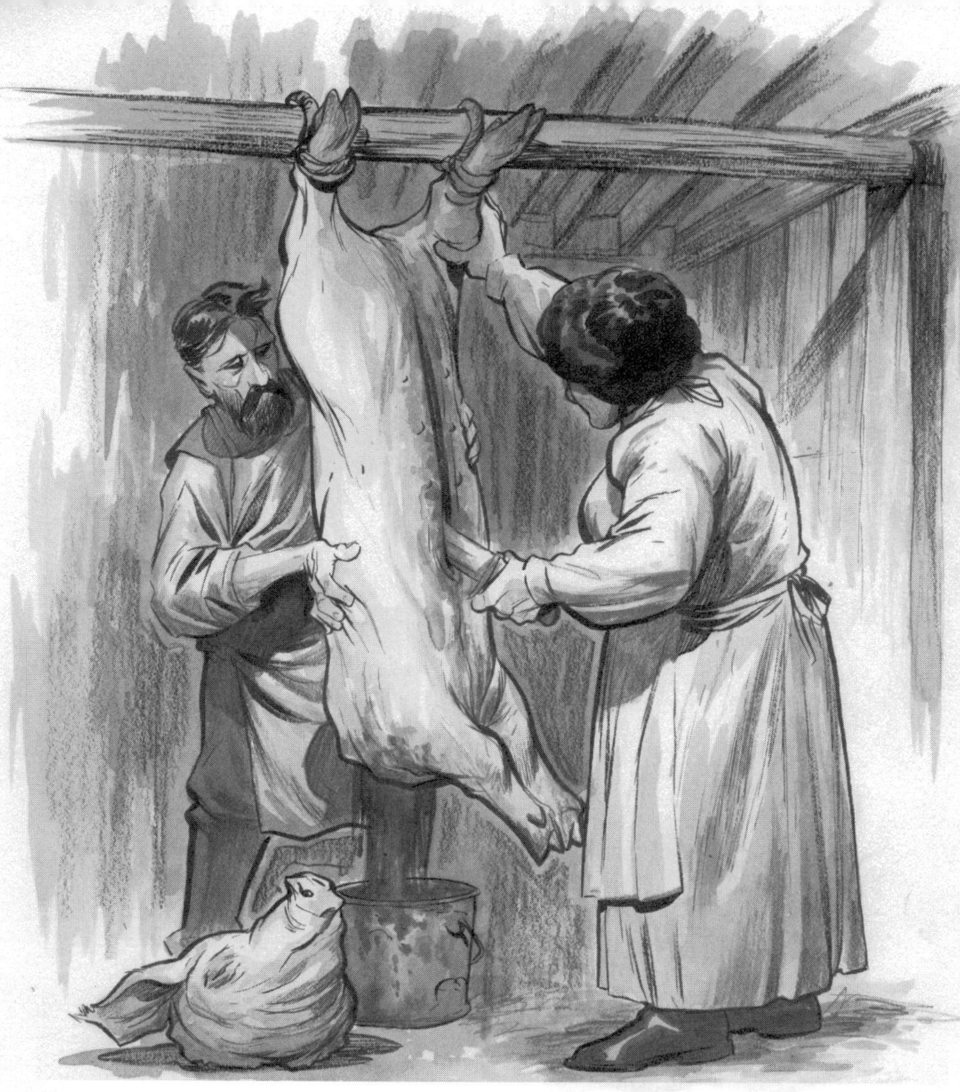

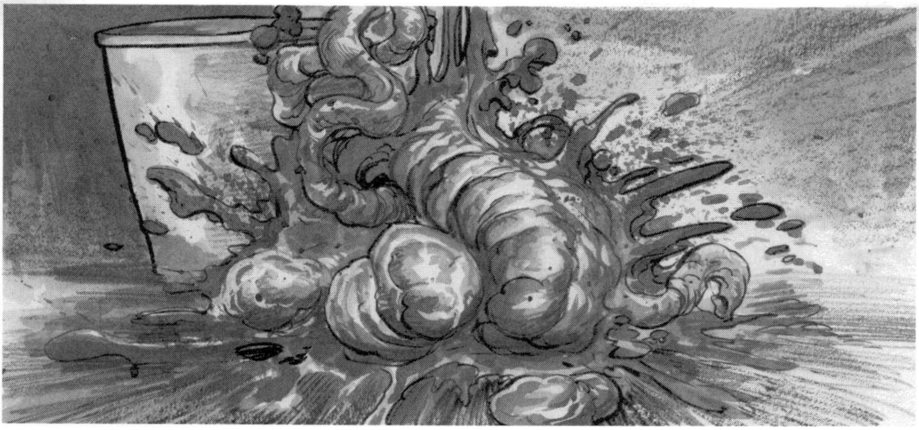

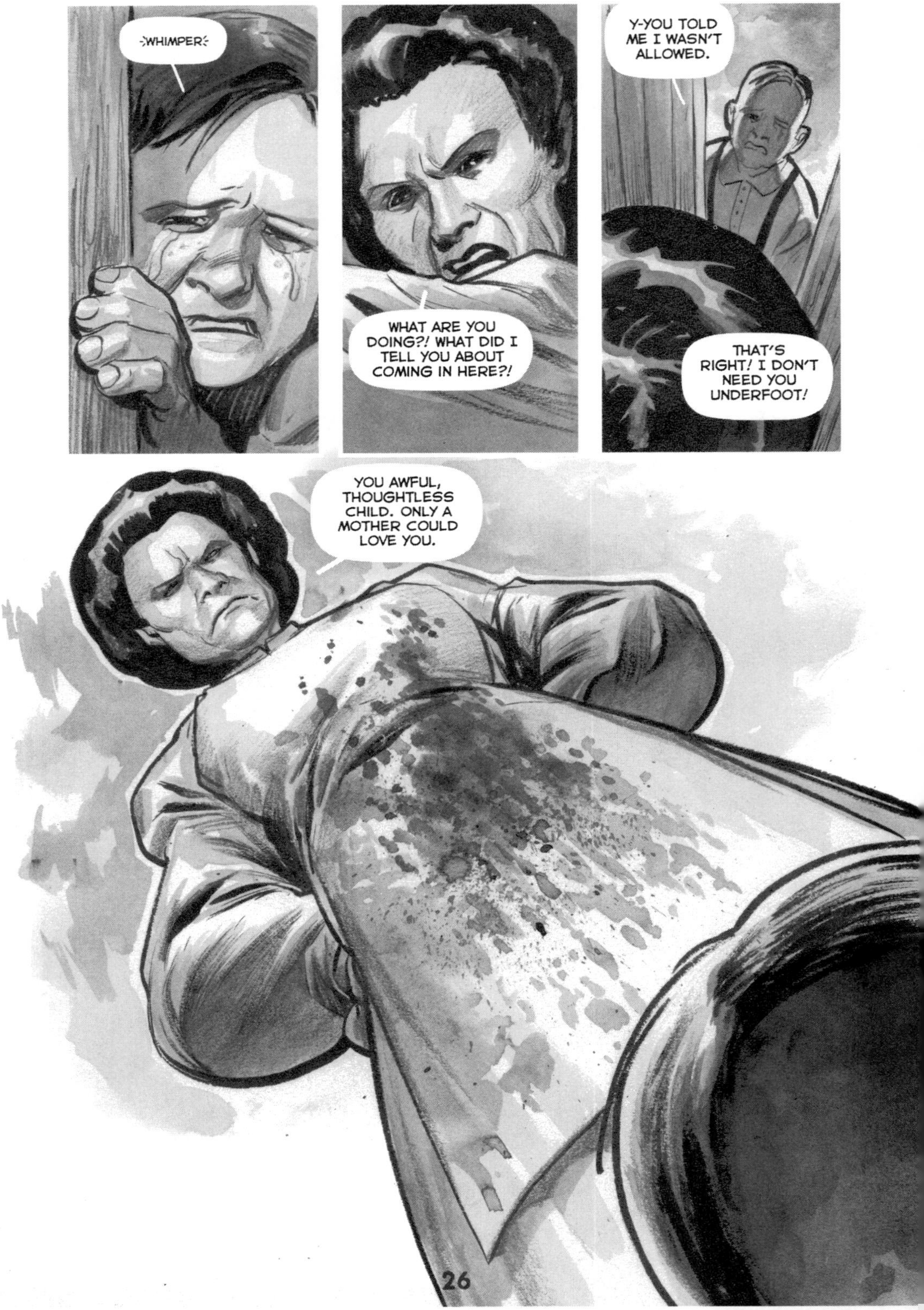

WHIMPER
WHAT ARE YOU DOING?! WHAT DID I TELL YOU ABOUT COMING IN HERE?!
Y-YOU TOLD ME I WASN'T ALLOWED.
THAT'S RIGHT! I DON'T NEED YOU UNDERFOOT!
YOU AWFUL, THOUGHTLESS CHILD. ONLY A MOTHER COULD LOVE YOU.

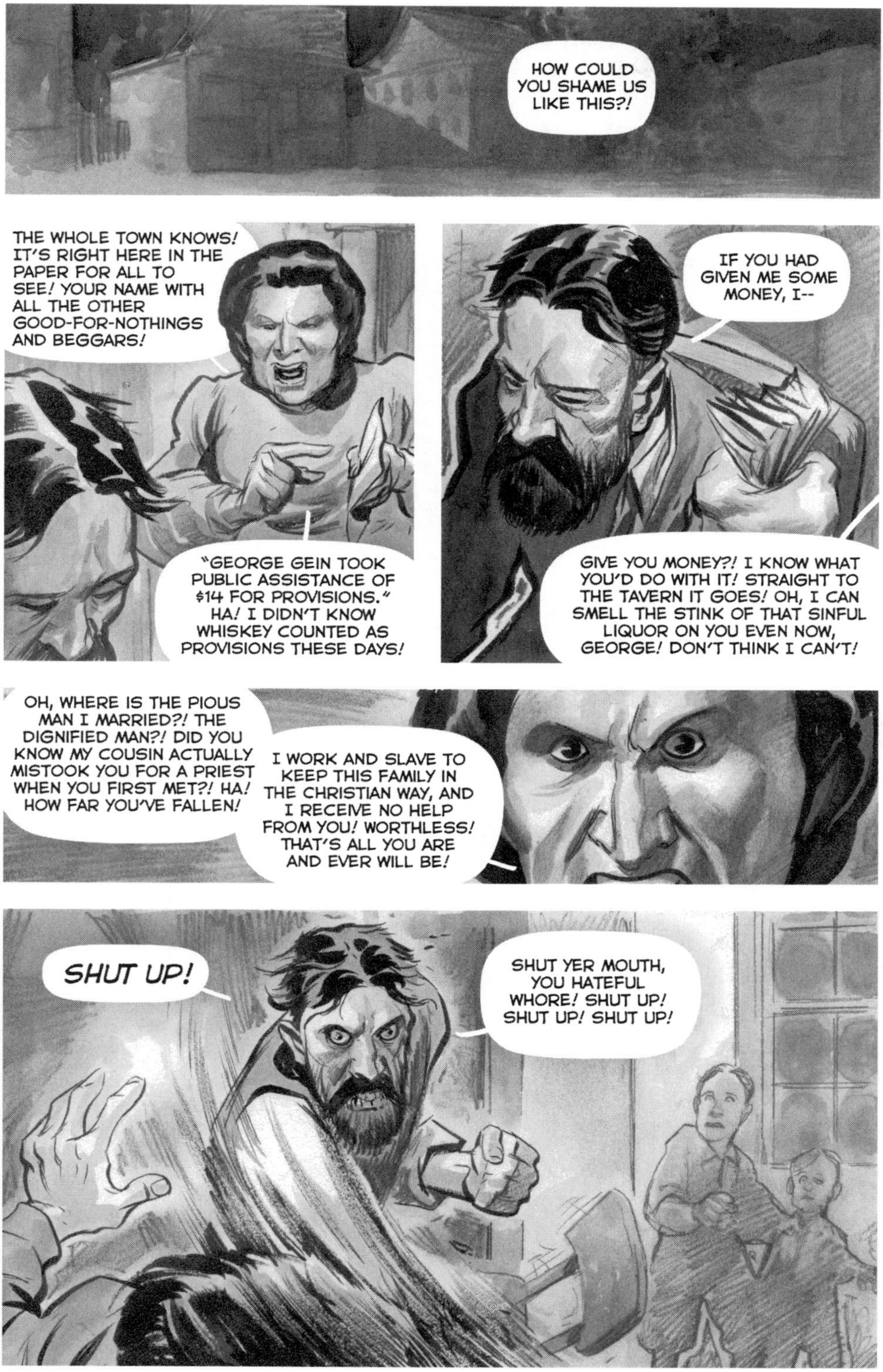
HOW COULD YOU SHAME US LIKE THIS?!
THE WHOLE TOWN KNOWS! IT'S RIGHT HERE IN THE PAPER FOR ALL TO SEE! YOUR NAME WITH ALL THE OTHER GOOD-FOR-NOTHINGS AND BEGGARS!
"GEORGE GEIN TOOK PUBLIC ASSISTANCE OF $14 FOR PROVISIONS." HA! I DIDN'T KNOW WHISKEY COUNTED AS PROVISIONS THESE DAYS!
IF YOU HAD GIVEN ME SOME MONEY, I--
GIVE YOU MONEY?! I KNOW WHAT YOU'D DO WITH IT! STRAIGHT TO THE TAVERN IT GOES! OH, I CAN SMELL THE STINK OF THAT SINFUL LIQUOR ON YOU EVEN NOW, GEORGE! DON'T THINK I CAN'T!
OH, WHERE IS THE PIOUS MAN I MARRIED?! THE DIGNIFIED MAN?! DID YOU KNOW MY COUSIN ACTUALLY MISTOOK YOU FOR A PRIEST WHEN YOU FIRST MET?! HA! HOW FAR YOU'VE FALLEN!
I WORK AND SLAVE TO KEEP THIS FAMILY IN THE CHRISTIAN WAY, AND I RECEIVE NO HELP FROM YOU! WORTHLESS! THAT'S ALL YOU ARE AND EVER WILL BE!
SHUT UP!
SHUT YER MOUTH, YOU HATEFUL WHORE! SHUT UP! SHUT UP! SHUT UP!

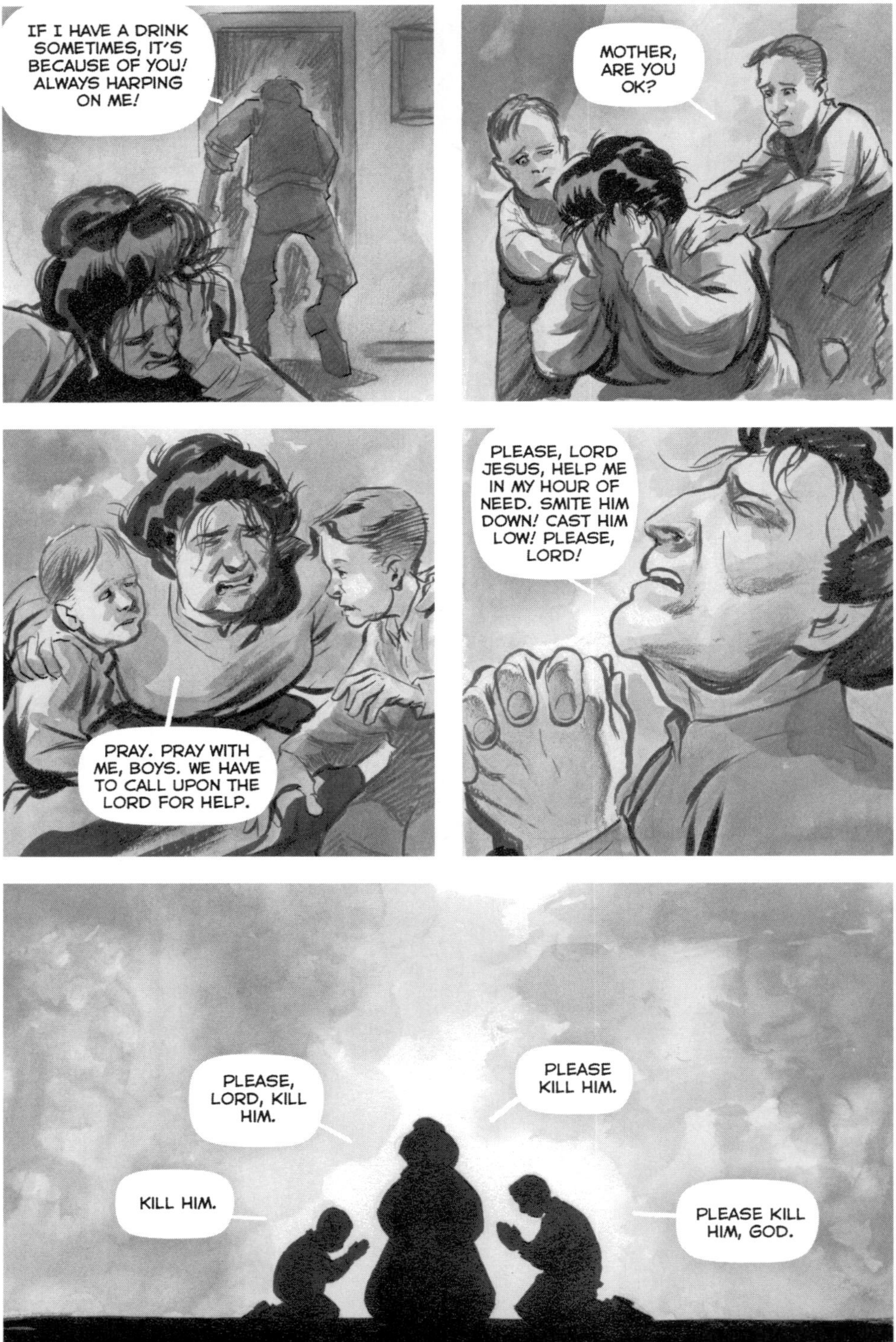
IF I HAVE A DRINK SOMETIMES, IT'S BECAUSE OF YOU! ALWAYS HARPING ON ME!
MOTHER, ARE YOU OK?
PRAY. PRAY WITH ME, BOYS. WE HAVE TO CALL UPON THE LORD FOR HELP.
PLEASE, LORD JESUS, HELP ME IN MY HOUR OF NEED. SMITE HIM DOWN! CAST HIM LOW! PLEASE, LORD!
PLEASE, LORD, KILL HIM.
PLEASE KILL HIM.
KILL HIM.
PLEASE KILL HIM, GOD.

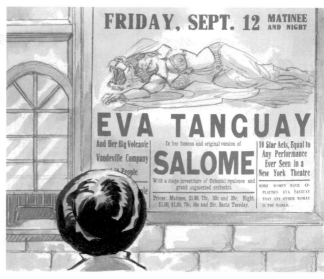

FRIDAY, SEPT. 12 MATINEE AND NIGHT

EVA TANGUAY

And Her Big Volcanic Vaudeville Company

In her famous and original version of

SALOME

With a stage investiture of Oriental opulence and grand augmented orchestra

10 Star Acts, Equal to Any Performance Ever Seen in a New York Theatre

MORE WOMEN HAVE APPLAUDED EVA TANGUAY THAN ANY OTHER WOMAN IN THE WORLD.

Prices: Matinee, $1.00, 75c, 50c and 25c; Night, $1.50, $1.00, 75c, 50c and 25c. Seats Tuesday.

BY 1913, AUGUSTA WAS FINISHED WITH LA CROSSE. THROUGH HER SKEWED IDEALS, IT WAS NO LESS THAN A LATTER-DAY SODOM. AND THE ONLY WAY TO SAVE HER SONS WAS TO PUT AS MUCH DISTANCE BETWEEN THEM AND THE SINNERS AS POSSIBLE.

PLAINFIELD, WISCONSIN. MAY 1914.

WELCOME TO PLAINFIELD
POPULATION 380

HER OVERZEALOUS WORK ETHIC AND PENNY-PINCHING HAD PAID OFF. SHE HAD MANAGED TO SAVE ENOUGH MONEY FOR A MODEST FARM. THE GEINS WOULD BECOME LANDOWNERS.

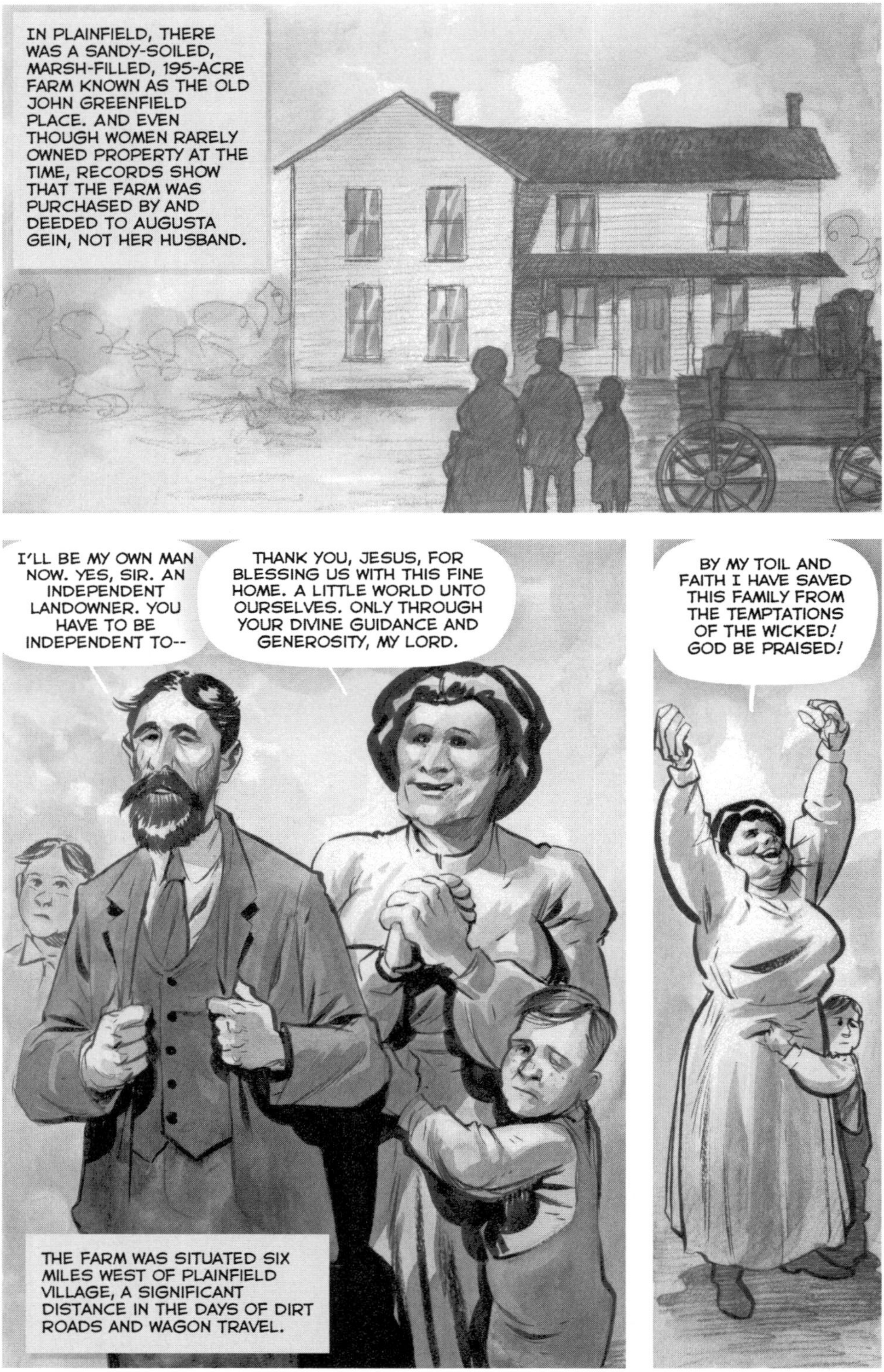
IN PLAINFIELD, THERE WAS A SANDY-SOILED, MARSH-FILLED, 195-ACRE FARM KNOWN AS THE OLD JOHN GREENFIELD PLACE. AND EVEN THOUGH WOMEN RARELY OWNED PROPERTY AT THE TIME, RECORDS SHOW THAT THE FARM WAS PURCHASED BY AND DEEDED TO AUGUSTA GEIN, NOT HER HUSBAND.
I'LL BE MY OWN MAN NOW. YES, SIR. AN INDEPENDENT LANDOWNER. YOU HAVE TO BE INDEPENDENT TO--
THANK YOU, JESUS, FOR BLESSING US WITH THIS FINE HOME. A LITTLE WORLD UNTO OURSELVES. ONLY THROUGH YOUR DIVINE GUIDANCE AND GENEROSITY, MY LORD.
THE FARM WAS SITUATED SIX MILES WEST OF PLAINFIELD VILLAGE, A SIGNIFICANT DISTANCE IN THE DAYS OF DIRT ROADS AND WAGON TRAVEL.
BY MY TOIL AND FAITH I HAVE SAVED THIS FAMILY FROM THE TEMPTATIONS OF THE WICKED! GOD BE PRAISED!

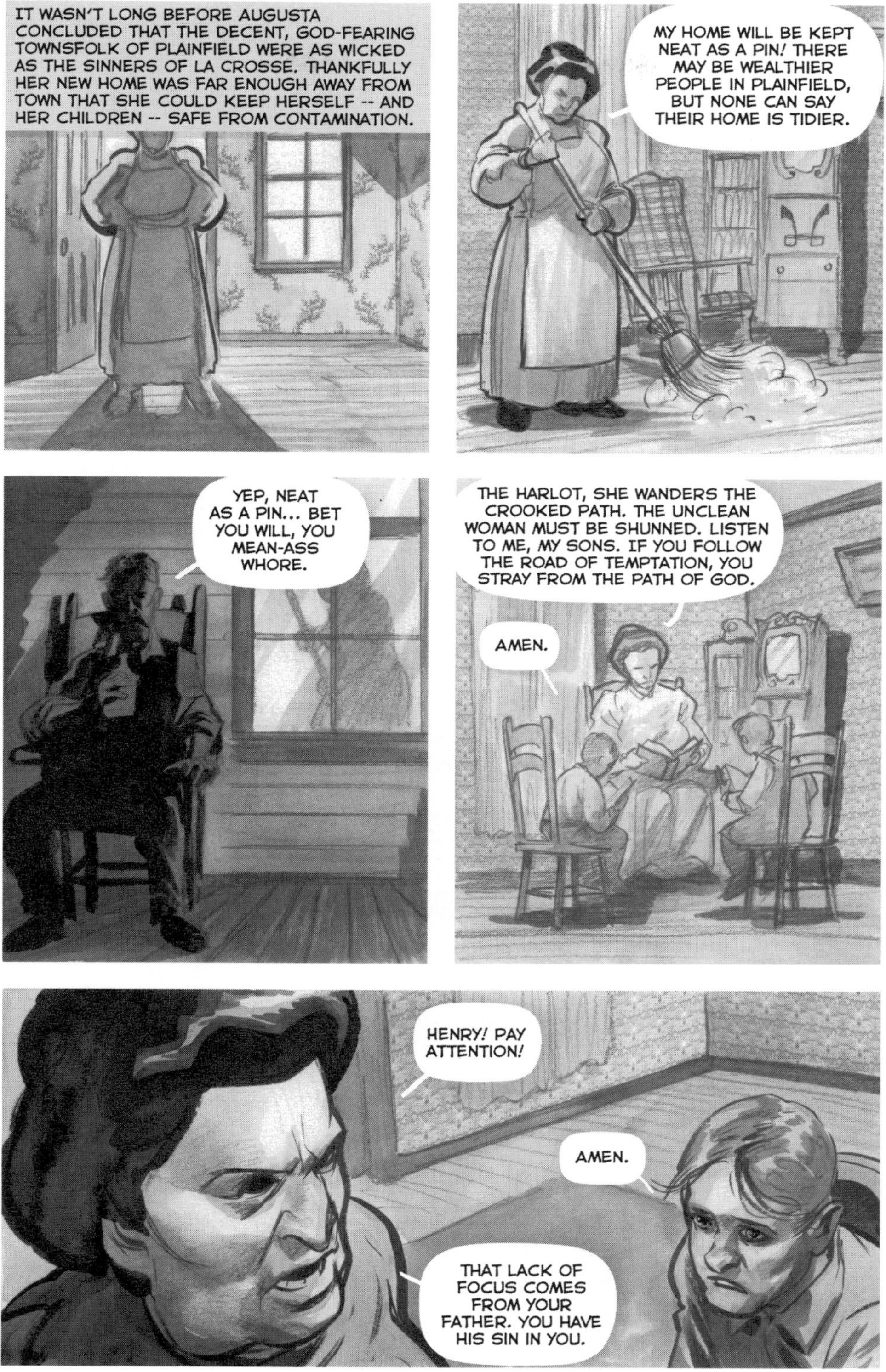
IT WASN'T LONG BEFORE AUGUSTA CONCLUDED THAT THE DECENT, GOD-FEARING TOWNSFOLK OF PLAINFIELD WERE AS WICKED AS THE SINNERS OF LA CROSSE. THANKFULLY HER NEW HOME WAS FAR ENOUGH AWAY FROM TOWN THAT SHE COULD KEEP HERSELF -- AND HER CHILDREN -- SAFE FROM CONTAMINATION.
MY HOME WILL BE KEPT NEAT AS A PIN! THERE MAY BE WEALTHIER PEOPLE IN PLAINFIELD, BUT NONE CAN SAY THEIR HOME IS TIDIER.
YEP, NEAT AS A PIN... BET YOU WILL, YOU MEAN-ASS WHORE.
THE HARLOT, SHE WANDERS THE CROOKED PATH. THE UNCLEAN WOMAN MUST BE SHUNNED. LISTEN TO ME, MY SONS. IF YOU FOLLOW THE ROAD OF TEMPTATION, YOU STRAY FROM THE PATH OF GOD.
AMEN.
HENRY! PAY ATTENTION!
AMEN.
THAT LACK OF FOCUS COMES FROM YOUR FATHER. YOU HAVE HIS SIN IN YOU.

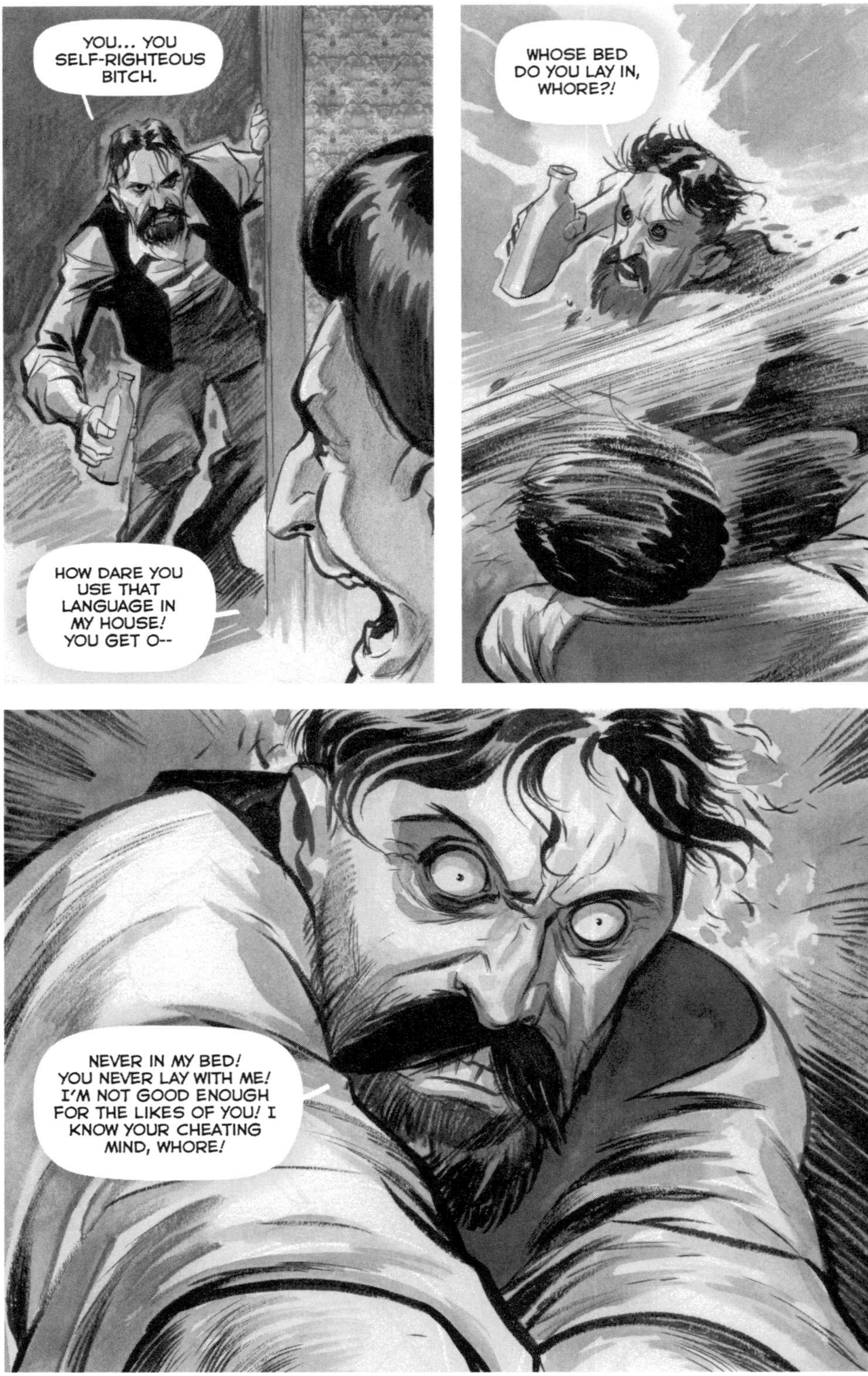
YOU... YOU SELF-RIGHTEOUS BITCH.
HOW DARE YOU USE THAT LANGUAGE IN MY HOUSE! YOU GET O--
WHOSE BED DO YOU LAY IN, WHORE?!
NEVER IN MY BED! YOU NEVER LAY WITH ME! I'M NOT GOOD ENOUGH FOR THE LIKES OF YOU! I KNOW YOUR CHEATING MIND, WHORE!

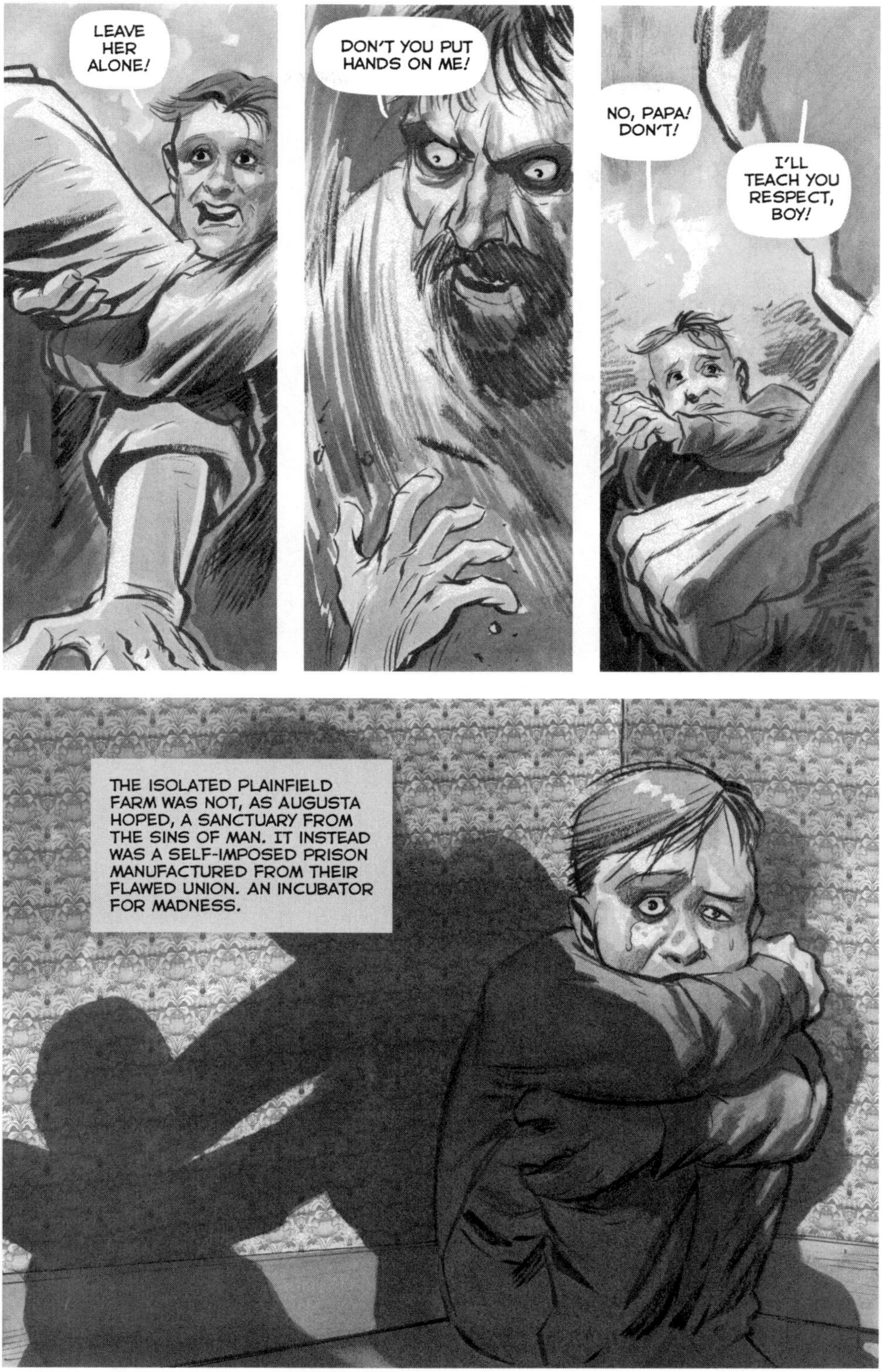
LEAVE HER ALONE!
DON'T YOU PUT HANDS ON ME!
NO, PAPA! DON'T!
I'LL TEACH YOU RESPECT, BOY!
THE ISOLATED PLAINFIELD FARM WAS NOT, AS AUGUSTA HOPED, A SANCTUARY FROM THE SINS OF MAN. IT INSTEAD WAS A SELF-IMPOSED PRISON MANUFACTURED FROM THEIR FLAWED UNION. AN INCUBATOR FOR MADNESS.

DAILY **CHAPTER 3**

Local Union
Talks Strike

Section 6a

10¢ ★ ★ ★

★ ★ ★ Monday, November 25th, 1957

MOTHER KNOWS BEST

By Dale Simons
Staff Reporter, City desk

Gein was in court again on Friday for a brief appearance before Circuit Judge Herbert A. Bunde. Dressed in baggy green work pants and a blue woolen jacket, Eddie, his stubbled face displaying no trace of emotion, was led into the large, high-ceilinged courtroom by Sheriff Schley. About eighty spectators, at least thirty of whom were women, had filled the courtroom. The crowd was hushed as the fragile-looking "ghoul-slayer" was brought before the bench, though the news photographers present were squirming with frustration. At Eddie's request, they had been barred by Judge Bunde, a stern, no-nonsense jurist, from taking pictures during the proceedings. Throughout the week, rumors had continued to circulate that certain individuals in Plainfield were outraged at the notion that Gein, by pleading insanity, might evade punishment for his crimes. District Attorney Kileen best sought to reassure the public by stating categorically that "Gein would never walk the streets of Plainfield again." Still, there was a good deal of bitterness at the thought that Gein might end up in a mental hospital, which, as far as certain people were concerned, would be

thirty-day examination period and remanded him to the custody of Sheriff Schley, who led Eddie back to the jailhouse to await transportation to the mental institution.

Though Gein was a wiry fellow, it seemed impossible that he could have had the strength to dig up a grave by himself, break open the casket, remove the corpse, and perform his grisly operations on it, then rebury the coffin and smooth over the sandy soil so that no trace of his crime remained—all in the space of a few hours.

Moreover, the townspeople didn't see how such an activity could possibly have gone undetected, particularly over the course of several years. Gein, they argued, would have had to perform his nocturnal pillaging by lantern light, and even in an area as isolated and lonely as Plainfield, it hardly seemed credible that no one would have once spotted a suspicious glow coming from the cemetery or noticed Gein's pickup parked there in the night and wondered what the strange little recluse was up to. One person eminently qualified to comment on the situation was the sexton who personally dismantled Gein's story. Dismas insisted that during the time he'd been caretaker, no grave had ever been

that Waushara County was not about to conduct any exhumations. "I want no part in opening any graves to prove anything," he told the newsmen. "Just think how the poor relatives would feel." He repeated that his county had no unsolved missing-persons cases. From his point of view, therefore, a check of the cemeteries wasn't necessary. "If other counties want to get court orders to open graves," Kileen said, "it's up to them," though he added that if the survivors "don't like it, I'll do everything possible to stop it."

For a while, it seemed as if the Crime Lab might offer the best solution to the problem. Charles Wilson had nine of his men working full-time on the case, analyzing the evidence and employing the most up-to-date techniques for identifying the victims from their remains. By comparing dirt particles gathered at the crime scene with soil samples from local cemeteries, the technicians hoped to determine the validity of Gein's claim.

But the sheer quantity of evidence—by far the largest amount ever handled by the ten-year-old Crime Lab—made it hard for Wilson to promise a quick resolution. Though Kileen urged the director to give the soil analysis top priority, it was clear that a final answer might take weeks,

Butcher Slayer Ed Gein Faces Murder Charge

By Kent Blake
Staff Reporter, City desk

Gein was in court again on Friday for a brief appearance before Circuit Judge Herbert A. Bunde. Dressed in baggy green work pants and a blue woolen jacket, Eddie, his stubbled face displaying no trace of emotion, was led into the large, high-ceilinged courtroom by Sheriff Schley. About eighty spectators, at least thirty of them newsmen, half filled the courtroom. The crowd was hushed as the fragile-looking "ghoul-slayer" was brought before the bench, though the news photographers present were squirming with frustration. At Eddie's request, they had been barred by Judge Bunde, a stern, no-nonsense jurist, from taking pictures during the proceedings.

Throughout the week, rumors had continued to circulate that certain individuals in Plainfield

smooth over the sandy soil so that no trace of his crime remained—all in the space of a few hours.

Moreover, the townspeople didn't see how such an activity could possibly have gone undetected, particularly over the course of several years, Gein, his nocturnal pillaging by lantern light, and even in an area as isolated and lonely as Plainfield, it hardly seemed credible that no one would have once spotted a suspicious glow coming from the cemetery or noticed Gein's pickup truck parked there in the night and wondered what the strange little recluse was up to. One person eminently qualified to comment on the situation was the sexton of the Plainfield cemetery, Pat Dismas, who completely dismantled Gein's story. Dismas insisted that during the time he'd been caretaker, no grave had ever been

the technicians hoped to determine the validity of Gein's claim.

But the sheer quantity of evidence—by far the largest amount ever handled by the ten-year-old Crime Lab—made it hard for Wilson to promise a quick resolution. Though Kileen urged the director to give the soil analysis top priority, it was clear that a final answer might take weeks, even months.

In the meantime, Kileen was under growing pressure from the Plainfield citizenry to determine the truth of Gein's assertion. It was becoming increasingly obvious that the townsfolk would never be able to rest without knowing whether their loved ones had, in fact, been ravaged in their graves.

On Friday afternoon, therefore, following his meeting with Judge Bunde and the other officials, Kileen called a press conference

Appear Before Judge Bunde

By Leland Nyingdorf
Local Desk Reporter

such as people didn't see possibly could not see how such an activity could possibly have gone undetected, particularly over the course of several years. Gein, they argued, would have had to perform his nocturnal pillaging by lantern light, and even in an area as isolated and lonely as Plainfield, it hardly seemed credible to the concern of the judge about the offices of the

Handy Man Is Grilled by DA
Body of Missing Plainfield Woman Discovered at Farm Home of Ed Gein

"You shouldn't say such
things about Mother."

THE ROCHE-A-CRI GRADE SCHOOL, A SMALL ONE-ROOM SCHOOLHOUSE WITH NO MORE THAN A DOZEN OR SO STUDENTS, WAS NO SHELTER FOR YOUNG EDWARD THEODORE GEIN.

YOU READ THE NEWEST TARZAN IN *ALL-STORY*?

DID I EVER! WHADDAYA THINK'LL HAPPEN IN THE NEXT PART?

ED WATCHED THE OTHER CHILDREN FROM AFAR. STUDYING THEIR BEHAVIOR. WISHING TO IMITATE IT.

TARZAN'LL RESCUE JANE FROM THOSE KIDNAPPERS FOR SURE.

'COURSE HE WILL. BUT HOW?

BUT HE COULD NEVER GRASP HOW TO FIT IN.

BETCHA HIS MOTHER CAN HELP HIM. GIVE HIM ADVICE LIKE.

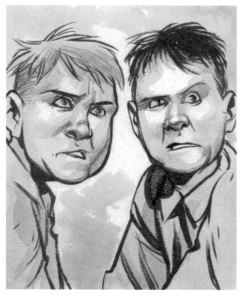

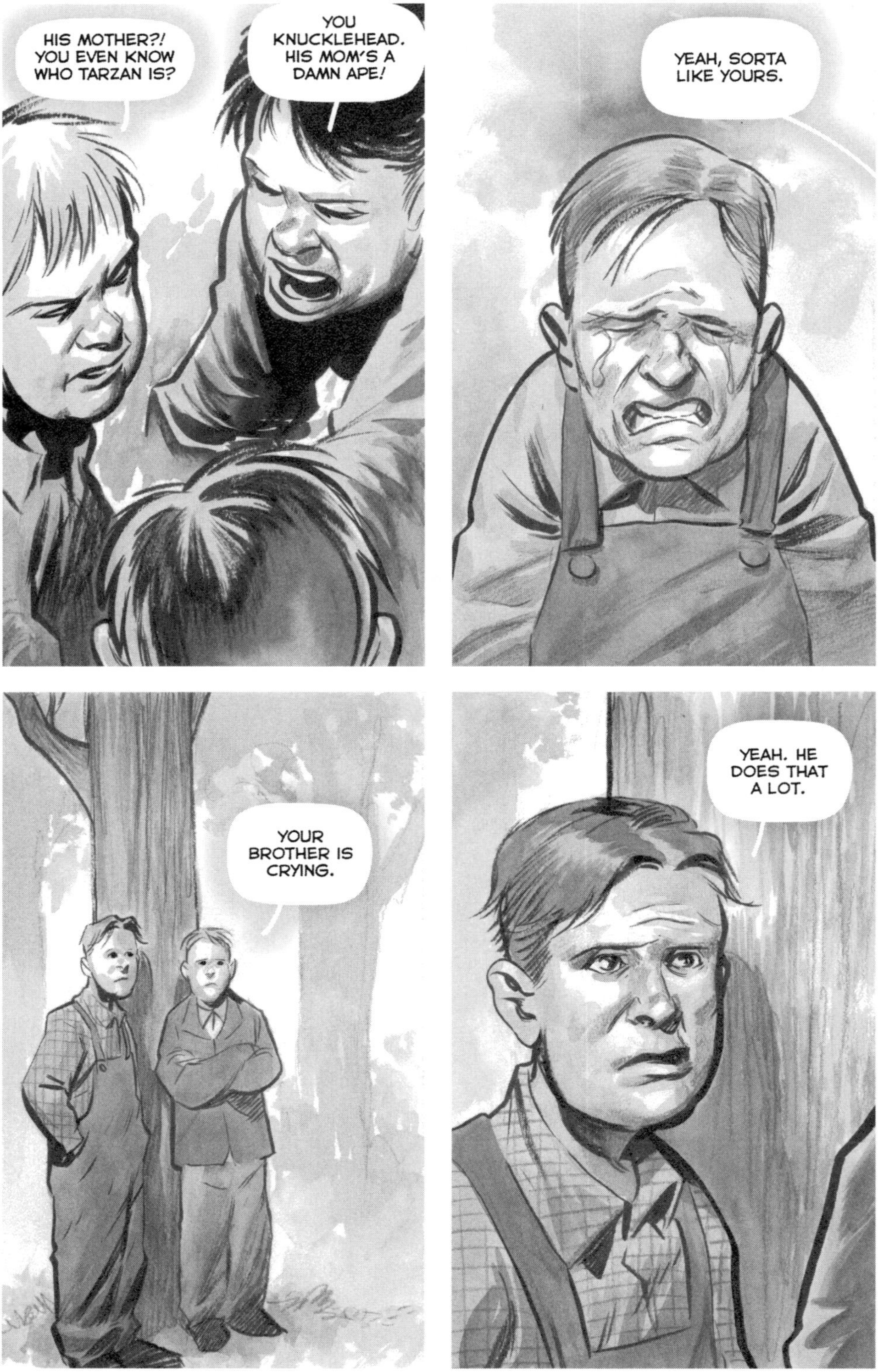
HIS MOTHER?! YOU EVEN KNOW WHO TARZAN IS?
YOU KNUCKLEHEAD. HIS MOM'S A DAMN APE!
YEAH, SORTA LIKE YOURS.
YOUR BROTHER IS CRYING.
YEAH. HE DOES THAT A LOT.

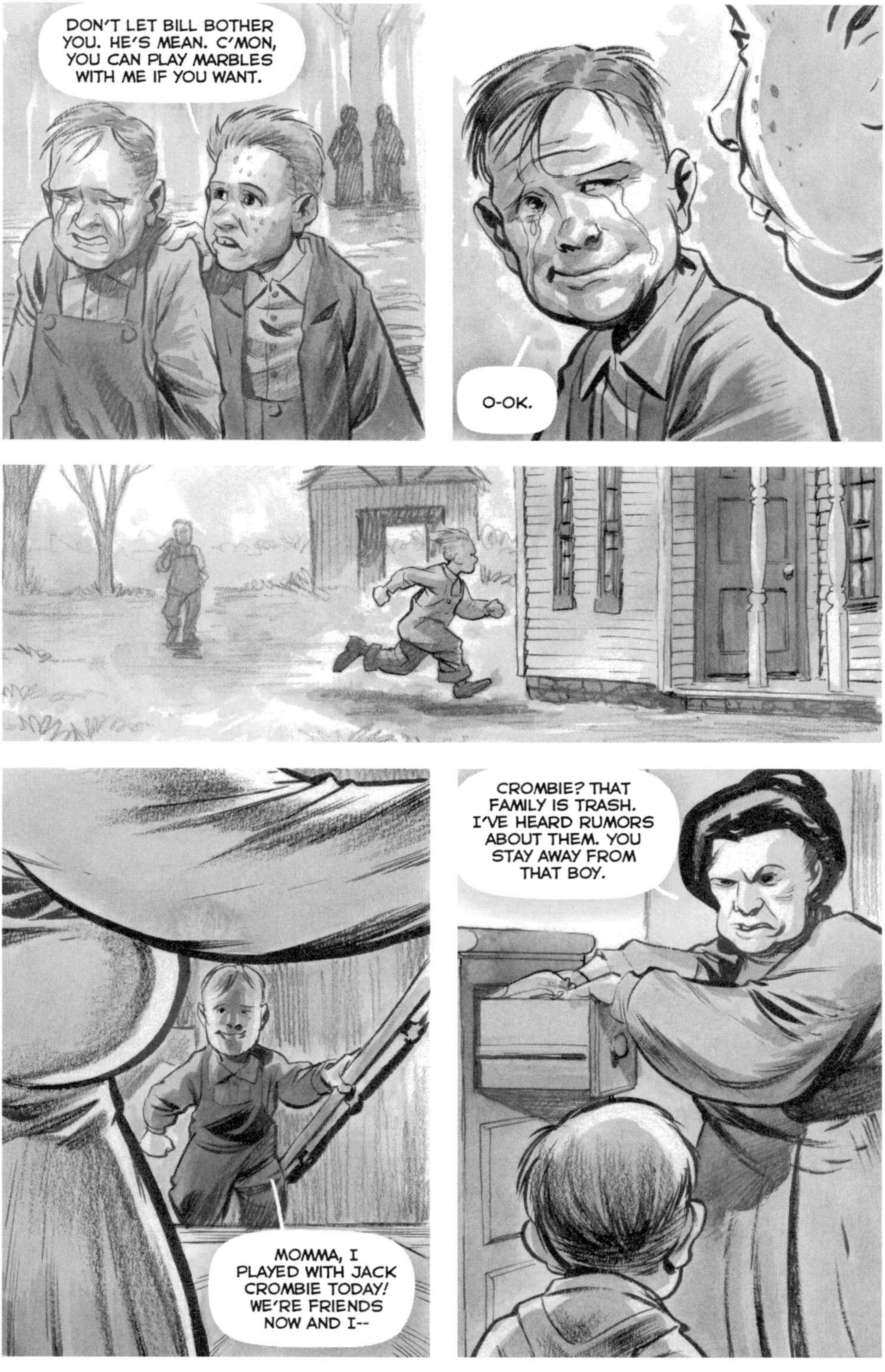
DON'T LET BILL BOTHER YOU. HE'S MEAN. C'MON, YOU CAN PLAY MARBLES WITH ME IF YOU WANT.
O-OK.
MOMMA, I PLAYED WITH JACK CROMBIE TODAY! WE'RE FRIENDS NOW AND I--
CROMBIE? THAT FAMILY IS TRASH. I'VE HEARD RUMORS ABOUT THEM. YOU STAY AWAY FROM THAT BOY.

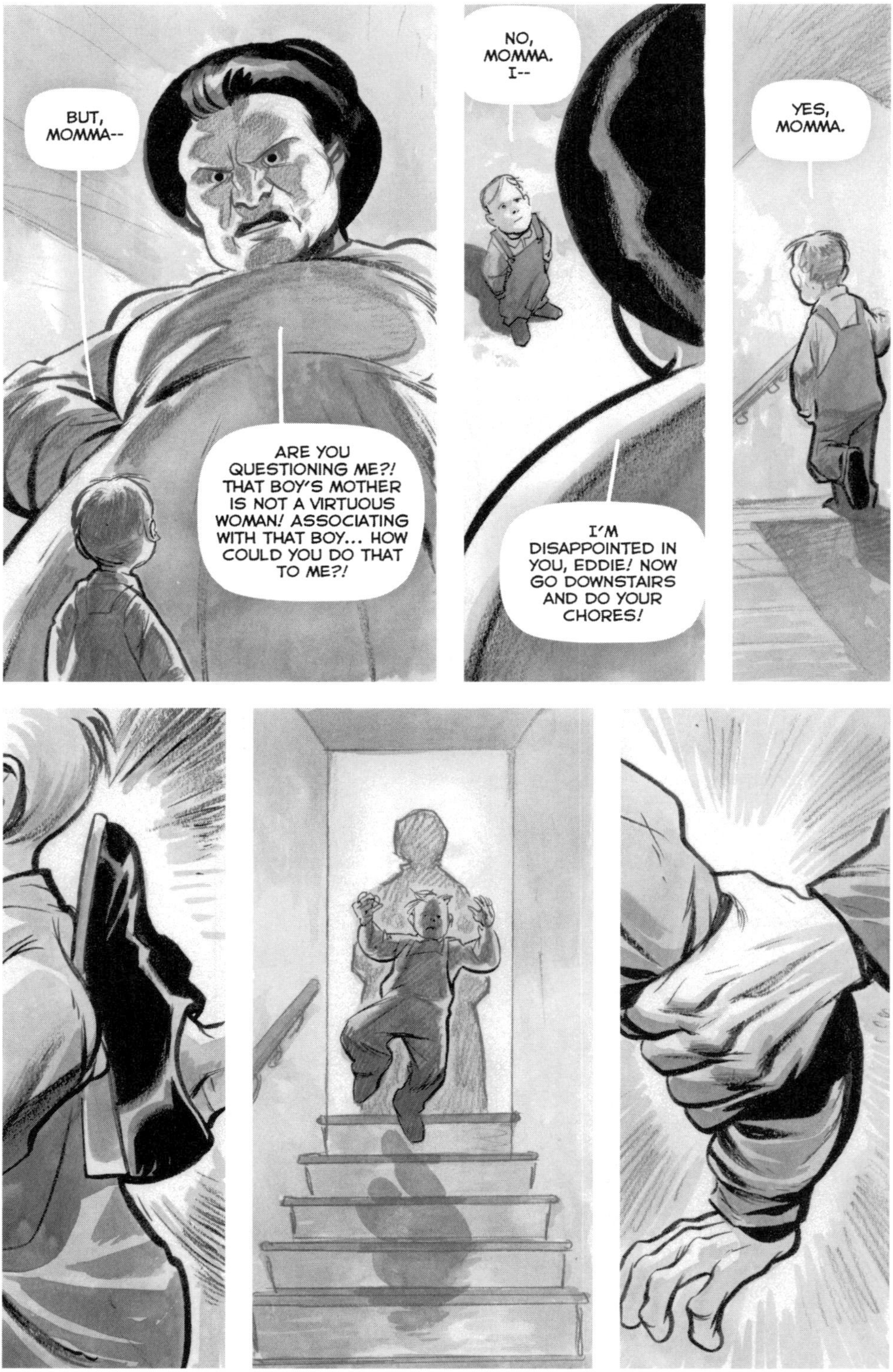
BUT, MOMMA--
ARE YOU QUESTIONING ME?! THAT BOY'S MOTHER IS NOT A VIRTUOUS WOMAN! ASSOCIATING WITH THAT BOY... HOW COULD YOU DO THAT TO ME?!
NO, MOMMA. I--
I'M DISAPPOINTED IN YOU, EDDIE! NOW GO DOWNSTAIRS AND DO YOUR CHORES!
YES, MOMMA.

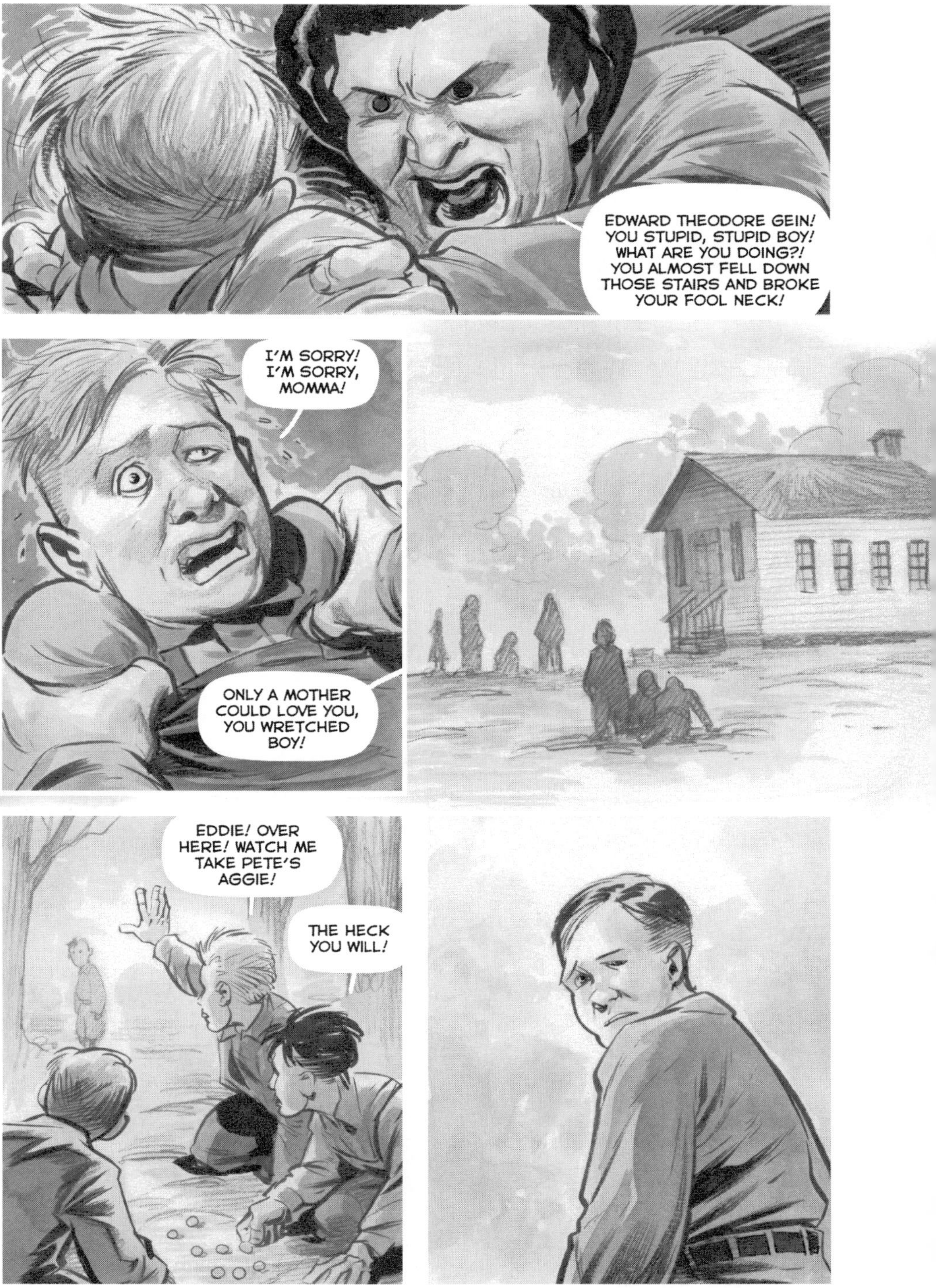
EDWARD THEODORE GEIN! YOU STUPID, STUPID BOY! WHAT ARE YOU DOING?! YOU ALMOST FELL DOWN THOSE STAIRS AND BROKE YOUR FOOL NECK!
I'M SORRY! I'M SORRY, MOMMA!
ONLY A MOTHER COULD LOVE YOU, YOU WRETCHED BOY!
EDDIE! OVER HERE! WATCH ME TAKE PETE'S AGGIE!
THE HECK YOU WILL!

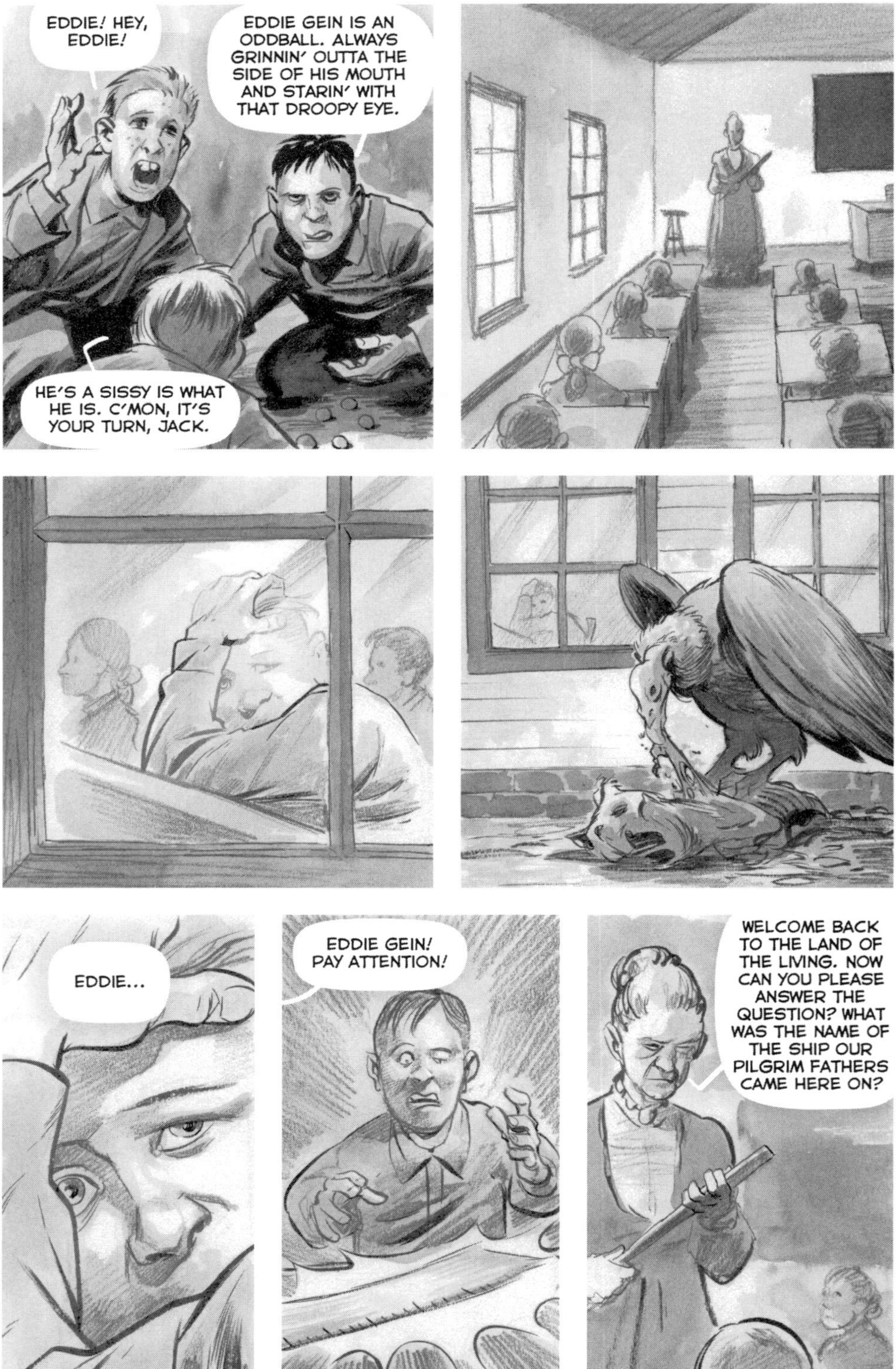
EDDIE! HEY, EDDIE!
EDDIE GEIN IS AN ODDBALL. ALWAYS GRINNIN' OUTTA THE SIDE OF HIS MOUTH AND STARIN' WITH THAT DROOPY EYE.
HE'S A SISSY IS WHAT HE IS. C'MON, IT'S YOUR TURN, JACK.
EDDIE...
EDDIE GEIN! PAY ATTENTION!
WELCOME BACK TO THE LAND OF THE LIVING. NOW CAN YOU PLEASE ANSWER THE QUESTION? WHAT WAS THE NAME OF THE SHIP OUR PILGRIM FATHERS CAME HERE ON?

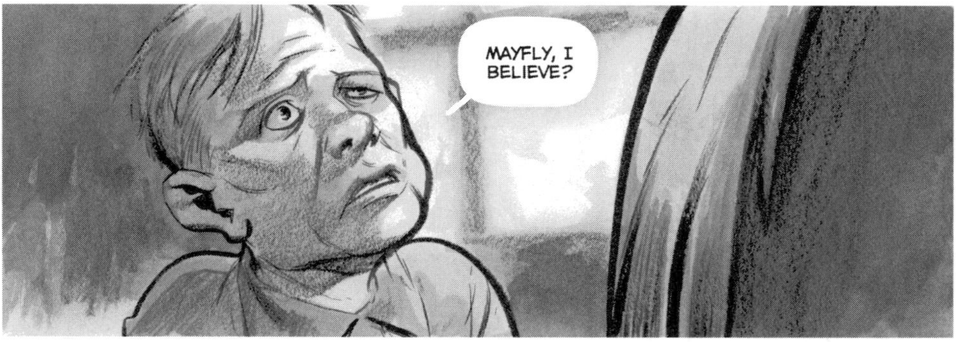
MAYFLY, I BELIEVE?

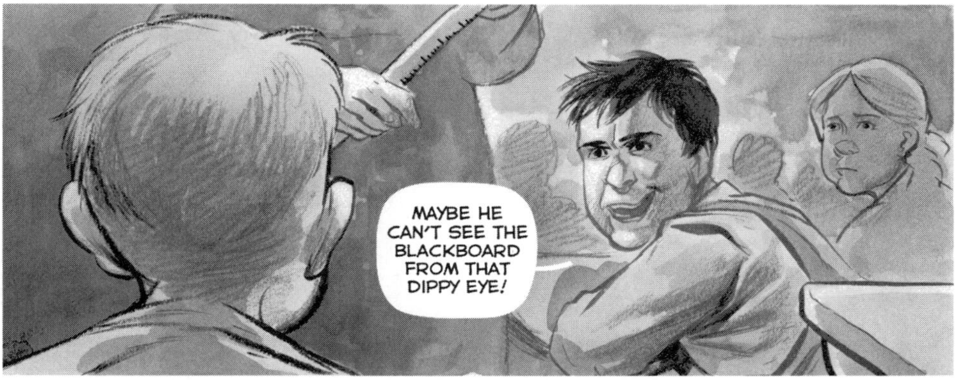
MAYBE HE CAN'T SEE THE BLACKBOARD FROM THAT DIPPY EYE!

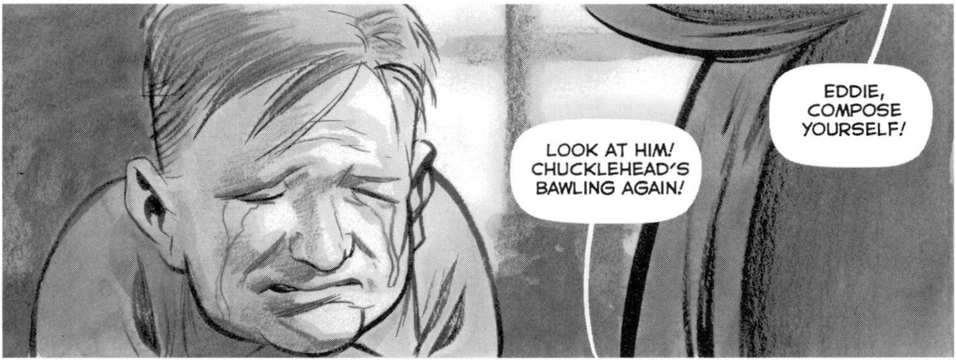
LOOK AT HIM! CHUCKLEHEAD'S BAWLING AGAIN!
EDDIE, COMPOSE YOURSELF!

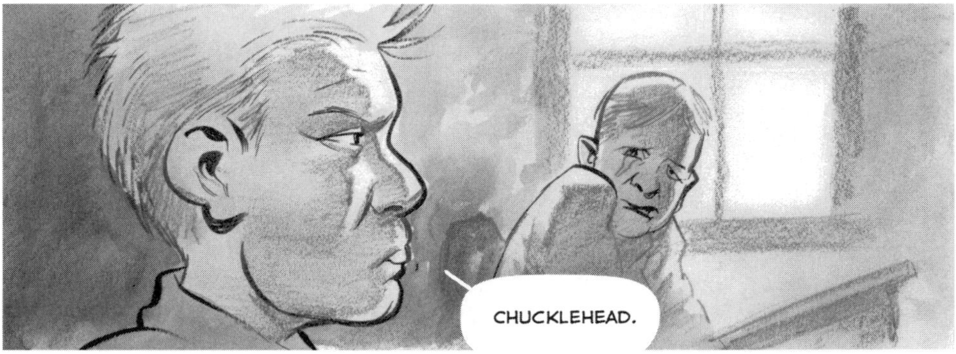
CHUCKLEHEAD.

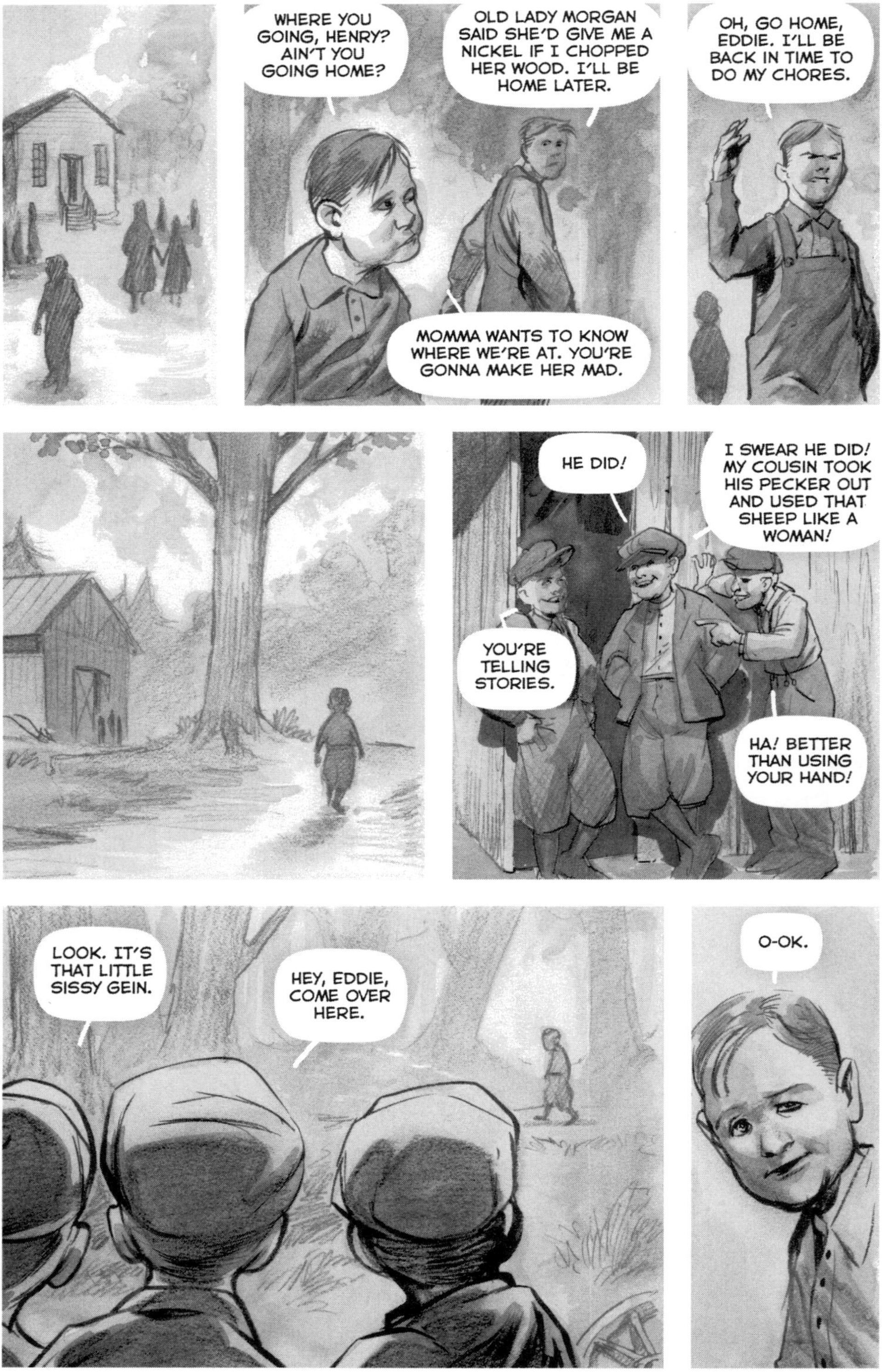
WHERE YOU GOING, HENRY? AIN'T YOU GOING HOME?
OLD LADY MORGAN SAID SHE'D GIVE ME A NICKEL IF I CHOPPED HER WOOD. I'LL BE HOME LATER.
MOMMA WANTS TO KNOW WHERE WE'RE AT. YOU'RE GONNA MAKE HER MAD.
OH, GO HOME, EDDIE. I'LL BE BACK IN TIME TO DO MY CHORES.
HE DID!
I SWEAR HE DID! MY COUSIN TOOK HIS PECKER OUT AND USED THAT SHEEP LIKE A WOMAN!
YOU'RE TELLING STORIES.
HA! BETTER THAN USING YOUR HAND!
LOOK. IT'S THAT LITTLE SISSY GEIN.
HEY, EDDIE, COME OVER HERE.
O-OK.

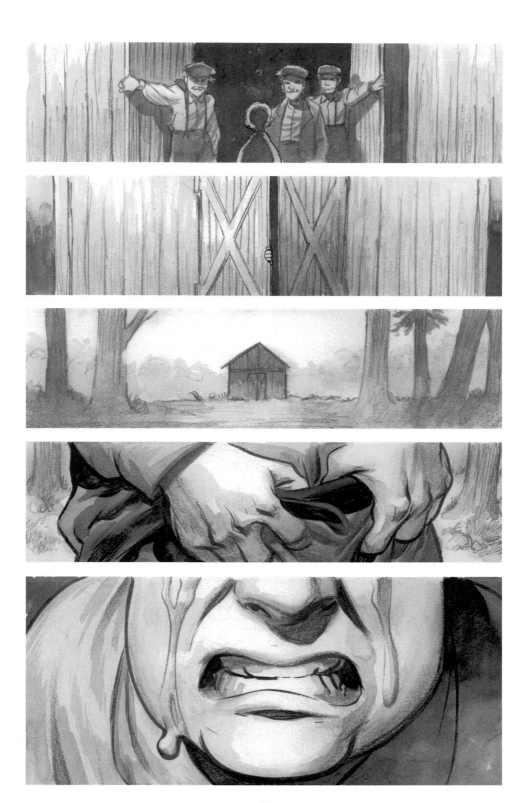

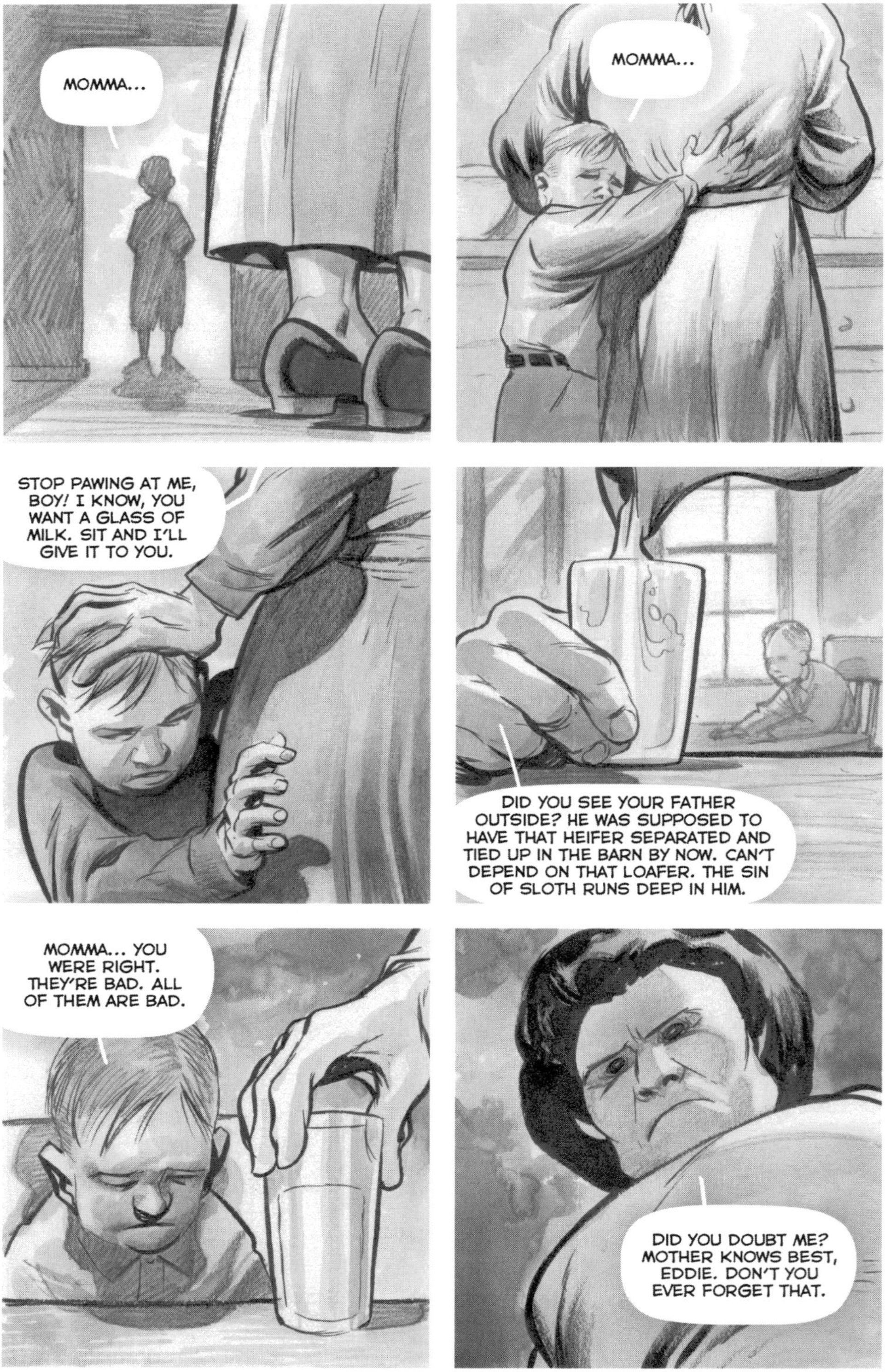
MOMMA...
MOMMA...
STOP PAWING AT ME, BOY! I KNOW, YOU WANT A GLASS OF MILK. SIT AND I'LL GIVE IT TO YOU.
DID YOU SEE YOUR FATHER OUTSIDE? HE WAS SUPPOSED TO HAVE THAT HEIFER SEPARATED AND TIED UP IN THE BARN BY NOW. CAN'T DEPEND ON THAT LOAFER. THE SIN OF SLOTH RUNS DEEP IN HIM.
MOMMA... YOU WERE RIGHT. THEY'RE BAD. ALL OF THEM ARE BAD.
DID YOU DOUBT ME? MOTHER KNOWS BEST, EDDIE. DON'T YOU EVER FORGET THAT.

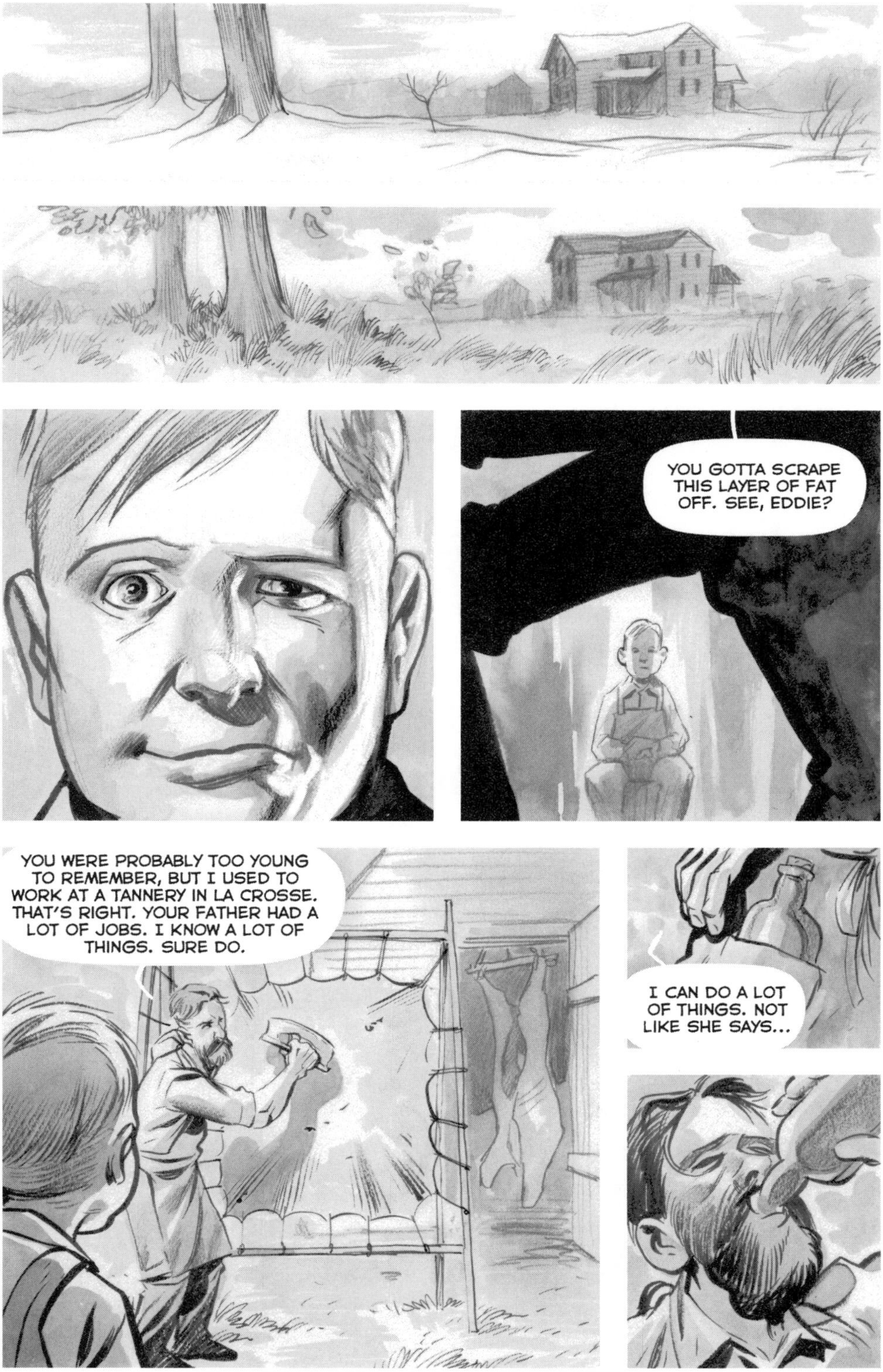
YOU GOTTA SCRAPE THIS LAYER OF FAT OFF. SEE, EDDIE?
YOU WERE PROBABLY TOO YOUNG TO REMEMBER, BUT I USED TO WORK AT A TANNERY IN LA CROSSE. THAT'S RIGHT. YOUR FATHER HAD A LOT OF JOBS. I KNOW A LOT OF THINGS. SURE DO.
I CAN DO A LOT OF THINGS. NOT LIKE SHE SAYS...

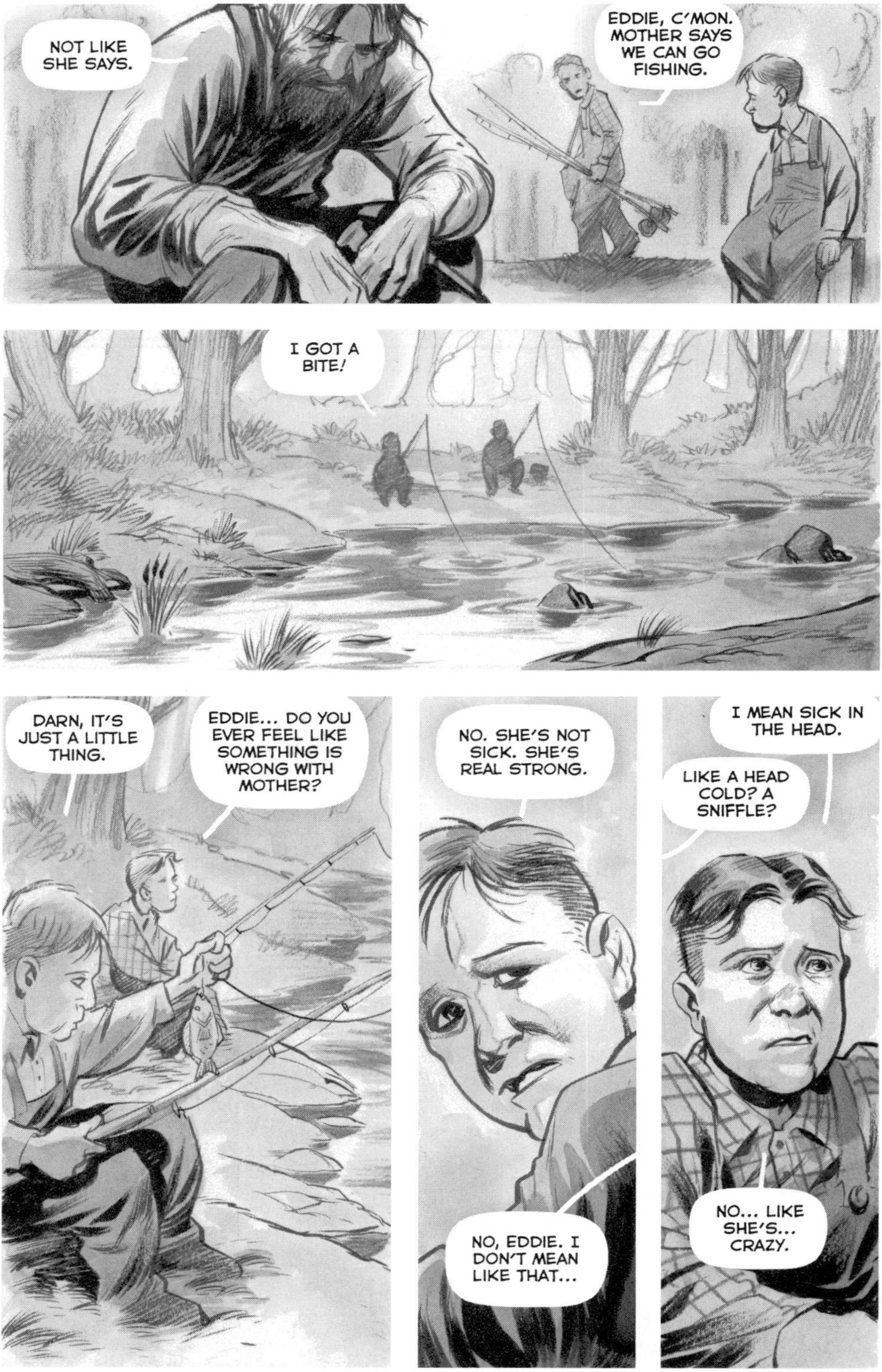
NOT LIKE SHE SAYS.
EDDIE, C'MON. MOTHER SAYS WE CAN GO FISHING.
I GOT A BITE!
DARN, IT'S JUST A LITTLE THING.
EDDIE... DO YOU EVER FEEL LIKE SOMETHING IS WRONG WITH MOTHER?
NO. SHE'S NOT SICK. SHE'S REAL STRONG.
NO, EDDIE. I DON'T MEAN LIKE THAT...
I MEAN SICK IN THE HEAD.
LIKE A HEAD COLD? A SNIFFLE?
NO... LIKE SHE'S... CRAZY.

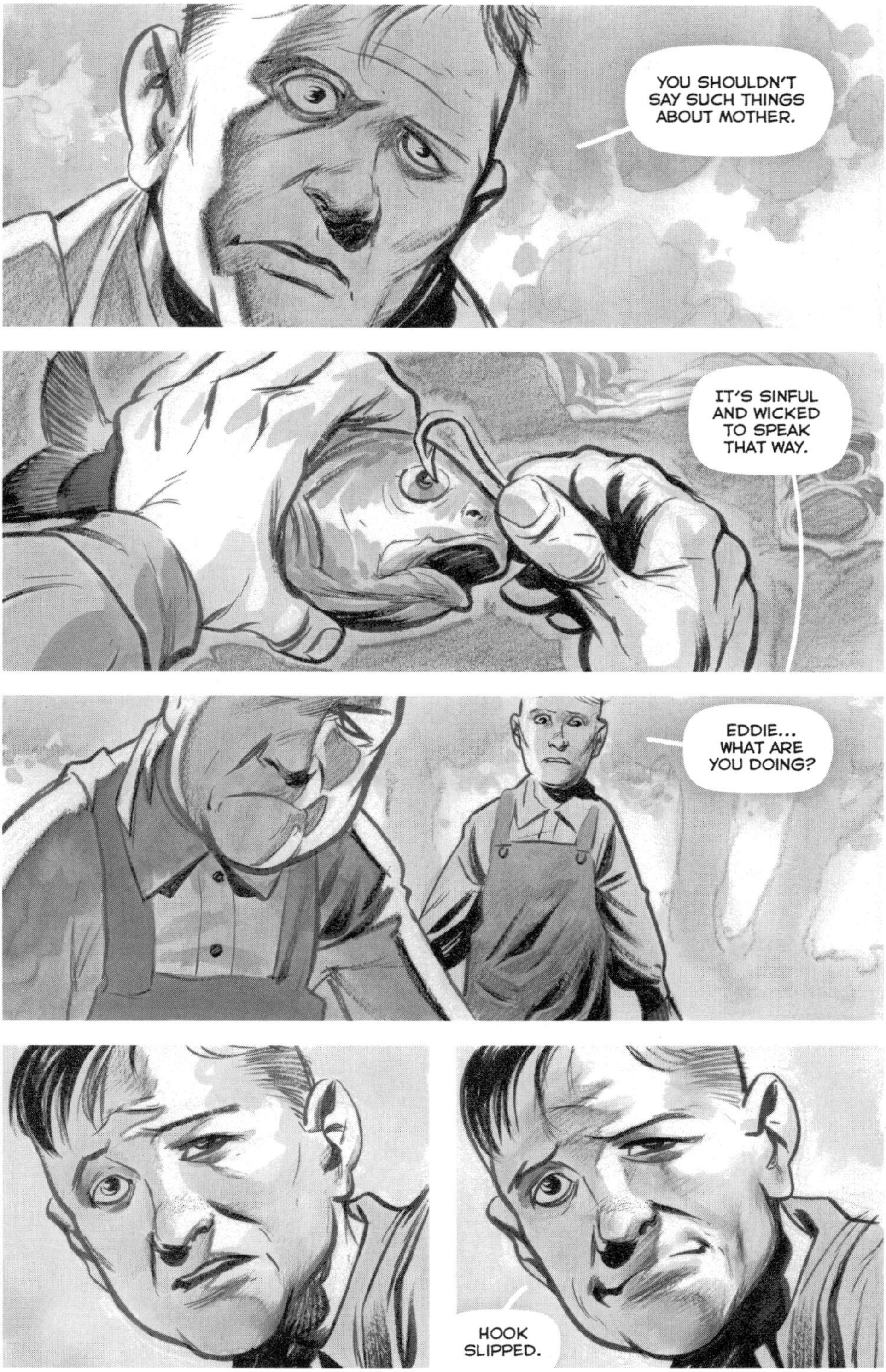
YOU SHOULDN'T SAY SUCH THINGS ABOUT MOTHER.
IT'S SINFUL AND WICKED TO SPEAK THAT WAY.
EDDIE... WHAT ARE YOU DOING?
HOOK SLIPPED.

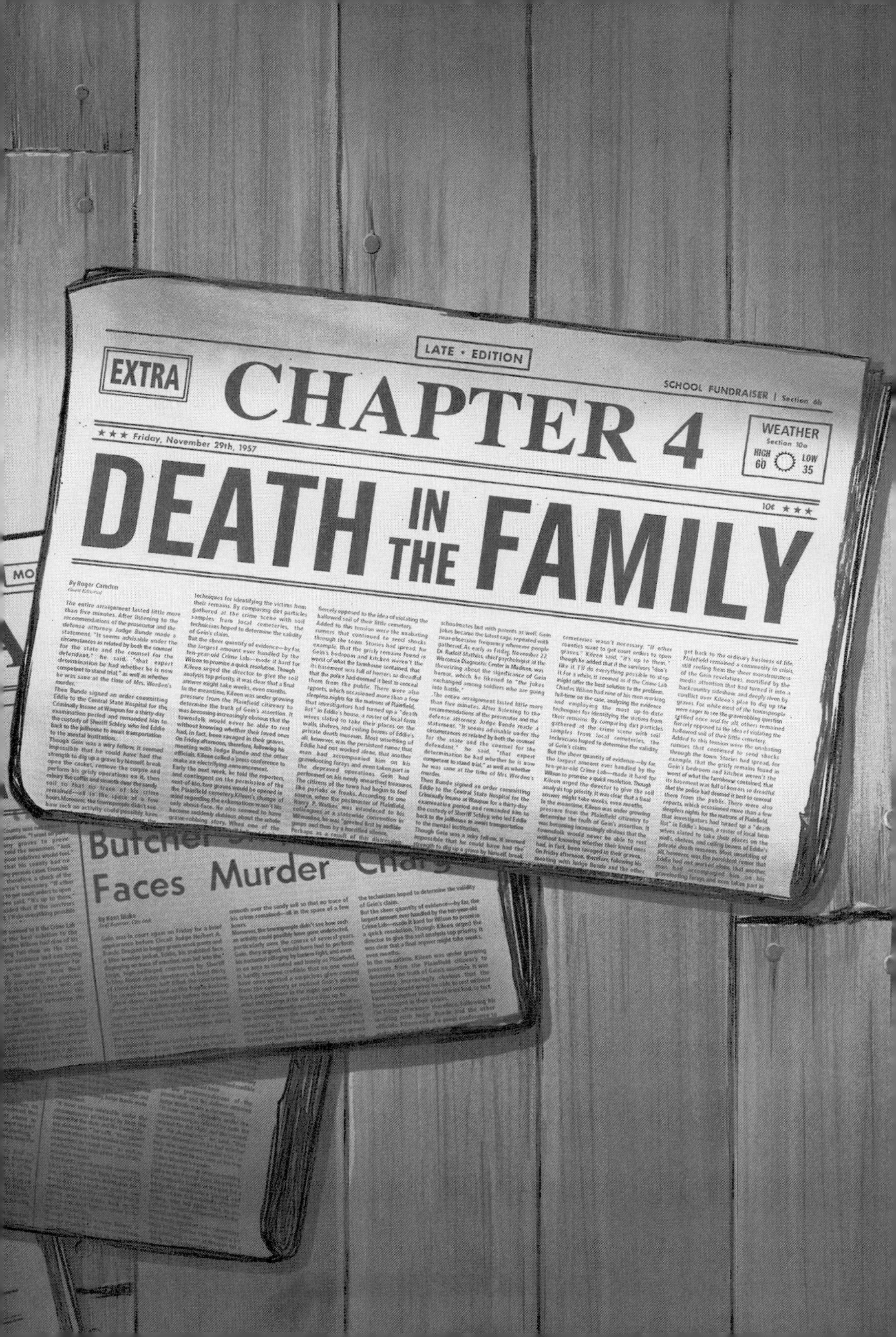

EXTRA
LATE • EDITION
CHAPTER 4
SCHOOL FUNDRAISER | Section 6b
Friday, November 29th, 1957
WEATHER
Section 10a
HIGH 60
LOW 35
10¢
DEATH IN THE FAMILY
By Roger Camden
Butcher
Faces Murder

"A boy's place is
with his mother."

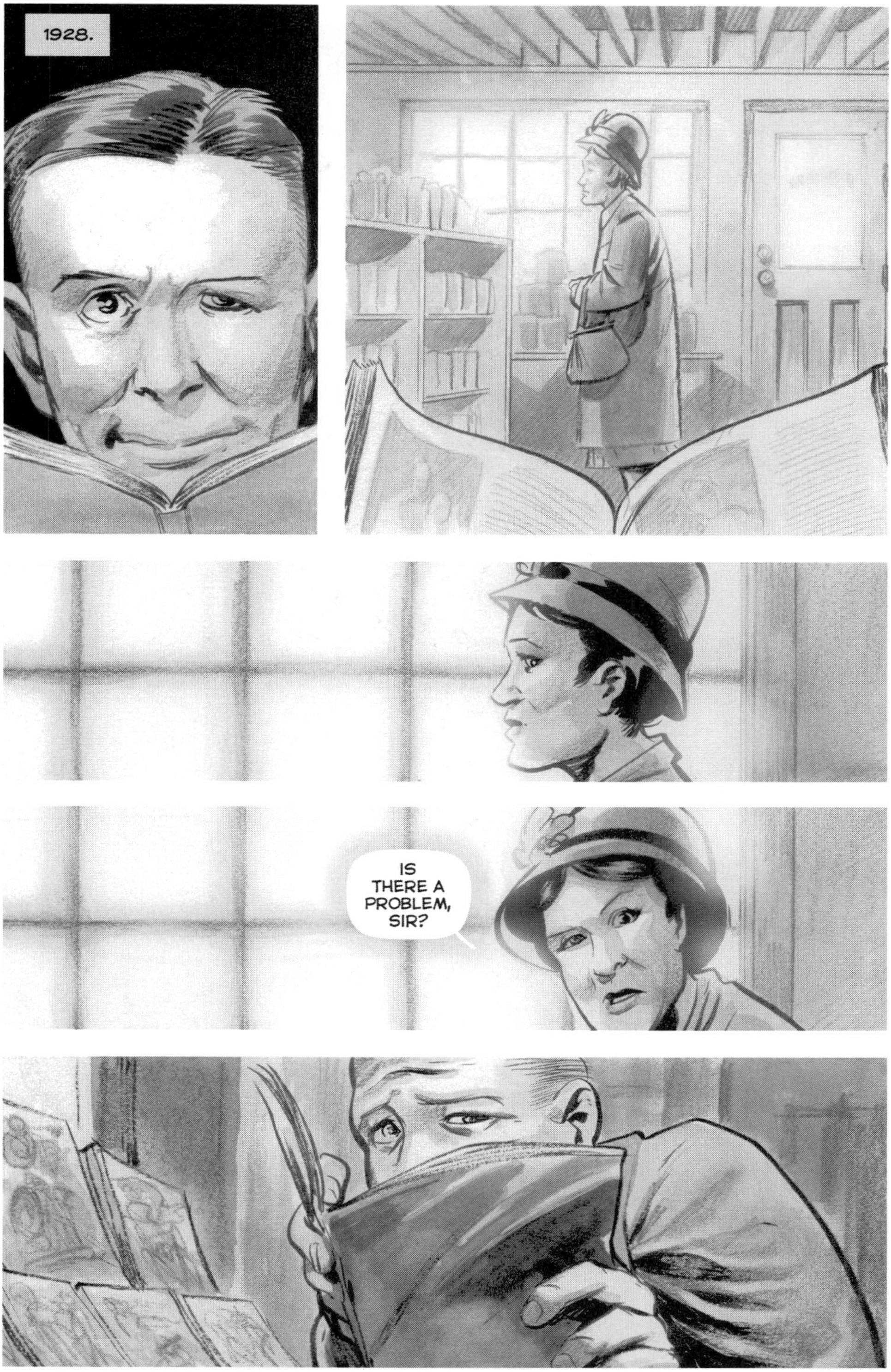
1928.
IS THERE A PROBLEM, SIR?

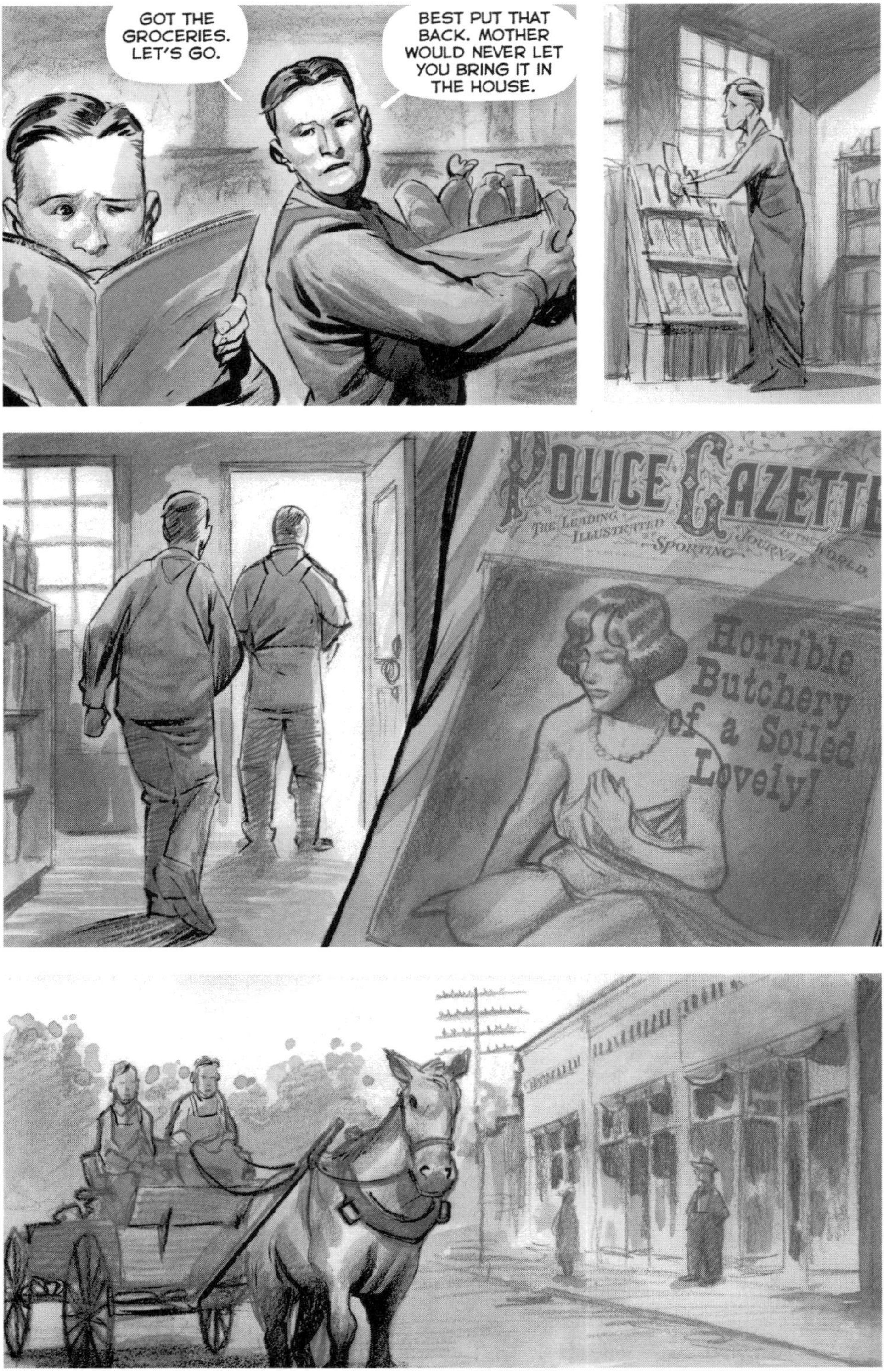
GOT THE GROCERIES. LET'S GO.
BEST PUT THAT BACK. MOTHER WOULD NEVER LET YOU BRING IT IN THE HOUSE.
POLICE GAZETTE
THE LEADING ILLUSTRATED SPORTING JOURNAL IN THE WORLD.
Horrible Butchery of a Soiled Lovely!

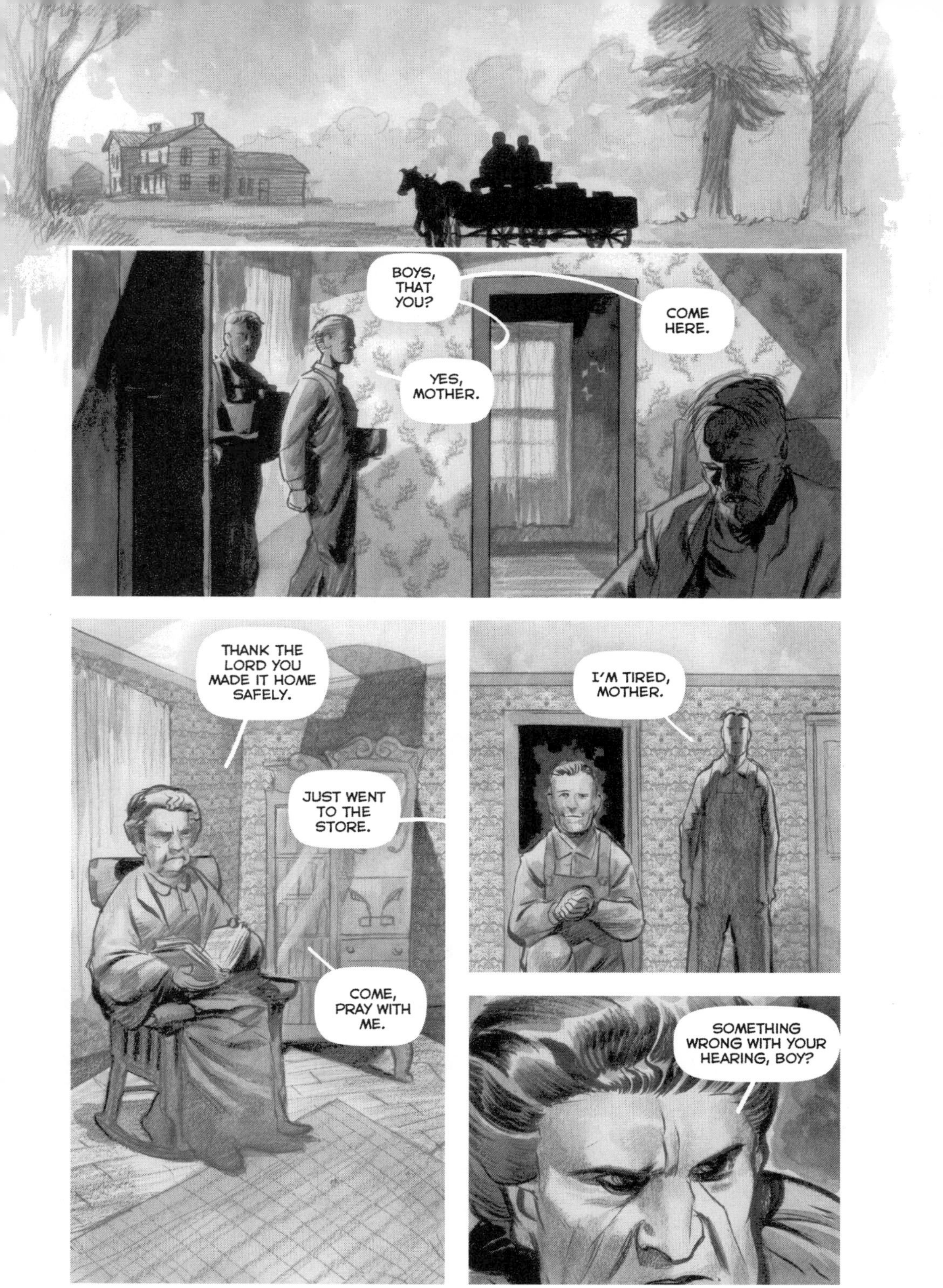
BOYS, THAT YOU?
COME HERE.
YES, MOTHER.
THANK THE LORD YOU MADE IT HOME SAFELY.
JUST WENT TO THE STORE.
COME, PRAY WITH ME.
I'M TIRED, MOTHER.
SOMETHING WRONG WITH YOUR HEARING, BOY?

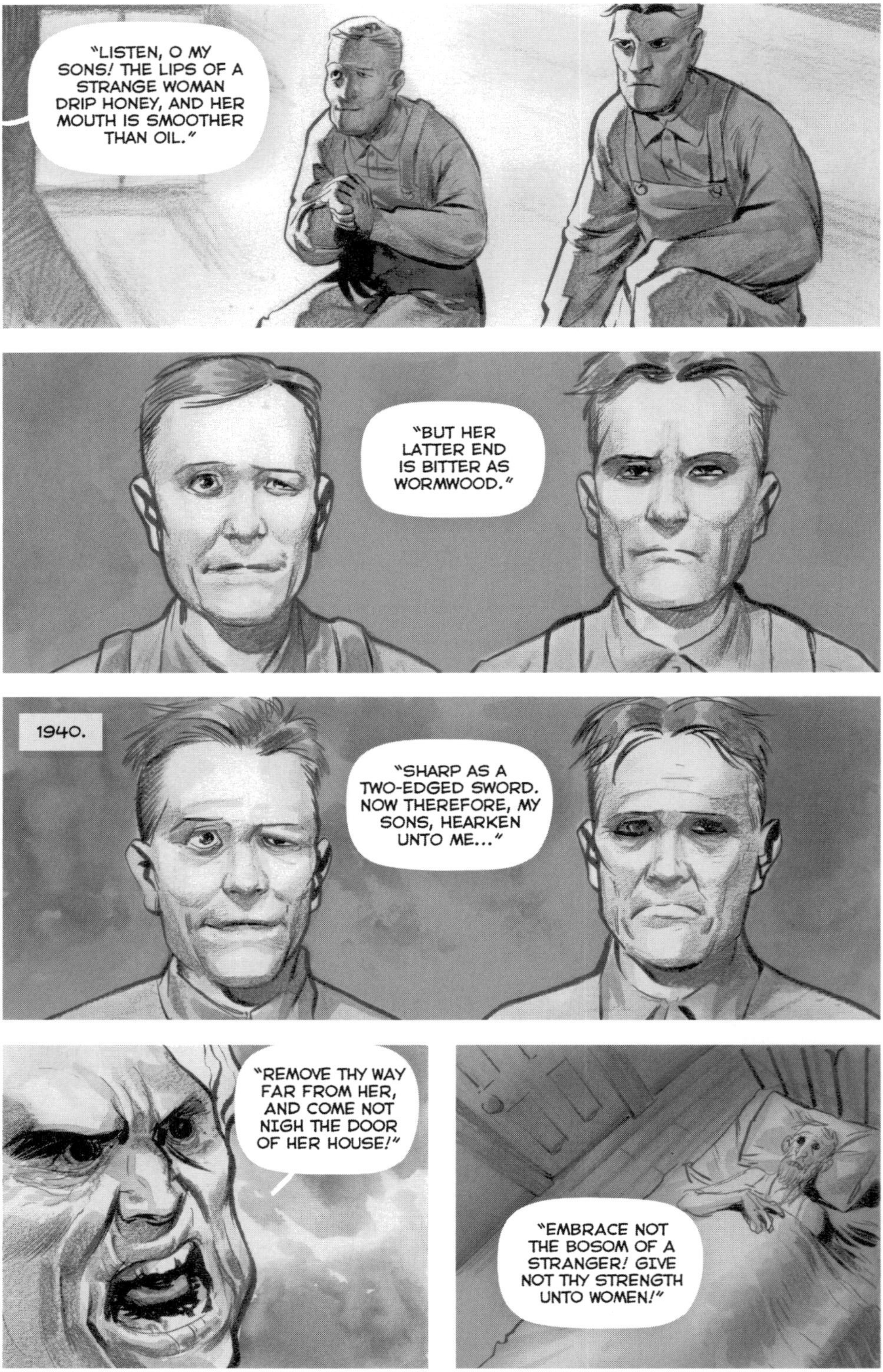
"LISTEN, O MY SONS! THE LIPS OF A STRANGE WOMAN DRIP HONEY, AND HER MOUTH IS SMOOTHER THAN OIL."
"BUT HER LATTER END IS BITTER AS WORMWOOD."
1940.
"SHARP AS A TWO-EDGED SWORD. NOW THEREFORE, MY SONS, HEARKEN UNTO ME..."
"REMOVE THY WAY FAR FROM HER, AND COME NOT NIGH THE DOOR OF HER HOUSE!"
"EMBRACE NOT THE BOSOM OF A STRANGER! GIVE NOT THY STRENGTH UNTO WOMEN!"

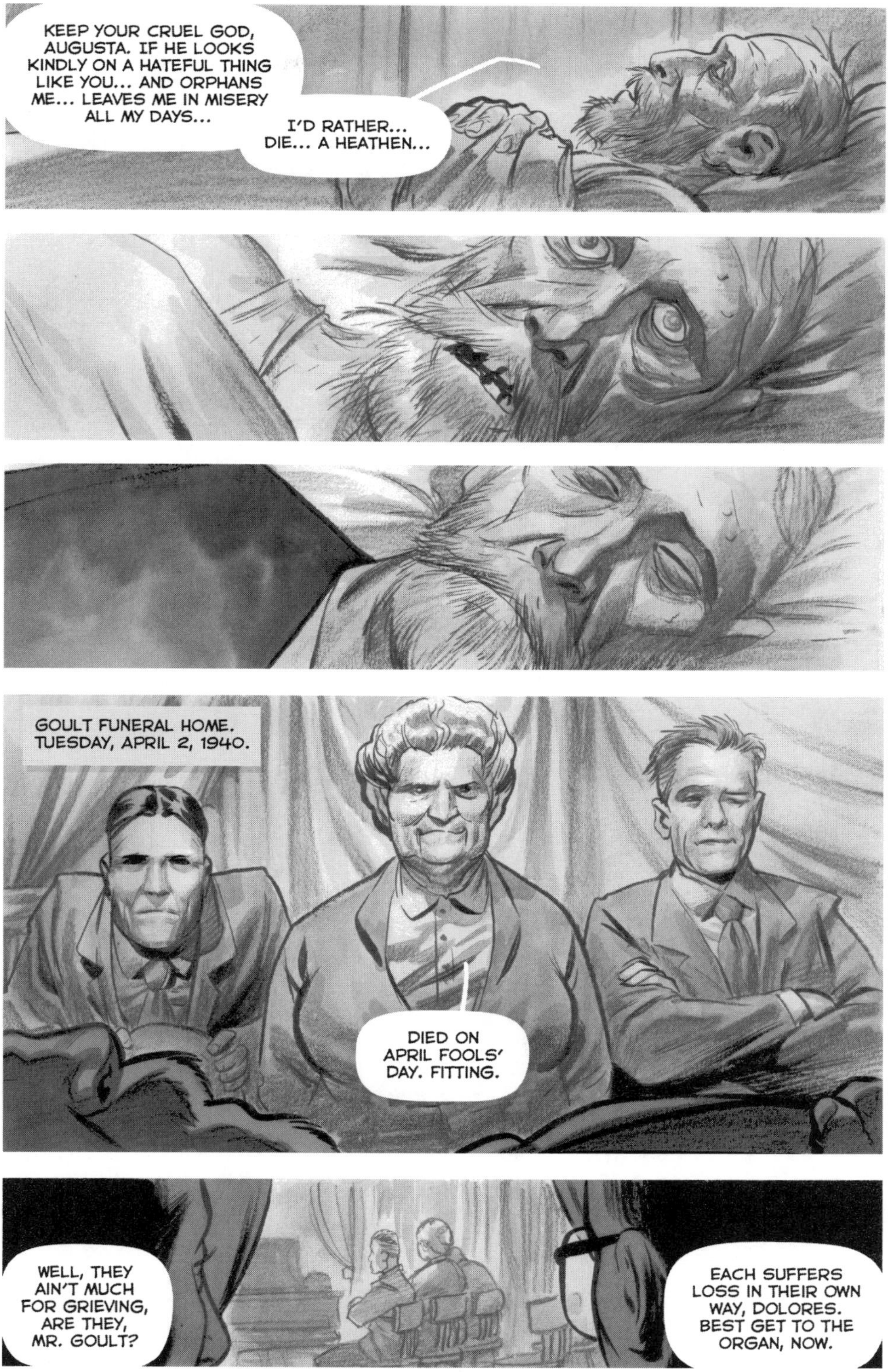
KEEP YOUR CRUEL GOD, AUGUSTA. IF HE LOOKS KINDLY ON A HATEFUL THING LIKE YOU... AND ORPHANS ME... LEAVES ME IN MISERY ALL MY DAYS...
I'D RATHER... DIE... A HEATHEN...
GOULT FUNERAL HOME. TUESDAY, APRIL 2, 1940.
DIED ON APRIL FOOLS' DAY. FITTING.
WELL, THEY AIN'T MUCH FOR GRIEVING, ARE THEY, MR. GOULT?
EACH SUFFERS LOSS IN THEIR OWN WAY, DOLORES. BEST GET TO THE ORGAN, NOW.

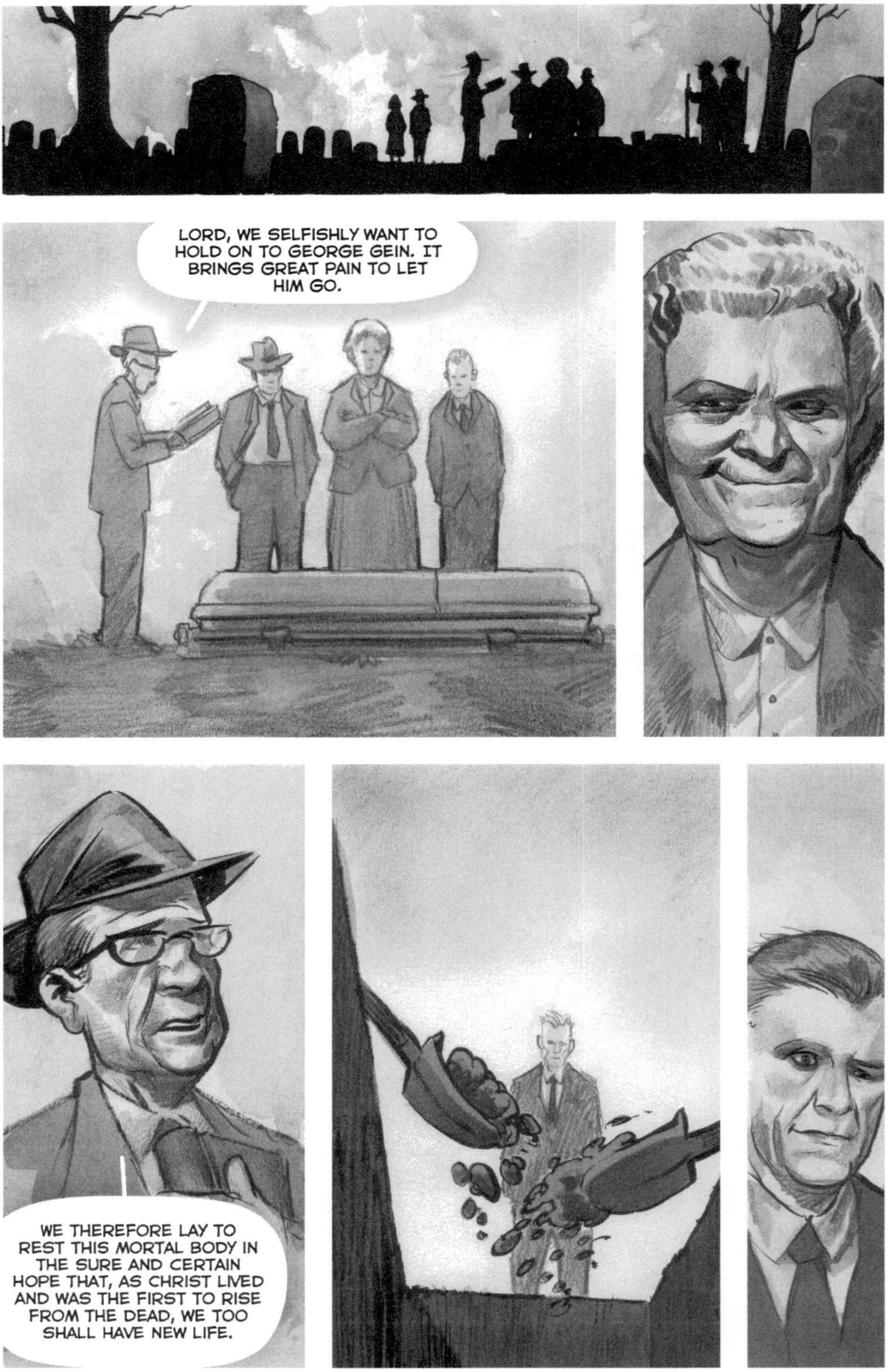
LORD, WE SELFISHLY WANT TO HOLD ON TO GEORGE GEIN. IT BRINGS GREAT PAIN TO LET HIM GO.
WE THEREFORE LAY TO REST THIS MORTAL BODY IN THE SURE AND CERTAIN HOPE THAT, AS CHRIST LIVED AND WAS THE FIRST TO RISE FROM THE DEAD, WE TOO SHALL HAVE NEW LIFE.

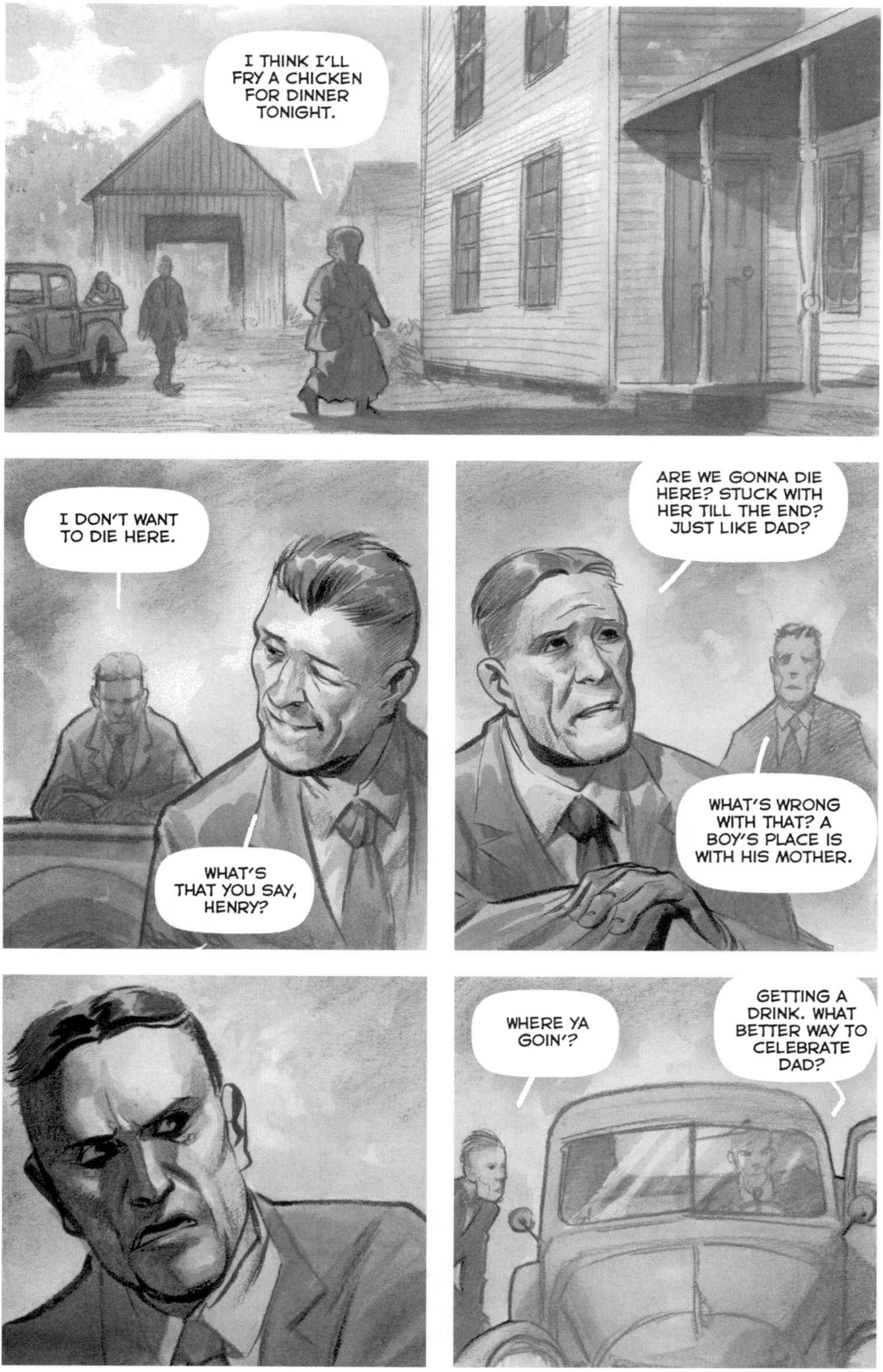
I THINK I'LL FRY A CHICKEN FOR DINNER TONIGHT.
I DON'T WANT TO DIE HERE.
WHAT'S THAT YOU SAY, HENRY?
ARE WE GONNA DIE HERE? STUCK WITH HER TILL THE END? JUST LIKE DAD?
WHAT'S WRONG WITH THAT? A BOY'S PLACE IS WITH HIS MOTHER.
WHERE YA GOIN'?
GETTING A DRINK. WHAT BETTER WAY TO CELEBRATE DAD?

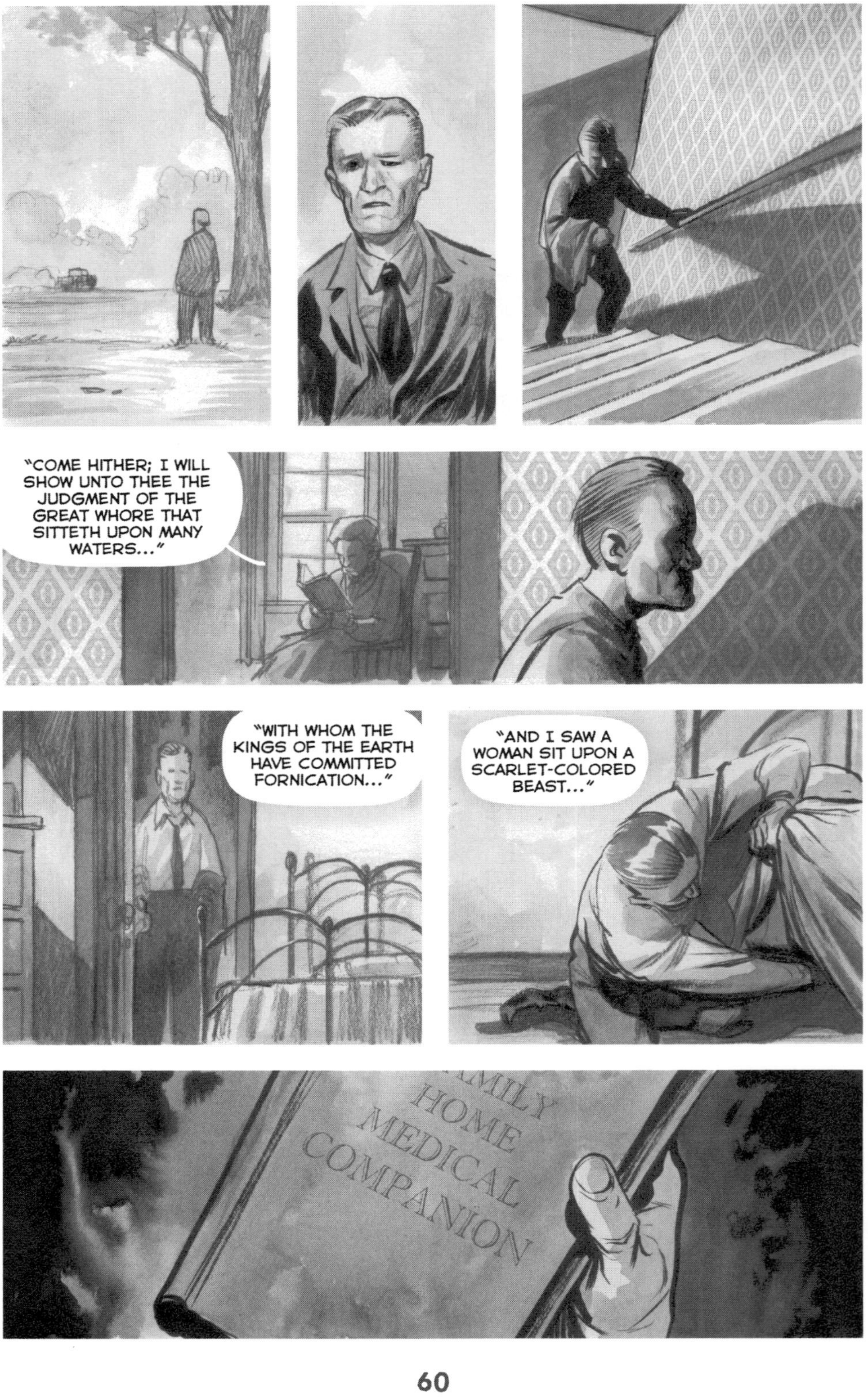
"COME HITHER; I WILL SHOW UNTO THEE THE JUDGMENT OF THE GREAT WHORE THAT SITTETH UPON MANY WATERS..."
"WITH WHOM THE KINGS OF THE EARTH HAVE COMMITTED FORNICATION..."
"AND I SAW A WOMAN SIT UPON A SCARLET-COLORED BEAST..."
HOME
MEDICAL
COMPANION

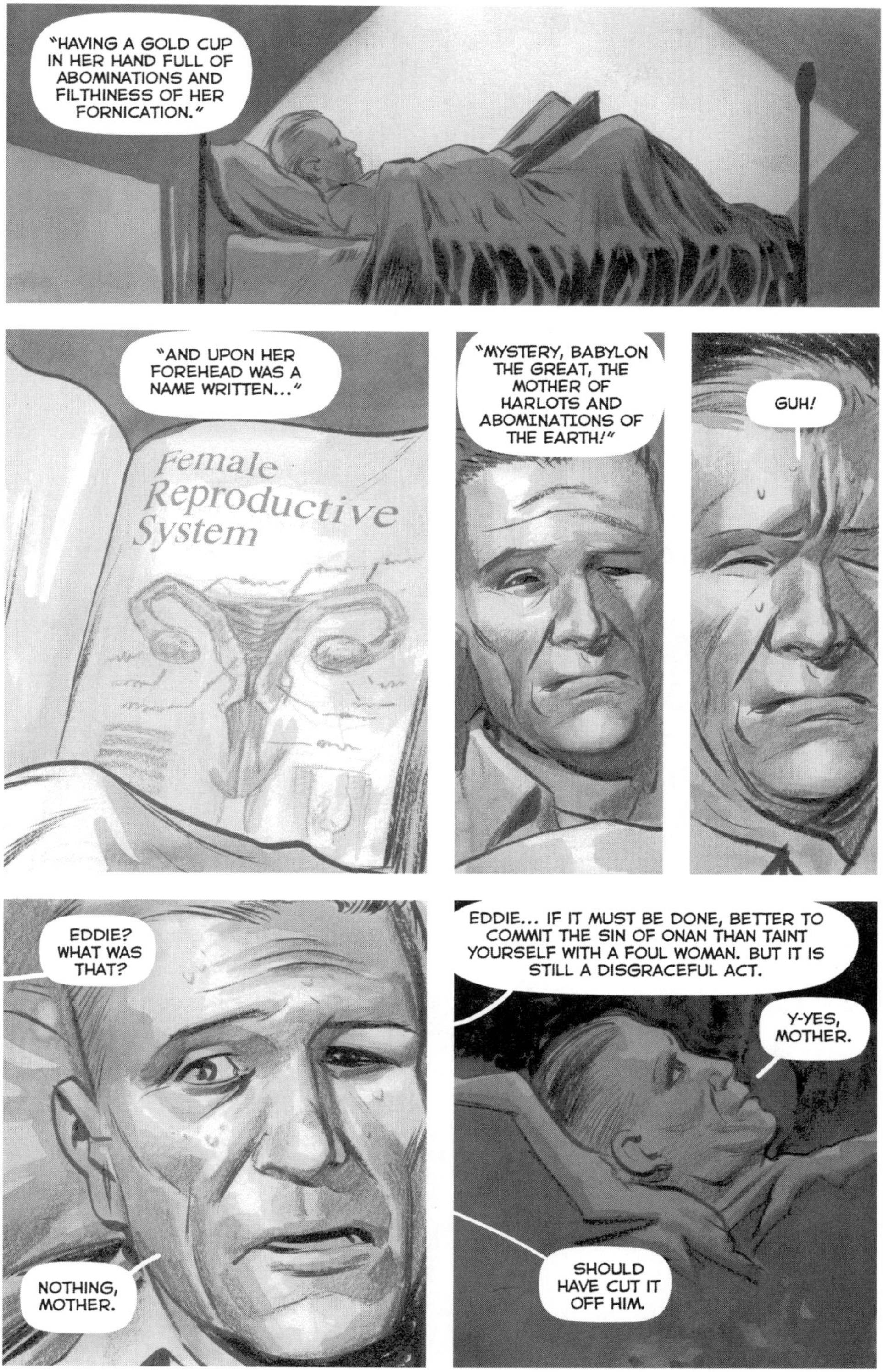
"HAVING A GOLD CUP IN HER HAND FULL OF ABOMINATIONS AND FILTHINESS OF HER FORNICATION."
"AND UPON HER FOREHEAD WAS A NAME WRITTEN..."
Female Reproductive System
"MYSTERY, BABYLON THE GREAT, THE MOTHER OF HARLOTS AND ABOMINATIONS OF THE EARTH!"
GUH!
EDDIE? WHAT WAS THAT?
NOTHING, MOTHER.
EDDIE... IF IT MUST BE DONE, BETTER TO COMMIT THE SIN OF ONAN THAN TAINT YOURSELF WITH A FOUL WOMAN. BUT IT IS STILL A DISGRACEFUL ACT.
Y-YES, MOTHER.
SHOULD HAVE CUT IT OFF HIM.

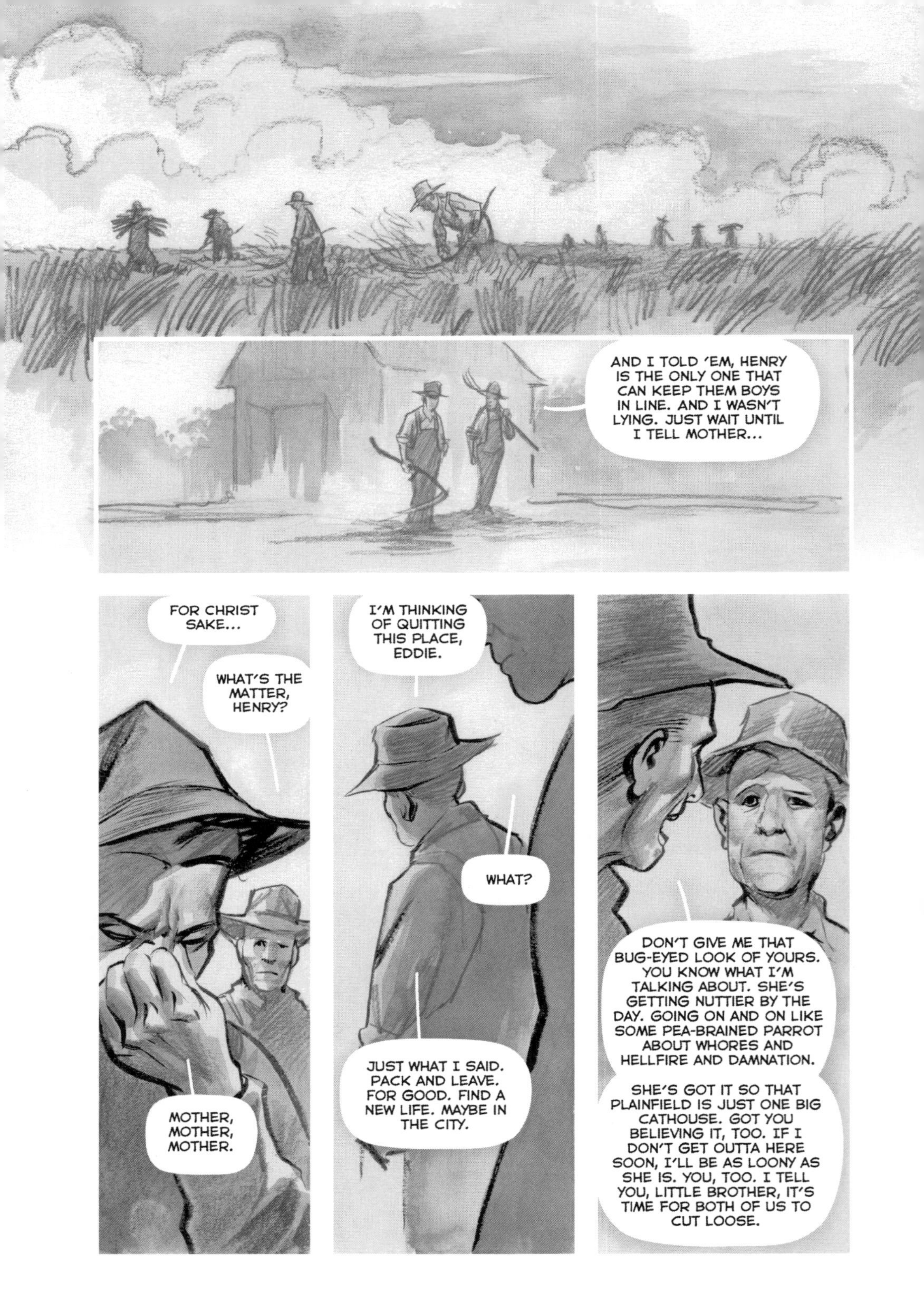
AND I TOLD 'EM, HENRY IS THE ONLY ONE THAT CAN KEEP THEM BOYS IN LINE. AND I WASN'T LYING. JUST WAIT UNTIL I TELL MOTHER...
FOR CHRIST SAKE...
WHAT'S THE MATTER, HENRY?
MOTHER, MOTHER, MOTHER.
I'M THINKING OF QUITTING THIS PLACE, EDDIE.
WHAT?
JUST WHAT I SAID. PACK AND LEAVE. FOR GOOD. FIND A NEW LIFE. MAYBE IN THE CITY.
DON'T GIVE ME THAT BUG-EYED LOOK OF YOURS. YOU KNOW WHAT I'M TALKING ABOUT. SHE'S GETTING NUTTIER BY THE DAY. GOING ON AND ON LIKE SOME PEA-BRAINED PARROT ABOUT WHORES AND HELLFIRE AND DAMNATION.
SHE'S GOT IT SO THAT PLAINFIELD IS JUST ONE BIG CATHOUSE. GOT YOU BELIEVING IT, TOO. IF I DON'T GET OUTTA HERE SOON, I'LL BE AS LOONY AS SHE IS. YOU, TOO. I TELL YOU, LITTLE BROTHER, IT'S TIME FOR BOTH OF US TO CUT LOOSE.

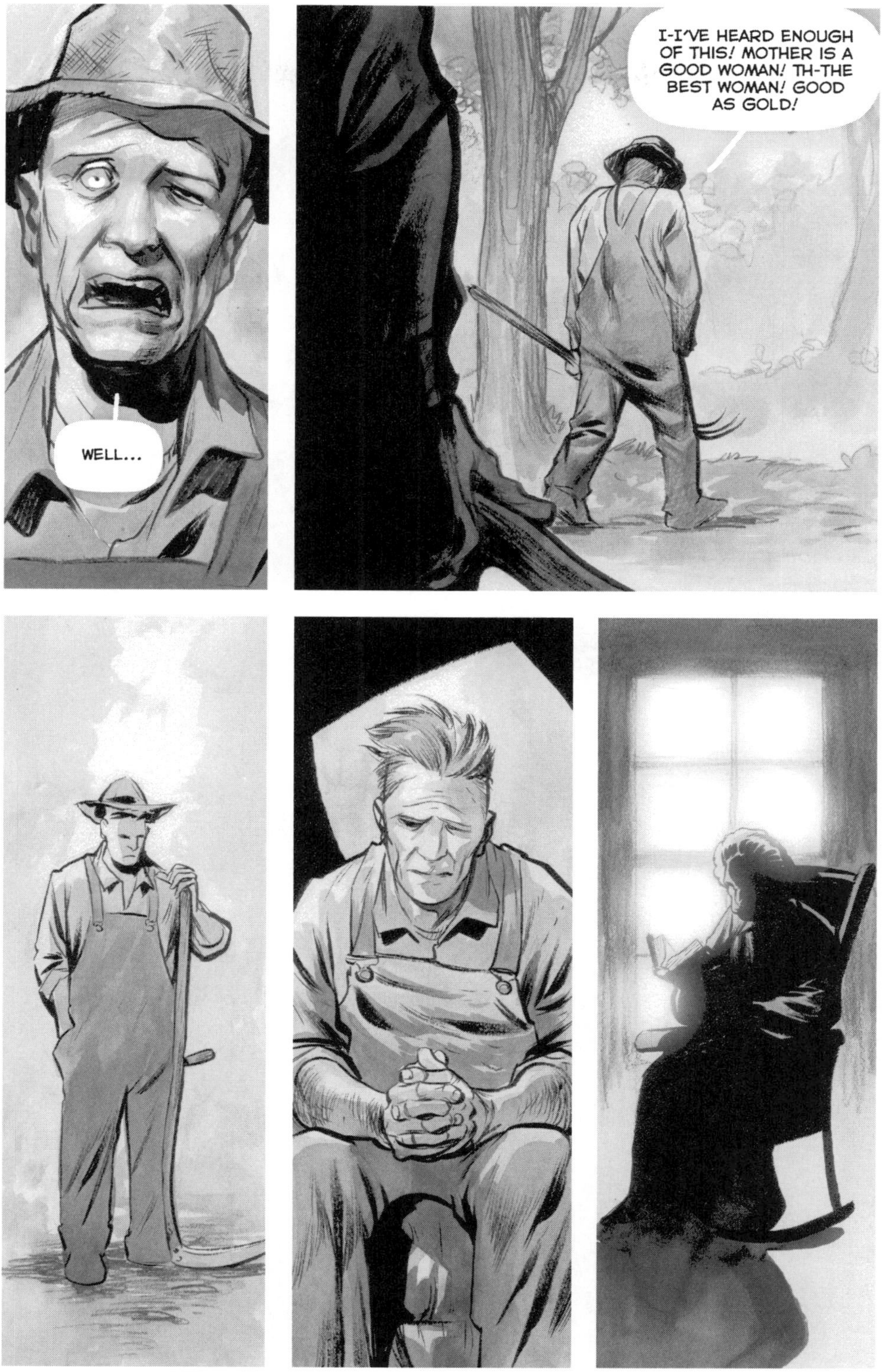
WELL...
I-I'VE HEARD ENOUGH OF THIS! MOTHER IS A GOOD WOMAN! TH-THE BEST WOMAN! GOOD AS GOLD!

MAY 16, 1944.

THERE ARE DIFFERING ACCOUNTS OF WHAT TOUCHED OFF THE MARSH FIRE. WHETHER IT WAS SET ACCIDENTALLY OR DELIBERATELY TO CLEAR THE FIELD. AND IF DELIBERATE, WHETHER IT WAS HENRY'S OR ED'S IDEA.

WHAT IS KNOWN IS THAT IT QUICKLY GOT OUT OF HAND. AND, ACCORDING TO ED, THE TWO BROTHERS BECAME SEPARATED AS THEY FOUGHT THE BLAZE.

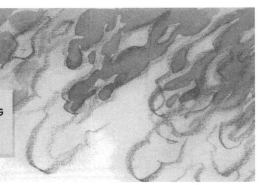

ED WOULD LATER CLAIM THAT SETTING THE FIRE WAS HENRY'S IDEA.

I COAXED HIM AND TRIED TO KEEP HIM HOME. BUT HE JUST KEPT AT ME TILL I TOOK HIM THERE.

AT THE TIME IT HAPPENED, THOUGH, NEWSPAPERS REPORTED THAT IT WAS ED WHO INSISTED ON BURNING THE MARSH THAT DAY, AND THAT HENRY HAD COME ALONG TO HELP.

ED TOLD THE SHERIFF THAT AFTER HE MANAGED TO PUT OUT THE FIRE, HE WENT BACK TO SEARCH FOR HENRY. BUT IT HAD GOTTEN DARK AND HE WAS UNABLE TO FIND HIM.

WHAT CAN I HELP YOU WITH, MR. GEIN?

I CAN'T FIND MY BROTHER.

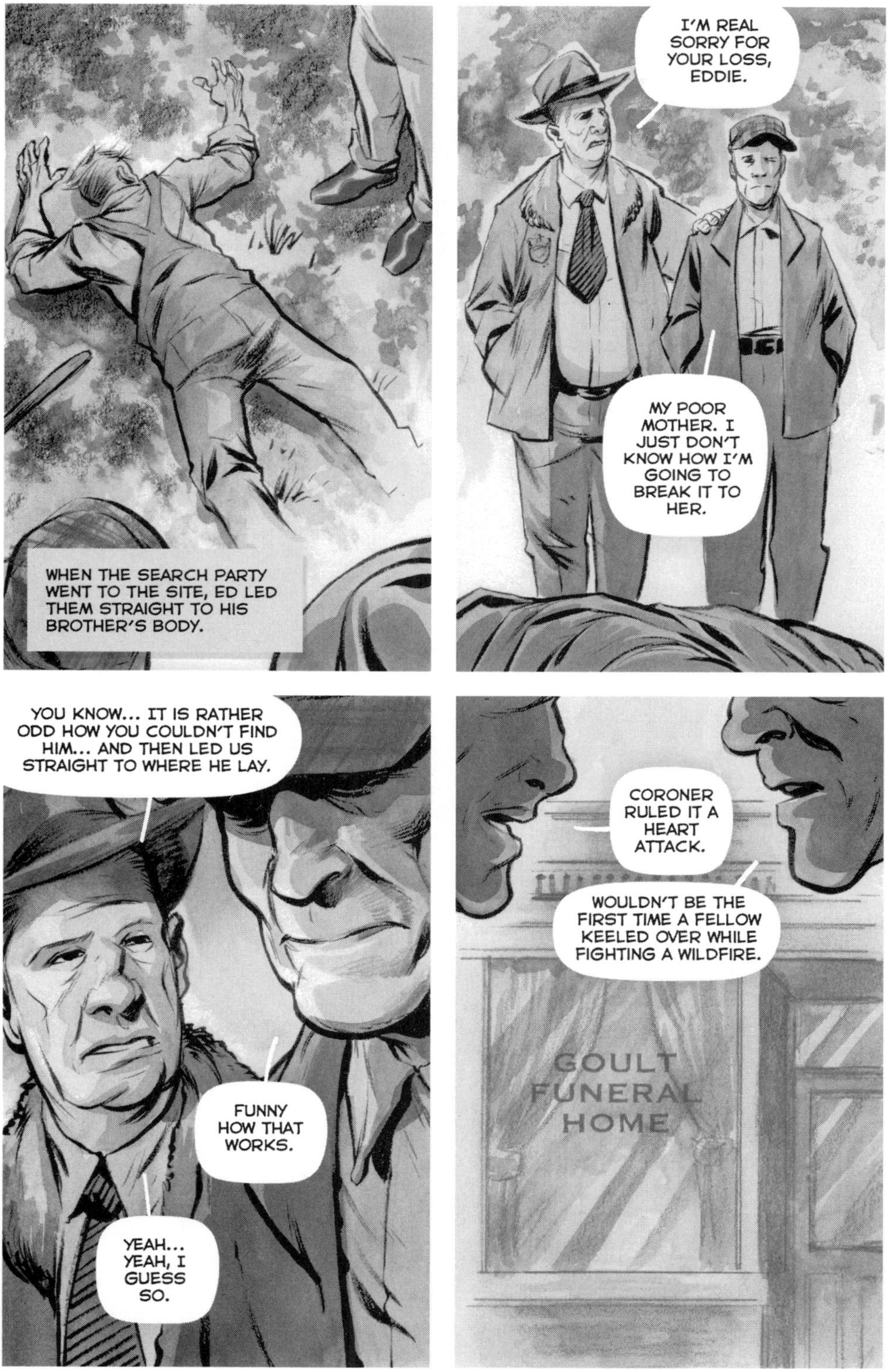
WHEN THE SEARCH PARTY WENT TO THE SITE, ED LED THEM STRAIGHT TO HIS BROTHER'S BODY.
I'M REAL SORRY FOR YOUR LOSS, EDDIE.
MY POOR MOTHER. I JUST DON'T KNOW HOW I'M GOING TO BREAK IT TO HER.
YOU KNOW... IT IS RATHER ODD HOW YOU COULDN'T FIND HIM... AND THEN LED US STRAIGHT TO WHERE HE LAY.
FUNNY HOW THAT WORKS.
YEAH... YEAH, I GUESS SO.
CORONER RULED IT A HEART ATTACK.
WOULDN'T BE THE FIRST TIME A FELLOW KEELED OVER WHILE FIGHTING A WILDFIRE.
GOULT FUNERAL HOME

I DON'T KNOW. I HEARD THERE WERE SOME MIGHTY PECULIAR MARKS ON THE BACK OF HIS SKULL.

WELL, SURE. A MAN DROPS DEAD OF A HEART ATTACK, HE'S LIABLE TO HIT HIS HEAD ON THE WAY DOWN.

YOU ASK ME, THAT BROTHER OF HIS HAD SOMETHING TO DO WITH IT.

EDDIE? THAT MILQUETOAST? HELL, HE'S MEEK AS A SCHOOLGIRL.

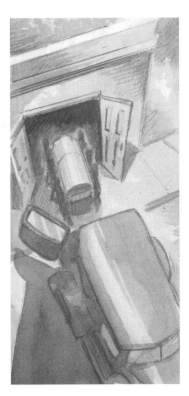

I'M SO SORRY ABOUT YOUR BOY, MRS. GEIN.

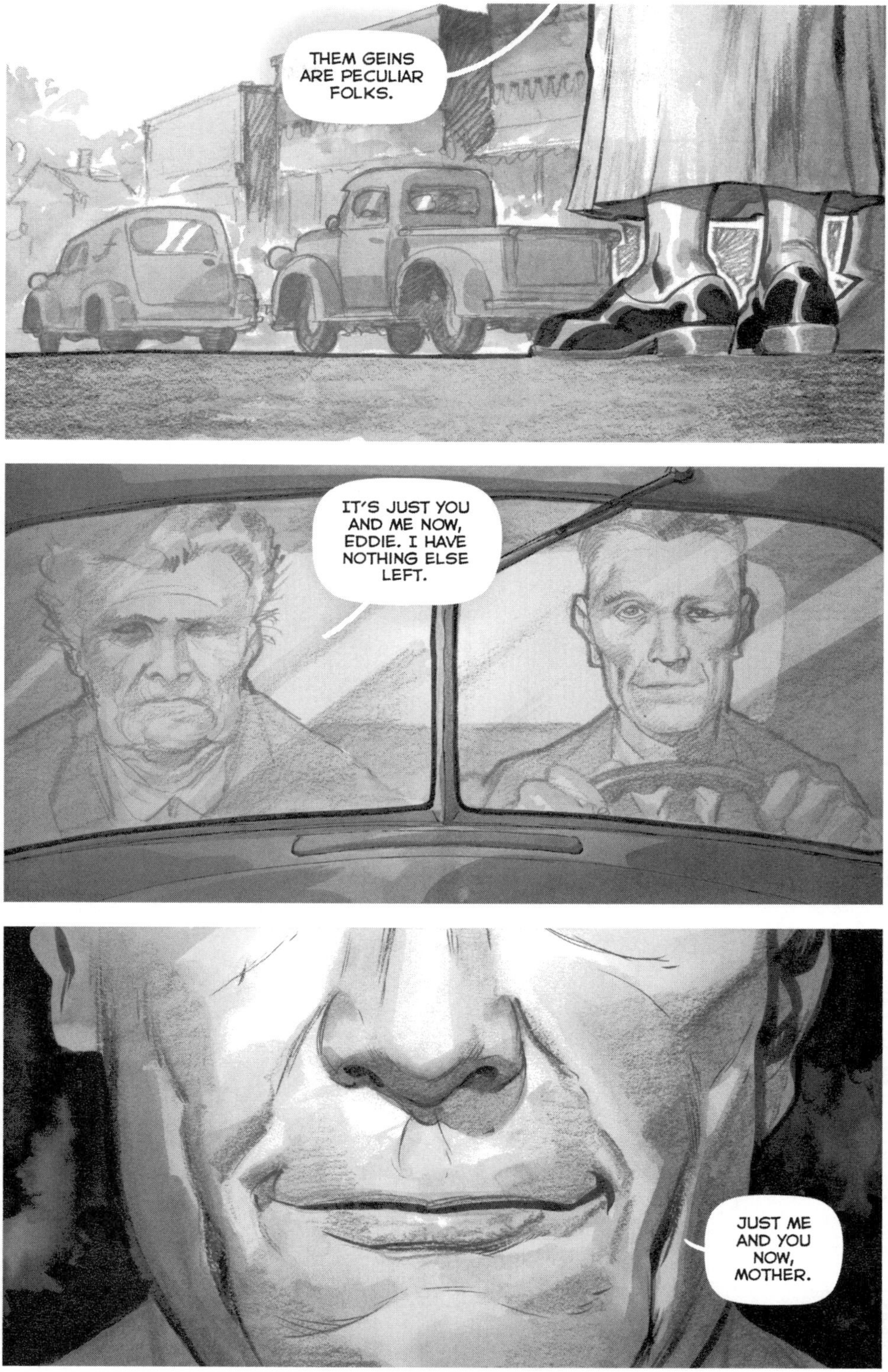
THEM GEINS ARE PECULIAR FOLKS.
IT'S JUST YOU AND ME NOW, EDDIE. I HAVE NOTHING ELSE LEFT.
JUST ME AND YOU NOW, MOTHER.

MORNING · EDITION

DAILY CHAPTER 5

WEATHER
Section 10a
HIGH 28 · LOW 7

10¢ ★ ★ ★

★ ★ ★ Monday, December 2nd, 1957

ALONE AT LAST

Residents Recall Her Influence on 'Mild' Man's Life

By Leland Rynquist
Lead reporter Cos And

The entire arraignment lasted little more than five minutes. After listening to the recommendations of the prosecutor and the defense attorneys, Judge Burde made a statement. "It seems advisable under the circumstances as related in both the counsel for the state and the counsel for the defendant," he said, "that expert determination be tried, whether he is now competent to stand trial," as well as whether he was sane at the time of Mrs. Worden's murder.

Then Burde signed an order committing Eddie to the Central State Hospital for the Criminally Insane at Rogues for a thirty-day examination period and remanded him to the custody of Sheriff Schley, who led Eddie back to the jailhouse.

techniques for identifying the victims from their remains. By comparing dirt particles gathered at the crime scene with soil samples from local cemeteries, the technicians hoped to determine the validity of Gein's claim.

But the sheer quantity of evidence—by far the largest amount ever handled by the ten-year-old Crime Lab—made it hard for Wilton to promise a quick resolution. Though Kileen urged the director to give the soil analysis top priority, it was clear that the answer might take weeks, even months.

In the meantime, there was under growing pressure from the Plainfield attorney's office to resolve the truth of Gein's assertion. It was becoming increasingly obvious that the only way to conclusively answer their loved ones without knowing whether their loved ones had, in fact, become ravaged in their graves.

On Friday afternoon, therefore, following his meeting with Judge Burde and the other...

cemeteries wasn't necessary. "If either counter wants to get court orders to open graves," Kileen said, "it's up to them." Though he added that if the evidence was like it, "I'll do everything necessary to stop it. For a while, it seemed possible to stop the ghoulish rumors that were plaguing the...

get back to the ordinary business of life. Still reeling from the mass excavations of the Gein revelation, mortified by the media attention that had turned it into a backcountry abbadon...

"It was the happiest
time of his life."

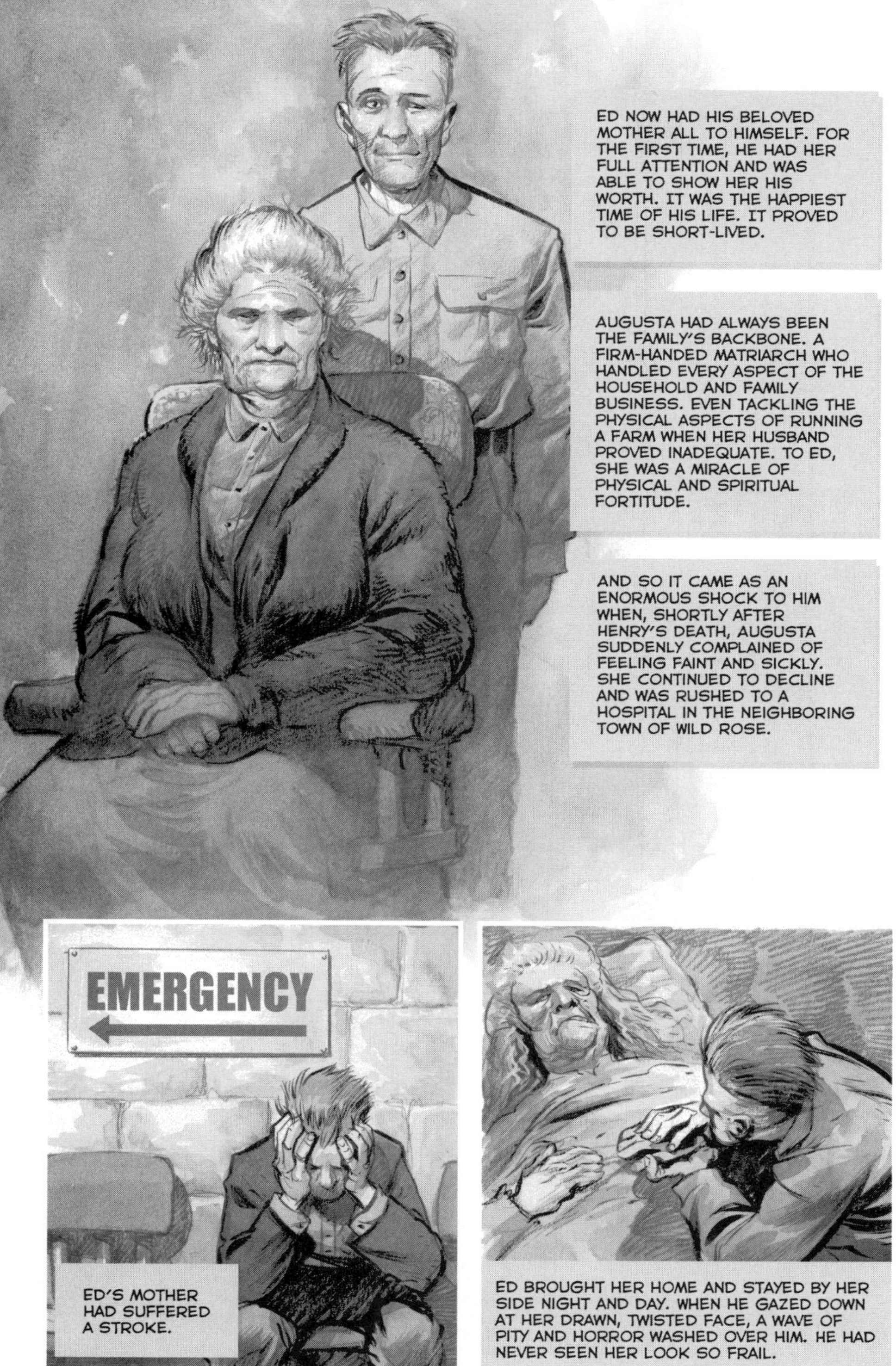
ED NOW HAD HIS BELOVED MOTHER ALL TO HIMSELF. FOR THE FIRST TIME, HE HAD HER FULL ATTENTION AND WAS ABLE TO SHOW HER HIS WORTH. IT WAS THE HAPPIEST TIME OF HIS LIFE. IT PROVED TO BE SHORT-LIVED.
AUGUSTA HAD ALWAYS BEEN THE FAMILY'S BACKBONE. A FIRM-HANDED MATRIARCH WHO HANDLED EVERY ASPECT OF THE HOUSEHOLD AND FAMILY BUSINESS. EVEN TACKLING THE PHYSICAL ASPECTS OF RUNNING A FARM WHEN HER HUSBAND PROVED INADEQUATE. TO ED, SHE WAS A MIRACLE OF PHYSICAL AND SPIRITUAL FORTITUDE.
AND SO IT CAME AS AN ENORMOUS SHOCK TO HIM WHEN, SHORTLY AFTER HENRY'S DEATH, AUGUSTA SUDDENLY COMPLAINED OF FEELING FAINT AND SICKLY. SHE CONTINUED TO DECLINE AND WAS RUSHED TO A HOSPITAL IN THE NEIGHBORING TOWN OF WILD ROSE.
EMERGENCY
ED'S MOTHER HAD SUFFERED A STROKE.
ED BROUGHT HER HOME AND STAYED BY HER SIDE NIGHT AND DAY. WHEN HE GAZED DOWN AT HER DRAWN, TWISTED FACE, A WAVE OF PITY AND HORROR WASHED OVER HIM. HE HAD NEVER SEEN HER LOOK SO FRAIL.

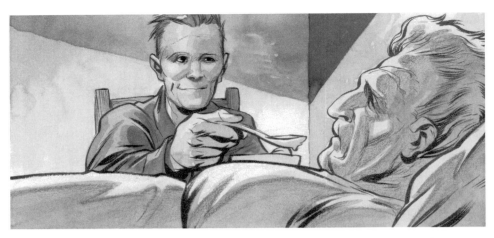

BUT AT THE SAME TIME, HE FELT STRANGELY EXHILARATED BY HER HELPLESSNESS. SHE WAS ENTIRELY IN HIS CARE. COMPLETELY IN HIS POWER.

FROM HER BED, SHE GAVE ED INSTRUCTION ON WHAT NEEDED TO BE DONE AROUND THE FARM. AT NIGHT, HE READ TO HER FROM THE BIBLE. SHE OFTEN REQUESTED HE RECITE PSALM 6.

"O LORD, REBUKE ME NOT IN THINE ANGER, NEITHER CHASTEN ME IN THY HOT DISPLEASURE. HAVE MERCY UPON ME, O LORD; FOR I AM WEAK: O LORD, HEAL ME; FOR MY BONES ARE VEXED."

"MY SOUL IS ALSO SORE VEXED: BUT THOU, O LORD, HOW LONG? RETURN, O LORD, DELIVER MY SOUL: O SAVE ME FOR THY MERCIES' SAKE. FOR IN DEATH THERE IS NO REMEMBRANCE OF THEE: IN THE GRAVE WHO SHALL GIVE THEE THANKS?"

"I AM WEARY WITH MY GROANING; ALL THE NIGHT MAKE I MY BED TO SWIM; I WATER MY COUCH WITH MY TEARS. MINE EYE IS CONSUMED BECAUSE OF GRIEF; IT WAXETH OLD BECAUSE OF ALL MINE ENEMIES. DEPART FROM ME, ALL YE WORKERS OF INIQUITY; FOR THE LORD HATH HEARD THE VOICE OF MY WEEPING. THE LORD HATH HEARD MY SUPPLICATION. THE LORD WILL RECEIVE MY PRAYER."

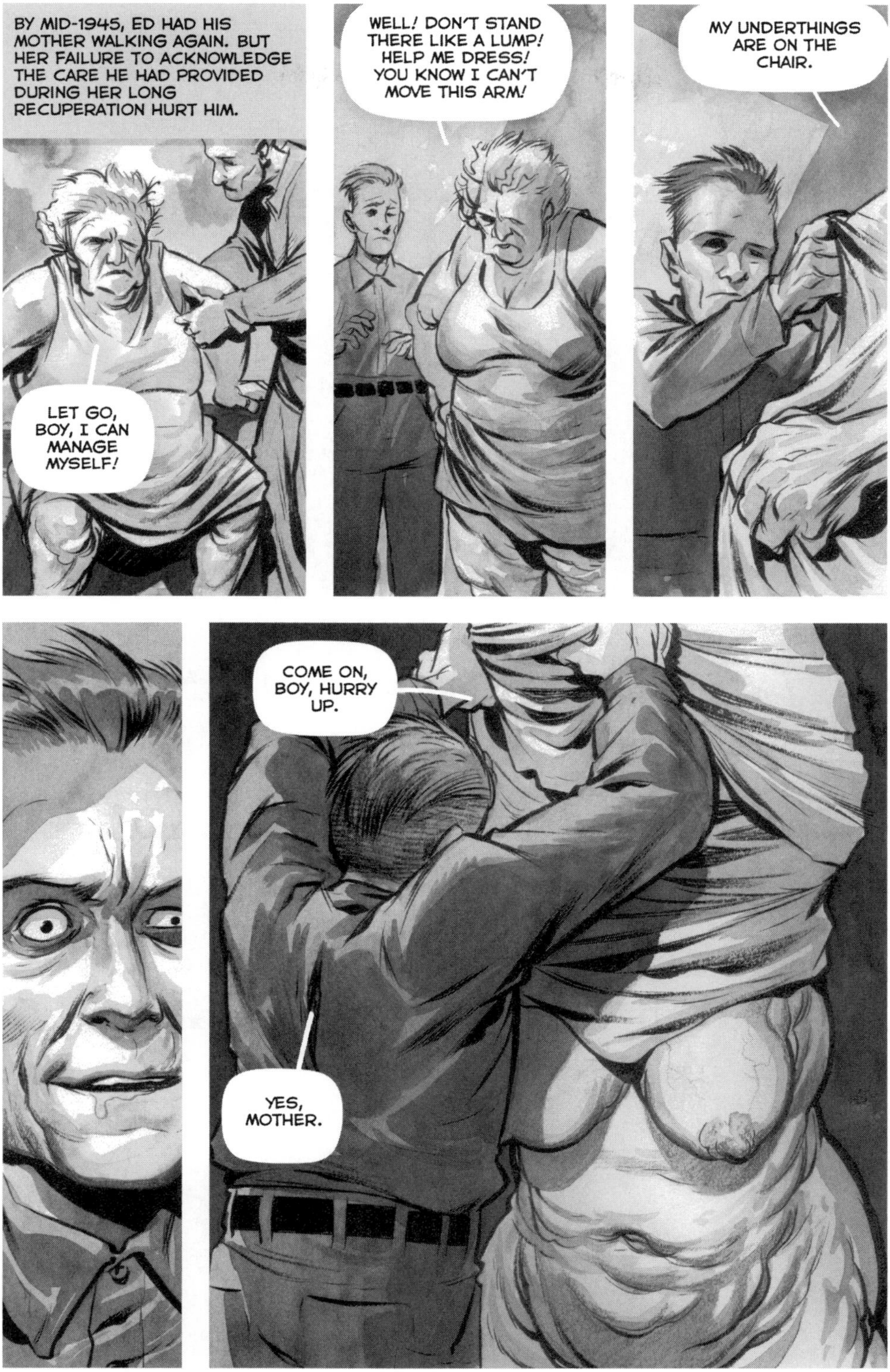
BY MID-1945, ED HAD HIS MOTHER WALKING AGAIN. BUT HER FAILURE TO ACKNOWLEDGE THE CARE HE HAD PROVIDED DURING HER LONG RECUPERATION HURT HIM.
LET GO, BOY, I CAN MANAGE MYSELF!
WELL! DON'T STAND THERE LIKE A LUMP! HELP ME DRESS! YOU KNOW I CAN'T MOVE THIS ARM!
MY UNDERTHINGS ARE ON THE CHAIR.
COME ON, BOY, HURRY UP.
YES, MOTHER.

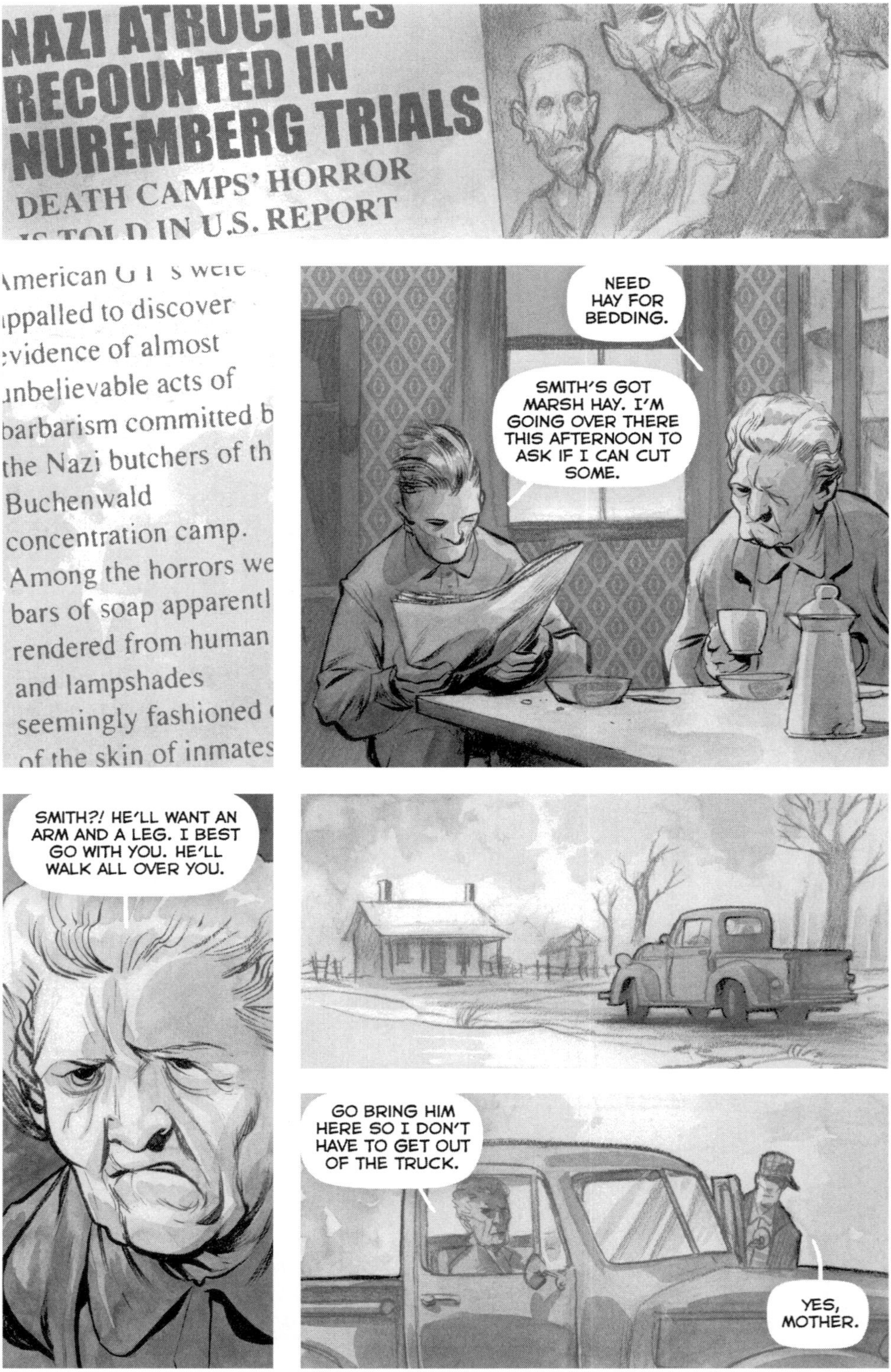
NAZI ATROCITIES RECOUNTED IN NUREMBERG TRIALS
DEATH CAMPS' HORROR IS TOLD IN U.S. REPORT
American G I 's were appalled to discover evidence of almost unbelievable acts of barbarism committed b the Nazi butchers of th Buchenwald concentration camp. Among the horrors we bars of soap apparentl rendered from human and lampshades seemingly fashioned of the skin of inmates
NEED HAY FOR BEDDING.
SMITH'S GOT MARSH HAY. I'M GOING OVER THERE THIS AFTERNOON TO ASK IF I CAN CUT SOME.
SMITH?! HE'LL WANT AN ARM AND A LEG. I BEST GO WITH YOU. HE'LL WALK ALL OVER YOU.
GO BRING HIM HERE SO I DON'T HAVE TO GET OUT OF THE TRUCK.
YES, MOTHER.

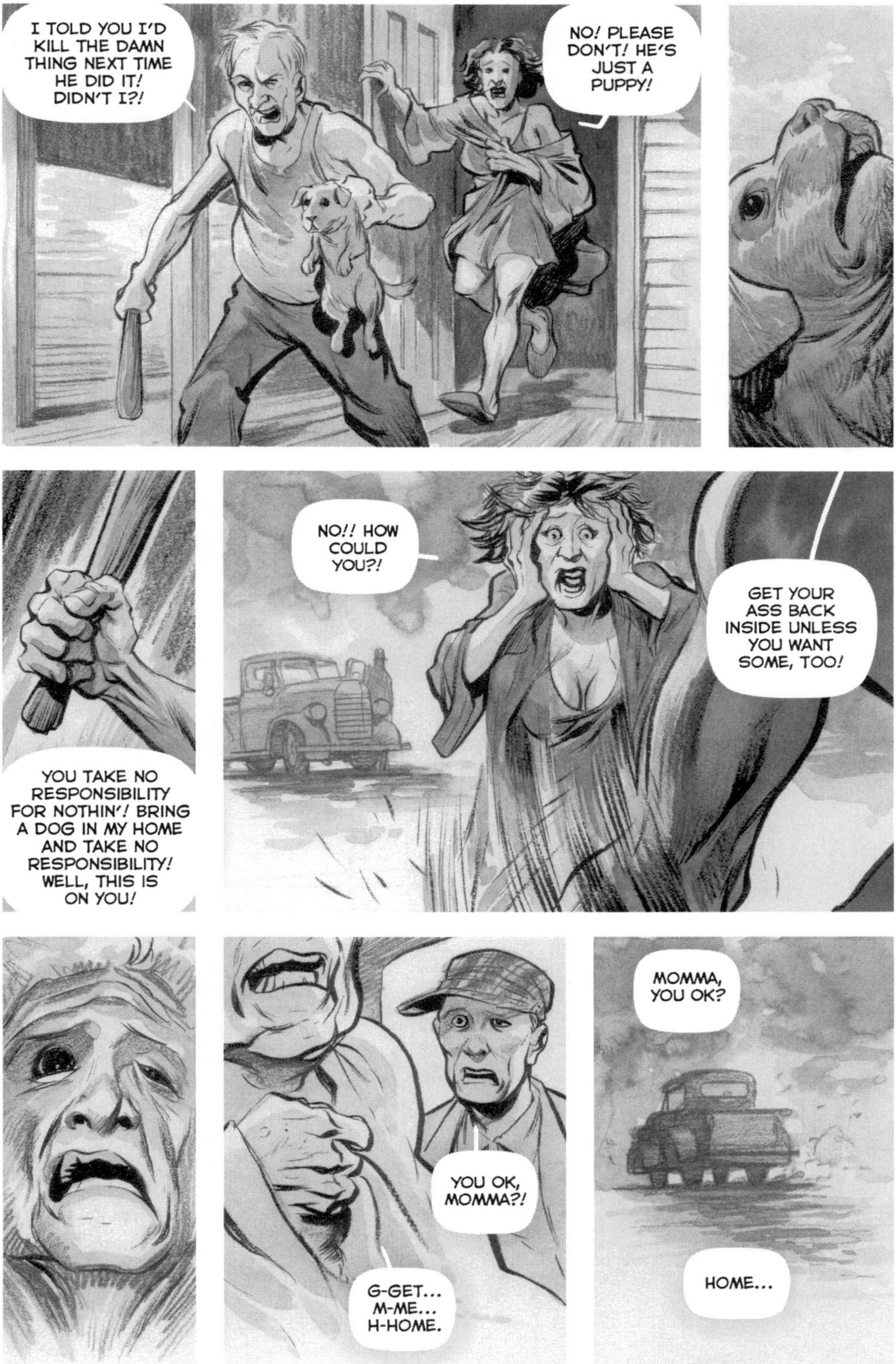
I TOLD YOU I'D KILL THE DAMN THING NEXT TIME HE DID IT! DIDN'T I?!
NO! PLEASE DON'T! HE'S JUST A PUPPY!
NO!! HOW COULD YOU?!
GET YOUR ASS BACK INSIDE UNLESS YOU WANT SOME, TOO!
YOU TAKE NO RESPONSIBILITY FOR NOTHIN'! BRING A DOG IN MY HOME AND TAKE NO RESPONSIBILITY! WELL, THIS IS ON YOU!
YOU OK, MOMMA?!
G-GET... M-ME... H-HOME.
MOMMA, YOU OK?
HOME...

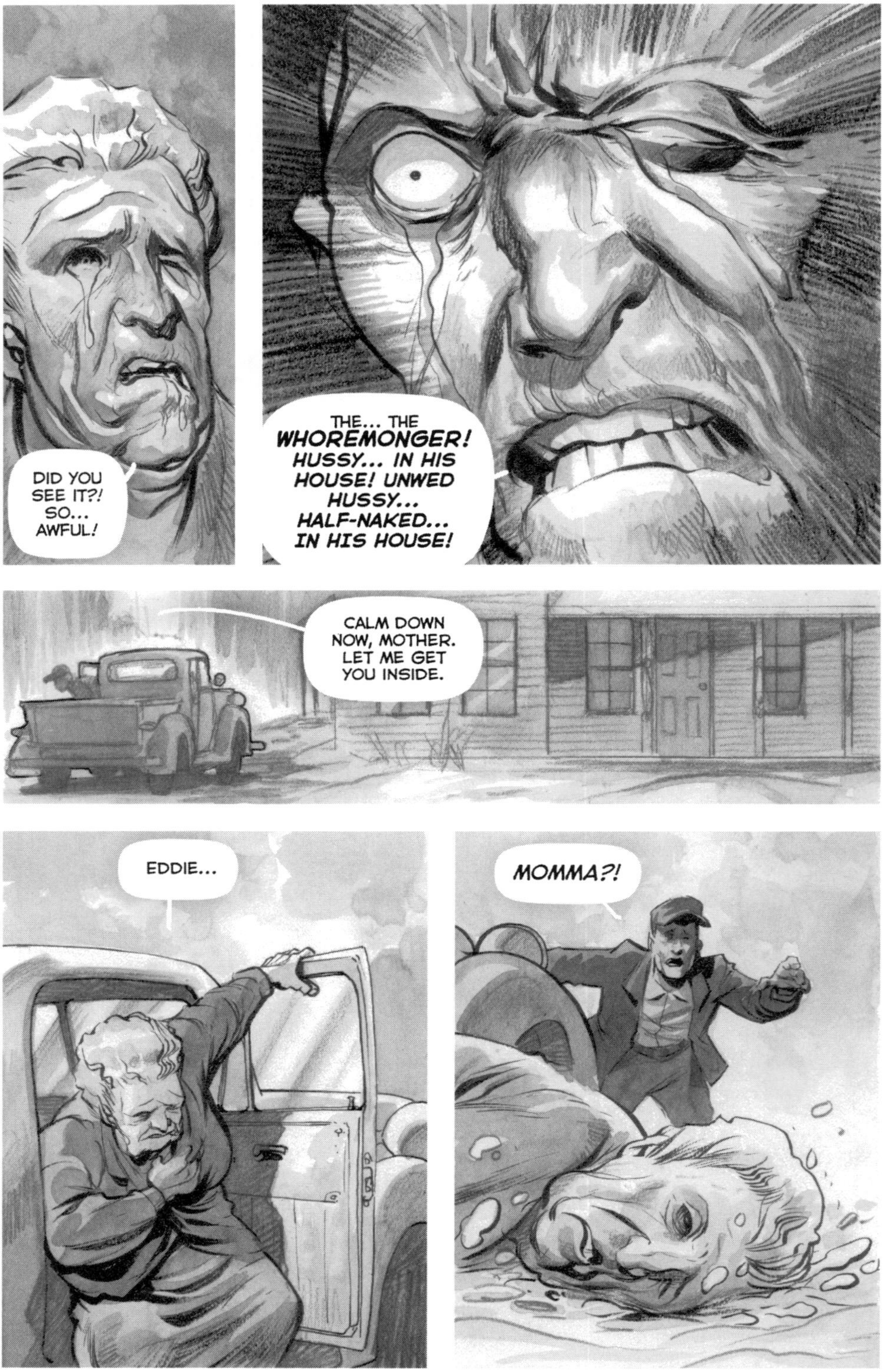
DID YOU SEE IT?! SO... AWFUL!
THE... THE WHOREMONGER! HUSSY... IN HIS HOUSE! UNWED HUSSY... HALF-NAKED... IN HIS HOUSE!
CALM DOWN NOW, MOTHER. LET ME GET YOU INSIDE.
EDDIE...
MOMMA?!

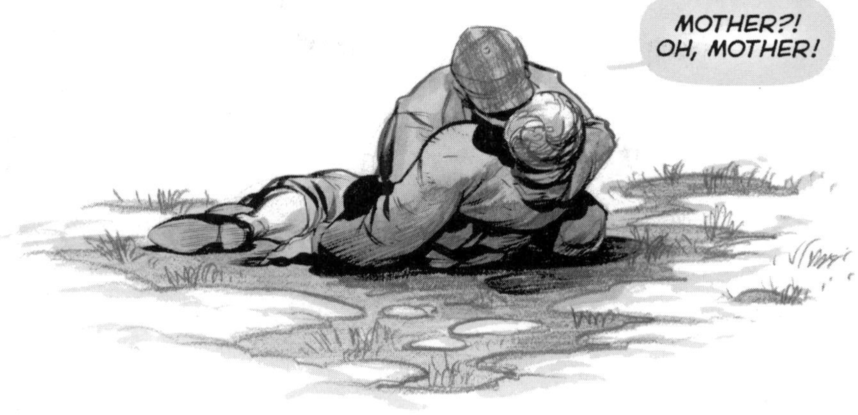
MOTHER?!
OH, MOTHER!

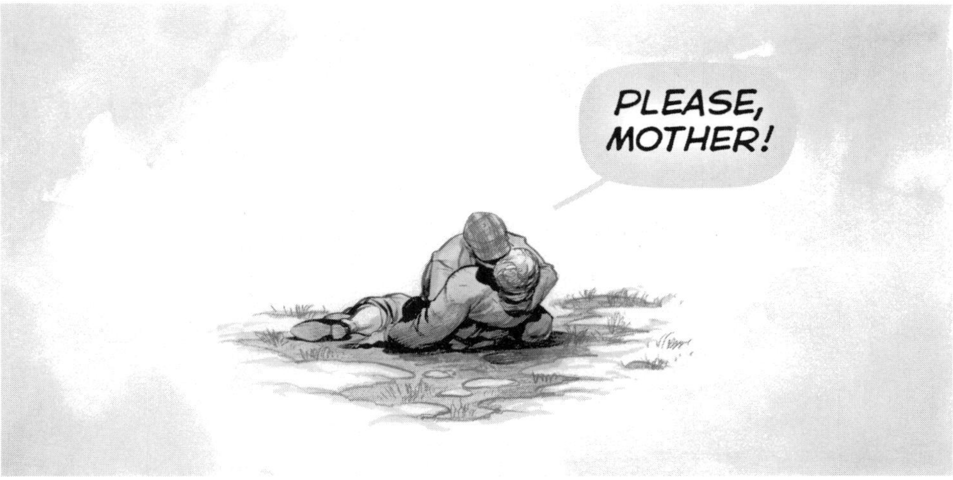
PLEASE,
MOTHER!

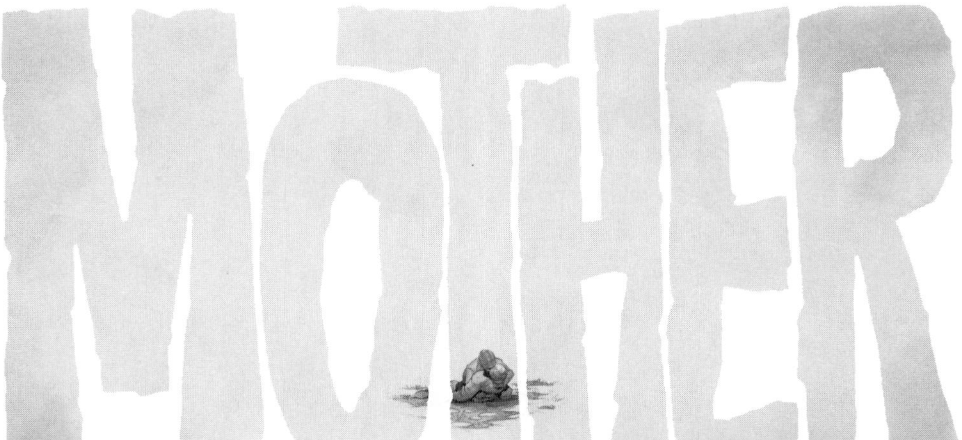
MOTHER

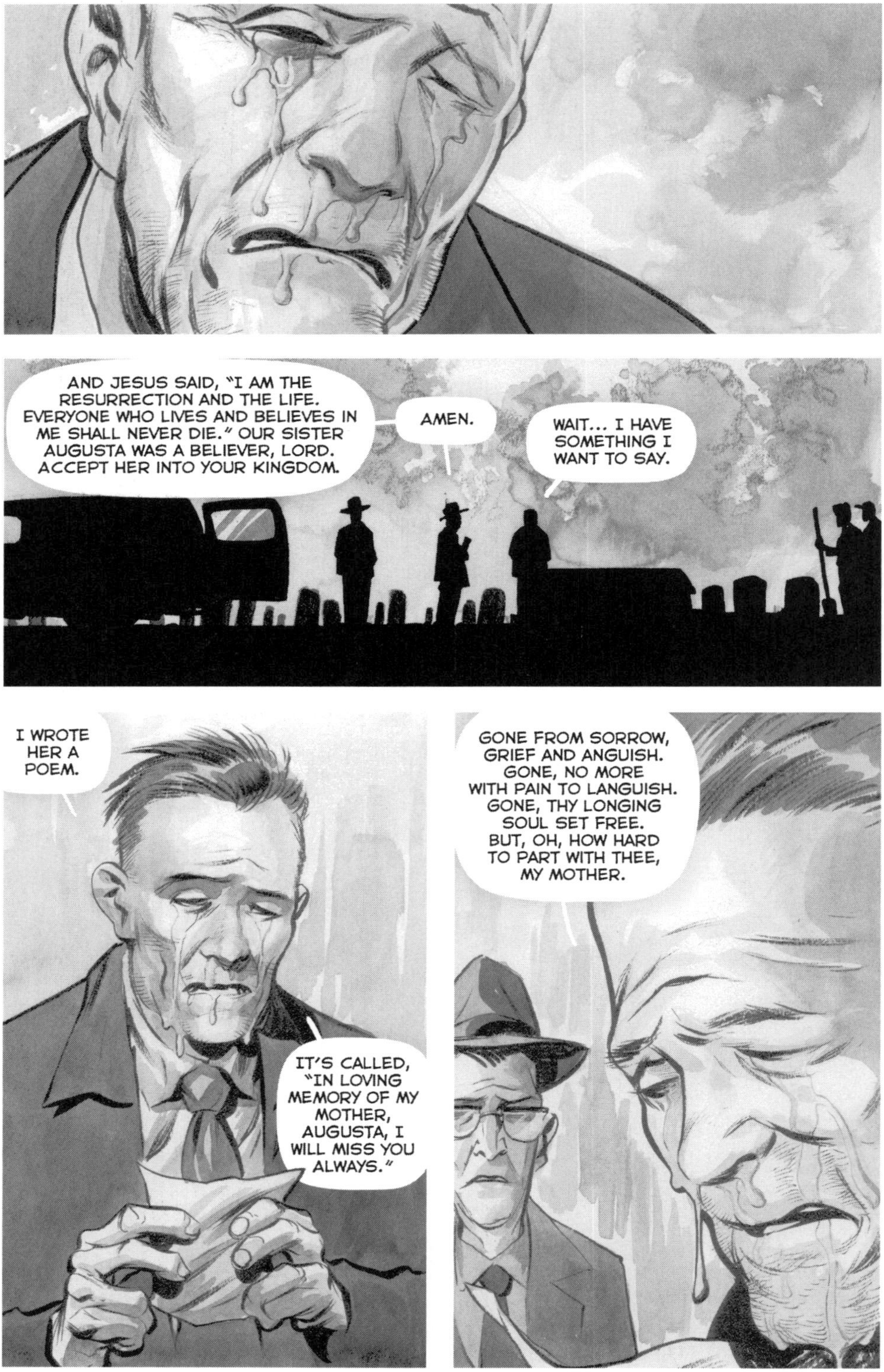
AND JESUS SAID, "I AM THE RESURRECTION AND THE LIFE. EVERYONE WHO LIVES AND BELIEVES IN ME SHALL NEVER DIE." OUR SISTER AUGUSTA WAS A BELIEVER, LORD. ACCEPT HER INTO YOUR KINGDOM.
AMEN.
WAIT... I HAVE SOMETHING I WANT TO SAY.
I WROTE HER A POEM.
IT'S CALLED, "IN LOVING MEMORY OF MY MOTHER, AUGUSTA, I WILL MISS YOU ALWAYS."
GONE FROM SORROW, GRIEF AND ANGUISH. GONE, NO MORE WITH PAIN TO LANGUISH. GONE, THY LONGING SOUL SET FREE. BUT, OH, HOW HARD TO PART WITH THEE, MY MOTHER.

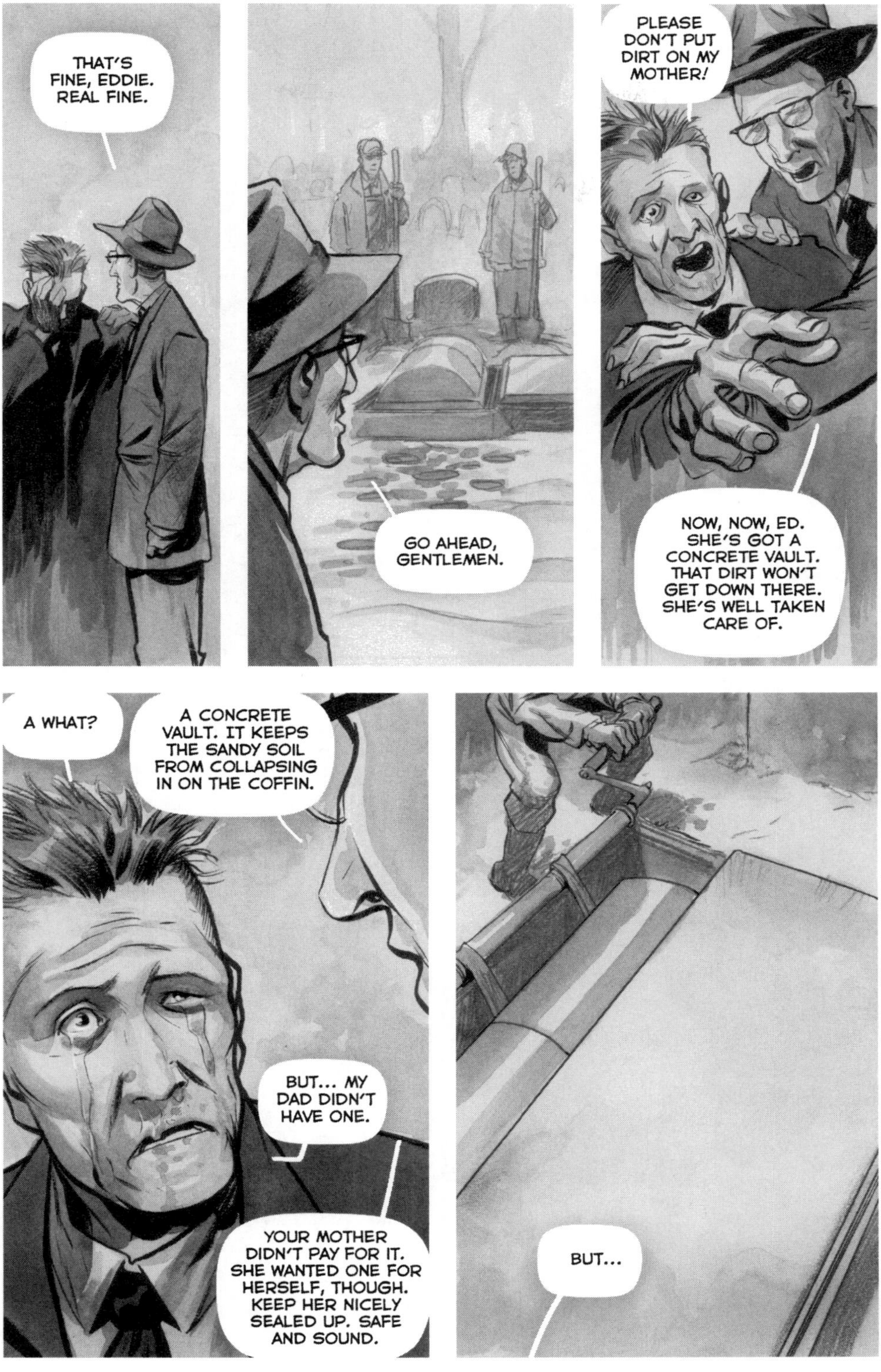
THAT'S FINE, EDDIE. REAL FINE.
GO AHEAD, GENTLEMEN.
PLEASE DON'T PUT DIRT ON MY MOTHER!
NOW, NOW, ED. SHE'S GOT A CONCRETE VAULT. THAT DIRT WON'T GET DOWN THERE. SHE'S WELL TAKEN CARE OF.
A WHAT?
A CONCRETE VAULT. IT KEEPS THE SANDY SOIL FROM COLLAPSING IN ON THE COFFIN.
BUT... MY DAD DIDN'T HAVE ONE.
YOUR MOTHER DIDN'T PAY FOR IT. SHE WANTED ONE FOR HERSELF, THOUGH. KEEP HER NICELY SEALED UP. SAFE AND SOUND.
BUT...

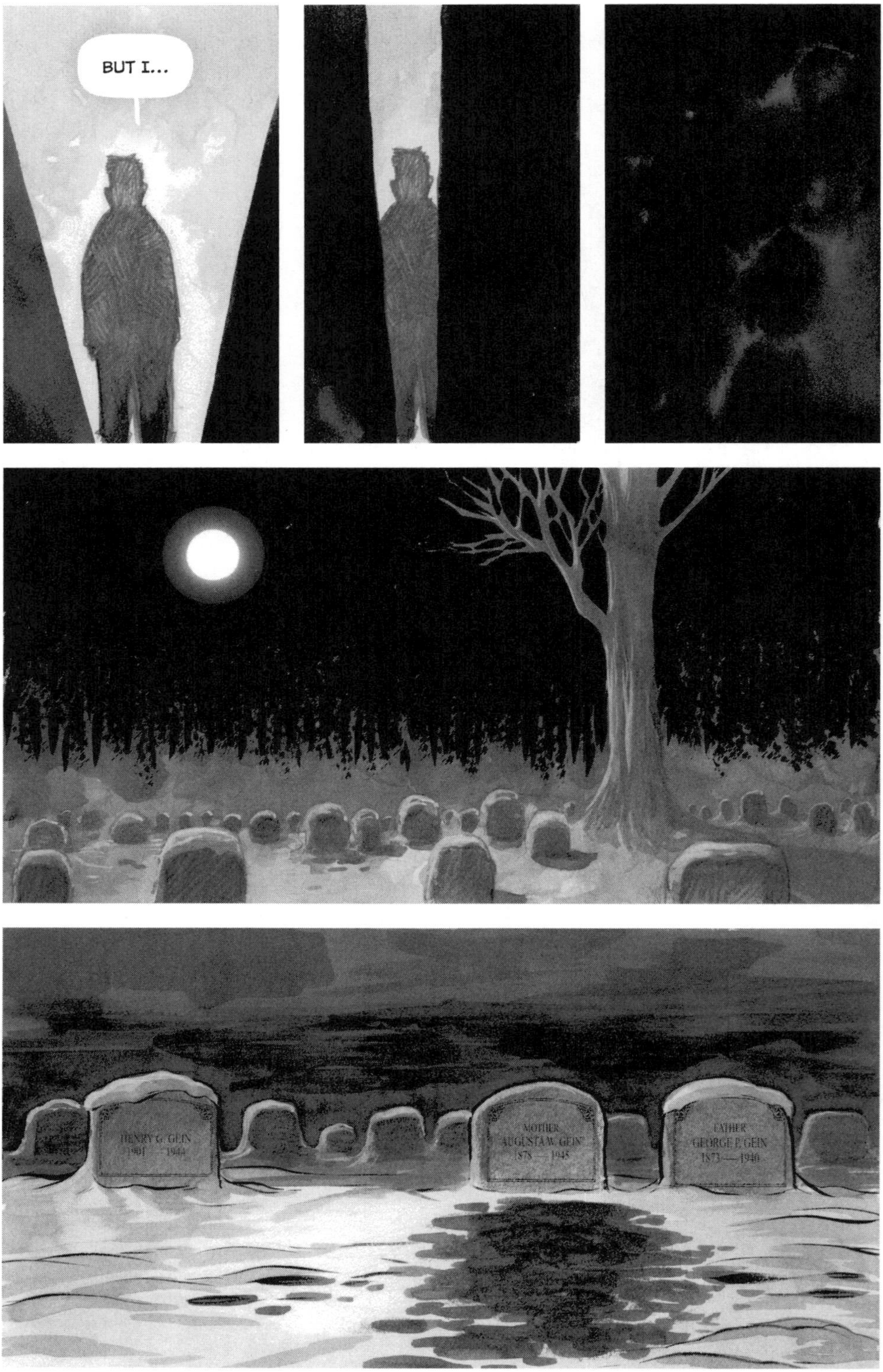
BUT I...
HENRY G. GEIN
1901 — 1944
MOTHER
AUGUSTA W. GEIN
1878 — 1945
FATHER
GEORGE P. GEIN
1873 — 1940

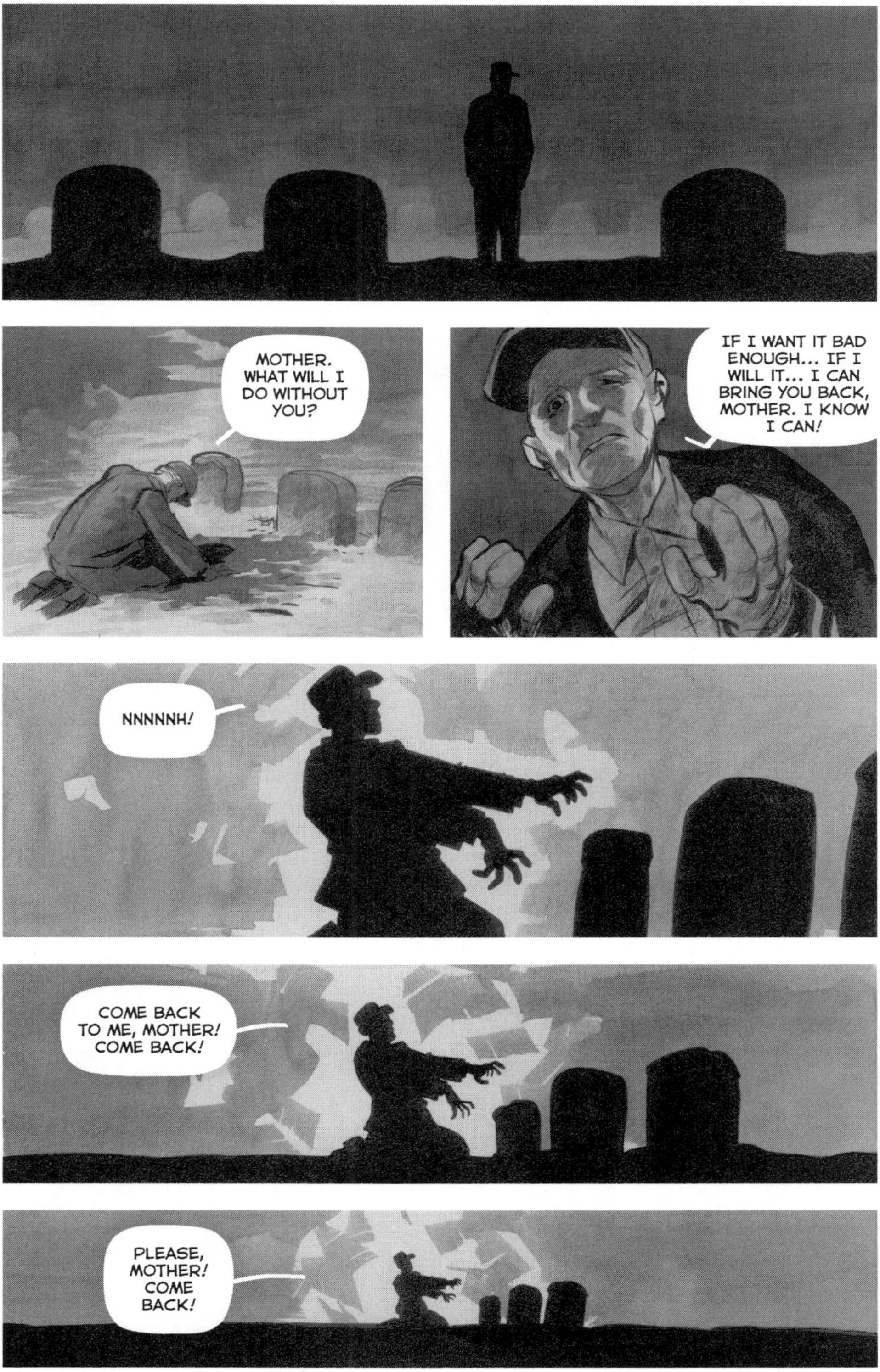
MOTHER. WHAT WILL I DO WITHOUT YOU?
IF I WANT IT BAD ENOUGH... IF I WILL IT... I CAN BRING YOU BACK, MOTHER. I KNOW I CAN!
NNNNNH!
COME BACK TO ME, MOTHER! COME BACK!
PLEASE, MOTHER! COME BACK!

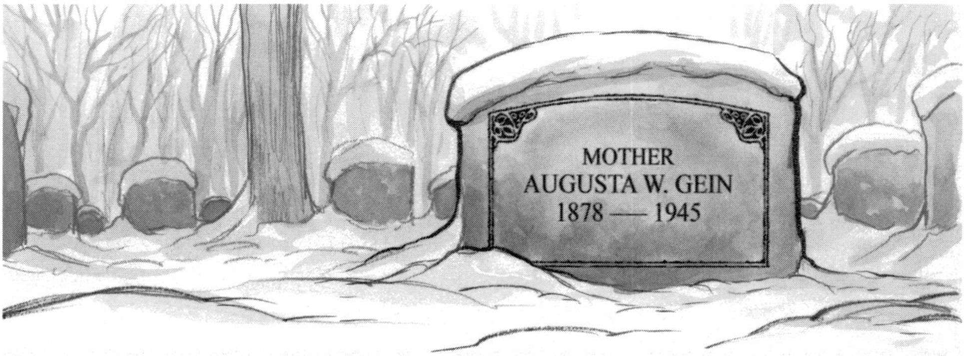
MOTHER
AUGUSTA W. GEIN
1878 —— 1945

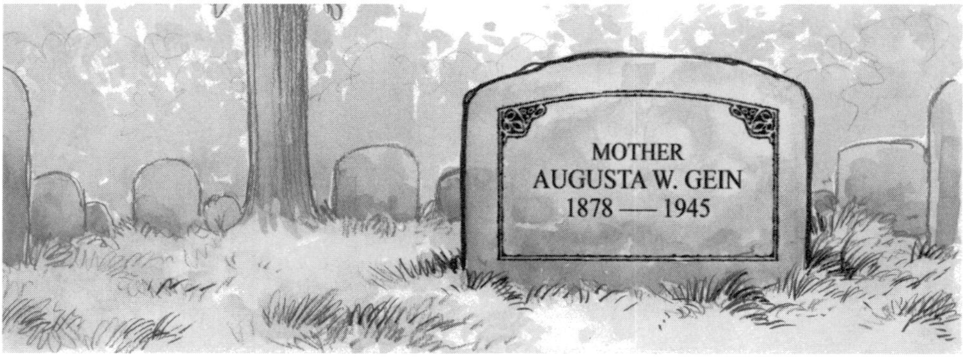
MOTHER
AUGUSTA W. GEIN
1878 —— 1945

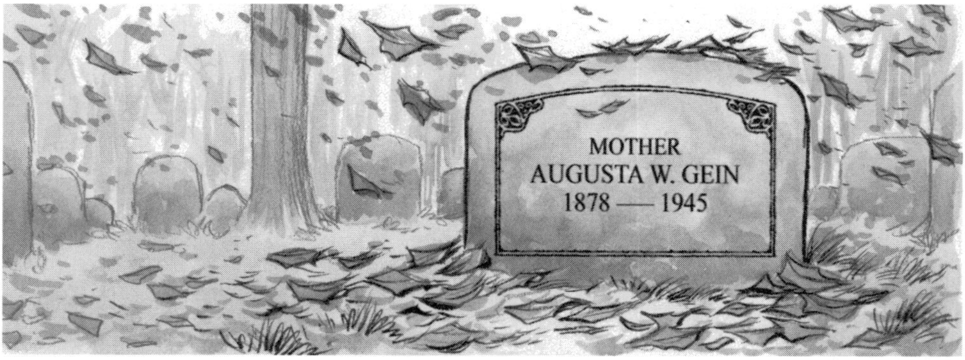
MOTHER
AUGUSTA W. GEIN
1878 —— 1945

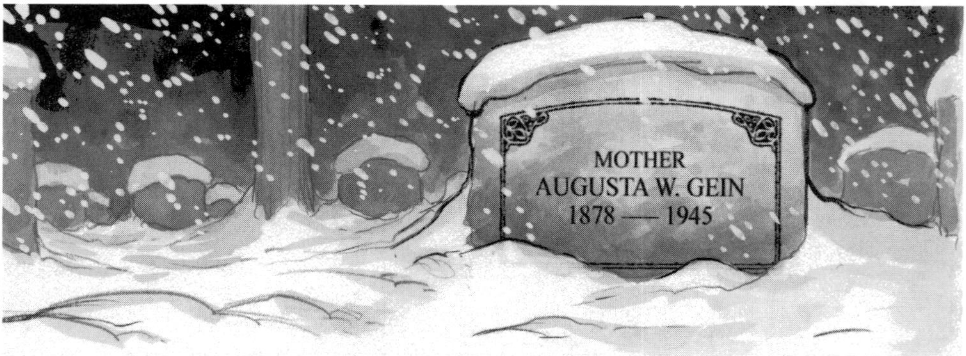
MOTHER
AUGUSTA W. GEIN
1878 —— 1945

DAILY

CHAPTER 6

INDEX
Politics 2
Television 5
Celebrity 9
Unusual 7
Personal ....
Finance 17
Sport 17
Cinema 18

★ ★ ★ Monday, December 9th, 1957

HUNTING SEASON

10¢ ★ ★ ★

Gein's Story As He Told It
Relates Events In Statement

By Kent Blake
Staff Reporter, City desk

The entire arraignment lasted little more than five minutes. After listening to the recommendations of the prosecutor and the defense attorney, Judge Boede made a statement. "It seems advisable under the circumstances as related by both the counsel for the state and the counsel for the defendant," he said, "that expert determination be had whether he is now competent to stand trial," as well as whether he was sane at the time of Mrs. Worden's murder.

Then Boede signed an order committing Eddie to the Central State Hospital for the Criminally Insane at Waupun for a thirty-day examination period and remanded him to the custody of Sheriff Schley, who led Eddie back to the jailhouse to await transportation to the mental institution.

Though Gein was a wiry fellow, it seemed impossible that he could have had the strength to dig up a grave by himself, knock open the casket, remove the corpse, and

it. For a while, it seemed as if the Crime Lab might offer the best solution to the problem. Charles Wilson had nine of his men working full-time on the case, analyzing the evidence and employing the most up-to-date techniques for identifying the victims from their remains. By comparing dirt particles gathered at the crime scene with soil samples from local cemeteries, the technicians hoped to determine the validity of Gein's claim.

But the sheer quantity of evidence—by far the largest amount ever handled by the ten-year-old Crime Lab—made it hard for Wilson to promise a quick resolution. Though Kileen urged the director to give the soil analysis top priority, it was clear that a final outcome might take weeks, even months. In the meantime, Kileen was under growing pressure from the Plainfield citizenry to determine the truth of Gein's assertion. It was becoming increasingly obvious that the townsfolk would never be able to rest without knowing whether their loved ones had, in fact, been ravaged in their graves. On Friday afternoon, therefore, following his

Photo / Kelly Conlen

Though his crimes were doing their best to get back to the ordinary business of life, Plainfield remained a community in crisis, still reeling from the sheer monstrousness of the Gein revelations, mortified by the

"produced on its first day of issue" through the Plainfield post office. By designating Plainfield as the place of issue for the prairie chicken stamp, the government would create favorable publicity for the town, [illegible], not only

of the Plainfield cemetery, Pat Danna, who completely discounted Gein's story. Danna insisted that during the time he'd been caretaker, no graves had ever been molested. He was not at the cemetery all the time,

was becoming increasingly obvious that the townsfolk would never be able to rest without knowing whether their loved ones had, in fact, been ravaged in their graves. On Friday afternoon, therefore, following his meeting with Judge Boede and the other officials, Kileen called a press conference to make an electrifying announcement.

Early the next week, he told the reporters, and contingent on the permission of the next-of-kin, two graves would be opened in the Plainfield cemetery. Kileen's change of mind regarding the exhumations wasn't his only about-face. He also seemed to have become suddenly dubious about the whole grave-robbing story. When one of the reporters asked him if he still believed Gein's claim, Kileen snorted. "Do you?" he asked in a heavily sarcastic tone that made his skepticism clear. For the first time, the district attorney revealed that Gein had supplied authorities with a list of "eight or nine" people whose corpses he had presumably violated. Kileen's intention was to dig up two of these graves, "unless the ground freezes." If nothing was found, he explained, no other bodies would be exhumed. On the other hand, if Gein turned out to be telling the truth, Kileen might go ahead and order the opening of "the other graves named by Gein."

When the reporters asked Kileen how he reconciled the "eight or nine" names with the significantly larger number of marks and

Her [illegible] 'Mild' Man's [illegible]

By Kent Blake

[column of illegible body text]

Butcher [illegible]
Faces Murder

"Must have been
somebody pretty
cold-blooded."

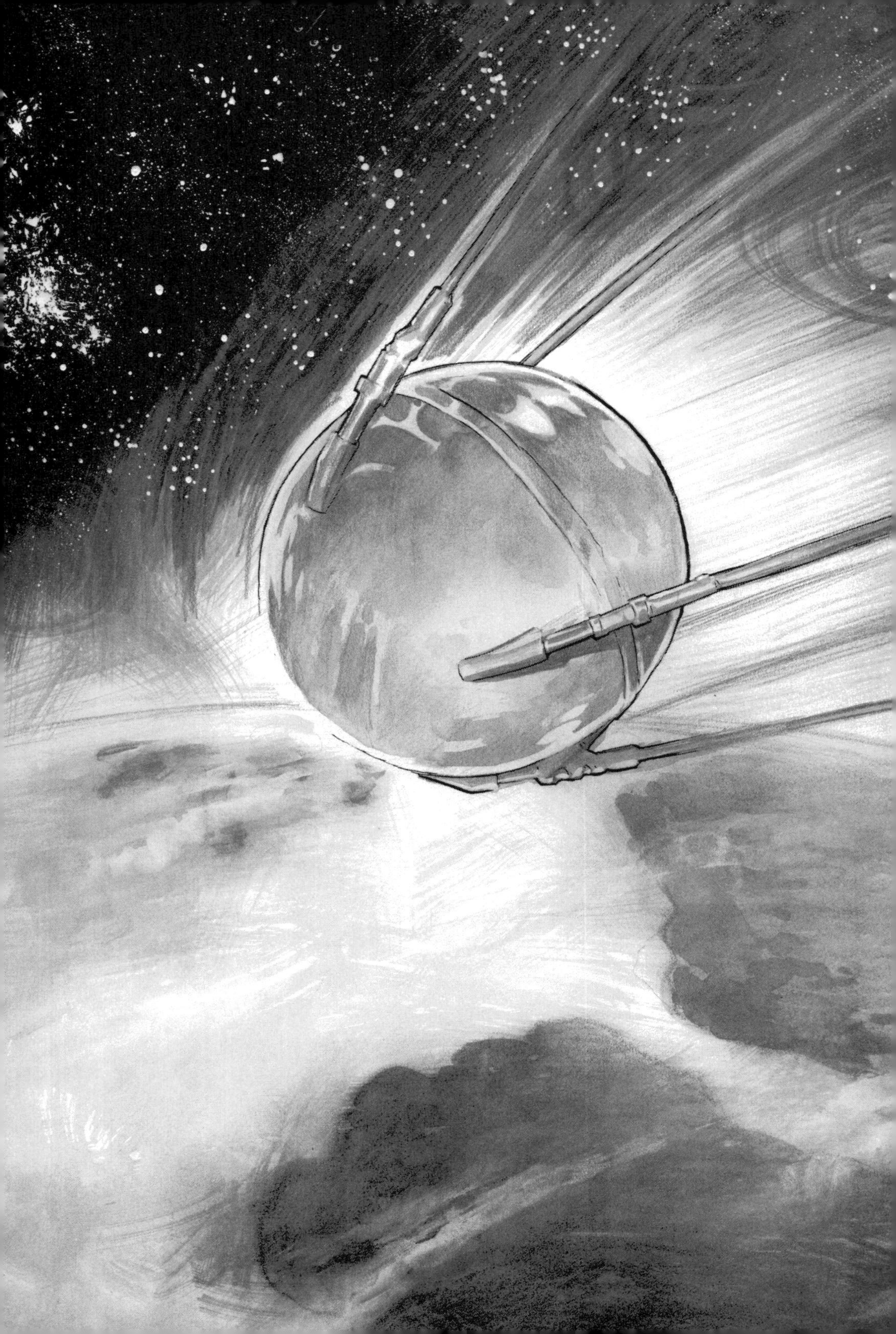

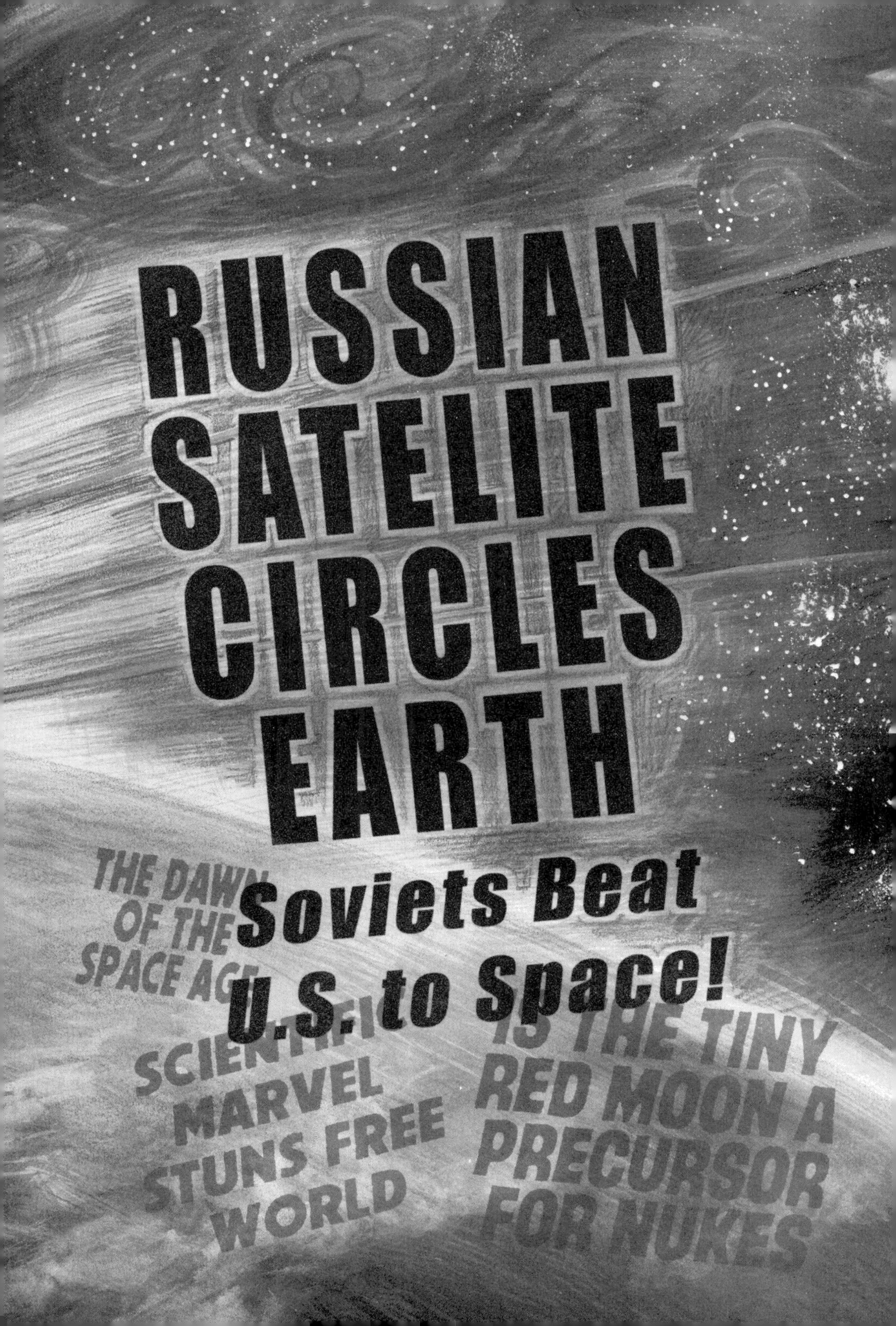
RUSSIAN SATELITE CIRCLES EARTH
Soviets Beat U.S. to Space!
THE DAWN OF THE SPACE AGE
SCIENTIFIC MARVEL STUNS FREE WORLD
IS THE TINY RED MOON A PRECURSOR FOR NUKES

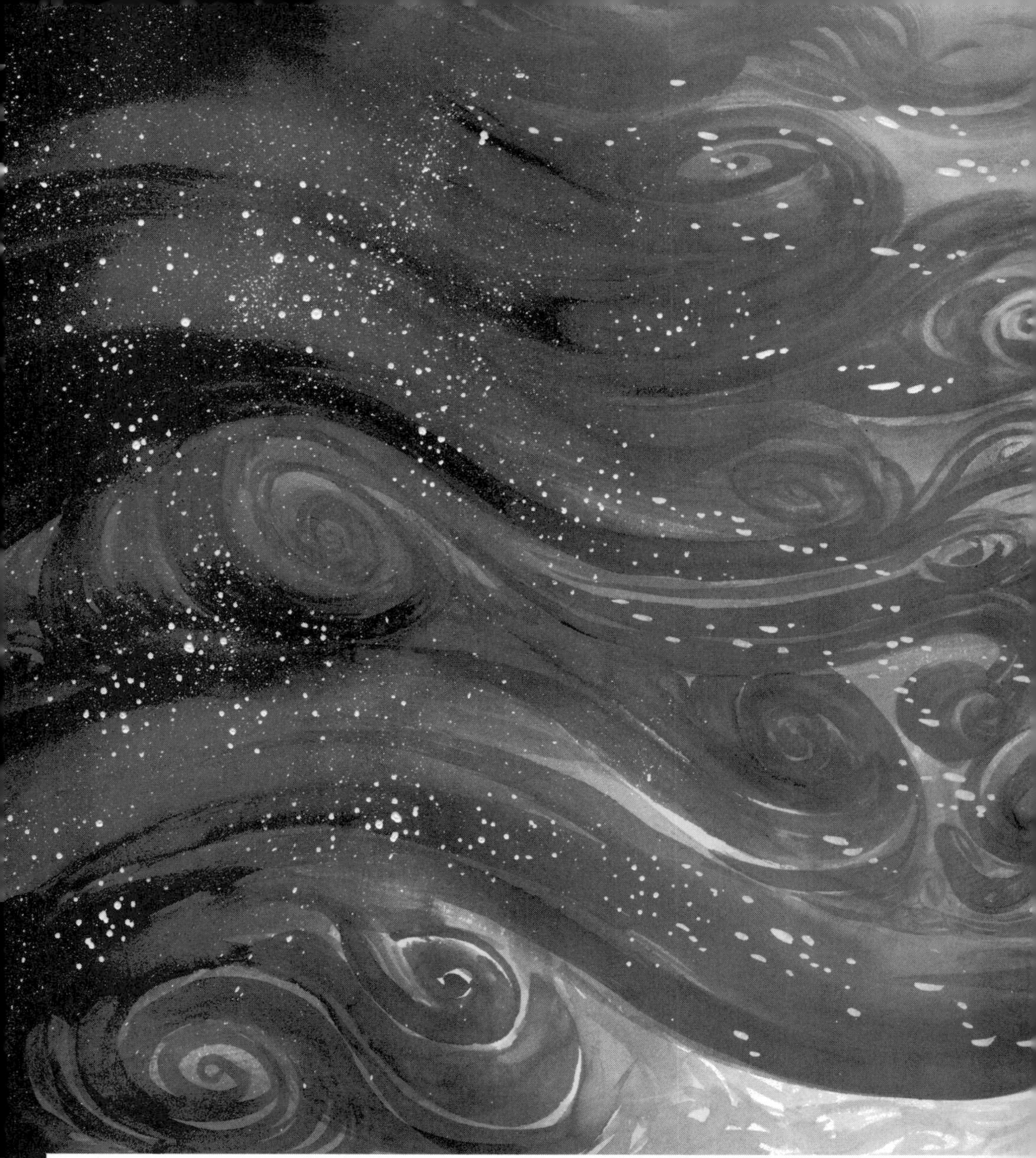

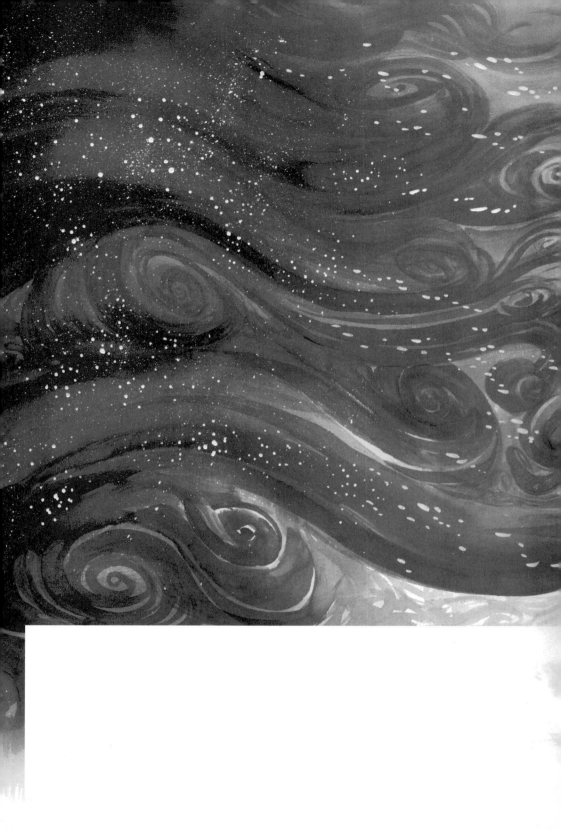

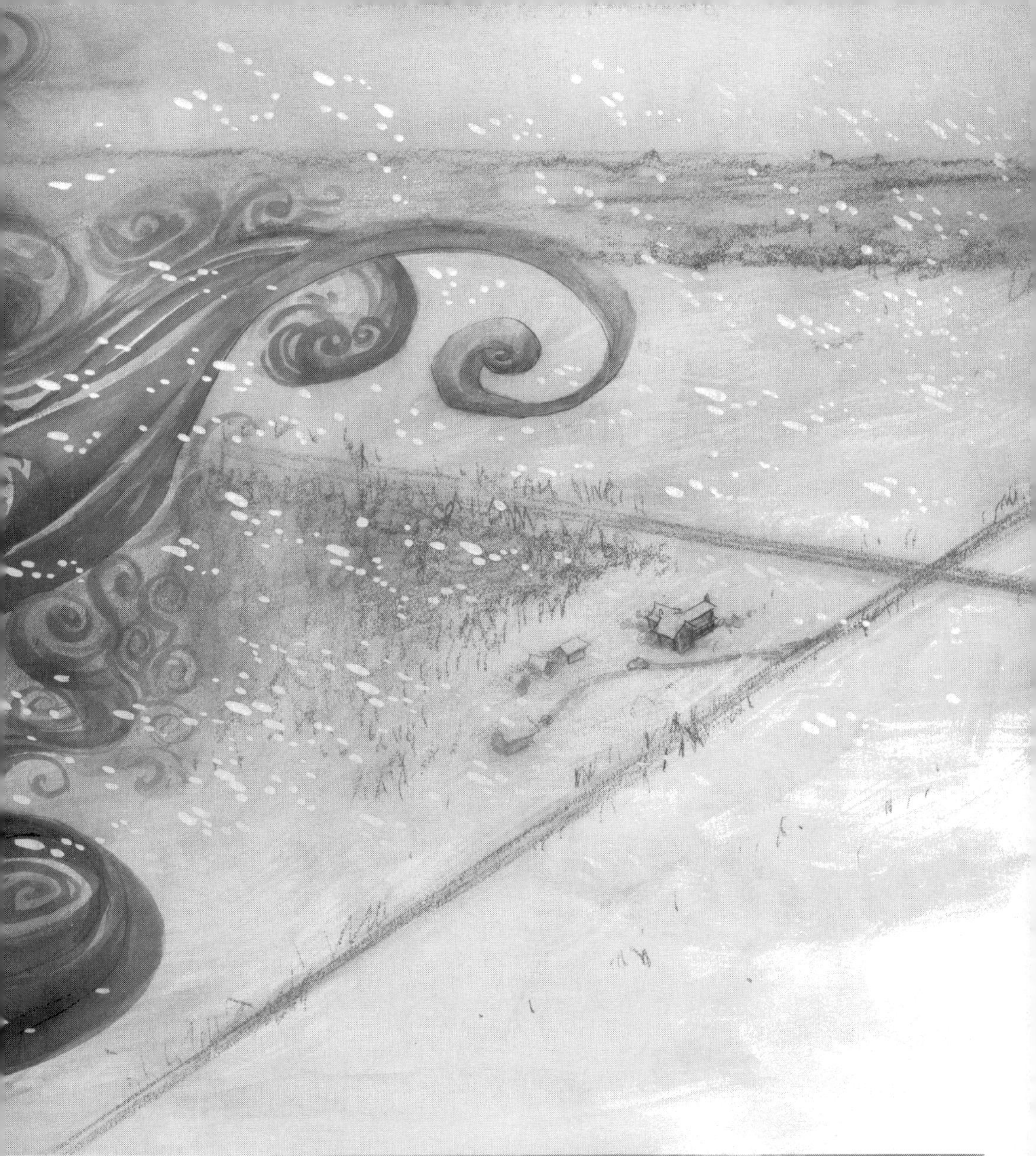
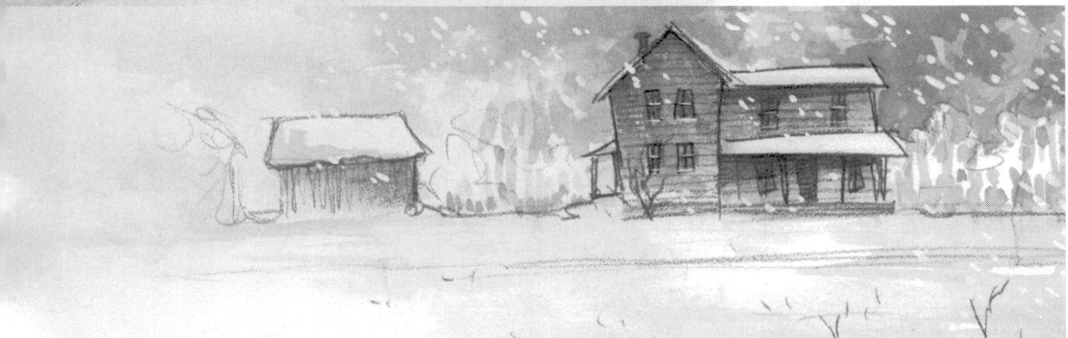

My Washdays are Holidays!

PUSH BUTTON TECHNOLOGY!

lows

up to 50x96"
except picture
windows

Aluminum!

g!

YEARS TO PAY!
specialized measure-
cial for 10 windows,

, subash; alo

Standout Picture

Far more restful to your eyes!

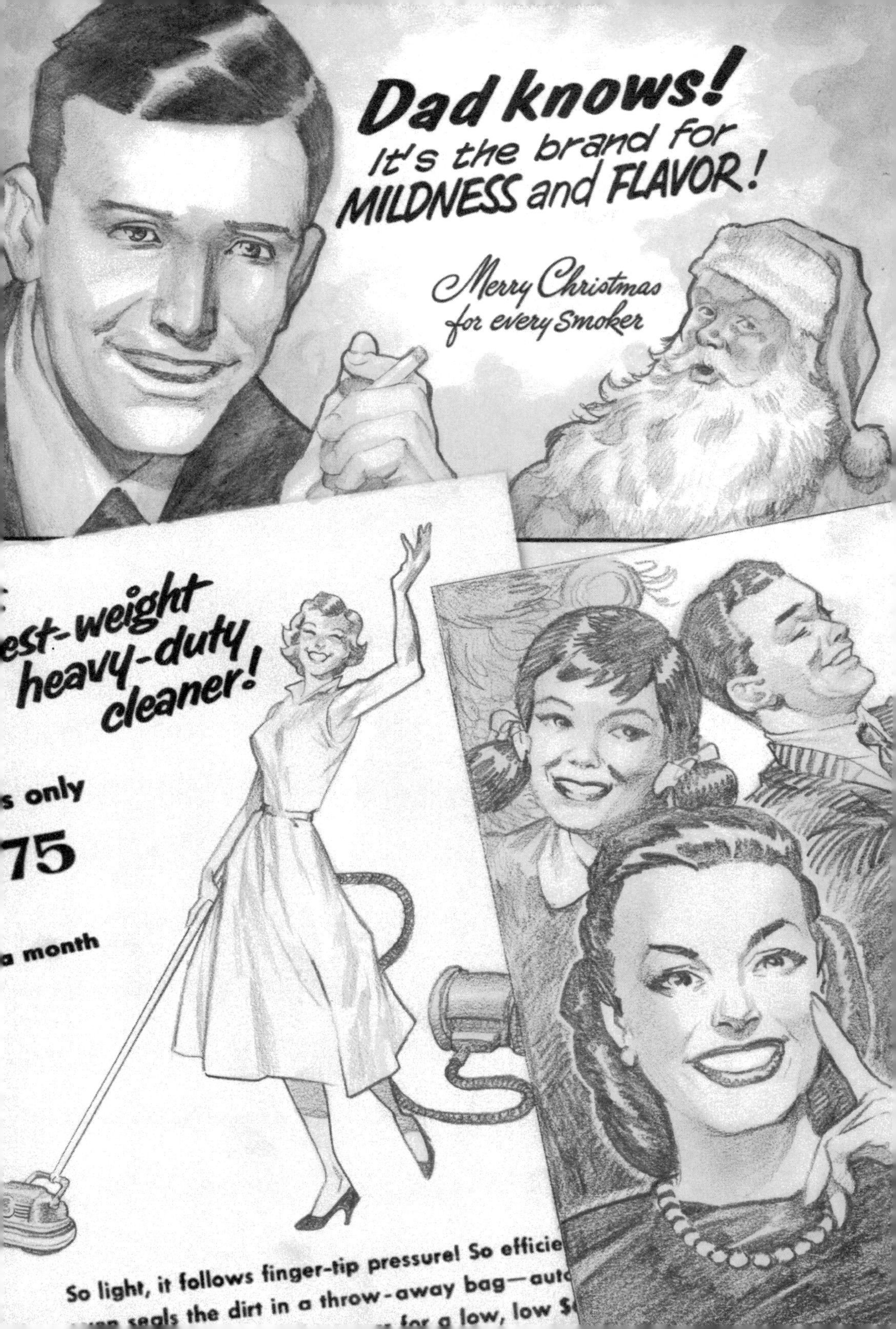
Dad knows!
It's the brand for
MILDNESS and FLAVOR!
Merry Christmas
for every Smoker
est-weight
heavy-duty
cleaner!
s only
75
a month
So light, it follows finger-tip pressure! So efficie
seals the dirt in a throw-away bag—auto
for a low, low S

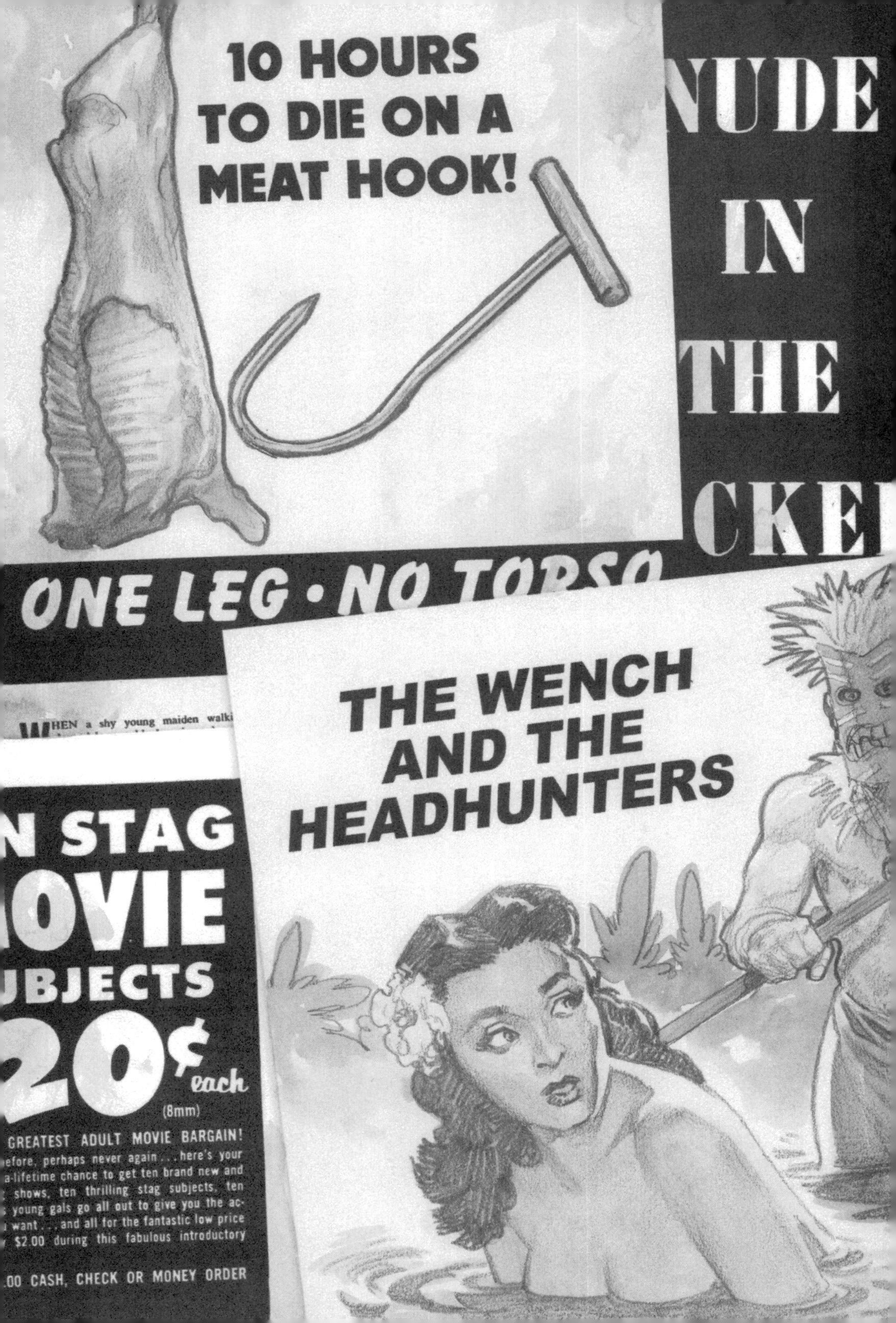
10 HOURS TO DIE ON A MEAT HOOK!
NUDE
IN
THE
CKE
ONE LEG • NO TORSO
HEN a shy young maiden walki
THE WENCH AND THE HEADHUNTERS
N STAG
OVIE
UBJECTS
20¢ each
(8mm)
GREATEST ADULT MOVIE BARGAIN!
efore, perhaps never again . . . here's your
a-lifetime chance to get ten brand new and
shows, ten thrilling stag subjects, ten
young gals go all out to give you the ac-
want . . . and all for the fantastic low price
$2.00 during this fabulous introductory
.00 CASH, CHECK OR MONEY ORDER

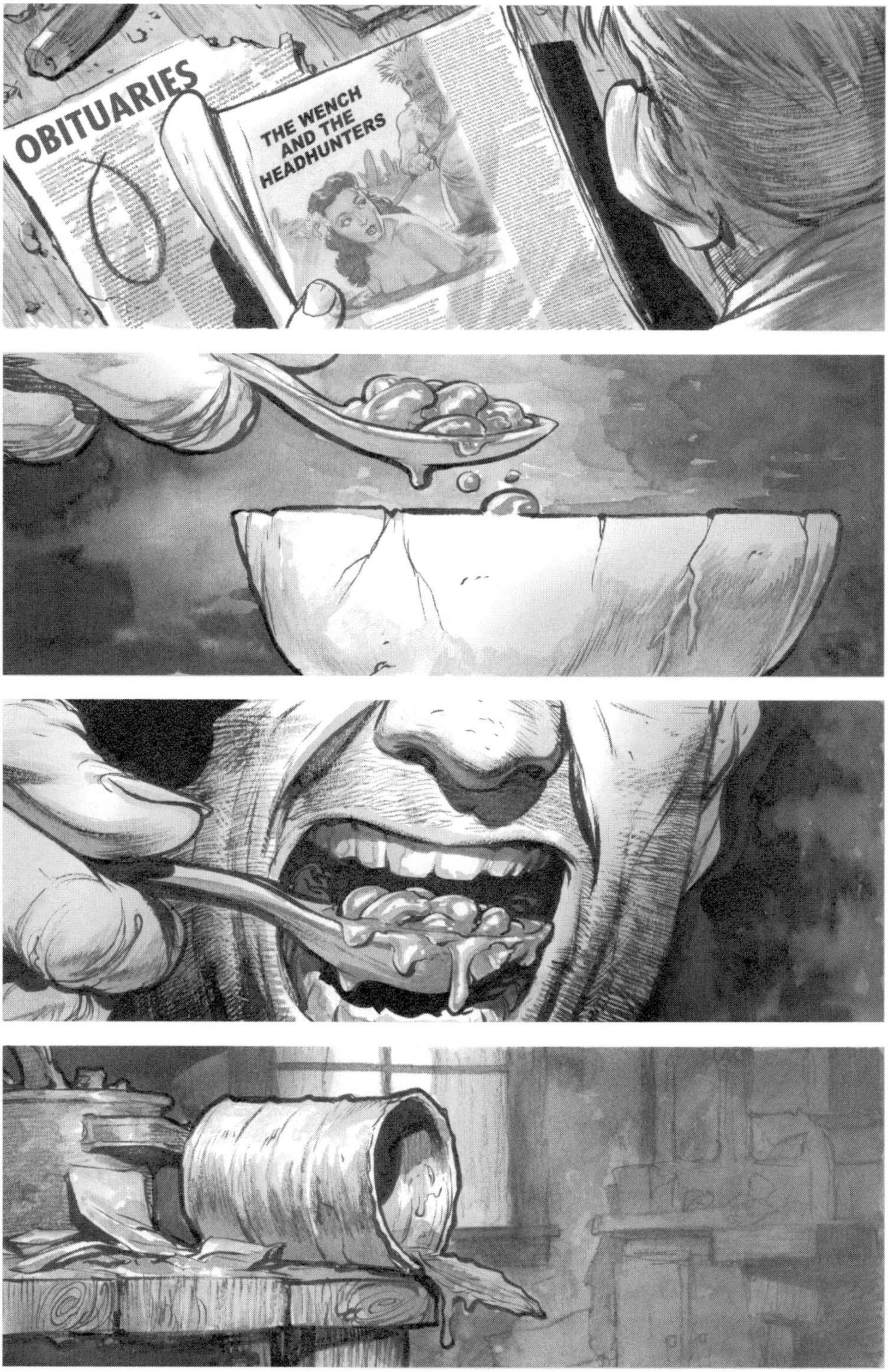
OBITUARIES
THE WENCH AND THE HEADHUNTERS

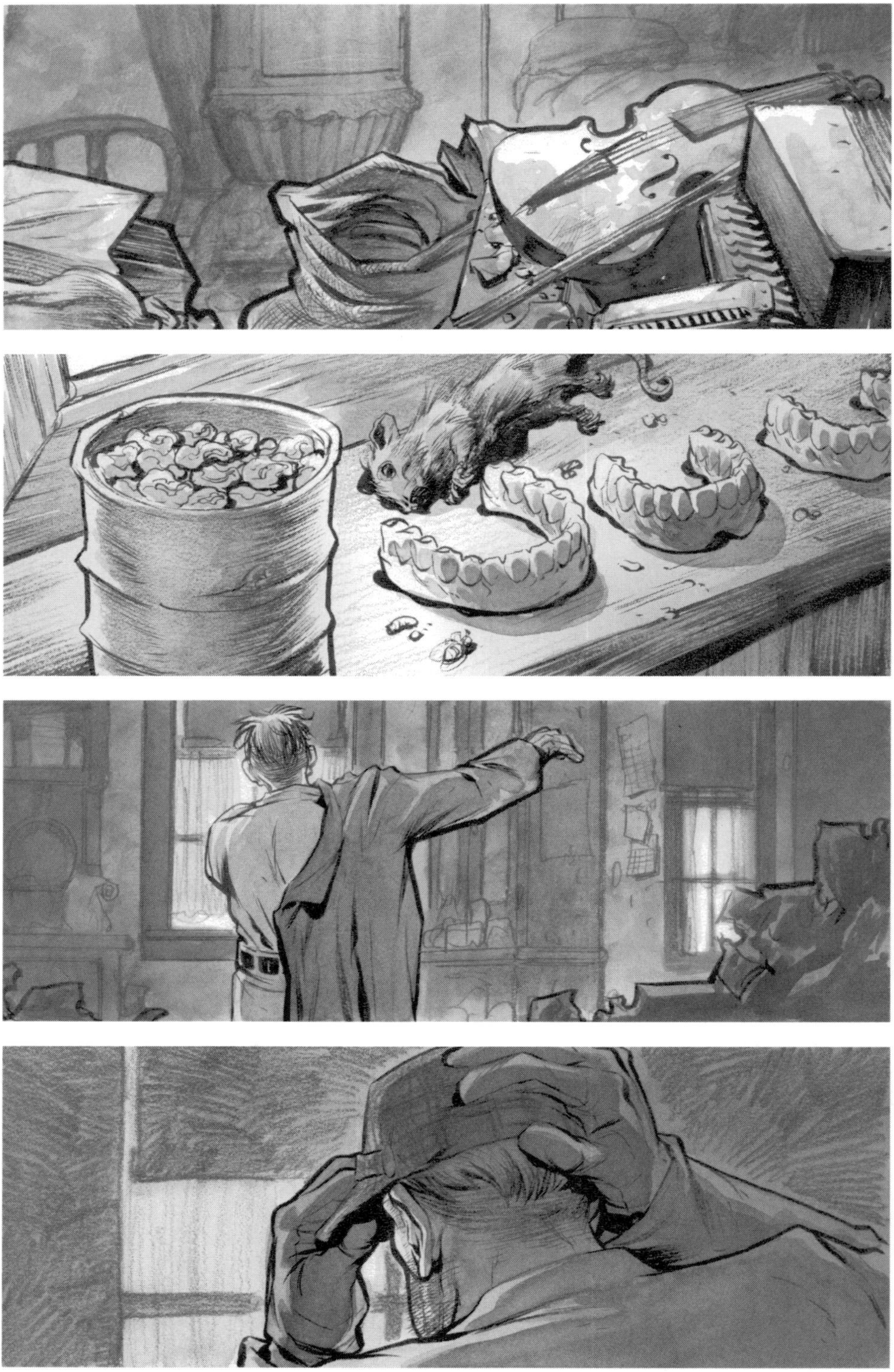

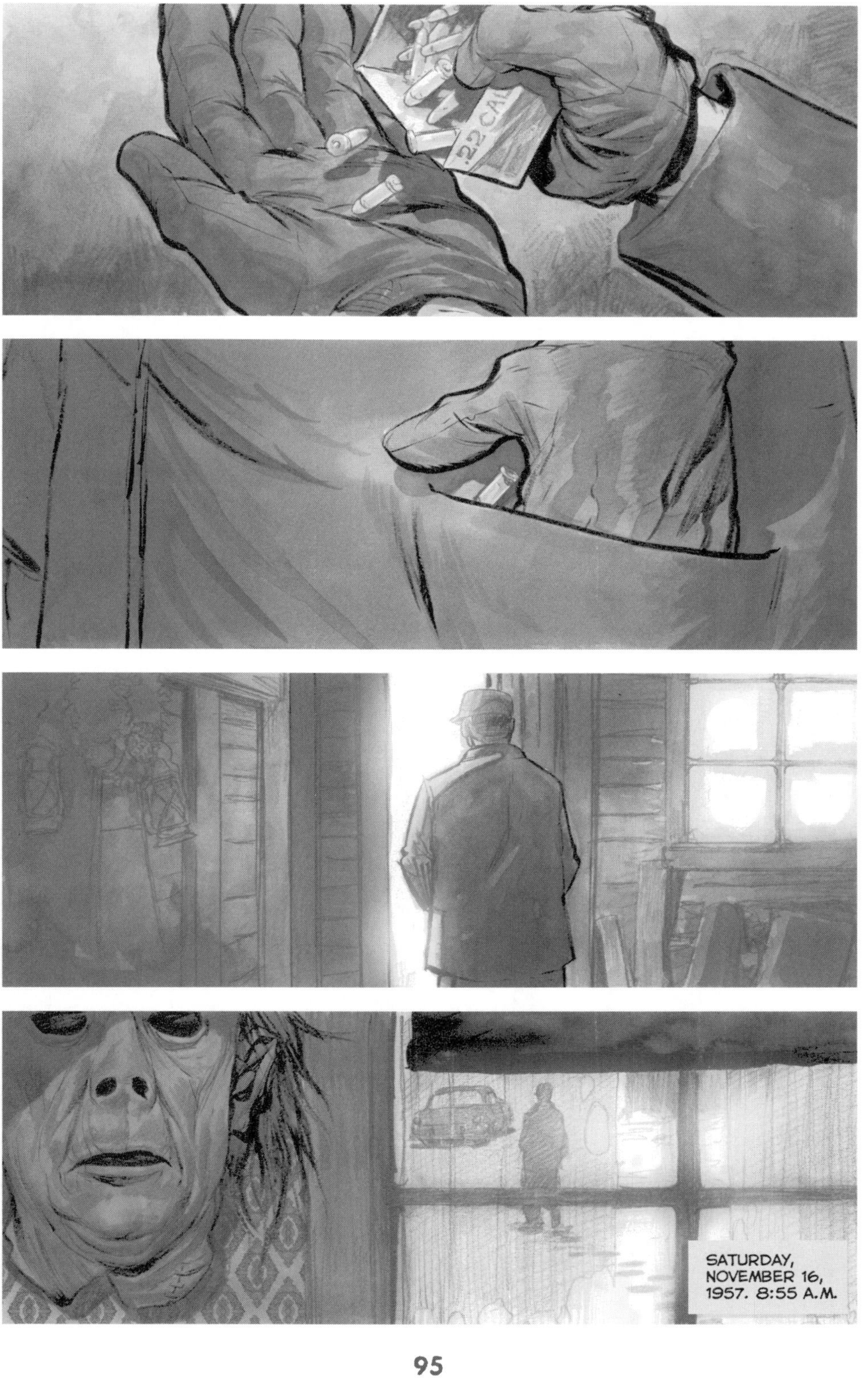
.22 CAL
SATURDAY, NOVEMBER 16, 1957. 8:55 A.M.

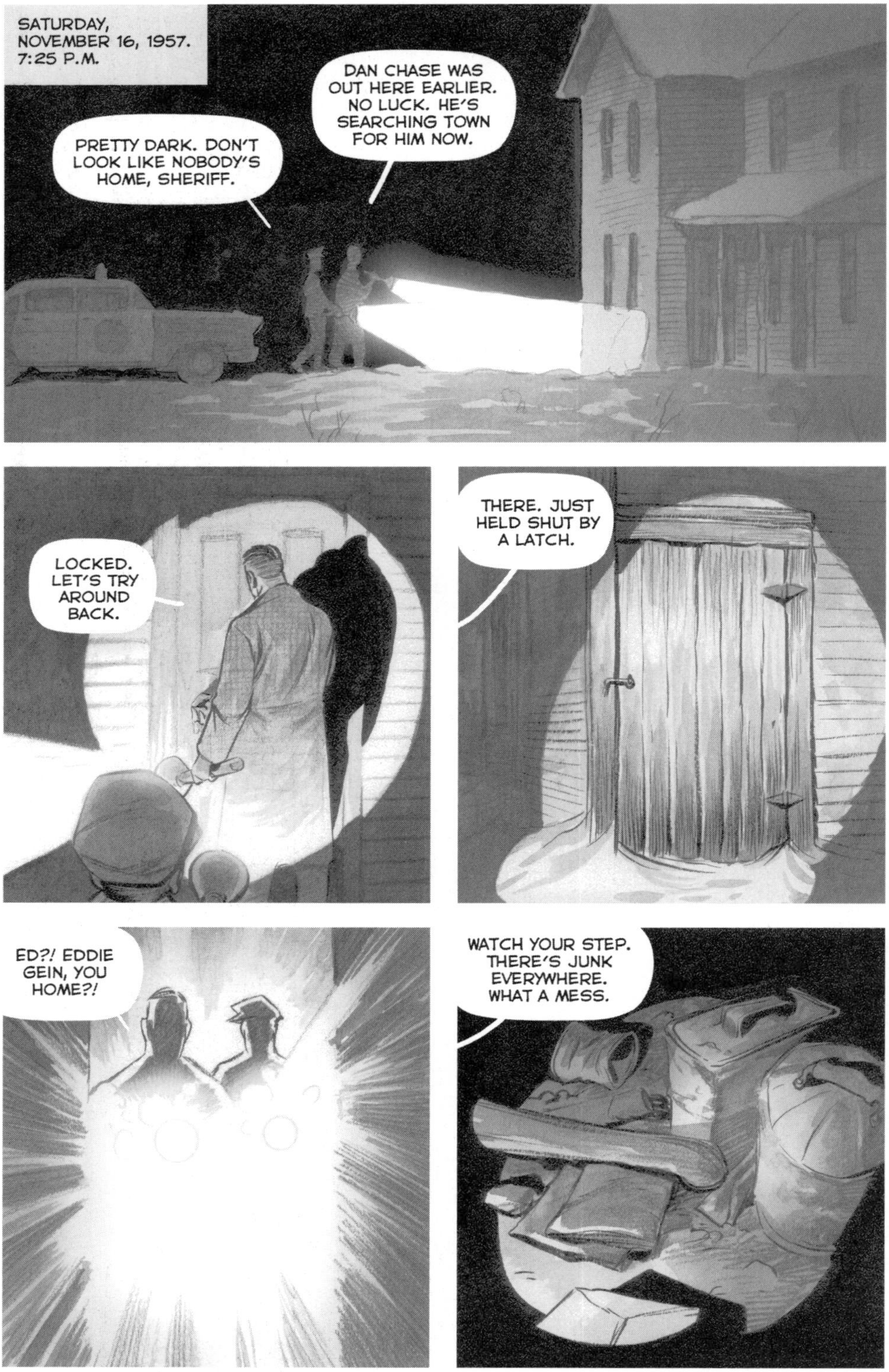
SATURDAY, NOVEMBER 16, 1957. 7:25 P.M.
PRETTY DARK. DON'T LOOK LIKE NOBODY'S HOME, SHERIFF.
DAN CHASE WAS OUT HERE EARLIER. NO LUCK. HE'S SEARCHING TOWN FOR HIM NOW.
LOCKED. LET'S TRY AROUND BACK.
THERE. JUST HELD SHUT BY A LATCH.
ED?! EDDIE GEIN, YOU HOME?!
WATCH YOUR STEP. THERE'S JUNK EVERYWHERE. WHAT A MESS.

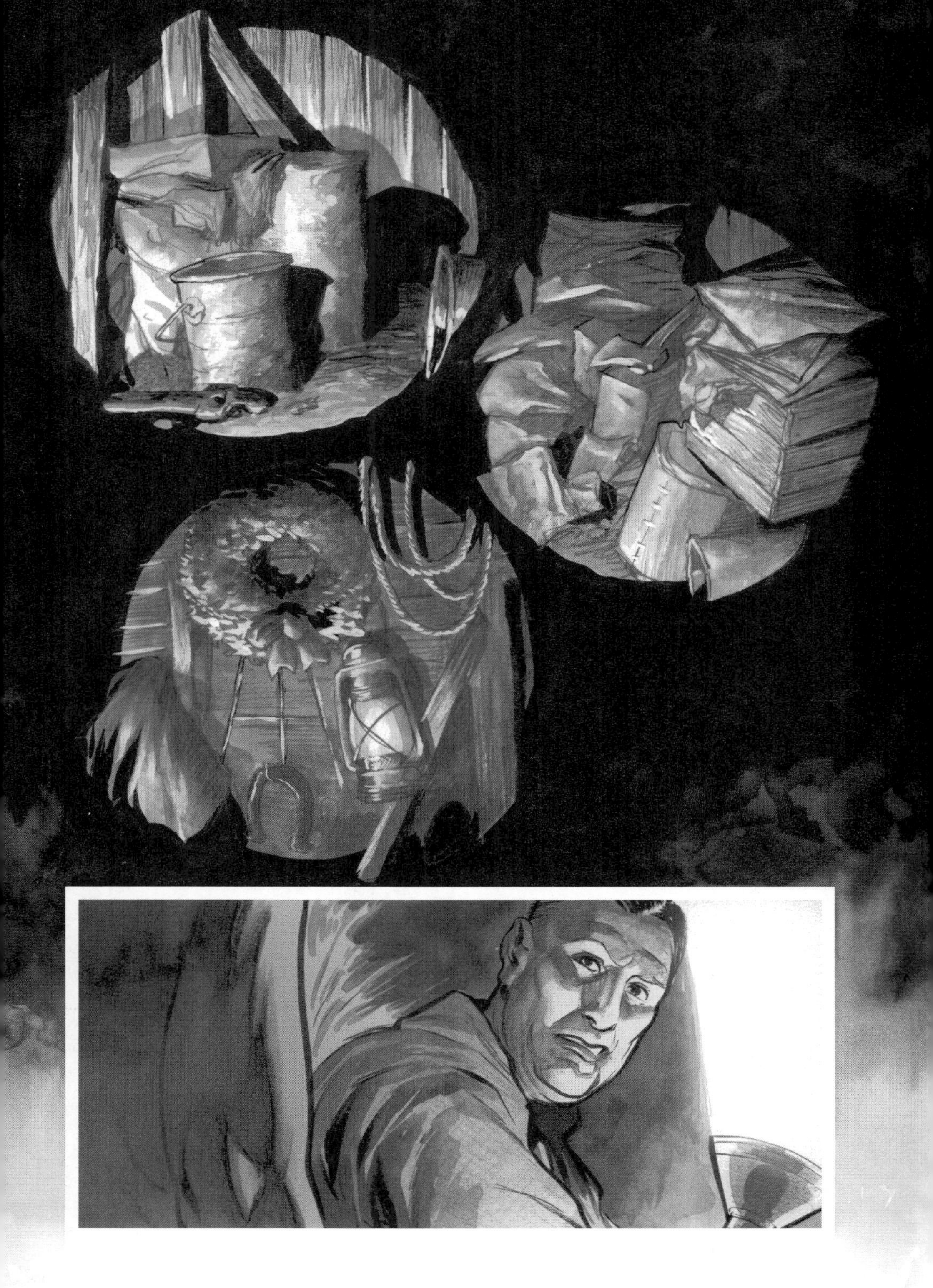

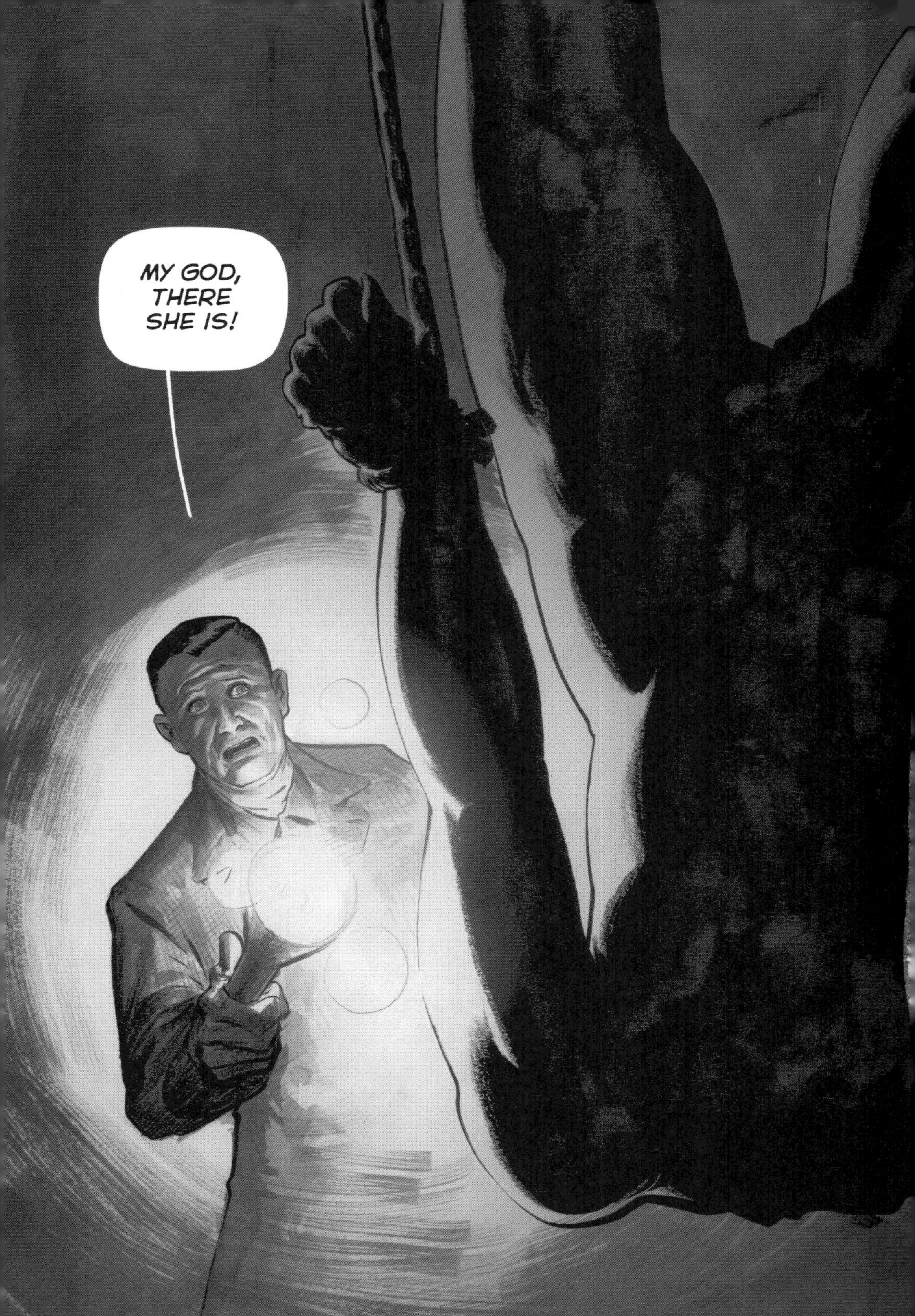
MY GOD, THERE SHE IS!

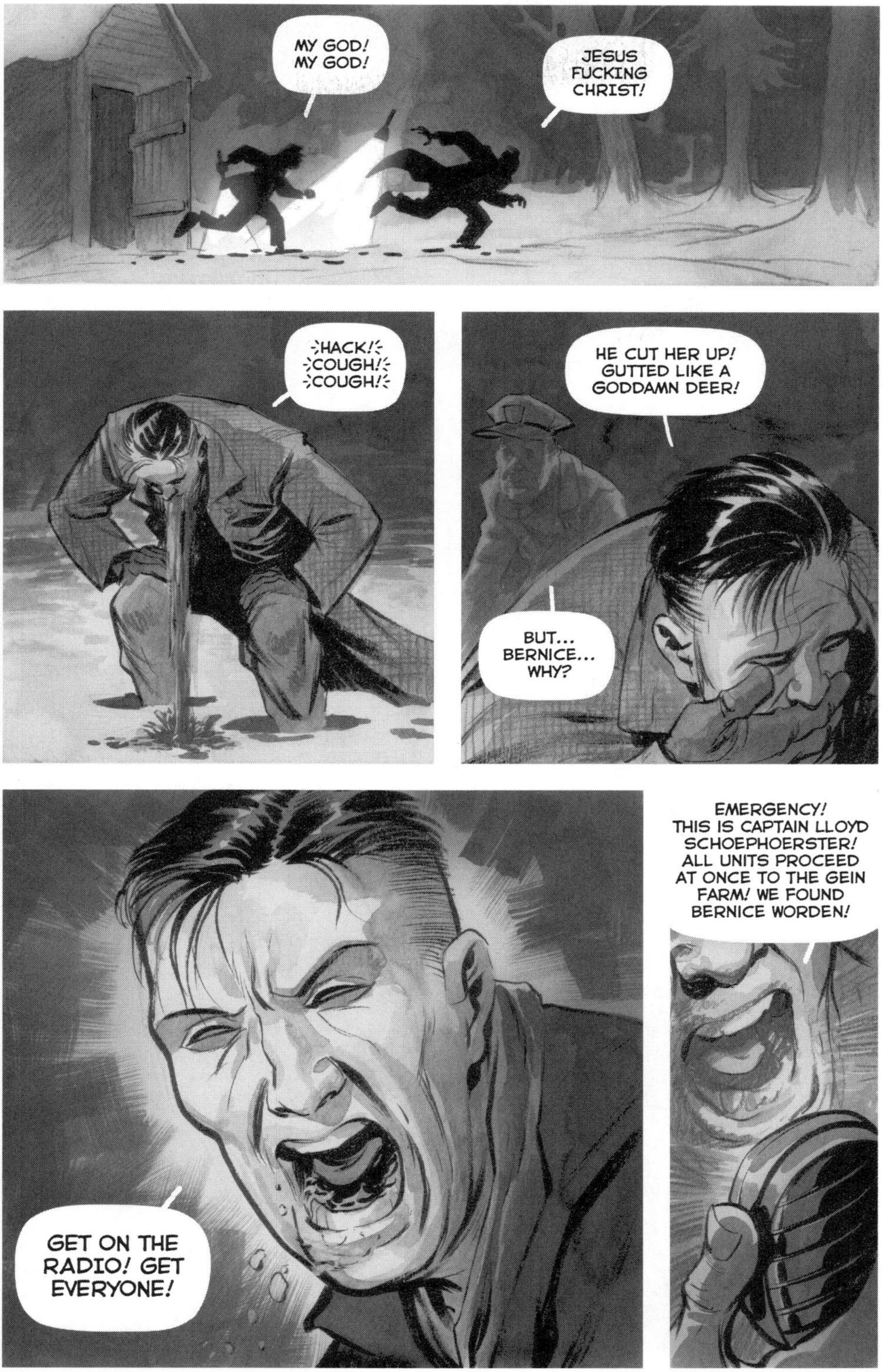
MY GOD! MY GOD!
JESUS FUCKING CHRIST!
HACK! COUGH! COUGH!
HE CUT HER UP! GUTTED LIKE A GODDAMN DEER!
BUT... BERNICE... WHY?
GET ON THE RADIO! GET EVERYONE!
EMERGENCY! THIS IS CAPTAIN LLOYD SCHOEPHOERSTER! ALL UNITS PROCEED AT ONCE TO THE GEIN FARM! WE FOUND BERNICE WORDEN!

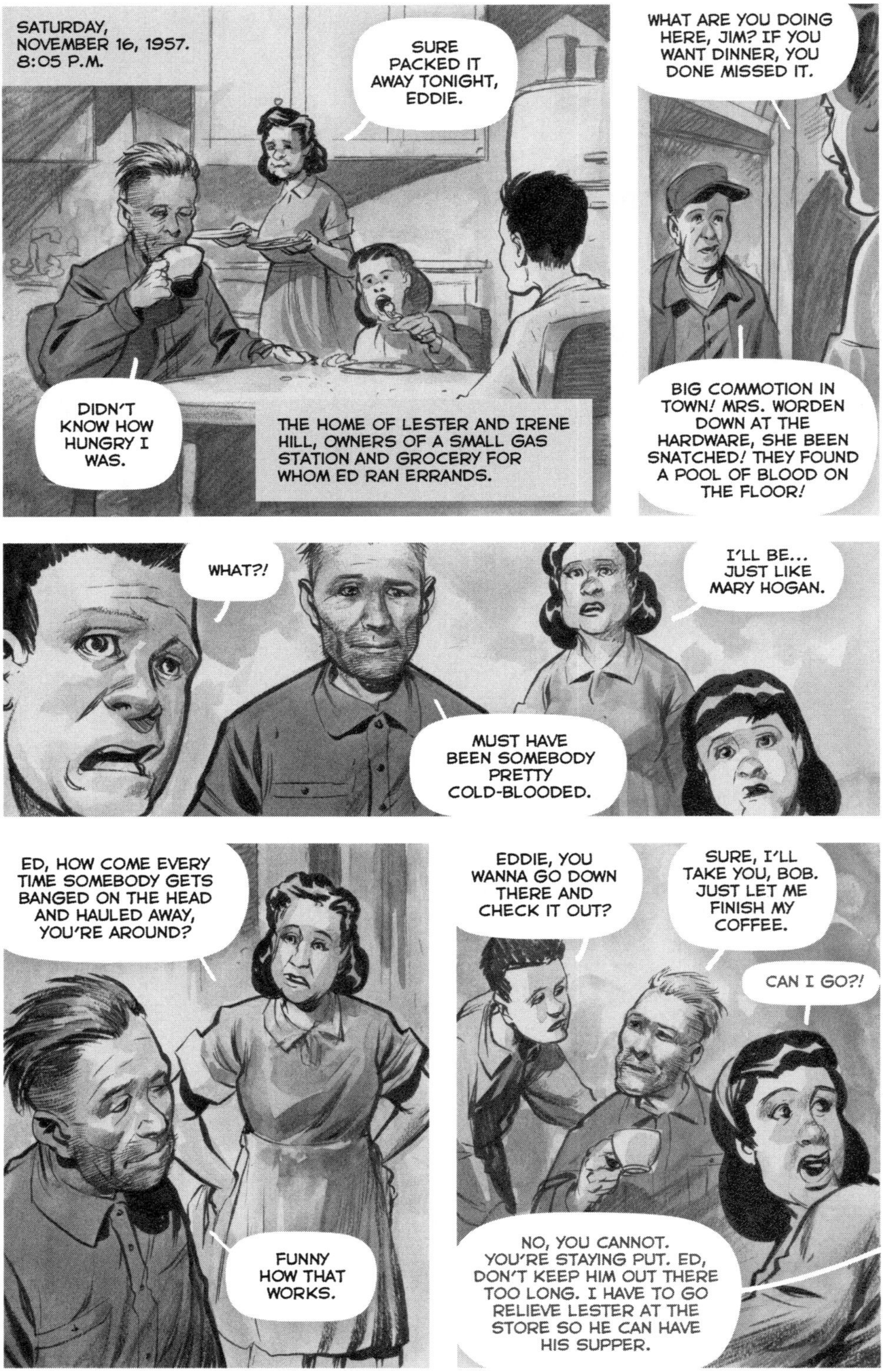
SATURDAY, NOVEMBER 16, 1957. 8:05 P.M.
SURE PACKED IT AWAY TONIGHT, EDDIE.
DIDN'T KNOW HOW HUNGRY I WAS.
THE HOME OF LESTER AND IRENE HILL, OWNERS OF A SMALL GAS STATION AND GROCERY FOR WHOM ED RAN ERRANDS.
WHAT ARE YOU DOING HERE, JIM? IF YOU WANT DINNER, YOU DONE MISSED IT.
BIG COMMOTION IN TOWN! MRS. WORDEN DOWN AT THE HARDWARE, SHE BEEN SNATCHED! THEY FOUND A POOL OF BLOOD ON THE FLOOR!
WHAT?!
MUST HAVE BEEN SOMEBODY PRETTY COLD-BLOODED.
I'LL BE... JUST LIKE MARY HOGAN.
ED, HOW COME EVERY TIME SOMEBODY GETS BANGED ON THE HEAD AND HAULED AWAY, YOU'RE AROUND?
FUNNY HOW THAT WORKS.
EDDIE, YOU WANNA GO DOWN THERE AND CHECK IT OUT?
SURE, I'LL TAKE YOU, BOB. JUST LET ME FINISH MY COFFEE.
CAN I GO?!
NO, YOU CANNOT. YOU'RE STAYING PUT. ED, DON'T KEEP HIM OUT THERE TOO LONG. I HAVE TO GO RELIEVE LESTER AT THE STORE SO HE CAN HAVE HIS SUPPER.

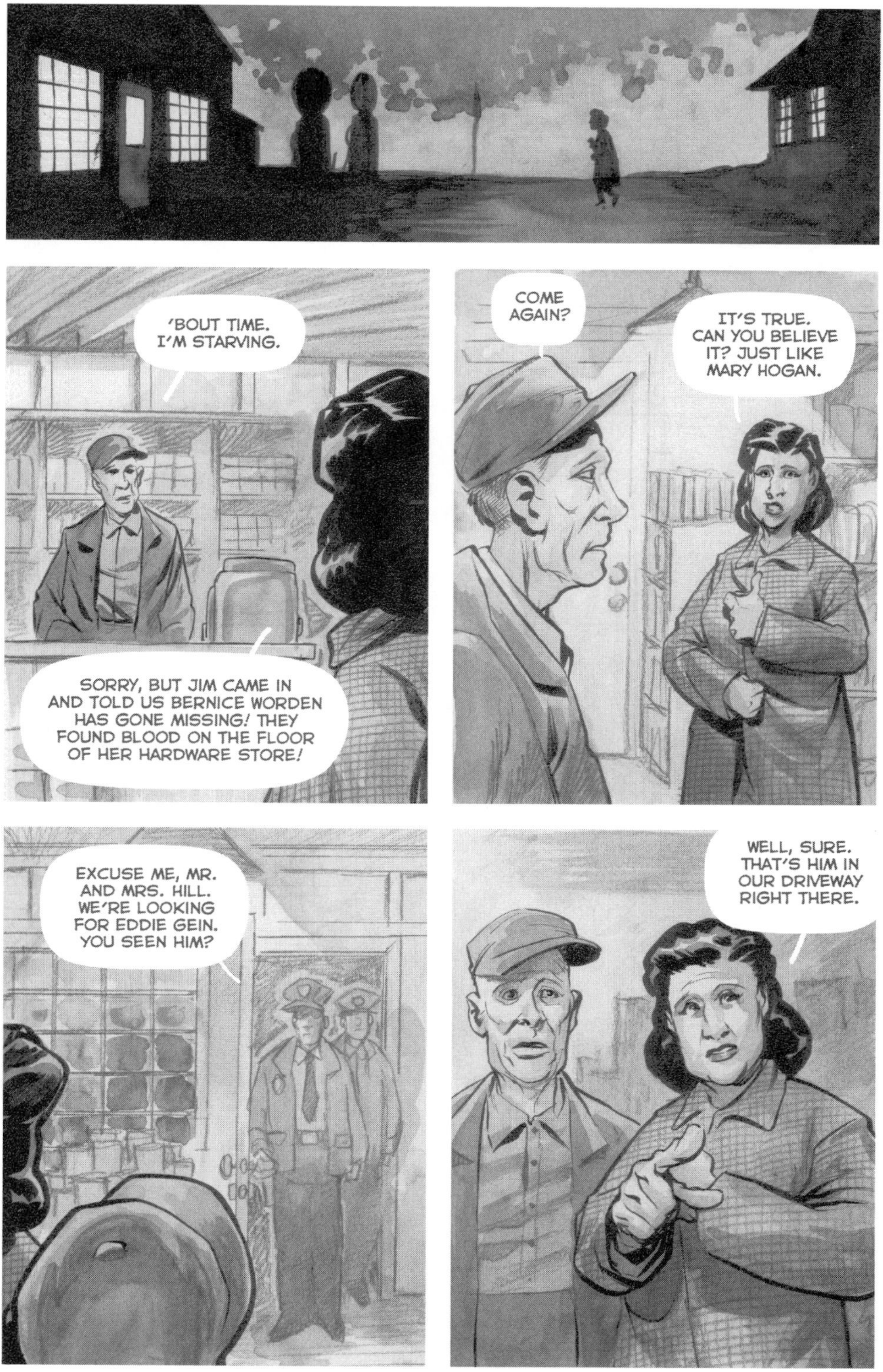
'BOUT TIME. I'M STARVING.
SORRY, BUT JIM CAME IN AND TOLD US BERNICE WORDEN HAS GONE MISSING! THEY FOUND BLOOD ON THE FLOOR OF HER HARDWARE STORE!
COME AGAIN?
IT'S TRUE. CAN YOU BELIEVE IT? JUST LIKE MARY HOGAN.
EXCUSE ME, MR. AND MRS. HILL. WE'RE LOOKING FOR EDDIE GEIN. YOU SEEN HIM?
WELL, SURE. THAT'S HIM IN OUR DRIVEWAY RIGHT THERE.

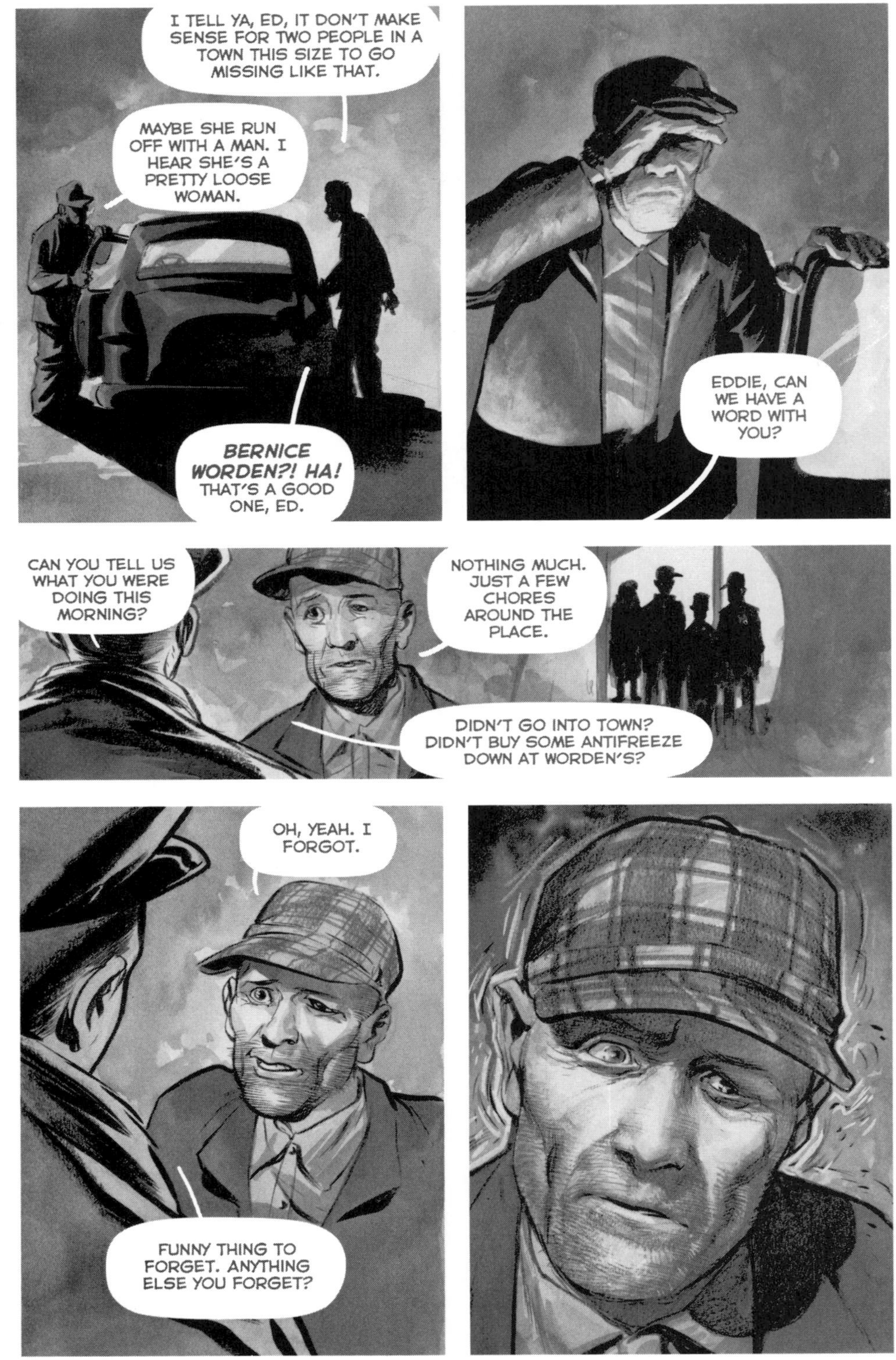
I TELL YA, ED, IT DON'T MAKE SENSE FOR TWO PEOPLE IN A TOWN THIS SIZE TO GO MISSING LIKE THAT.
MAYBE SHE RUN OFF WITH A MAN. I HEAR SHE'S A PRETTY LOOSE WOMAN.
BERNICE WORDEN?! HA! THAT'S A GOOD ONE, ED.
EDDIE, CAN WE HAVE A WORD WITH YOU?
CAN YOU TELL US WHAT YOU WERE DOING THIS MORNING?
NOTHING MUCH. JUST A FEW CHORES AROUND THE PLACE.
DIDN'T GO INTO TOWN? DIDN'T BUY SOME ANTIFREEZE DOWN AT WORDEN'S?
OH, YEAH. I FORGOT.
FUNNY THING TO FORGET. ANYTHING ELSE YOU FORGET?

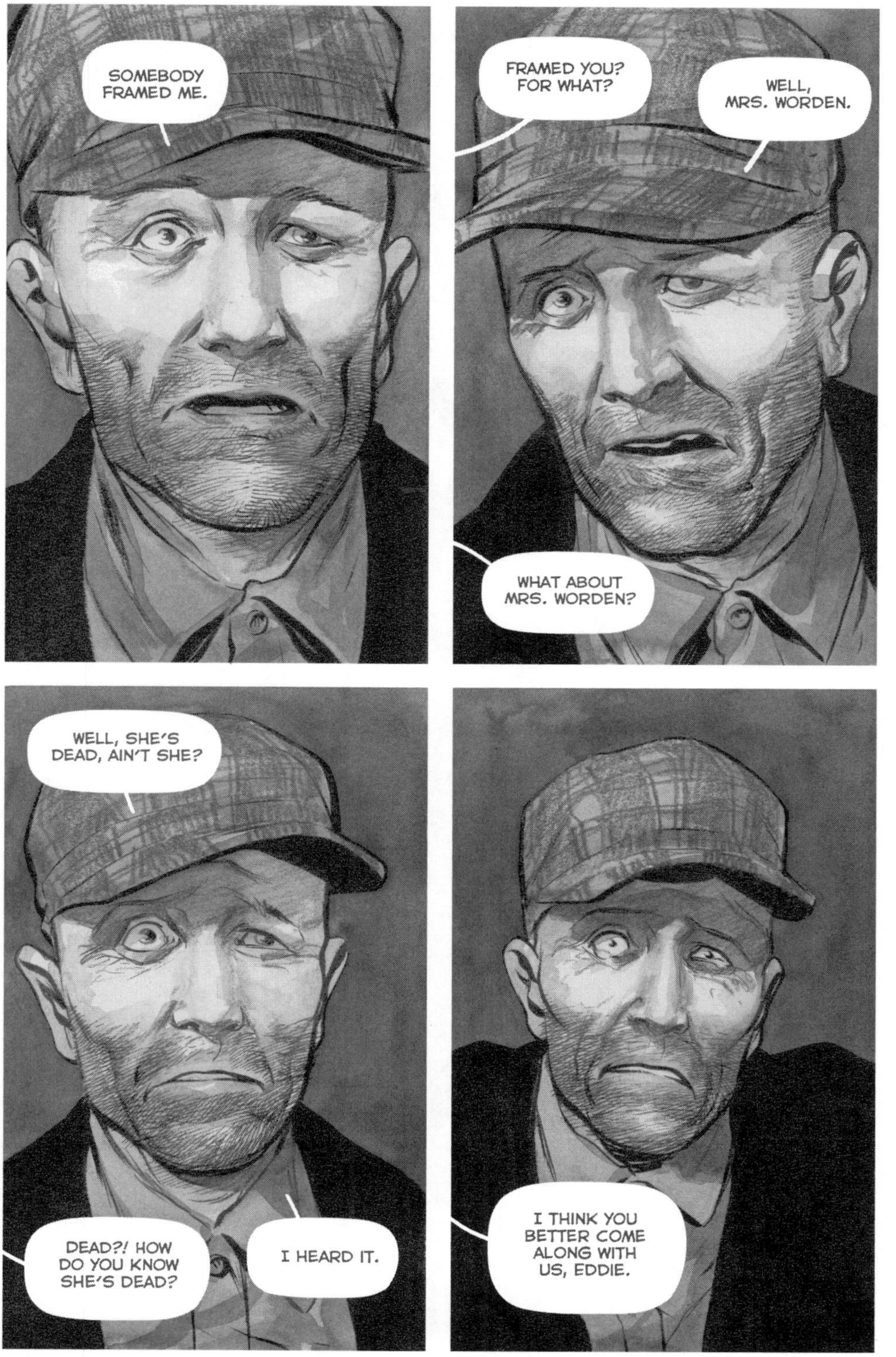
SOMEBODY FRAMED ME.
FRAMED YOU? FOR WHAT?
WELL, MRS. WORDEN.
WHAT ABOUT MRS. WORDEN?
WELL, SHE'S DEAD, AIN'T SHE?
DEAD?! HOW DO YOU KNOW SHE'S DEAD?
I HEARD IT.
I THINK YOU BETTER COME ALONG WITH US, EDDIE.

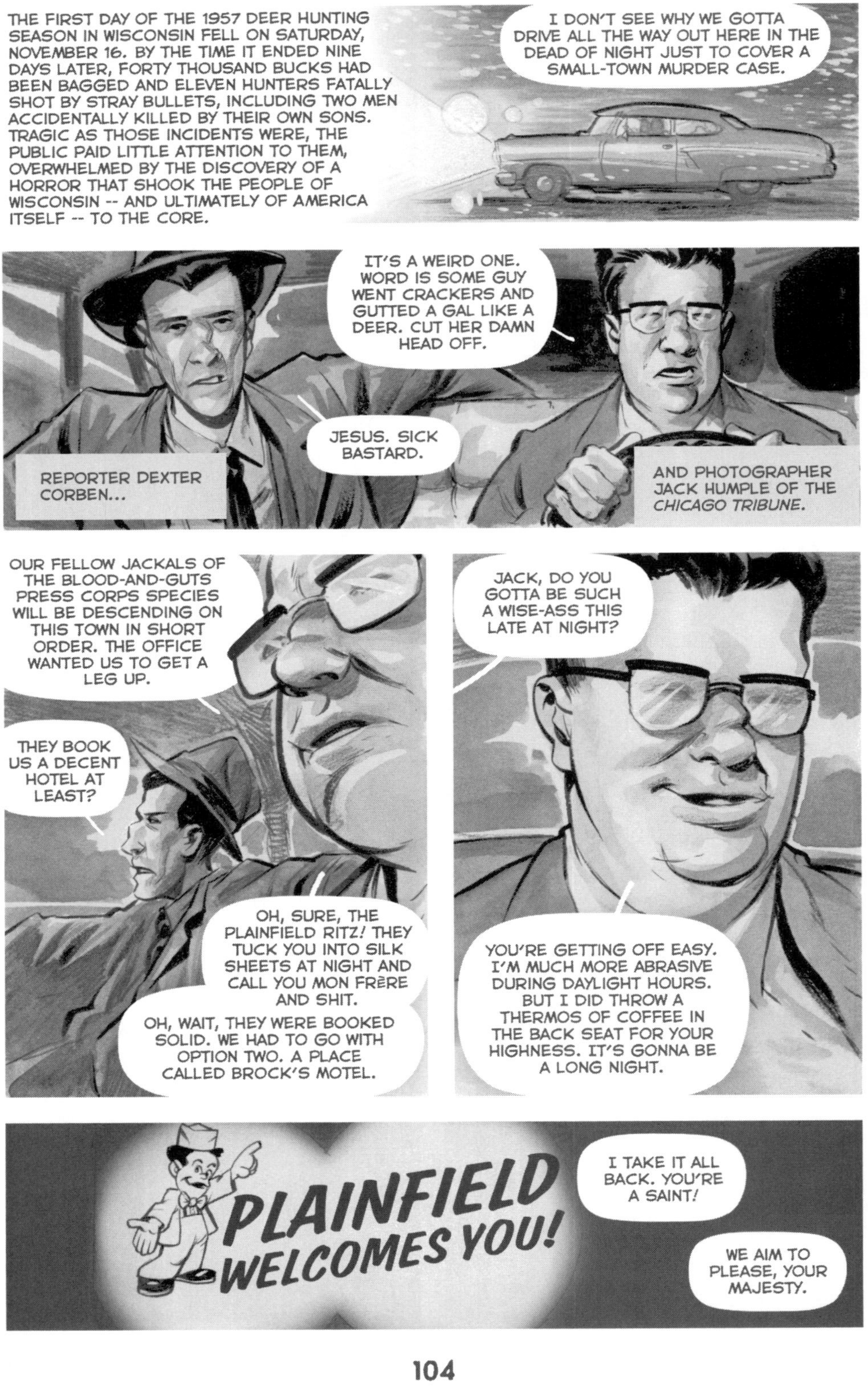
THE FIRST DAY OF THE 1957 DEER HUNTING SEASON IN WISCONSIN FELL ON SATURDAY, NOVEMBER 16. BY THE TIME IT ENDED NINE DAYS LATER, FORTY THOUSAND BUCKS HAD BEEN BAGGED AND ELEVEN HUNTERS FATALLY SHOT BY STRAY BULLETS, INCLUDING TWO MEN ACCIDENTALLY KILLED BY THEIR OWN SONS. TRAGIC AS THOSE INCIDENTS WERE, THE PUBLIC PAID LITTLE ATTENTION TO THEM, OVERWHELMED BY THE DISCOVERY OF A HORROR THAT SHOOK THE PEOPLE OF WISCONSIN -- AND ULTIMATELY OF AMERICA ITSELF -- TO THE CORE.
I DON'T SEE WHY WE GOTTA DRIVE ALL THE WAY OUT HERE IN THE DEAD OF NIGHT JUST TO COVER A SMALL-TOWN MURDER CASE.
IT'S A WEIRD ONE. WORD IS SOME GUY WENT CRACKERS AND GUTTED A GAL LIKE A DEER. CUT HER DAMN HEAD OFF.
JESUS. SICK BASTARD.
REPORTER DEXTER CORBEN...
AND PHOTOGRAPHER JACK HUMPLE OF THE *CHICAGO TRIBUNE*.
OUR FELLOW JACKALS OF THE BLOOD-AND-GUTS PRESS CORPS SPECIES WILL BE DESCENDING ON THIS TOWN IN SHORT ORDER. THE OFFICE WANTED US TO GET A LEG UP.
THEY BOOK US A DECENT HOTEL AT LEAST?
OH, SURE, THE PLAINFIELD RITZ! THEY TUCK YOU INTO SILK SHEETS AT NIGHT AND CALL YOU MON FRÈRE AND SHIT.
OH, WAIT, THEY WERE BOOKED SOLID. WE HAD TO GO WITH OPTION TWO. A PLACE CALLED BROCK'S MOTEL.
JACK, DO YOU GOTTA BE SUCH A WISE-ASS THIS LATE AT NIGHT?
YOU'RE GETTING OFF EASY. I'M MUCH MORE ABRASIVE DURING DAYLIGHT HOURS. BUT I DID THROW A THERMOS OF COFFEE IN THE BACK SEAT FOR YOUR HIGHNESS. IT'S GONNA BE A LONG NIGHT.
PLAINFIELD WELCOMES YOU!
I TAKE IT ALL BACK. YOU'RE A SAINT!
WE AIM TO PLEASE, YOUR MAJESTY.

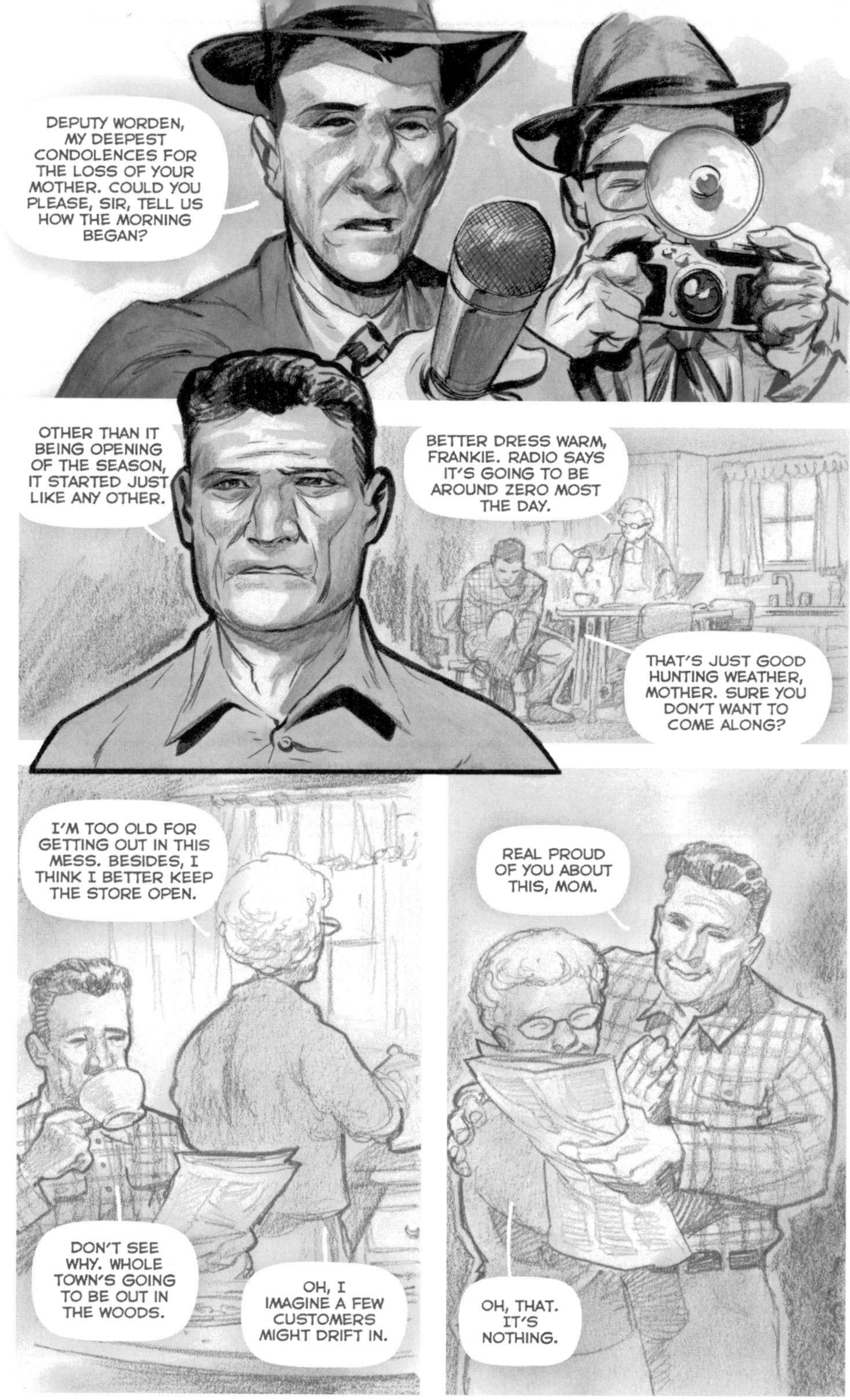
DEPUTY WORDEN, MY DEEPEST CONDOLENCES FOR THE LOSS OF YOUR MOTHER. COULD YOU PLEASE, SIR, TELL US HOW THE MORNING BEGAN?
OTHER THAN IT BEING OPENING OF THE SEASON, IT STARTED JUST LIKE ANY OTHER.
BETTER DRESS WARM, FRANKIE. RADIO SAYS IT'S GOING TO BE AROUND ZERO MOST THE DAY.
THAT'S JUST GOOD HUNTING WEATHER, MOTHER. SURE YOU DON'T WANT TO COME ALONG?
I'M TOO OLD FOR GETTING OUT IN THIS MESS. BESIDES, I THINK I BETTER KEEP THE STORE OPEN.
DON'T SEE WHY. WHOLE TOWN'S GOING TO BE OUT IN THE WOODS.
OH, I IMAGINE A FEW CUSTOMERS MIGHT DRIFT IN.
REAL PROUD OF YOU ABOUT THIS, MOM.
OH, THAT. IT'S NOTHING.

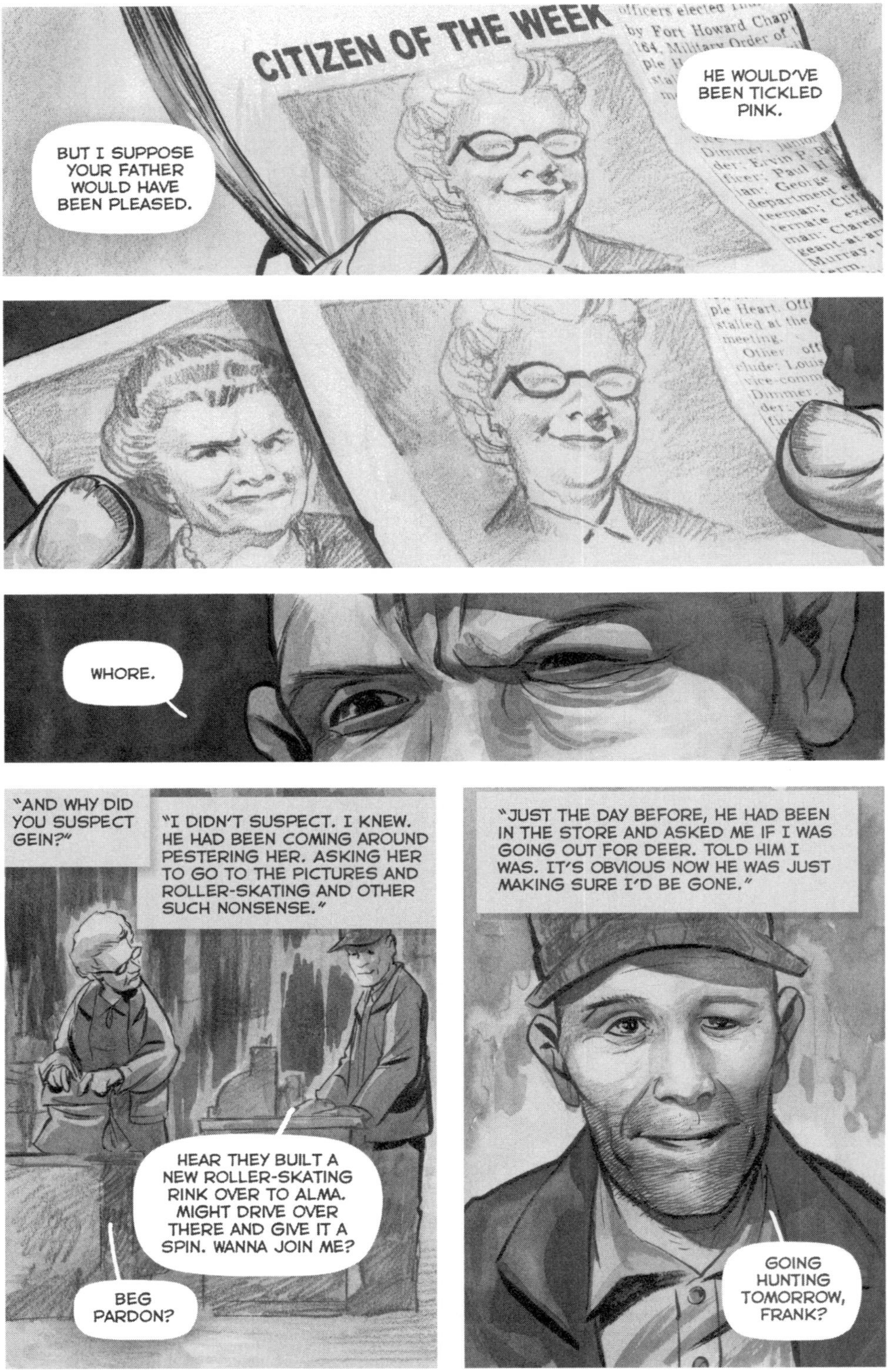
CITIZEN OF THE WEEK
BUT I SUPPOSE YOUR FATHER WOULD HAVE BEEN PLEASED.
HE WOULD'VE BEEN TICKLED PINK.
WHORE.
"AND WHY DID YOU SUSPECT GEIN?"
"I DIDN'T SUSPECT. I KNEW. HE HAD BEEN COMING AROUND PESTERING HER. ASKING HER TO GO TO THE PICTURES AND ROLLER-SKATING AND OTHER SUCH NONSENSE."
HEAR THEY BUILT A NEW ROLLER-SKATING RINK OVER TO ALMA. MIGHT DRIVE OVER THERE AND GIVE IT A SPIN. WANNA JOIN ME?
BEG PARDON?
"JUST THE DAY BEFORE, HE HAD BEEN IN THE STORE AND ASKED ME IF I WAS GOING OUT FOR DEER. TOLD HIM I WAS. IT'S OBVIOUS NOW HE WAS JUST MAKING SURE I'D BE GONE."
GOING HUNTING TOMORROW, FRANK?

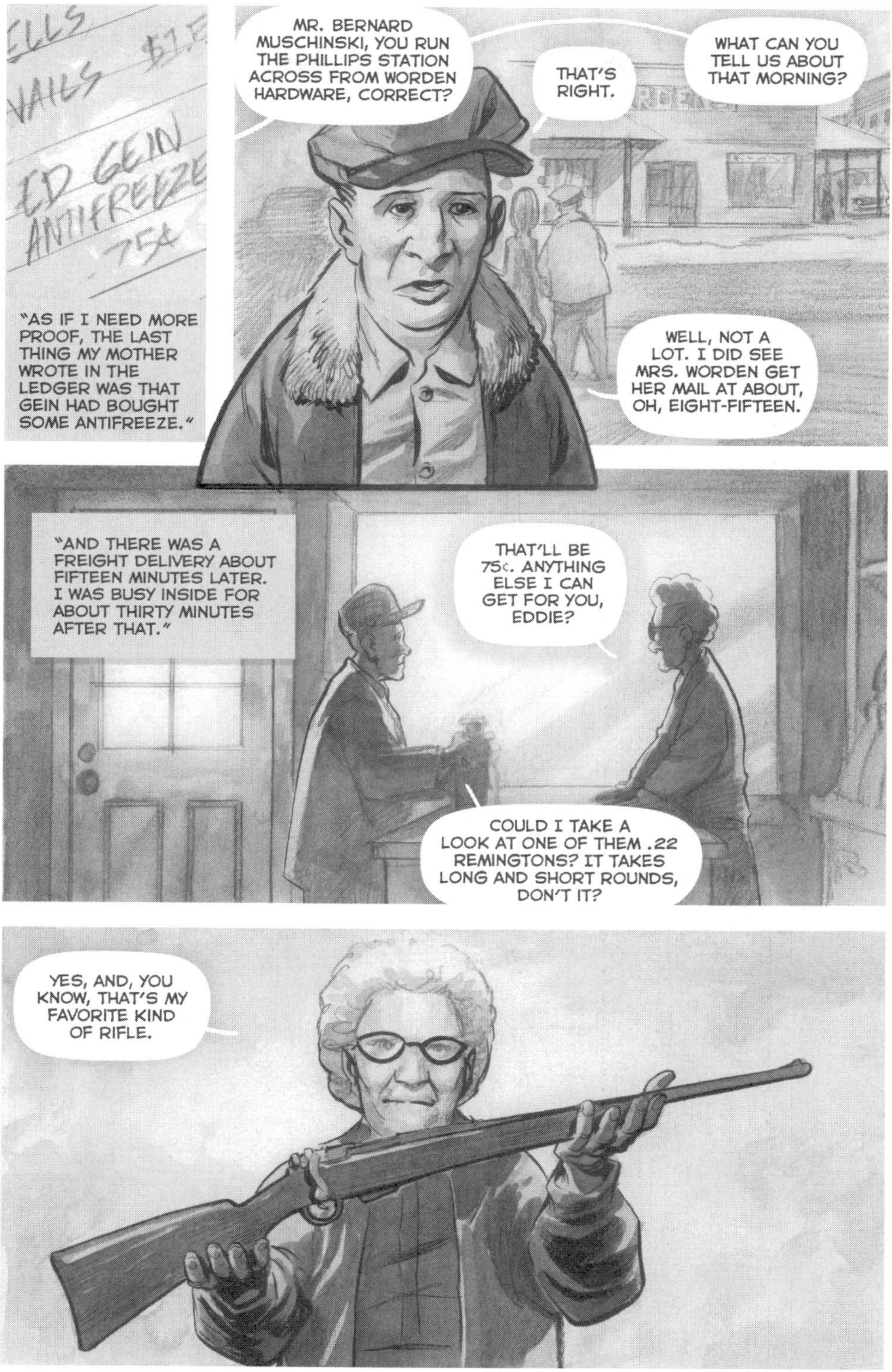
ED GEIN
ANTIFREEZE
75¢
"AS IF I NEED MORE PROOF, THE LAST THING MY MOTHER WROTE IN THE LEDGER WAS THAT GEIN HAD BOUGHT SOME ANTIFREEZE."
MR. BERNARD MUSCHINSKI, YOU RUN THE PHILLIPS STATION ACROSS FROM WORDEN HARDWARE, CORRECT?
THAT'S RIGHT.
WHAT CAN YOU TELL US ABOUT THAT MORNING?
WELL, NOT A LOT. I DID SEE MRS. WORDEN GET HER MAIL AT ABOUT, OH, EIGHT-FIFTEEN.
"AND THERE WAS A FREIGHT DELIVERY ABOUT FIFTEEN MINUTES LATER. I WAS BUSY INSIDE FOR ABOUT THIRTY MINUTES AFTER THAT."
THAT'LL BE 75¢. ANYTHING ELSE I CAN GET FOR YOU, EDDIE?
COULD I TAKE A LOOK AT ONE OF THEM .22 REMINGTONS? IT TAKES LONG AND SHORT ROUNDS, DON'T IT?
YES, AND, YOU KNOW, THAT'S MY FAVORITE KIND OF RIFLE.

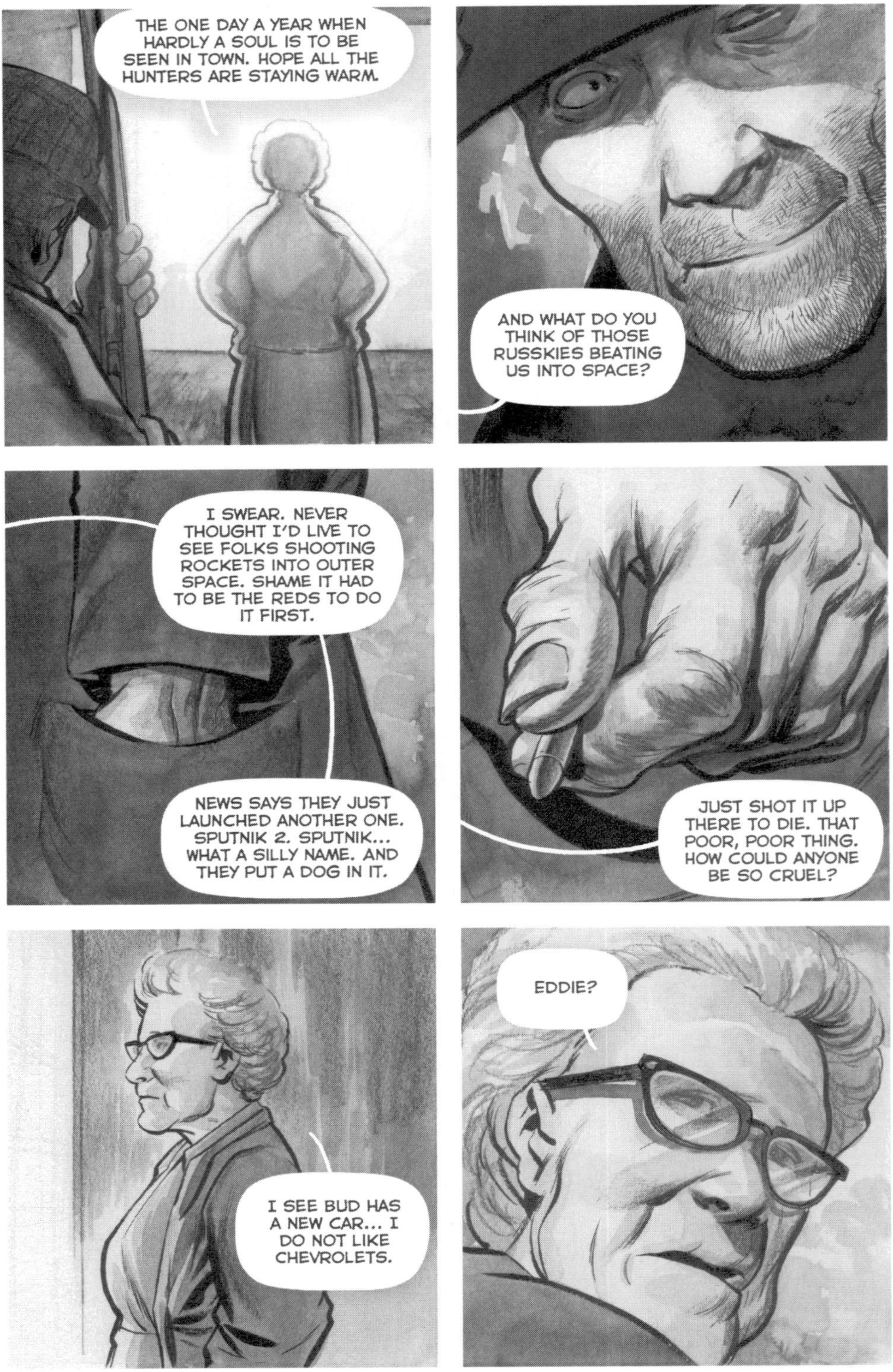
THE ONE DAY A YEAR WHEN HARDLY A SOUL IS TO BE SEEN IN TOWN. HOPE ALL THE HUNTERS ARE STAYING WARM.
AND WHAT DO YOU THINK OF THOSE RUSSKIES BEATING US INTO SPACE?
I SWEAR. NEVER THOUGHT I'D LIVE TO SEE FOLKS SHOOTING ROCKETS INTO OUTER SPACE. SHAME IT HAD TO BE THE REDS TO DO IT FIRST.
NEWS SAYS THEY JUST LAUNCHED ANOTHER ONE. SPUTNIK 2. SPUTNIK... WHAT A SILLY NAME. AND THEY PUT A DOG IN IT.
JUST SHOT IT UP THERE TO DIE. THAT POOR, POOR THING. HOW COULD ANYONE BE SO CRUEL?
I SEE BUD HAS A NEW CAR... I DO NOT LIKE CHEVROLETS.
EDDIE?

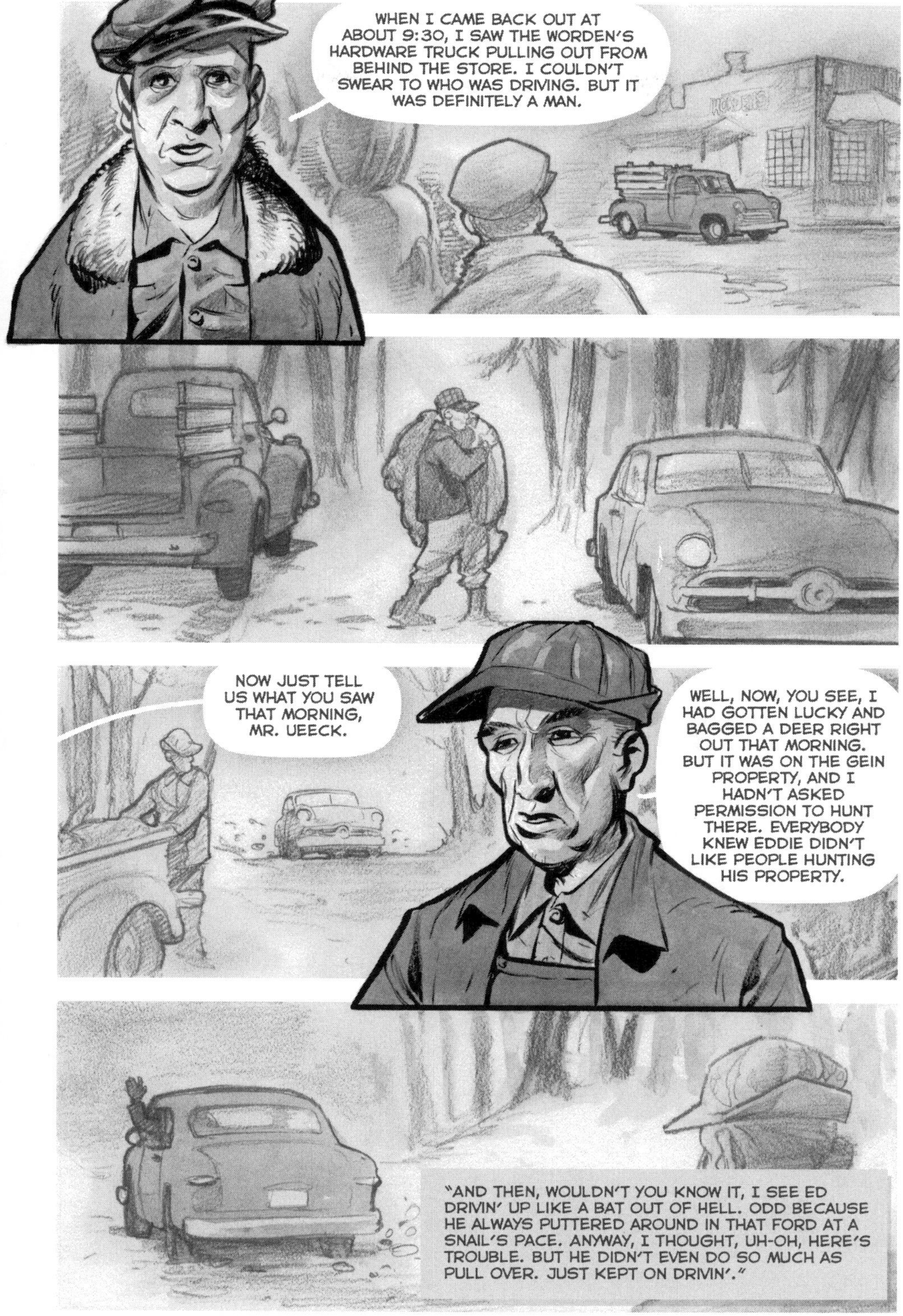
WHEN I CAME BACK OUT AT ABOUT 9:30, I SAW THE WORDEN'S HARDWARE TRUCK PULLING OUT FROM BEHIND THE STORE. I COULDN'T SWEAR TO WHO WAS DRIVING. BUT IT WAS DEFINITELY A MAN.
NOW JUST TELL US WHAT YOU SAW THAT MORNING, MR. UEECK.
WELL, NOW, YOU SEE, I HAD GOTTEN LUCKY AND BAGGED A DEER RIGHT OUT THAT MORNING. BUT IT WAS ON THE GEIN PROPERTY, AND I HADN'T ASKED PERMISSION TO HUNT THERE. EVERYBODY KNEW EDDIE DIDN'T LIKE PEOPLE HUNTING HIS PROPERTY.
"AND THEN, WOULDN'T YOU KNOW IT, I SEE ED DRIVIN' UP LIKE A BAT OUT OF HELL. ODD BECAUSE HE ALWAYS PUTTERED AROUND IN THAT FORD AT A SNAIL'S PACE. ANYWAY, I THOUGHT, UH-OH, HERE'S TROUBLE. BUT HE DIDN'T EVEN DO SO MUCH AS PULL OVER. JUST KEPT ON DRIVIN'."

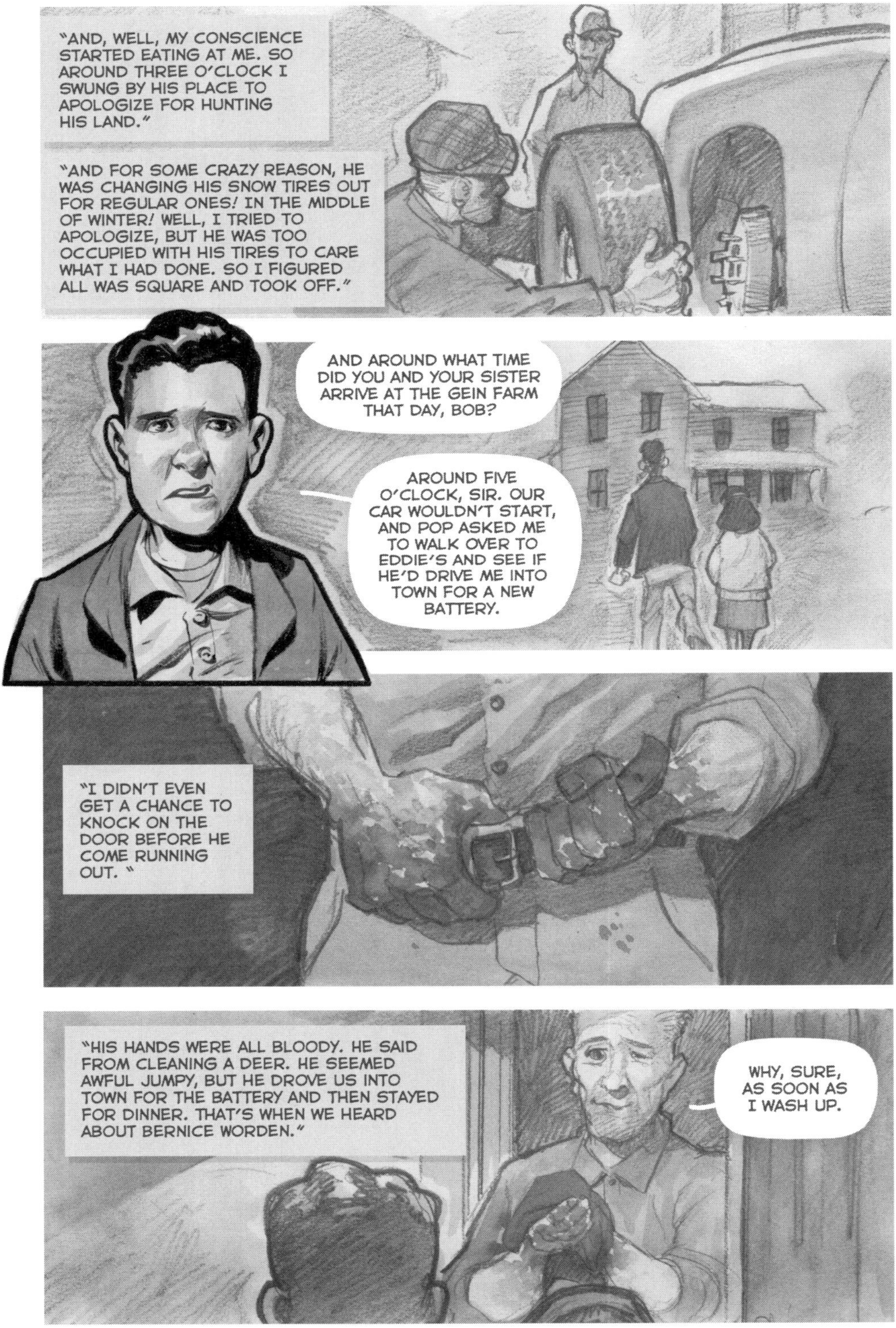
"AND, WELL, MY CONSCIENCE STARTED EATING AT ME. SO AROUND THREE O'CLOCK I SWUNG BY HIS PLACE TO APOLOGIZE FOR HUNTING HIS LAND."
"AND FOR SOME CRAZY REASON, HE WAS CHANGING HIS SNOW TIRES OUT FOR REGULAR ONES! IN THE MIDDLE OF WINTER! WELL, I TRIED TO APOLOGIZE, BUT HE WAS TOO OCCUPIED WITH HIS TIRES TO CARE WHAT I HAD DONE. SO I FIGURED ALL WAS SQUARE AND TOOK OFF."
AND AROUND WHAT TIME DID YOU AND YOUR SISTER ARRIVE AT THE GEIN FARM THAT DAY, BOB?
AROUND FIVE O'CLOCK, SIR. OUR CAR WOULDN'T START, AND POP ASKED ME TO WALK OVER TO EDDIE'S AND SEE IF HE'D DRIVE ME INTO TOWN FOR A NEW BATTERY.
"I DIDN'T EVEN GET A CHANCE TO KNOCK ON THE DOOR BEFORE HE COME RUNNING OUT."
"HIS HANDS WERE ALL BLOODY. HE SAID FROM CLEANING A DEER. HE SEEMED AWFUL JUMPY, BUT HE DROVE US INTO TOWN FOR THE BATTERY AND THEN STAYED FOR DINNER. THAT'S WHEN WE HEARD ABOUT BERNICE WORDEN."
WHY, SURE, AS SOON AS I WASH UP.

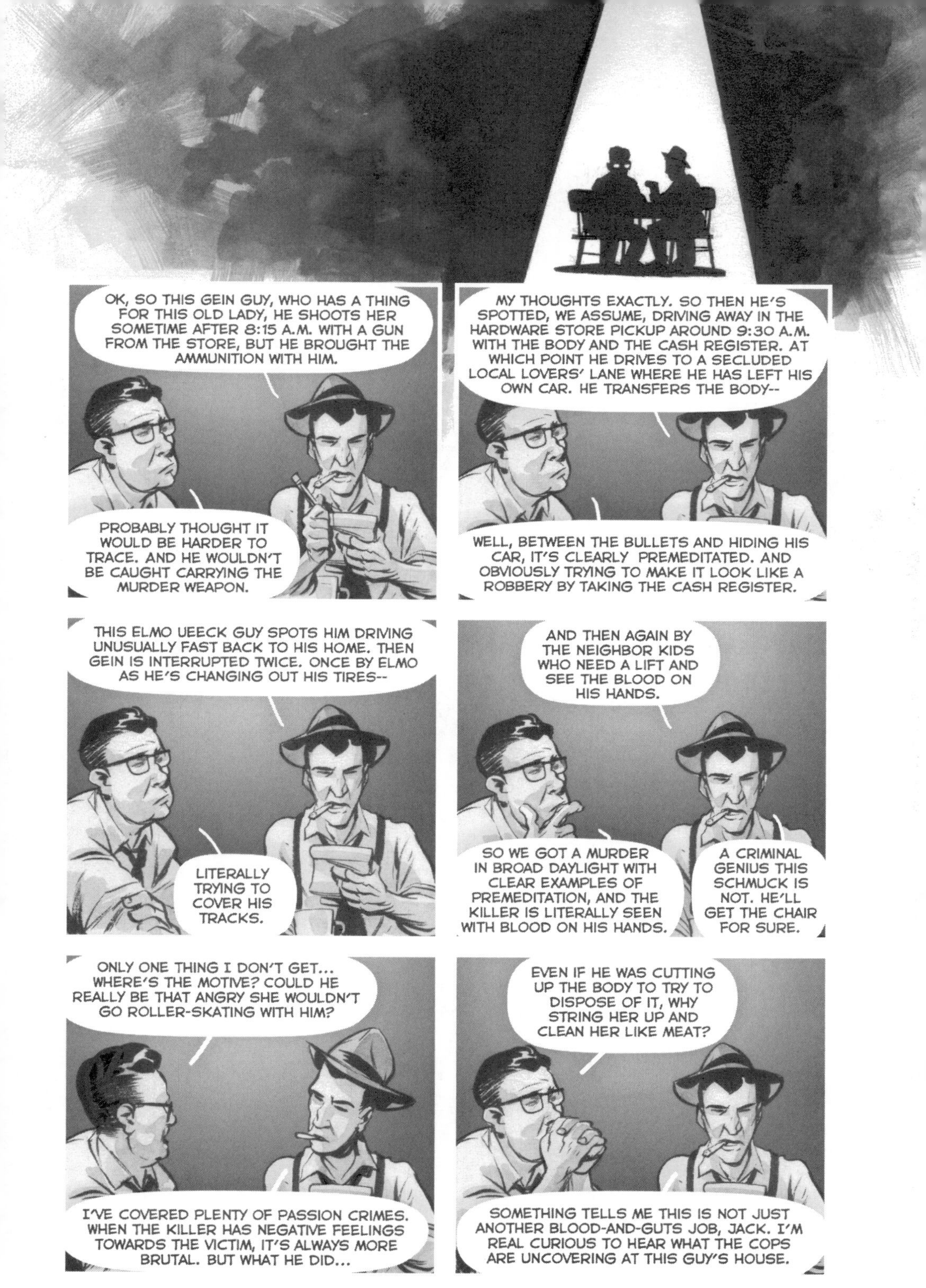
OK, SO THIS GEIN GUY, WHO HAS A THING FOR THIS OLD LADY, HE SHOOTS HER SOMETIME AFTER 8:15 A.M. WITH A GUN FROM THE STORE, BUT HE BROUGHT THE AMMUNITION WITH HIM.
PROBABLY THOUGHT IT WOULD BE HARDER TO TRACE. AND HE WOULDN'T BE CAUGHT CARRYING THE MURDER WEAPON.
MY THOUGHTS EXACTLY. SO THEN HE'S SPOTTED, WE ASSUME, DRIVING AWAY IN THE HARDWARE STORE PICKUP AROUND 9:30 A.M. WITH THE BODY AND THE CASH REGISTER. AT WHICH POINT HE DRIVES TO A SECLUDED LOCAL LOVERS' LANE WHERE HE HAS LEFT HIS OWN CAR. HE TRANSFERS THE BODY--
WELL, BETWEEN THE BULLETS AND HIDING HIS CAR, IT'S CLEARLY PREMEDITATED. AND OBVIOUSLY TRYING TO MAKE IT LOOK LIKE A ROBBERY BY TAKING THE CASH REGISTER.
THIS ELMO UEECK GUY SPOTS HIM DRIVING UNUSUALLY FAST BACK TO HIS HOME. THEN GEIN IS INTERRUPTED TWICE. ONCE BY ELMO AS HE'S CHANGING OUT HIS TIRES--
LITERALLY TRYING TO COVER HIS TRACKS.
AND THEN AGAIN BY THE NEIGHBOR KIDS WHO NEED A LIFT AND SEE THE BLOOD ON HIS HANDS.
SO WE GOT A MURDER IN BROAD DAYLIGHT WITH CLEAR EXAMPLES OF PREMEDITATION, AND THE KILLER IS LITERALLY SEEN WITH BLOOD ON HIS HANDS.
A CRIMINAL GENIUS THIS SCHMUCK IS NOT. HE'LL GET THE CHAIR FOR SURE.
ONLY ONE THING I DON'T GET... WHERE'S THE MOTIVE? COULD HE REALLY BE THAT ANGRY SHE WOULDN'T GO ROLLER-SKATING WITH HIM?
I'VE COVERED PLENTY OF PASSION CRIMES. WHEN THE KILLER HAS NEGATIVE FEELINGS TOWARDS THE VICTIM, IT'S ALWAYS MORE BRUTAL. BUT WHAT HE DID...
EVEN IF HE WAS CUTTING UP THE BODY TO TRY TO DISPOSE OF IT, WHY STRING HER UP AND CLEAN HER LIKE MEAT?
SOMETHING TELLS ME THIS IS NOT JUST ANOTHER BLOOD-AND-GUTS JOB, JACK. I'M REAL CURIOUS TO HEAR WHAT THE COPS ARE UNCOVERING AT THIS GUY'S HOUSE.

CHAPTER 7

10¢ ★★★

★★★ Friday, December 13th, 1957

ARCHEOLOGY IN HELL

By Roger Cahsdon
Guest Editorial

The entire arraignment lasted little more than five minutes. After listening to the recommendations of the prosecutor and the defense attorney, Judge Bunde made a statement. "It seems advisable under the circumstances as related by both the counsel for the state and the counsel for the defendant," he said, "that expert determination be had whether he is now competent to stand trial," as well as whether he was sane at the time of Mrs. Worden's murder.

Then Bunde signed an order committing Eddie to the Central State Hospital for the Criminally Insane at Waupun for a thirty-day examination period and remanded him to the custody of Sheriff Schley, who led Eddie back to the jailhouse to await transportation to the mental institution.

Though Gein was a wily fellow, it seemed impossible that he could have had the strength to dig up a grave by himself, break open the casket, remove the corpse and perform his grisly operations on it, then rebury the coffin and smooth over the newly-turned earth — all in the space of a few hours. Moreover, the townspeople didn't see how such an activity could possibly have

techniques for identifying the victims from their remains. By comparing dirt particles gathered at the crime scene with soil samples from local cemeteries, the technicians hoped to determine the validity of Gein's claim.

But the sheer quantity of evidence—by far, the largest amount ever handled by the ten-year-old Crime Lab—made it hard for Wilson to promise a quick resolution. Though Kileen urged the director to give the soil analysis top priority, it was clear that a final analysis might take weeks, even months.

In the meantime, Kileen was under growing pressure from the Plainfield citizenry to determine the truth of Gein's assertion. It was becoming increasingly obvious that the townsfolk would never be able to rest without knowing whether their loved ones had, in fact, been ravaged in their graves. On Friday afternoon, therefore, following his meeting with Judge Bunde and the other officials, Kileen called a press conference to make an electrifying announcement.

Early the next week, he told the reporters, the soil analysis would be opened to the Plainfield cemetery. Kileen's charge of soil regarding the exhumations wasn't his only aboat-face. He also seemed to have become suddenly flustant about the whole grave-robbing story. When one of the

Within days of the discovery of the crimes, every youngster in Wisconsin, it seemed, was swapping "Gainers" for fun—not only with schoolmates but with parents as well. Grim jokes became the latest rage, repeated with near obsessive frequency wherever people gathered. As early as Friday November 22, Dr. Rudolf Mathias, chief psychologist at the Wisconsin Diagnostic Center in Madison, was theorizing about the significance of Gein humor, which he likened to "the jokes exchanged among soldiers who are going into battle." Fiercely opposed to the idea of violating the hallowed soil of their little

cemetery. Added to this tension were the unabating rumors that continued to send shocks through the town. Styles had spread, for example, that the grisly remains found in Gein's bedroom and kitchen weren't the worst of what the farmhouse contained, that its basement was full of horrors so dreadful that the police had deemed it best to conceal them from the public. There were also reports, which occasioned more than a few sleepless nights for the matrons of Plainfield, that investigators had turned up a "death list" in Eddie's house, a roster of local farm wives slated to take their places on the

walls, shelves, and ceiling beams of Eddie's private death museum. Most unsettling of all, however, was the persistent rumor that Eddie had not worked alone, that another man had accompanied him on his archeolology forays and even taken part in the depraved operations Gein had performed on his newly unearthed treasures, the citizens of the town had begun to feel the pariah or freaks. According to one source, when the postmaster of Plainfield, Harry P. Walker, was introduced to his colleagues at a statewide convention in Milwaukee. —CONTINUED on page 3

10 Skulls Found in House of Horror

By Leland Bynquist
Lead reporter, City desk

Within days of the discovery of the crimes, every youngster in Wisconsin, it seemed, was swapping "Gainers" not only with schoolmates but with parents as well. Grim jokes became the latest rage, repeated with near-obsessive frequency wherever people gathered. As early as Friday, November 22, Dr. Rudolf Mathias, Chief of the

commemorative postage stamp honoring the prairie chicken, which would be "introduced on its first day of issue" through the Plainfield post office. By designating Plainfield as the place of issue for the prairie chicken stamp, the government would create favorable publicity for the town, not only among the country's millions of philatelists, but also to the national press.

Just how seriously Walker's proposal was

the custody of Sheriff Schley who led Eddie back to the jailhouse to await transportation to the mental institution.

Though Gein was a wily fellow, it seemed impossible that he could have had the strength to dig up a grave by himself, break open the casket, remove the corpse and perform his grisly operations on it, then rebury the coffin and smooth over the newly-turned earth—all in the space of a few hours. When one of the

"I hear it's going to be a long night."

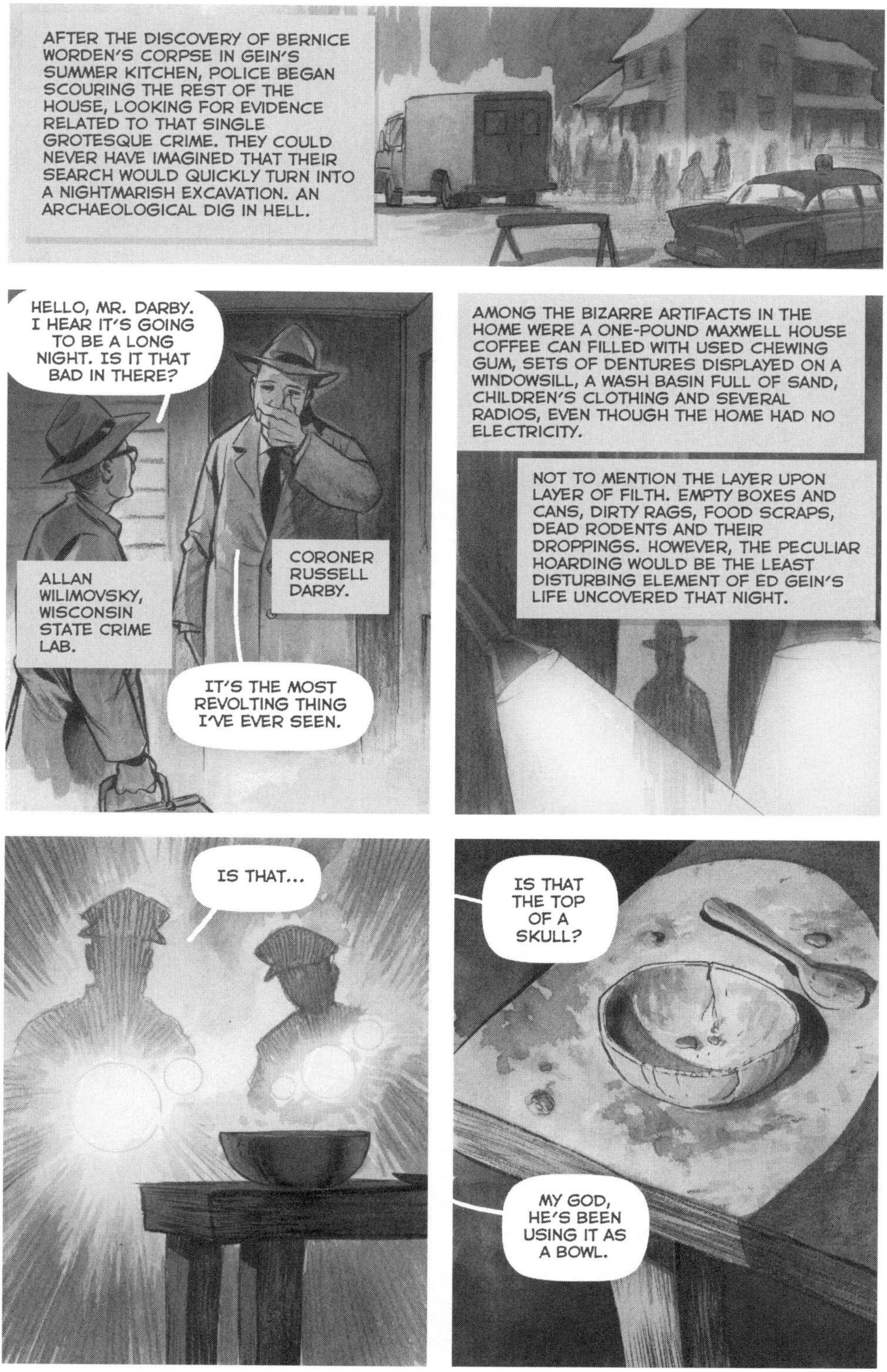
AFTER THE DISCOVERY OF BERNICE WORDEN'S CORPSE IN GEIN'S SUMMER KITCHEN, POLICE BEGAN SCOURING THE REST OF THE HOUSE, LOOKING FOR EVIDENCE RELATED TO THAT SINGLE GROTESQUE CRIME. THEY COULD NEVER HAVE IMAGINED THAT THEIR SEARCH WOULD QUICKLY TURN INTO A NIGHTMARISH EXCAVATION. AN ARCHAEOLOGICAL DIG IN HELL.
HELLO, MR. DARBY. I HEAR IT'S GOING TO BE A LONG NIGHT. IS IT THAT BAD IN THERE?
ALLAN WILIMOVSKY, WISCONSIN STATE CRIME LAB.
CORONER RUSSELL DARBY.
IT'S THE MOST REVOLTING THING I'VE EVER SEEN.
AMONG THE BIZARRE ARTIFACTS IN THE HOME WERE A ONE-POUND MAXWELL HOUSE COFFEE CAN FILLED WITH USED CHEWING GUM, SETS OF DENTURES DISPLAYED ON A WINDOWSILL, A WASH BASIN FULL OF SAND, CHILDREN'S CLOTHING AND SEVERAL RADIOS, EVEN THOUGH THE HOME HAD NO ELECTRICITY.
NOT TO MENTION THE LAYER UPON LAYER OF FILTH. EMPTY BOXES AND CANS, DIRTY RAGS, FOOD SCRAPS, DEAD RODENTS AND THEIR DROPPINGS. HOWEVER, THE PECULIAR HOARDING WOULD BE THE LEAST DISTURBING ELEMENT OF ED GEIN'S LIFE UNCOVERED THAT NIGHT.
IS THAT...
IS THAT THE TOP OF A SKULL?
MY GOD, HE'S BEEN USING IT AS A BOWL.

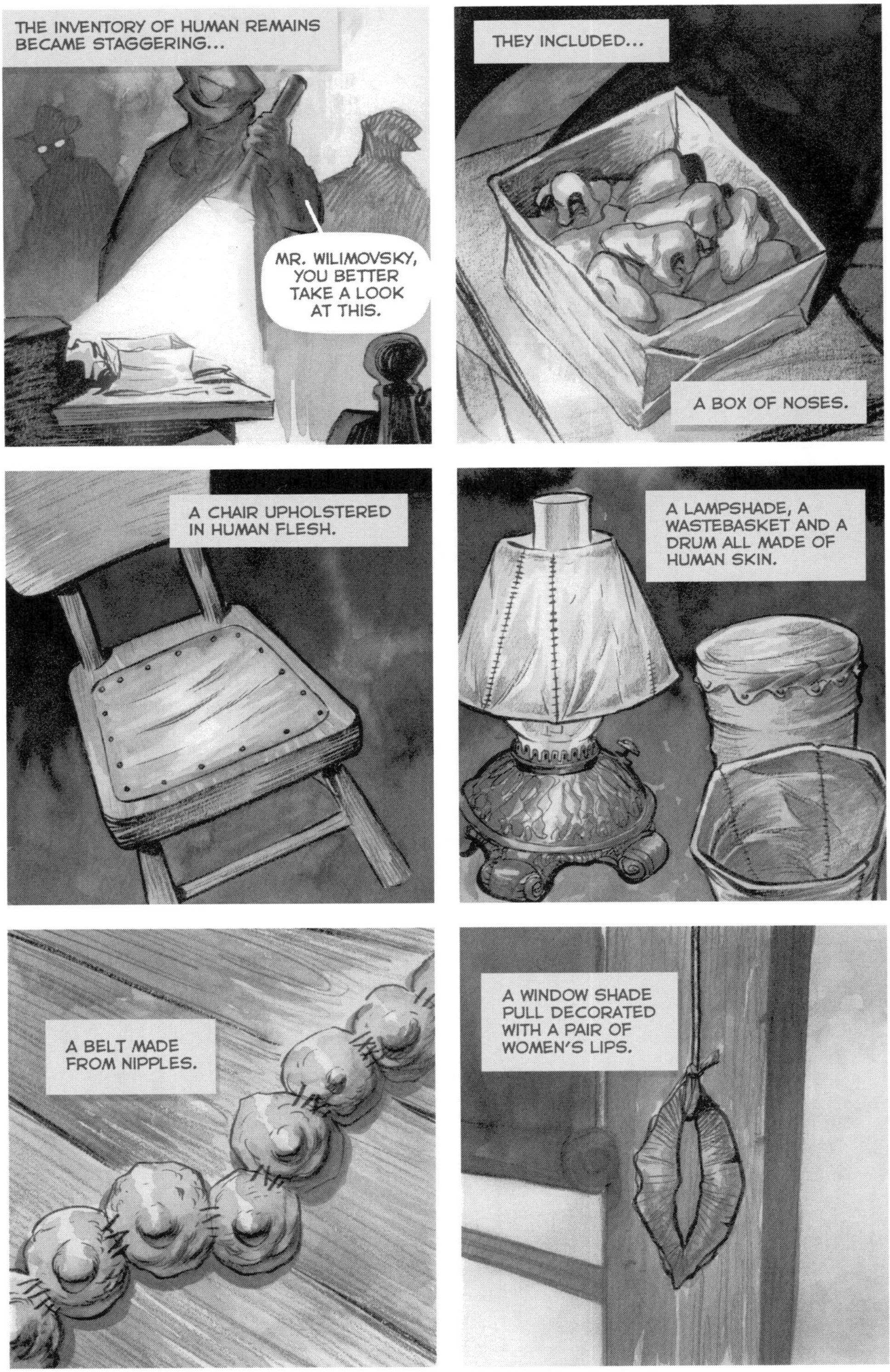
THE INVENTORY OF HUMAN REMAINS BECAME STAGGERING...
MR. WILIMOVSKY, YOU BETTER TAKE A LOOK AT THIS.
THEY INCLUDED...
A BOX OF NOSES.
A CHAIR UPHOLSTERED IN HUMAN FLESH.
A LAMPSHADE, A WASTEBASKET AND A DRUM ALL MADE OF HUMAN SKIN.
A BELT MADE FROM NIPPLES.
A WINDOW SHADE PULL DECORATED WITH A PAIR OF WOMEN'S LIPS.

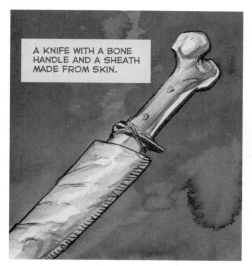

A KNIFE WITH A BONE HANDLE AND A SHEATH MADE FROM SKIN.

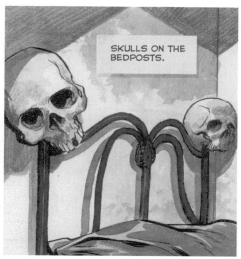

SKULLS ON THE BEDPOSTS.

FOUR FACE MASKS HANGING FROM THE WALL.

FIVE MORE MASKS IN BAGS.

GENTLEMEN, THIS SHOEBOX APPEARS TO CONTAIN A SIZABLE COLLECTION OF FEMALE GENITALIA.

SOME OF THE VAGINAS IN THE BOX WERE DRIED WITH SALT. ONE WAS DAUBED WITH SILVER PAINT AND TRIMMED WITH RED RIBBON. AND ONE WAS SO FRESH IT HAD CLEARLY BEEN NEWLY EXCISED.

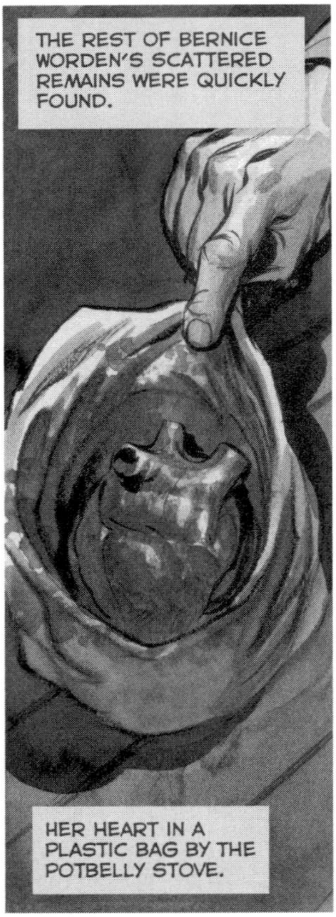
THE REST OF BERNICE WORDEN'S SCATTERED REMAINS WERE QUICKLY FOUND.
HER HEART IN A PLASTIC BAG BY THE POTBELLY STOVE.

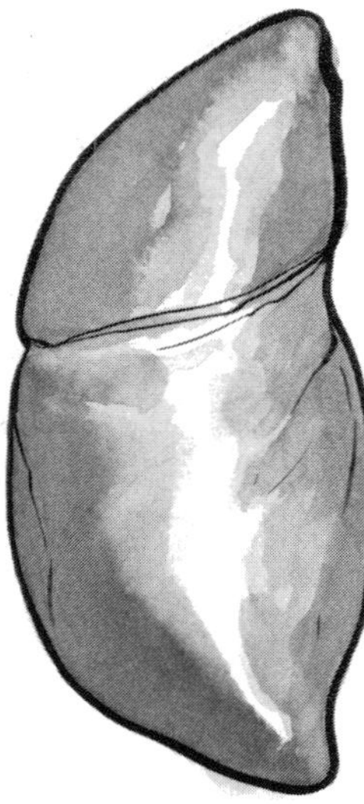
HER LIVER, WHOSE LOCATION WAS NOT DOCUMENTED.

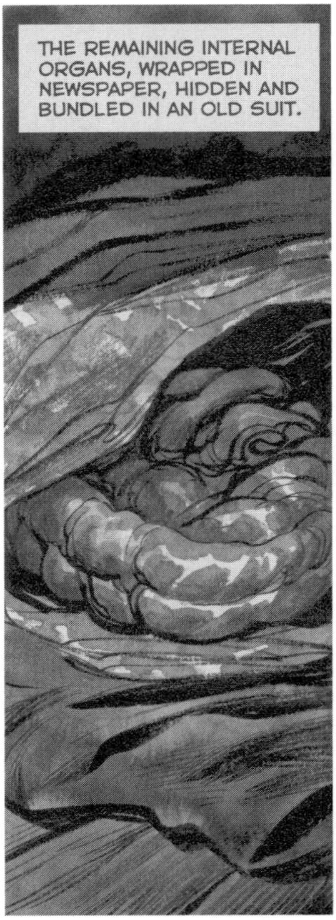
THE REMAINING INTERNAL ORGANS, WRAPPED IN NEWSPAPER, HIDDEN AND BUNDLED IN AN OLD SUIT.

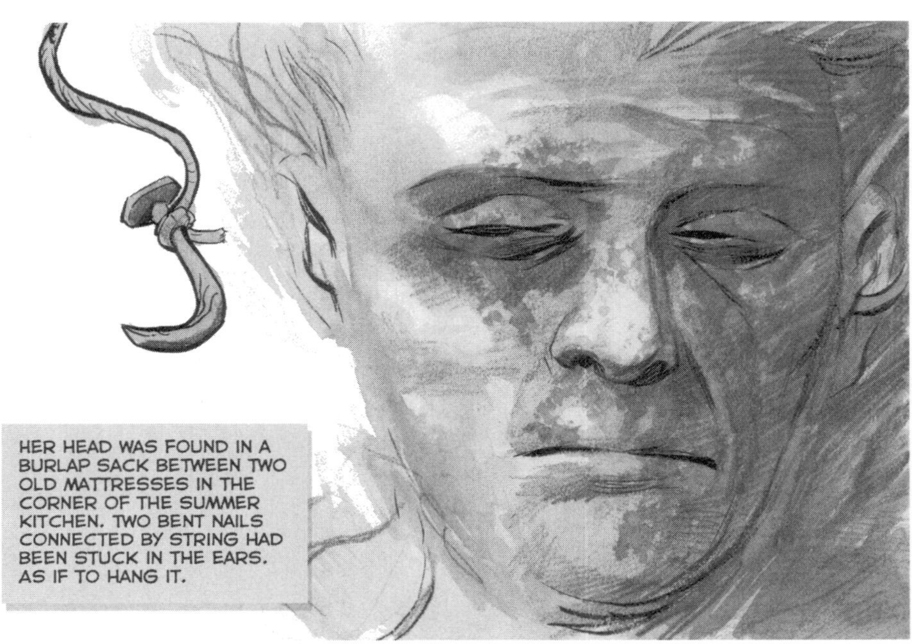
HER HEAD WAS FOUND IN A BURLAP SACK BETWEEN TWO OLD MATTRESSES IN THE CORNER OF THE SUMMER KITCHEN. TWO BENT NAILS CONNECTED BY STRING HAD BEEN STUCK IN THE EARS. AS IF TO HANG IT.

IT WAS DEPUTY ARNIE FRITZ WHO STUMBLED UPON A MOTH-EATEN HORSEHIDE ROBE CRUMPLED UP BEHIND THE KITCHEN DOOR. WRAPPED IN THE ROBE WAS A BROWN PAPER BAG.

LATER IN LIFE, DEPUTY FRITZ WOULD LOOK BACK AND WONDER WHAT POSSESSED HIM TO PUT HIS HAND IN THAT BAG.

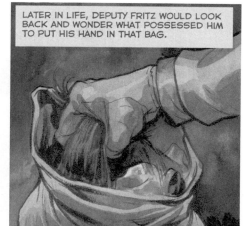

BUT WHEN HIS HAND CLOSED ON A CLUMP OF HAIR, HE WITHDREW IT, AND A MYSTERY THAT HAD PLAGUED THE TOWN FOR THREE YEARS WAS FINALLY SOLVED.

BY GOD... IT'S MARY HOGAN!

BUT THAT WASN'T THE LAST MORBID REVELATION OF THE NIGHT.

LEGS? LIKE HE WAS SEWING PANTS OR SOMETHING.

I GOT YOU ONE BETTER. LOOK AT THIS.

WHAT IN GOD'S NAME WAS HE DOING WITH THAT?

THE CORD WAS TO PUT AROUND HIS NECK. HE WAS WEARING IT.

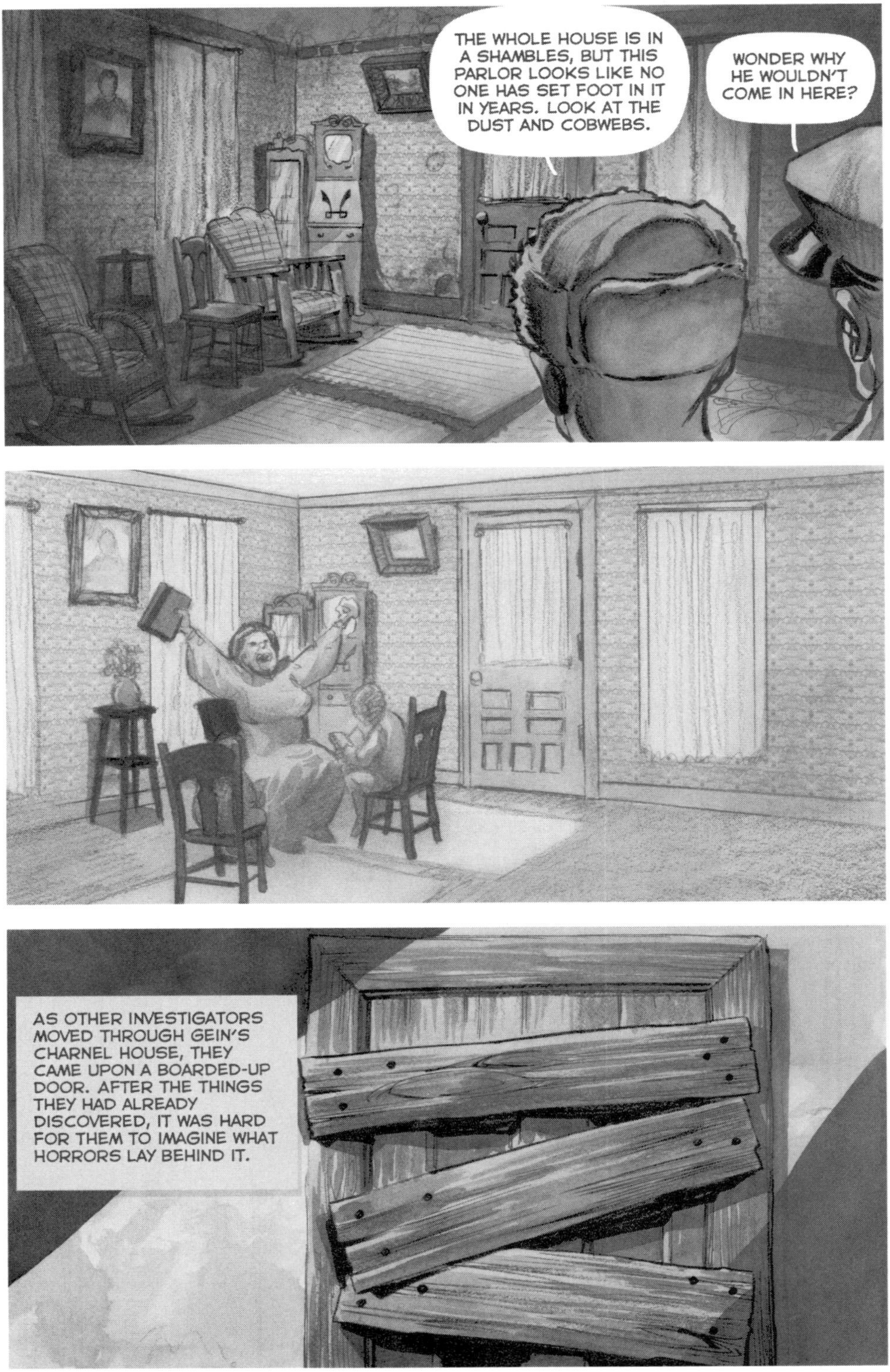
THE WHOLE HOUSE IS IN A SHAMBLES, BUT THIS PARLOR LOOKS LIKE NO ONE HAS SET FOOT IN IT IN YEARS. LOOK AT THE DUST AND COBWEBS.
WONDER WHY HE WOULDN'T COME IN HERE?
AS OTHER INVESTIGATORS MOVED THROUGH GEIN'S CHARNEL HOUSE, THEY CAME UPON A BOARDED-UP DOOR. AFTER THE THINGS THEY HAD ALREADY DISCOVERED, IT WAS HARD FOR THEM TO IMAGINE WHAT HORRORS LAY BEHIND IT.

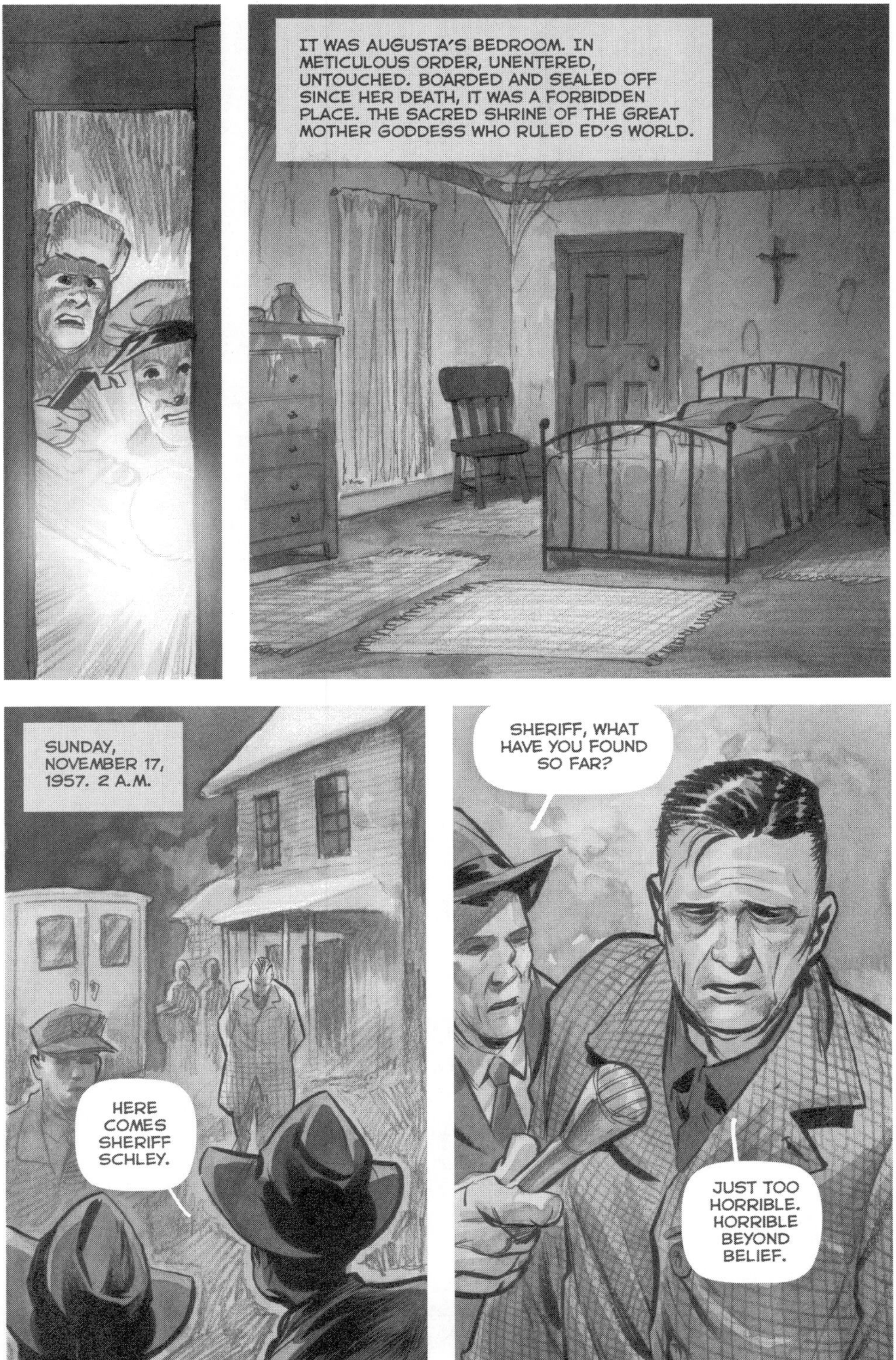
IT WAS AUGUSTA'S BEDROOM. IN METICULOUS ORDER, UNENTERED, UNTOUCHED. BOARDED AND SEALED OFF SINCE HER DEATH, IT WAS A FORBIDDEN PLACE. THE SACRED SHRINE OF THE GREAT MOTHER GODDESS WHO RULED ED'S WORLD.
SUNDAY, NOVEMBER 17, 1957. 2 A.M.
HERE COMES SHERIFF SCHLEY.
SHERIFF, WHAT HAVE YOU FOUND SO FAR?
JUST TOO HORRIBLE. HORRIBLE BEYOND BELIEF.

CHAPTER 8

★★★ Wednesday, December 18th, 1957 · 10¢

DAILY

ISOLATION

Plainfield Cemetery Is Blocked Off to Public

By Leland Rynquist
Staff reporter, City desk

Artist rendering of alleged events

Waushara County's DA Won't Open More Graves

By Kent Elako
Staff Reporter, City desk

ouse of Horror

WEATHER
HIGH 28 LOW 4

LAST

Residents Recall
Her

"HOW MANY?!"

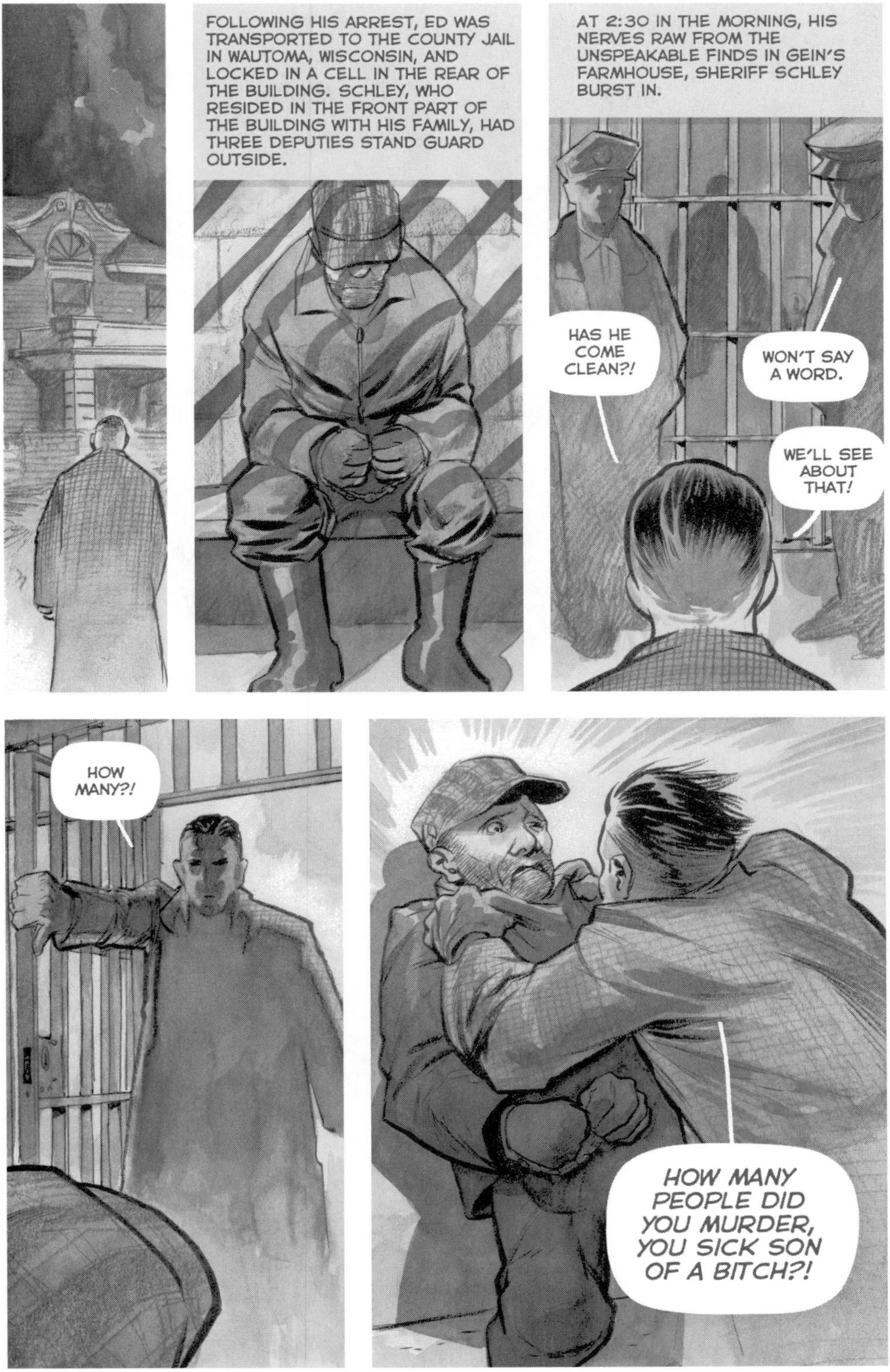
FOLLOWING HIS ARREST, ED WAS TRANSPORTED TO THE COUNTY JAIL IN WAUTOMA, WISCONSIN, AND LOCKED IN A CELL IN THE REAR OF THE BUILDING. SCHLEY, WHO RESIDED IN THE FRONT PART OF THE BUILDING WITH HIS FAMILY, HAD THREE DEPUTIES STAND GUARD OUTSIDE.
AT 2:30 IN THE MORNING, HIS NERVES RAW FROM THE UNSPEAKABLE FINDS IN GEIN'S FARMHOUSE, SHERIFF SCHLEY BURST IN.
HAS HE COME CLEAN?!
WON'T SAY A WORD.
WE'LL SEE ABOUT THAT!
HOW MANY?!
HOW MANY PEOPLE DID YOU MURDER, YOU SICK SON OF A BITCH?!

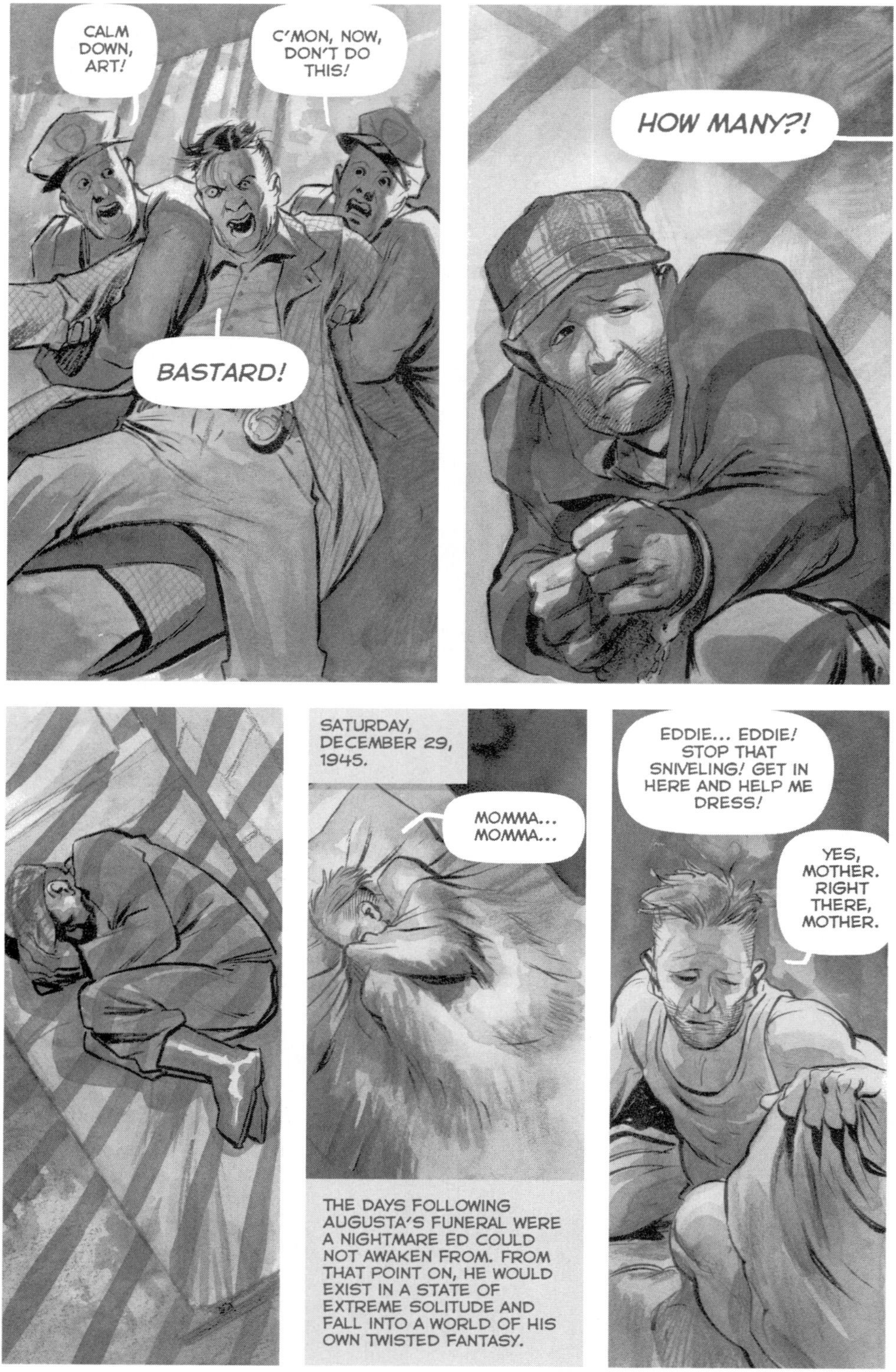
CALM DOWN, ART!
C'MON, NOW, DON'T DO THIS!
BASTARD!
HOW MANY?!
SATURDAY, DECEMBER 29, 1945.
MOMMA... MOMMA...
THE DAYS FOLLOWING AUGUSTA'S FUNERAL WERE A NIGHTMARE ED COULD NOT AWAKEN FROM. FROM THAT POINT ON, HE WOULD EXIST IN A STATE OF EXTREME SOLITUDE AND FALL INTO A WORLD OF HIS OWN TWISTED FANTASY.
EDDIE... EDDIE! STOP THAT SNIVELING! GET IN HERE AND HELP ME DRESS!
YES, MOTHER. RIGHT THERE, MOTHER.

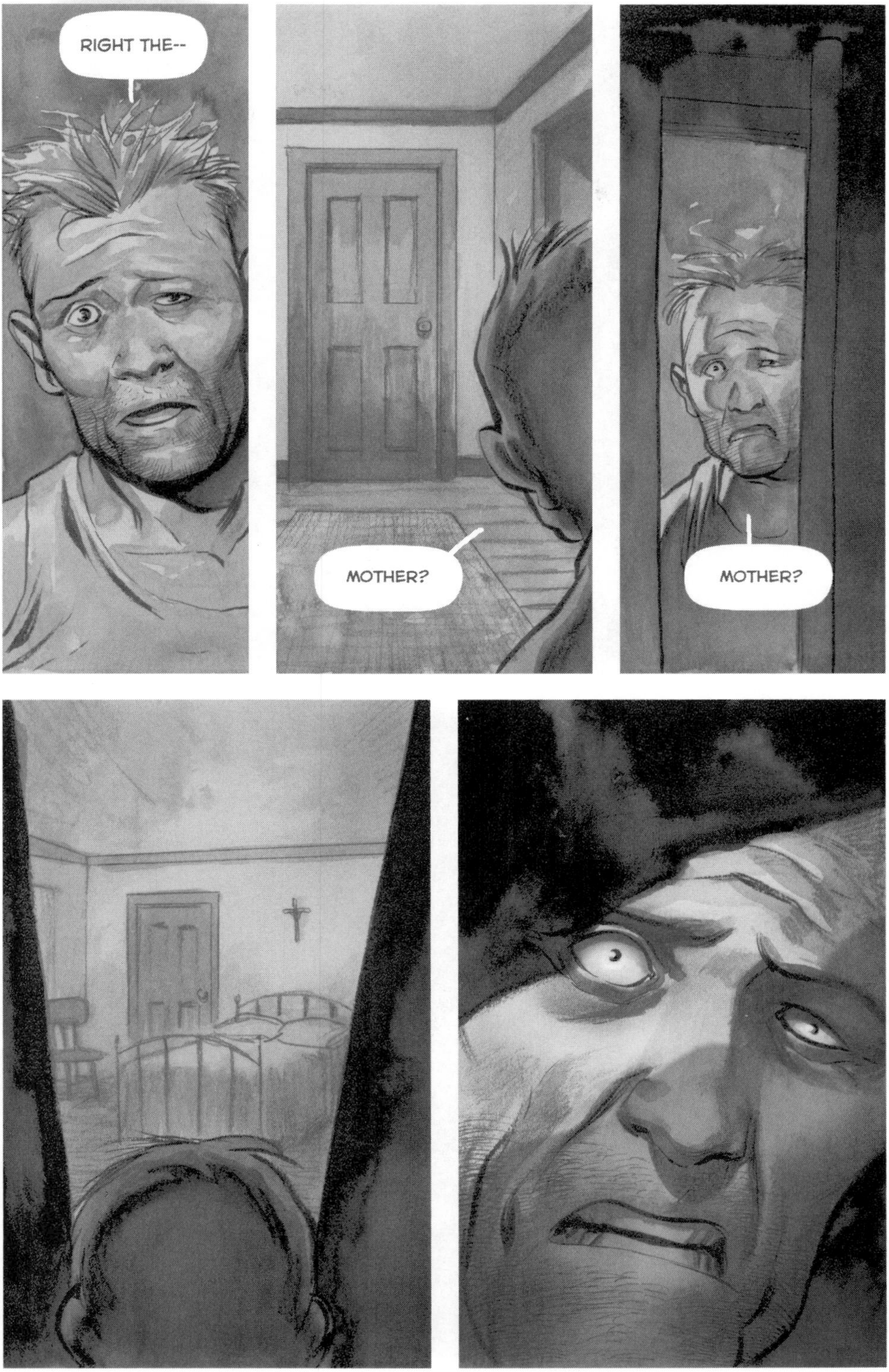
RIGHT THE--
MOTHER?
MOTHER?

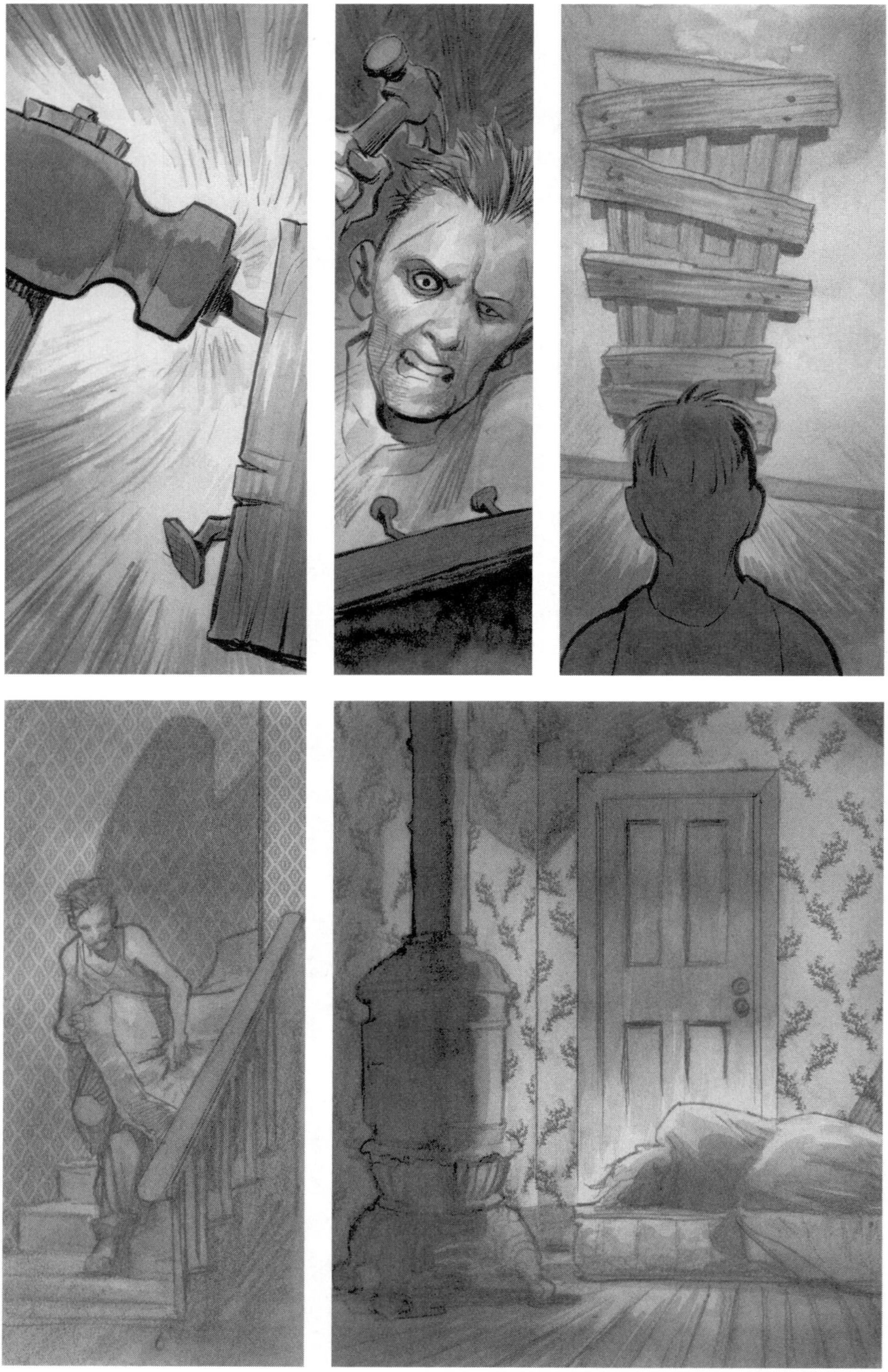

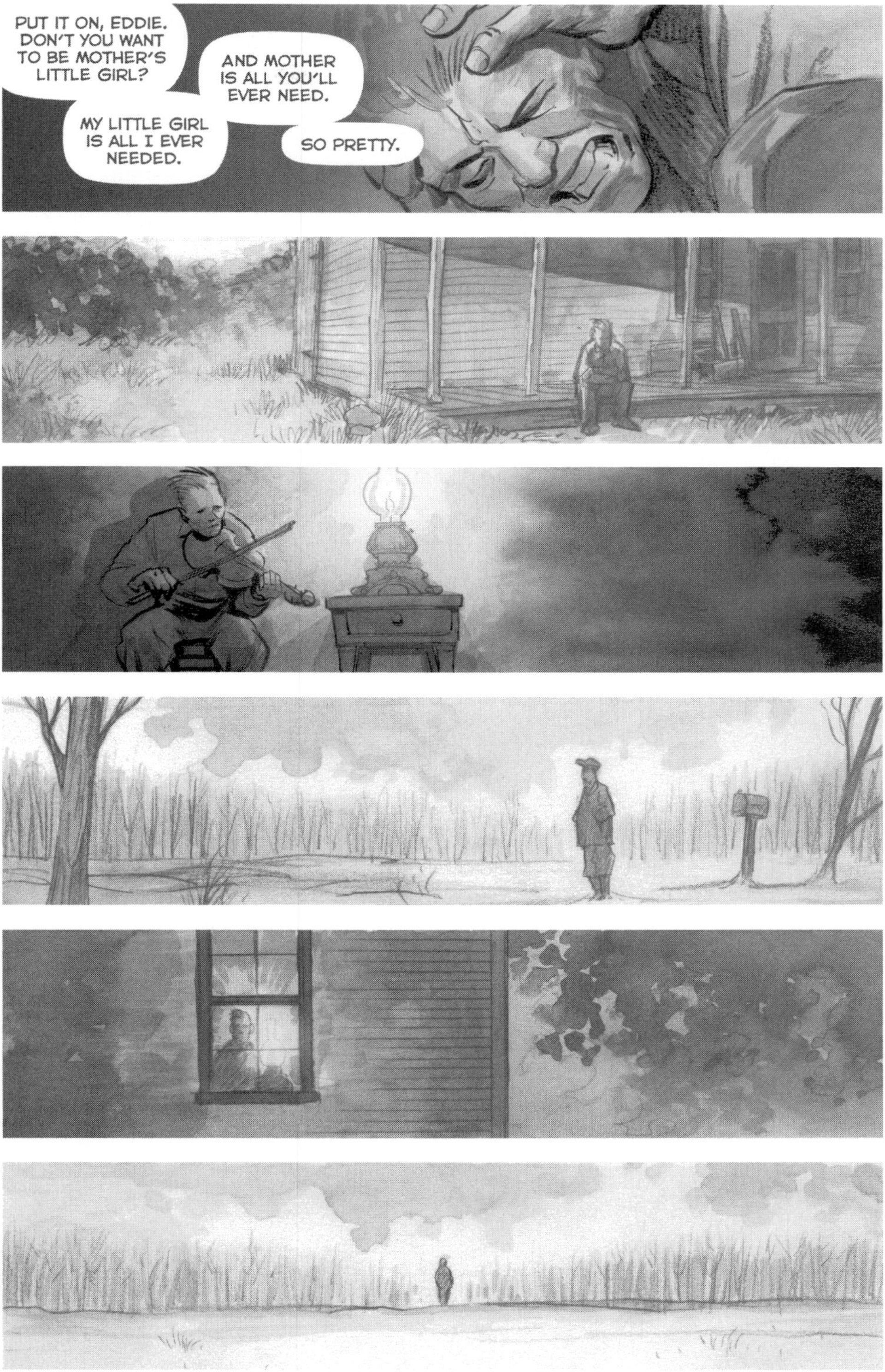
PUT IT ON, EDDIE. DON'T YOU WANT TO BE MOTHER'S LITTLE GIRL?
MY LITTLE GIRL IS ALL I EVER NEEDED.
AND MOTHER IS ALL YOU'LL EVER NEED.
SO PRETTY.

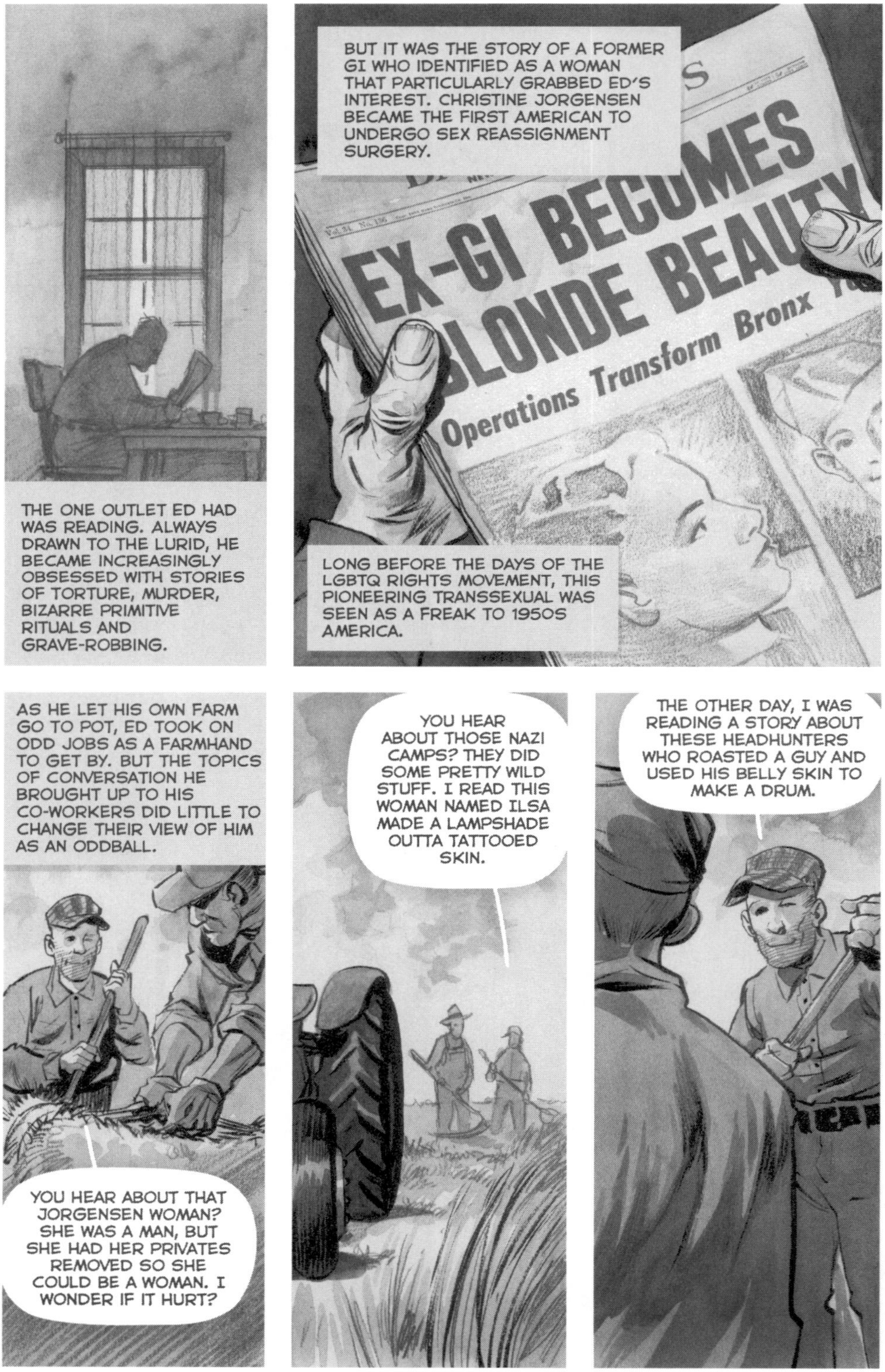
THE ONE OUTLET ED HAD WAS READING. ALWAYS DRAWN TO THE LURID, HE BECAME INCREASINGLY OBSESSED WITH STORIES OF TORTURE, MURDER, BIZARRE PRIMITIVE RITUALS AND GRAVE-ROBBING.
BUT IT WAS THE STORY OF A FORMER GI WHO IDENTIFIED AS A WOMAN THAT PARTICULARLY GRABBED ED'S INTEREST. CHRISTINE JORGENSEN BECAME THE FIRST AMERICAN TO UNDERGO SEX REASSIGNMENT SURGERY.
EX-GI BECOMES BLONDE BEAUTY
Operations Transform Bronx
LONG BEFORE THE DAYS OF THE LGBTQ RIGHTS MOVEMENT, THIS PIONEERING TRANSSEXUAL WAS SEEN AS A FREAK TO 1950S AMERICA.
AS HE LET HIS OWN FARM GO TO POT, ED TOOK ON ODD JOBS AS A FARMHAND TO GET BY. BUT THE TOPICS OF CONVERSATION HE BROUGHT UP TO HIS CO-WORKERS DID LITTLE TO CHANGE THEIR VIEW OF HIM AS AN ODDBALL.
YOU HEAR ABOUT THAT JORGENSEN WOMAN? SHE WAS A MAN, BUT SHE HAD HER PRIVATES REMOVED SO SHE COULD BE A WOMAN. I WONDER IF IT HURT?
YOU HEAR ABOUT THOSE NAZI CAMPS? THEY DID SOME PRETTY WILD STUFF. I READ THIS WOMAN NAMED ILSA MADE A LAMPSHADE OUTTA TATTOOED SKIN.
THE OTHER DAY, I WAS READING A STORY ABOUT THESE HEADHUNTERS WHO ROASTED A GUY AND USED HIS BELLY SKIN TO MAKE A DRUM.

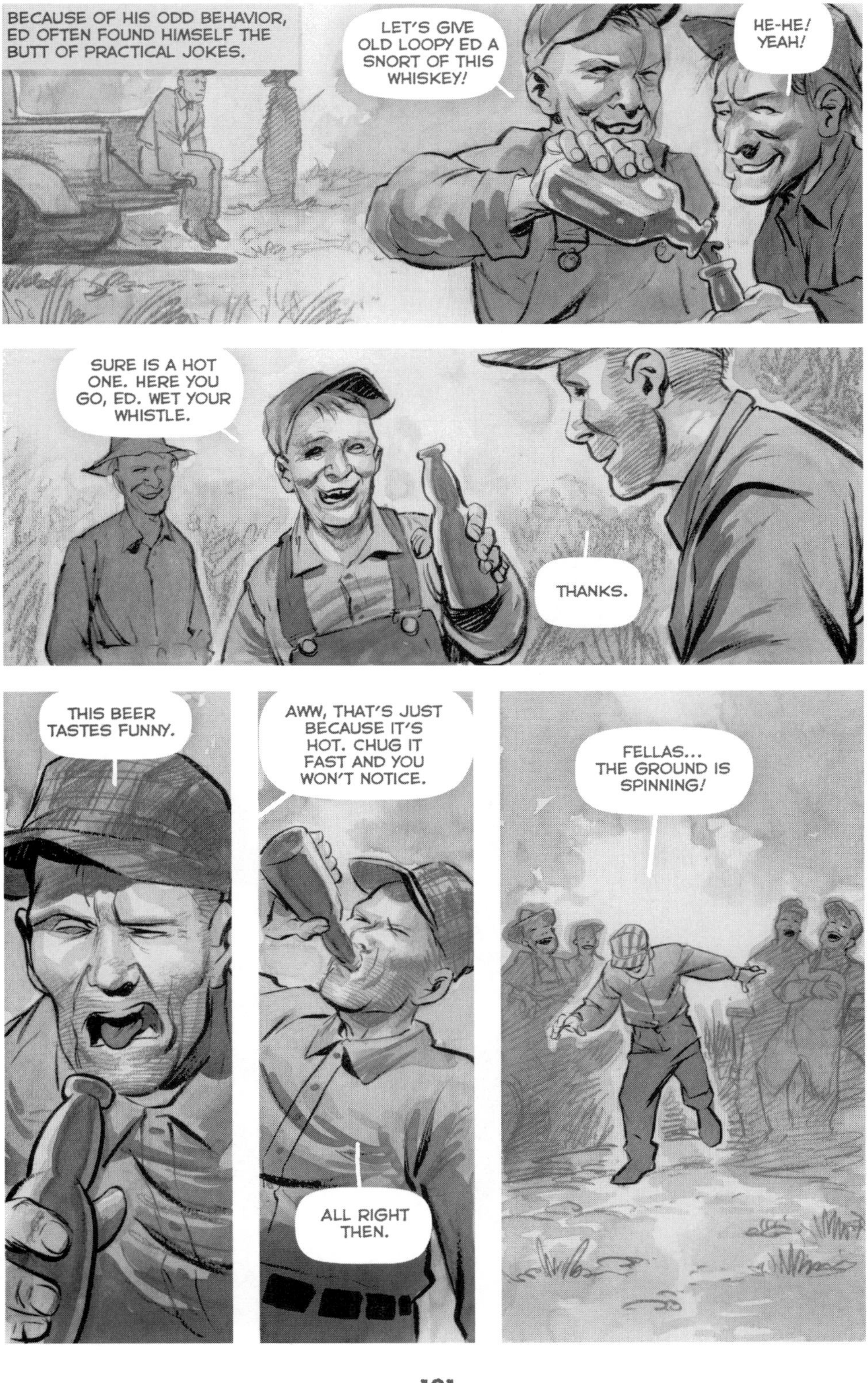
BECAUSE OF HIS ODD BEHAVIOR, ED OFTEN FOUND HIMSELF THE BUTT OF PRACTICAL JOKES.
LET'S GIVE OLD LOOPY ED A SNORT OF THIS WHISKEY!
HE-HE! YEAH!
SURE IS A HOT ONE. HERE YOU GO, ED. WET YOUR WHISTLE.
THANKS.
THIS BEER TASTES FUNNY.
AWW, THAT'S JUST BECAUSE IT'S HOT. CHUG IT FAST AND YOU WON'T NOTICE.
ALL RIGHT THEN.
FELLAS... THE GROUND IS SPINNING!

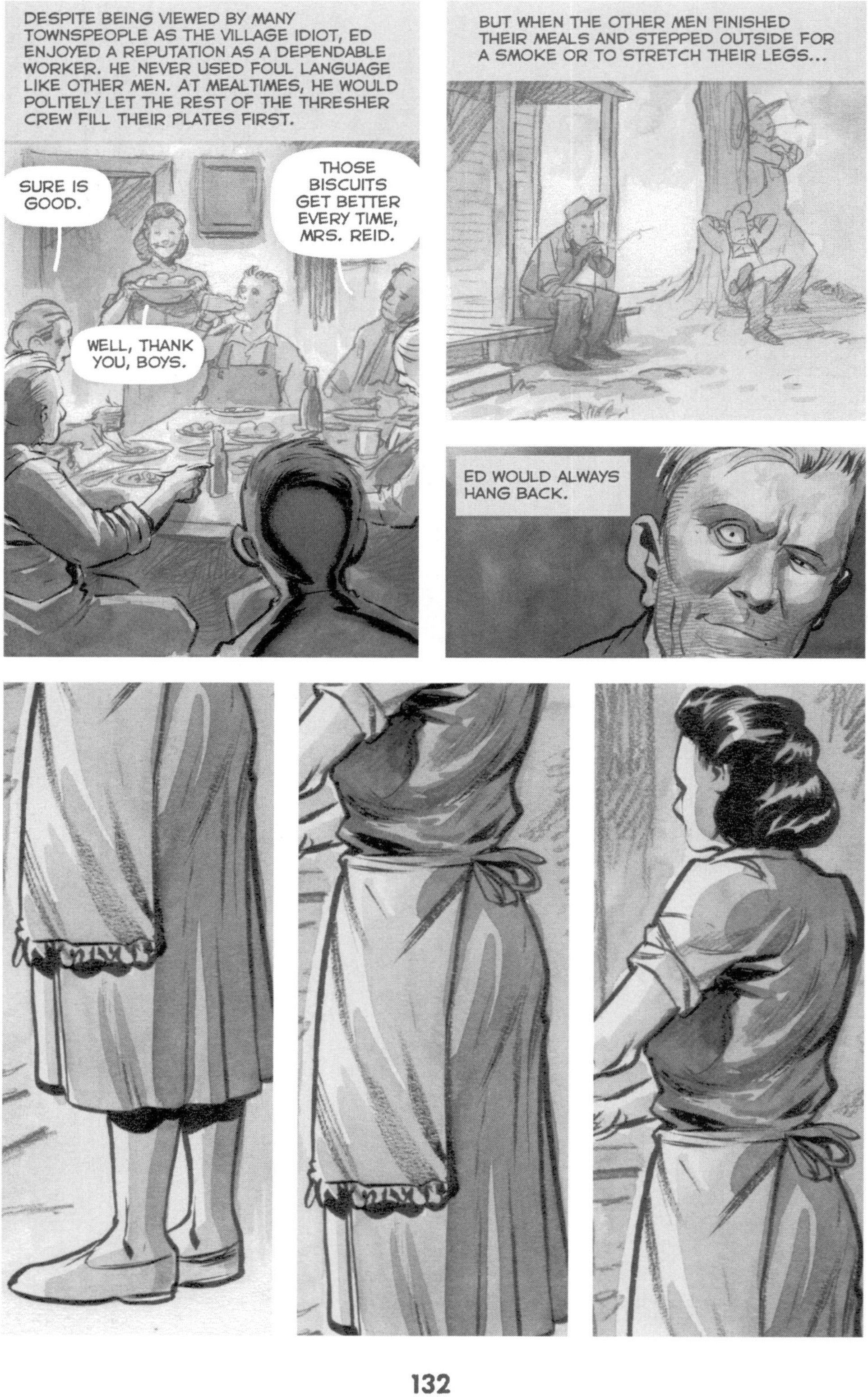
DESPITE BEING VIEWED BY MANY TOWNSPEOPLE AS THE VILLAGE IDIOT, ED ENJOYED A REPUTATION AS A DEPENDABLE WORKER. HE NEVER USED FOUL LANGUAGE LIKE OTHER MEN. AT MEALTIMES, HE WOULD POLITELY LET THE REST OF THE THRESHER CREW FILL THEIR PLATES FIRST.
SURE IS GOOD.
THOSE BISCUITS GET BETTER EVERY TIME, MRS. REID.
WELL, THANK YOU, BOYS.
BUT WHEN THE OTHER MEN FINISHED THEIR MEALS AND STEPPED OUTSIDE FOR A SMOKE OR TO STRETCH THEIR LEGS...
ED WOULD ALWAYS HANG BACK.

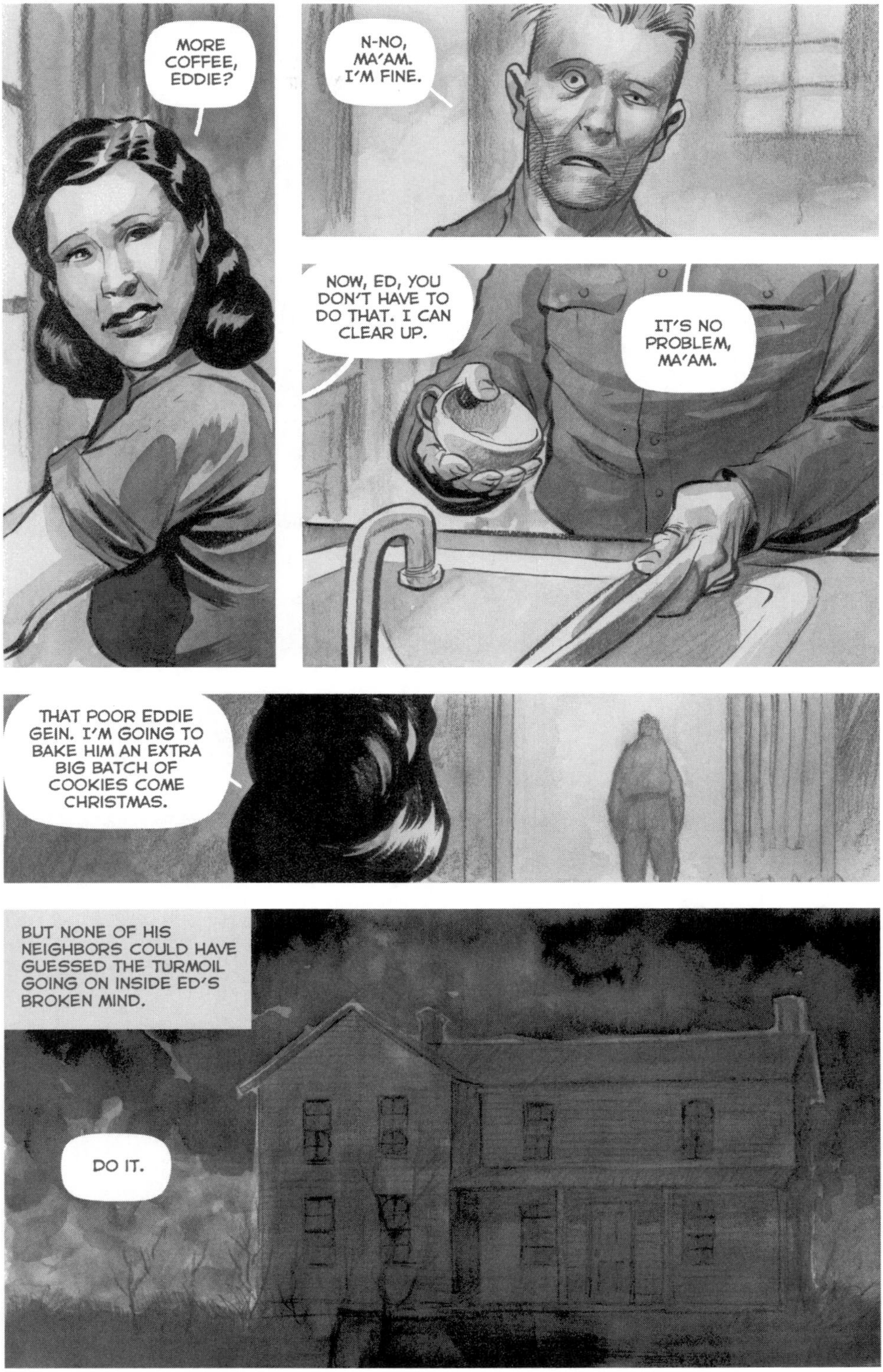
MORE COFFEE, EDDIE?
N-NO, MA'AM. I'M FINE.
NOW, ED, YOU DON'T HAVE TO DO THAT. I CAN CLEAR UP.
IT'S NO PROBLEM, MA'AM.
THAT POOR EDDIE GEIN. I'M GOING TO BAKE HIM AN EXTRA BIG BATCH OF COOKIES COME CHRISTMAS.
BUT NONE OF HIS NEIGHBORS COULD HAVE GUESSED THE TURMOIL GOING ON INSIDE ED'S BROKEN MIND.
DO IT.

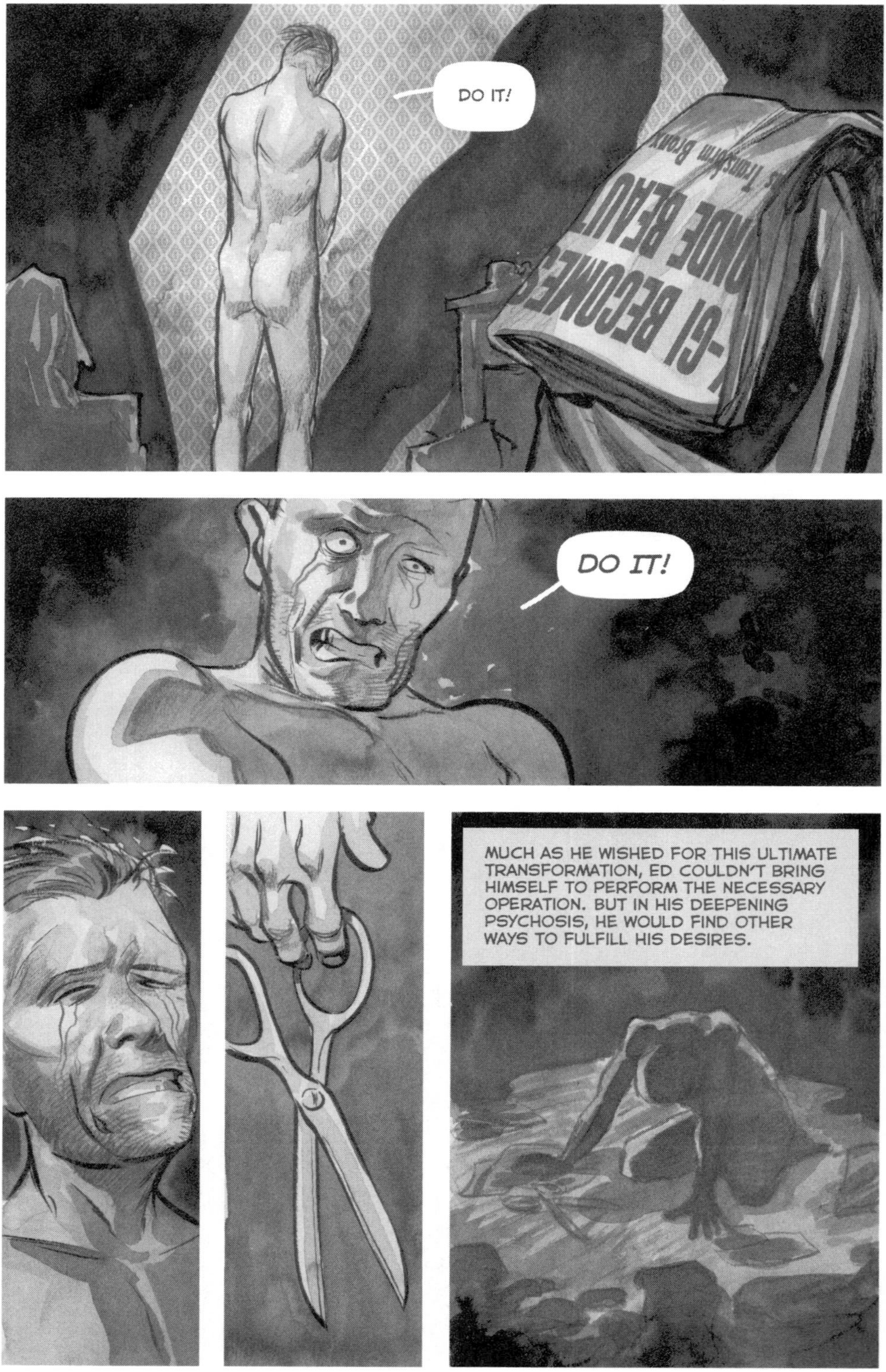
DO IT!
DO IT!
MUCH AS HE WISHED FOR THIS ULTIMATE TRANSFORMATION, ED COULDN'T BRING HIMSELF TO PERFORM THE NECESSARY OPERATION. BUT IN HIS DEEPENING PSYCHOSIS, HE WOULD FIND OTHER WAYS TO FULFILL HIS DESIRES.

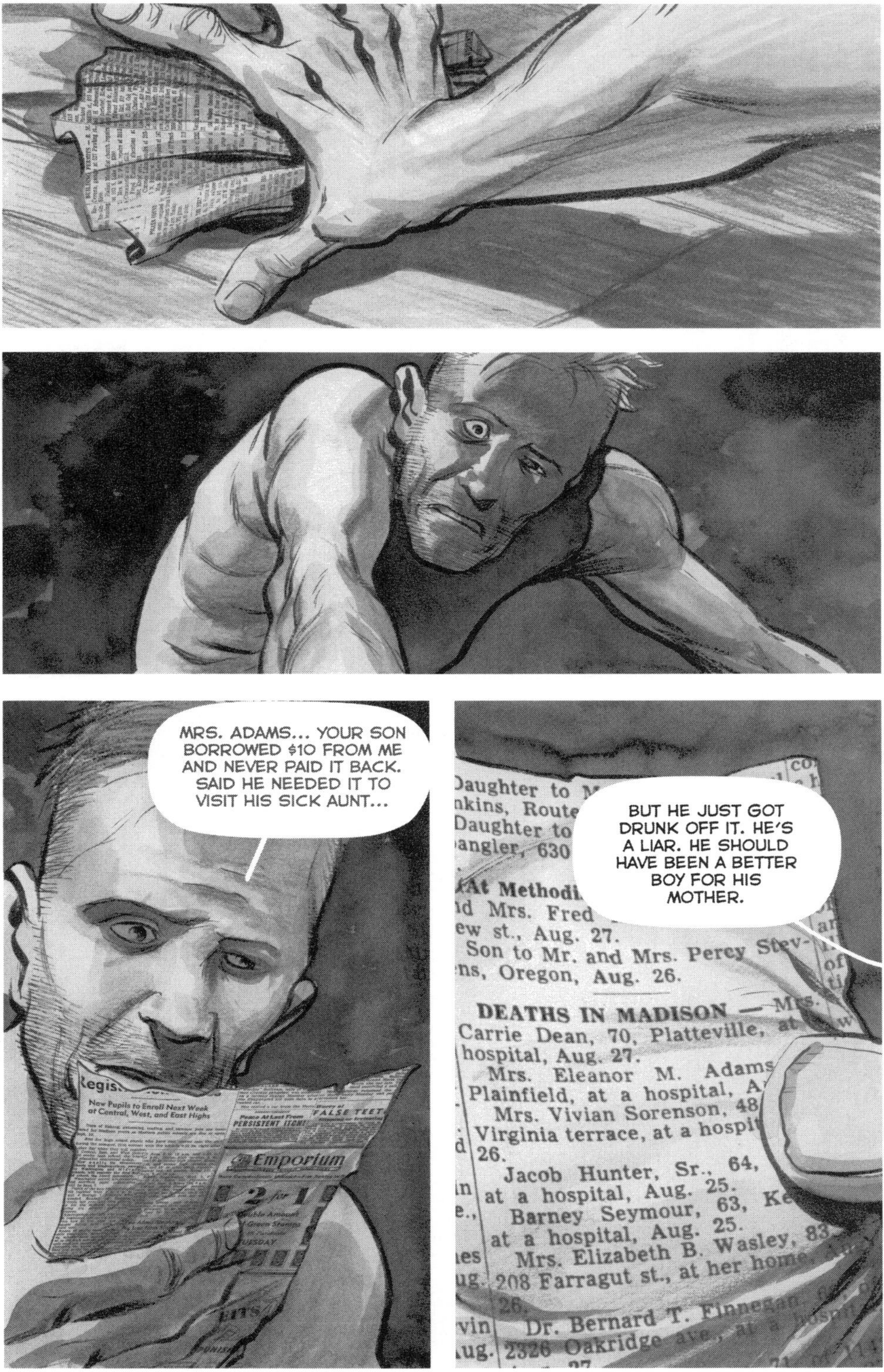

MRS. ADAMS... YOUR SON BORROWED $10 FROM ME AND NEVER PAID IT BACK. SAID HE NEEDED IT TO VISIT HIS SICK AUNT...
New Pupils to Enroll Next Week at Central, West, and East Highs
PERSISTENT ITCH!
FALSE TEETH
Emporium
2 for 1
BUT HE JUST GOT DRUNK OFF IT. HE'S A LIAR. HE SHOULD HAVE BEEN A BETTER BOY FOR HIS MOTHER.
Son to Mr. and Mrs. Percy Stev-
ns, Oregon, Aug. 26.
DEATHS IN MADISON —
Carrie Dean, 70, Platteville, at
hospital, Aug. 27.
Mrs. Eleanor M. Adams
Plainfield, at a hospital,
Mrs. Vivian Sorenson,
Virginia terrace, at a
26.
Jacob Hunter, Sr., 64,
at a hospital, Aug. 25.
Barney Seymour, 63,
at a hospital, Aug. 25.
Mrs. Elizabeth B. Wasley,
208 Farragut st., at her
Dr. Bernard T.
2326 Oakridge ave.,

ELEANOR ADAMS' GRAVE LAY
JUST BEFORE ED'S MOTHER'S.

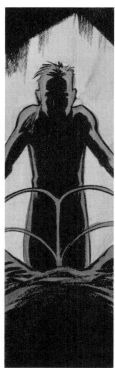

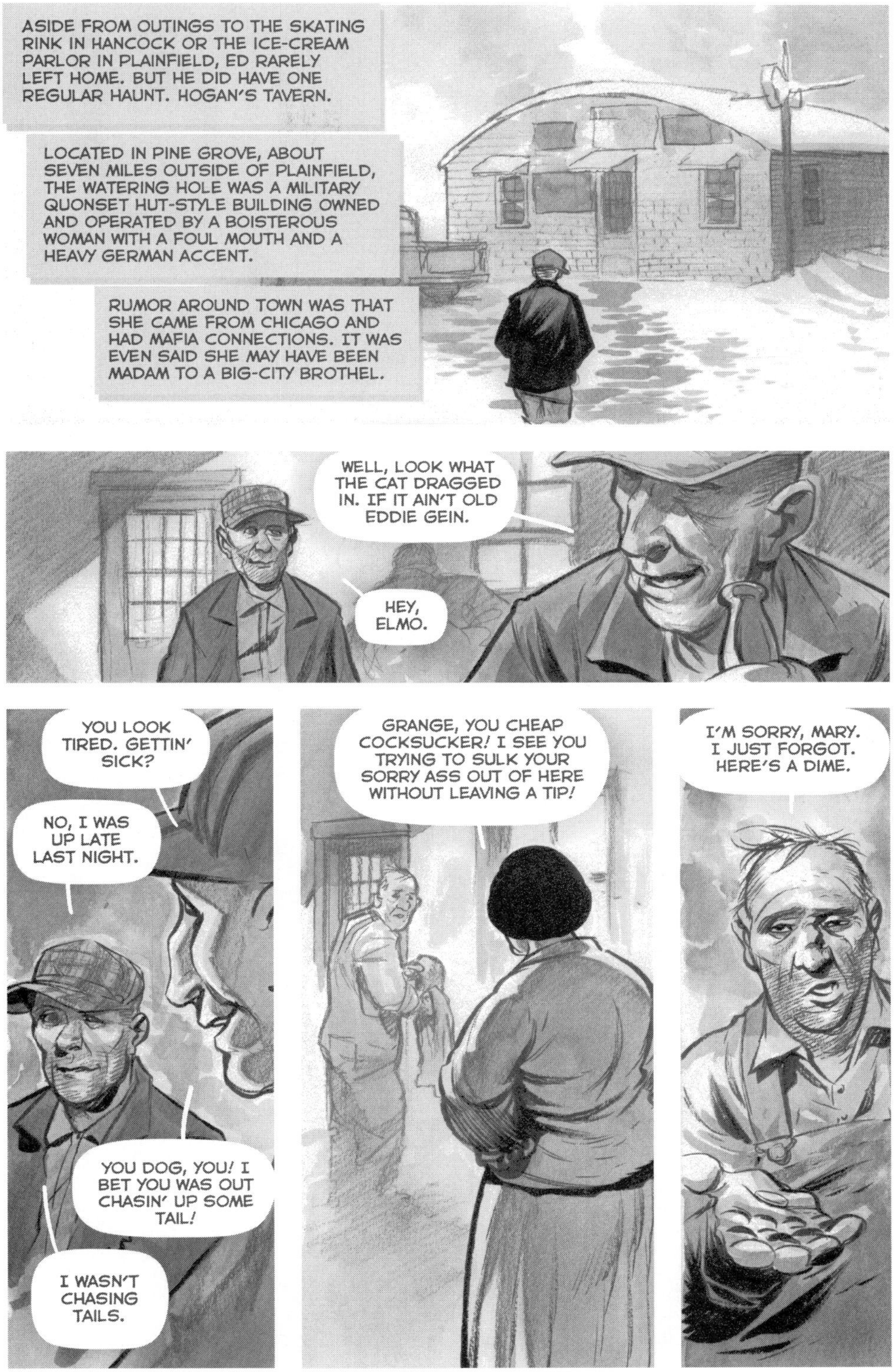
ASIDE FROM OUTINGS TO THE SKATING RINK IN HANCOCK OR THE ICE-CREAM PARLOR IN PLAINFIELD, ED RARELY LEFT HOME. BUT HE DID HAVE ONE REGULAR HAUNT. HOGAN'S TAVERN.
LOCATED IN PINE GROVE, ABOUT SEVEN MILES OUTSIDE OF PLAINFIELD, THE WATERING HOLE WAS A MILITARY QUONSET HUT-STYLE BUILDING OWNED AND OPERATED BY A BOISTEROUS WOMAN WITH A FOUL MOUTH AND A HEAVY GERMAN ACCENT.
RUMOR AROUND TOWN WAS THAT SHE CAME FROM CHICAGO AND HAD MAFIA CONNECTIONS. IT WAS EVEN SAID SHE MAY HAVE BEEN MADAM TO A BIG-CITY BROTHEL.
WELL, LOOK WHAT THE CAT DRAGGED IN. IF IT AIN'T OLD EDDIE GEIN.
HEY, ELMO.
YOU LOOK TIRED. GETTIN' SICK?
NO, I WAS UP LATE LAST NIGHT.
YOU DOG, YOU! I BET YOU WAS OUT CHASIN' UP SOME TAIL!
I WASN'T CHASING TAILS.
GRANGE, YOU CHEAP COCKSUCKER! I SEE YOU TRYING TO SULK YOUR SORRY ASS OUT OF HERE WITHOUT LEAVING A TIP!
I'M SORRY, MARY. I JUST FORGOT. HERE'S A DIME.

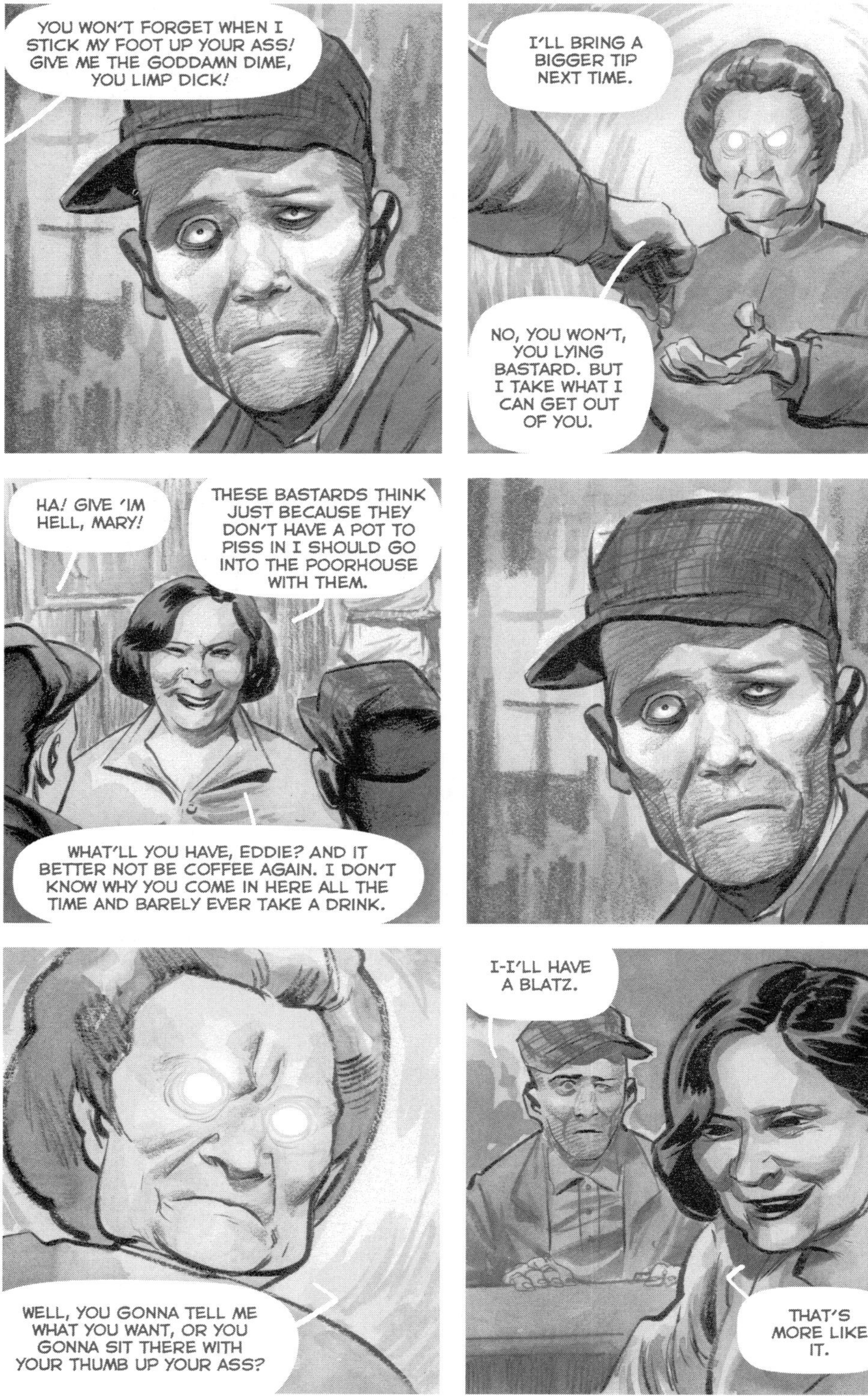
YOU WON'T FORGET WHEN I STICK MY FOOT UP YOUR ASS! GIVE ME THE GODDAMN DIME, YOU LIMP DICK!
I'LL BRING A BIGGER TIP NEXT TIME.
NO, YOU WON'T, YOU LYING BASTARD. BUT I TAKE WHAT I CAN GET OUT OF YOU.
HA! GIVE 'IM HELL, MARY!
THESE BASTARDS THINK JUST BECAUSE THEY DON'T HAVE A POT TO PISS IN I SHOULD GO INTO THE POORHOUSE WITH THEM.
WHAT'LL YOU HAVE, EDDIE? AND IT BETTER NOT BE COFFEE AGAIN. I DON'T KNOW WHY YOU COME IN HERE ALL THE TIME AND BARELY EVER TAKE A DRINK.
WELL, YOU GONNA TELL ME WHAT YOU WANT, OR YOU GONNA SIT THERE WITH YOUR THUMB UP YOUR ASS?
I-I'LL HAVE A BLATZ.
THAT'S MORE LIKE IT.

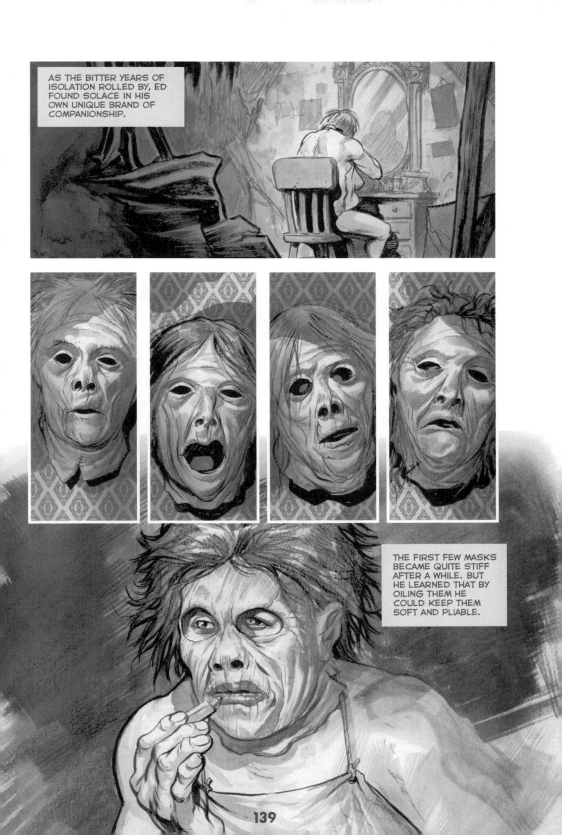

AS THE BITTER YEARS OF ISOLATION ROLLED BY, ED FOUND SOLACE IN HIS OWN UNIQUE BRAND OF COMPANIONSHIP.

THE FIRST FEW MASKS BECAME QUITE STIFF AFTER A WHILE. BUT HE LEARNED THAT BY OILING THEM HE COULD KEEP THEM SOFT AND PLIABLE.

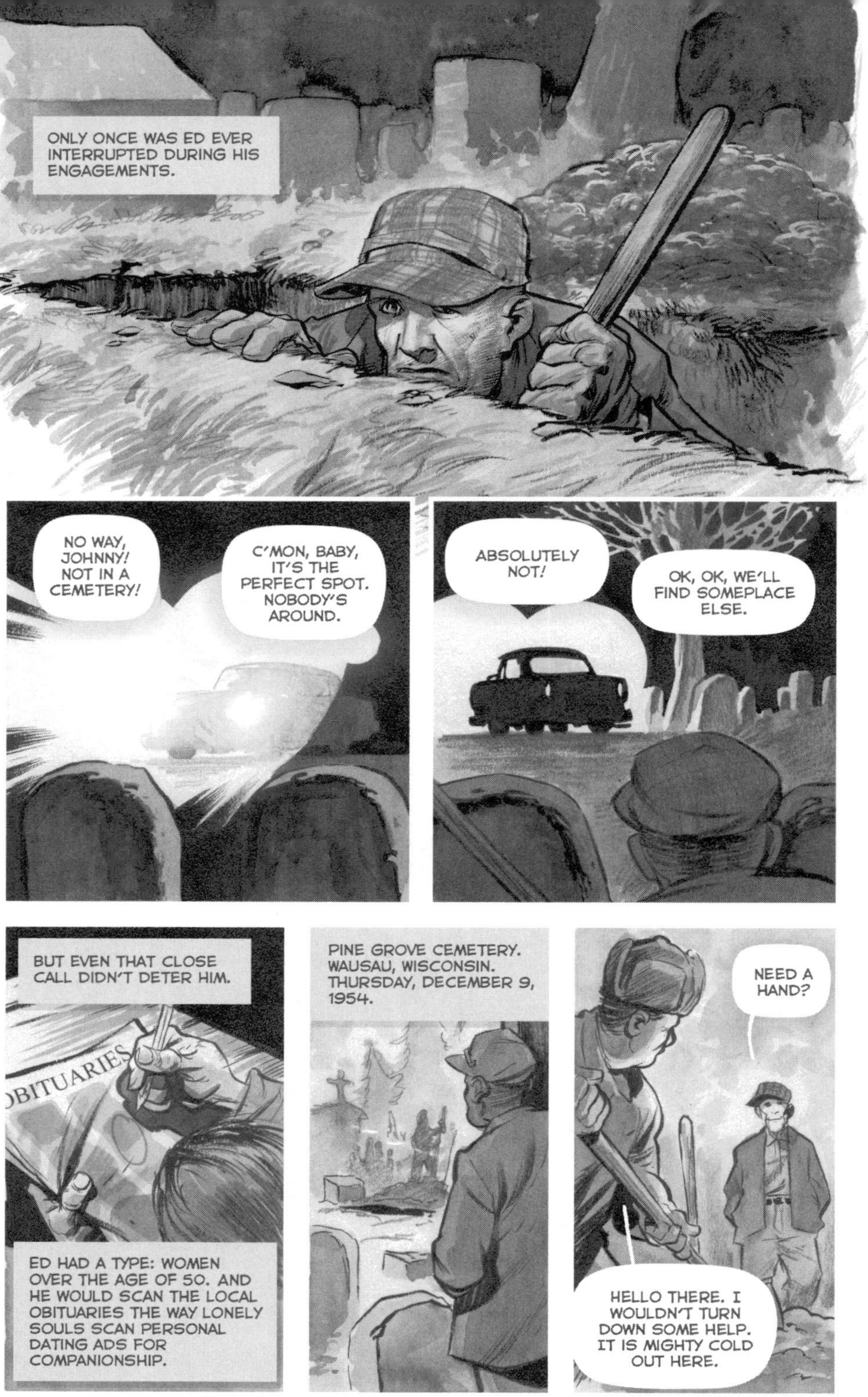
ONLY ONCE WAS ED EVER INTERRUPTED DURING HIS ENGAGEMENTS.
NO WAY, JOHNNY! NOT IN A CEMETERY!
C'MON, BABY, IT'S THE PERFECT SPOT. NOBODY'S AROUND.
ABSOLUTELY NOT!
OK, OK, WE'LL FIND SOMEPLACE ELSE.
BUT EVEN THAT CLOSE CALL DIDN'T DETER HIM.
OBITUARIES
ED HAD A TYPE: WOMEN OVER THE AGE OF 50. AND HE WOULD SCAN THE LOCAL OBITUARIES THE WAY LONELY SOULS SCAN PERSONAL DATING ADS FOR COMPANIONSHIP.
PINE GROVE CEMETERY. WAUSAU, WISCONSIN. THURSDAY, DECEMBER 9, 1954.
NEED A HAND?
HELLO THERE. I WOULDN'T TURN DOWN SOME HELP. IT IS MIGHTY COLD OUT HERE.

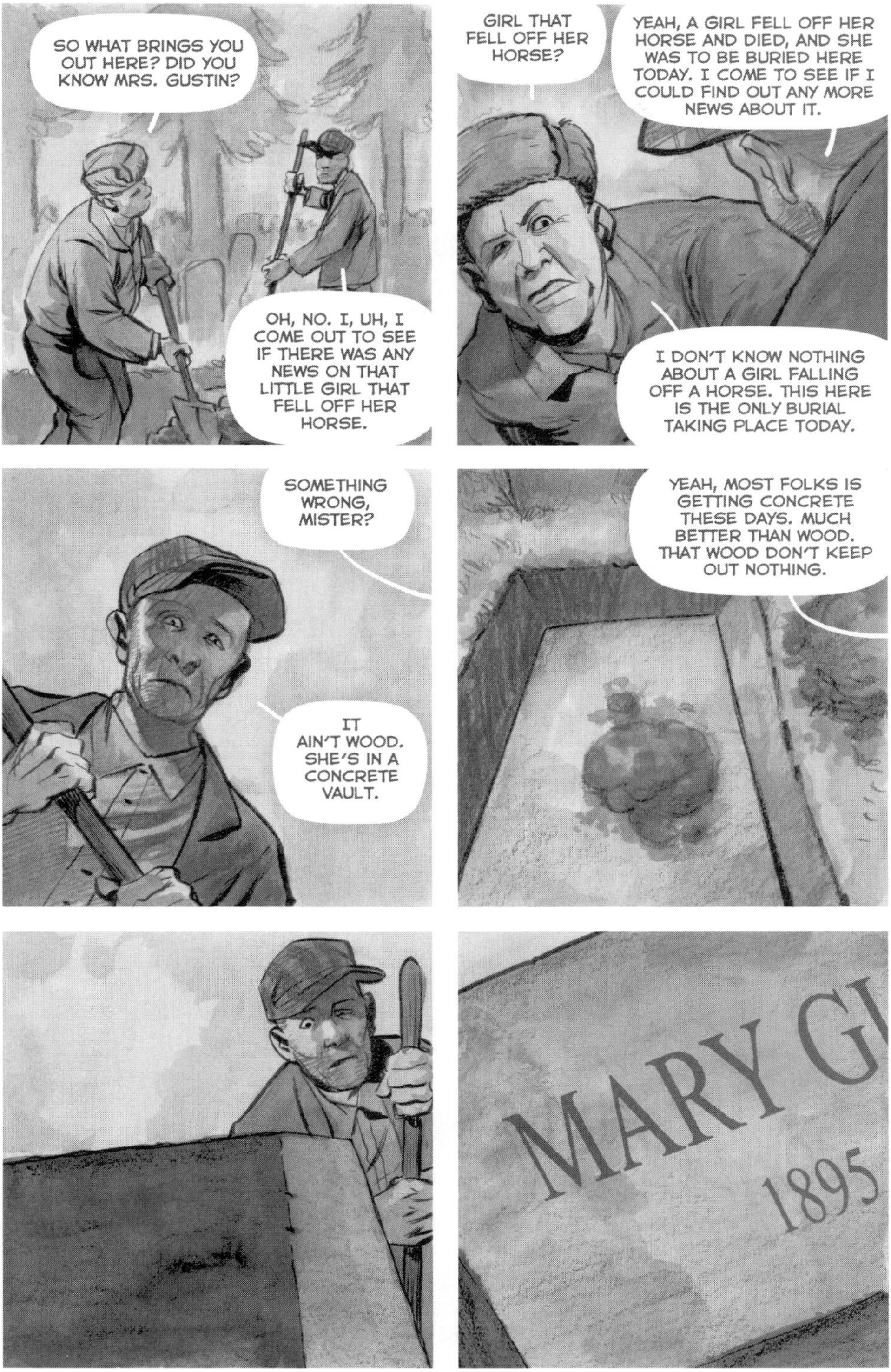
SO WHAT BRINGS YOU OUT HERE? DID YOU KNOW MRS. GUSTIN?
OH, NO. I, UH, I COME OUT TO SEE IF THERE WAS ANY NEWS ON THAT LITTLE GIRL THAT FELL OFF HER HORSE.
GIRL THAT FELL OFF HER HORSE?
YEAH, A GIRL FELL OFF HER HORSE AND DIED, AND SHE WAS TO BE BURIED HERE TODAY. I COME TO SEE IF I COULD FIND OUT ANY MORE NEWS ABOUT IT.
I DON'T KNOW NOTHING ABOUT A GIRL FALLING OFF A HORSE. THIS HERE IS THE ONLY BURIAL TAKING PLACE TODAY.
SOMETHING WRONG, MISTER?
IT AIN'T WOOD. SHE'S IN A CONCRETE VAULT.
YEAH, MOST FOLKS IS GETTING CONCRETE THESE DAYS. MUCH BETTER THAN WOOD. THAT WOOD DON'T KEEP OUT NOTHING.
MARY GU
1895

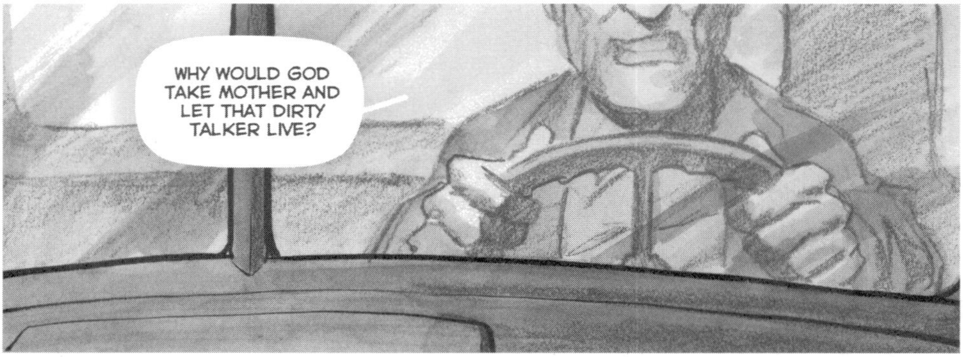
WHY WOULD GOD TAKE MOTHER AND LET THAT DIRTY TALKER LIVE?

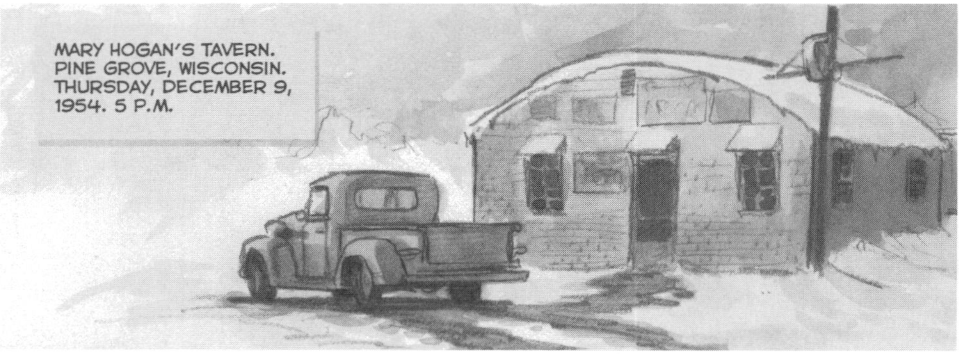
MARY HOGAN'S TAVERN. PINE GROVE, WISCONSIN. THURSDAY, DECEMBER 9, 1954. 5 P.M.

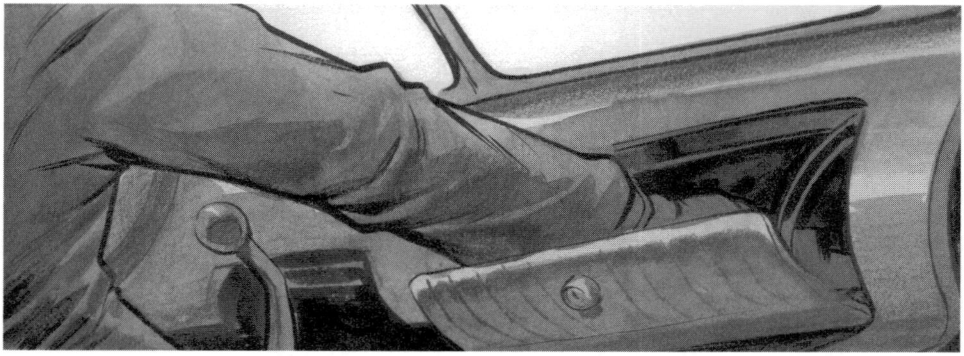

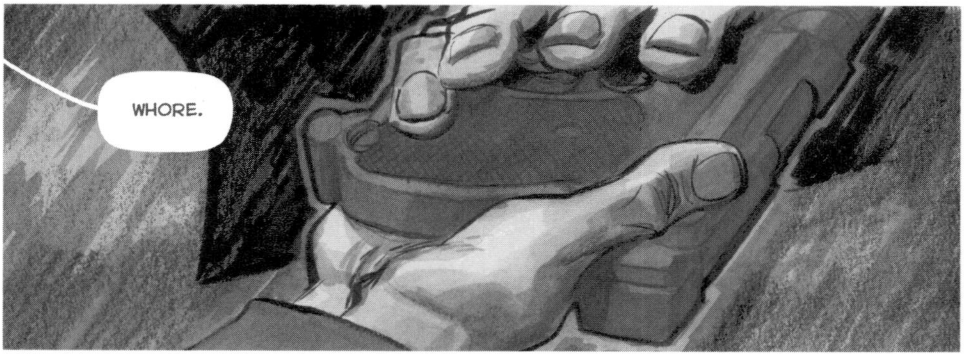
WHORE.

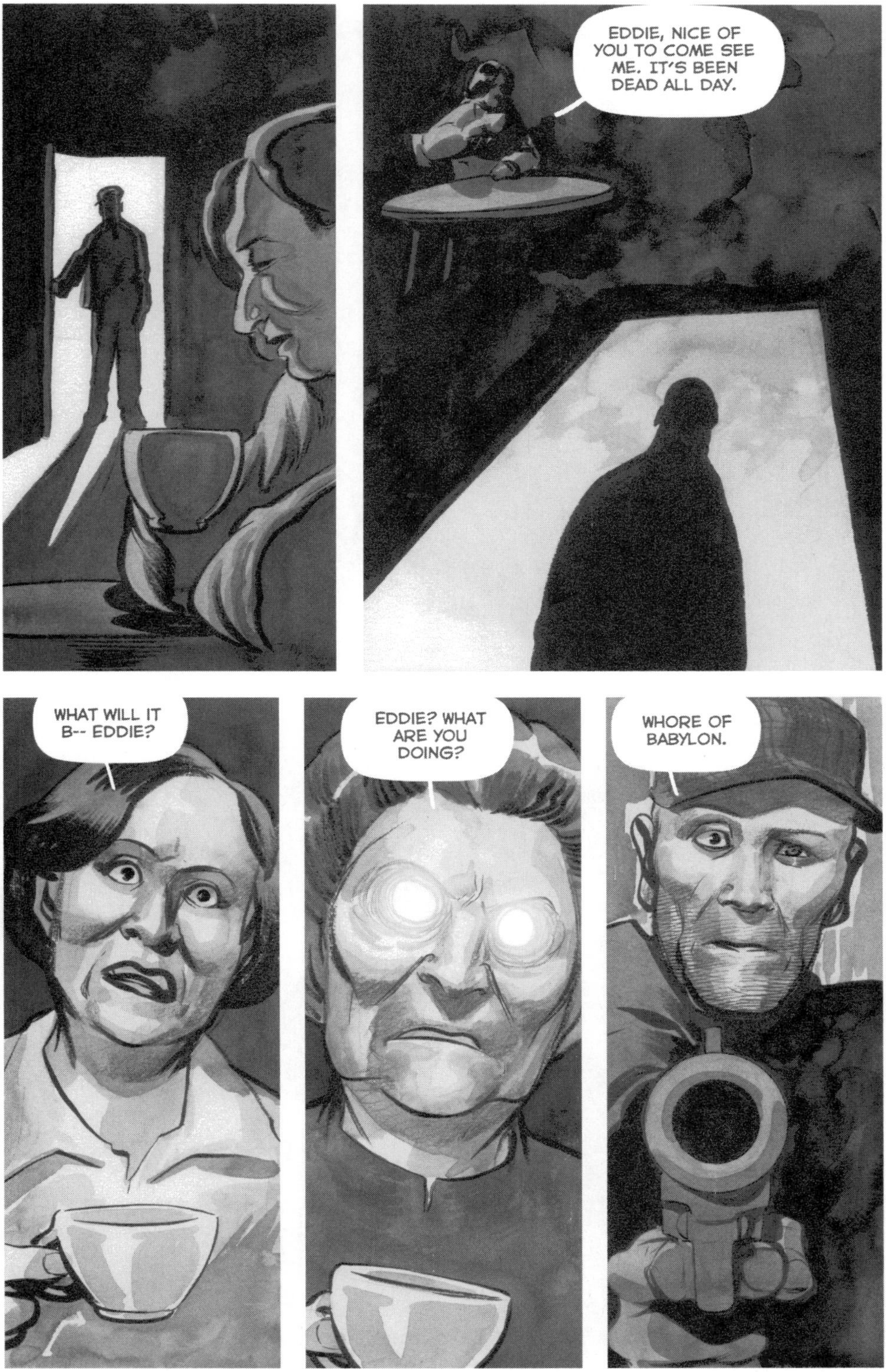
EDDIE, NICE OF YOU TO COME SEE ME. IT'S BEEN DEAD ALL DAY.
WHAT WILL IT B-- EDDIE?
EDDIE? WHAT ARE YOU DOING?
WHORE OF BABYLON.

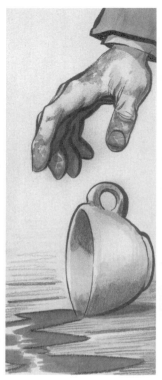

ADVENTURE
THE ISLAND OF SEX CRAZED WOMEN!
MAN'S
UHHH...
UHHH...
HEAD HUNTING SAVAGES!
AH...
AHHH...
-ADVENTURE
25¢
BEATING THE BANGTAILS

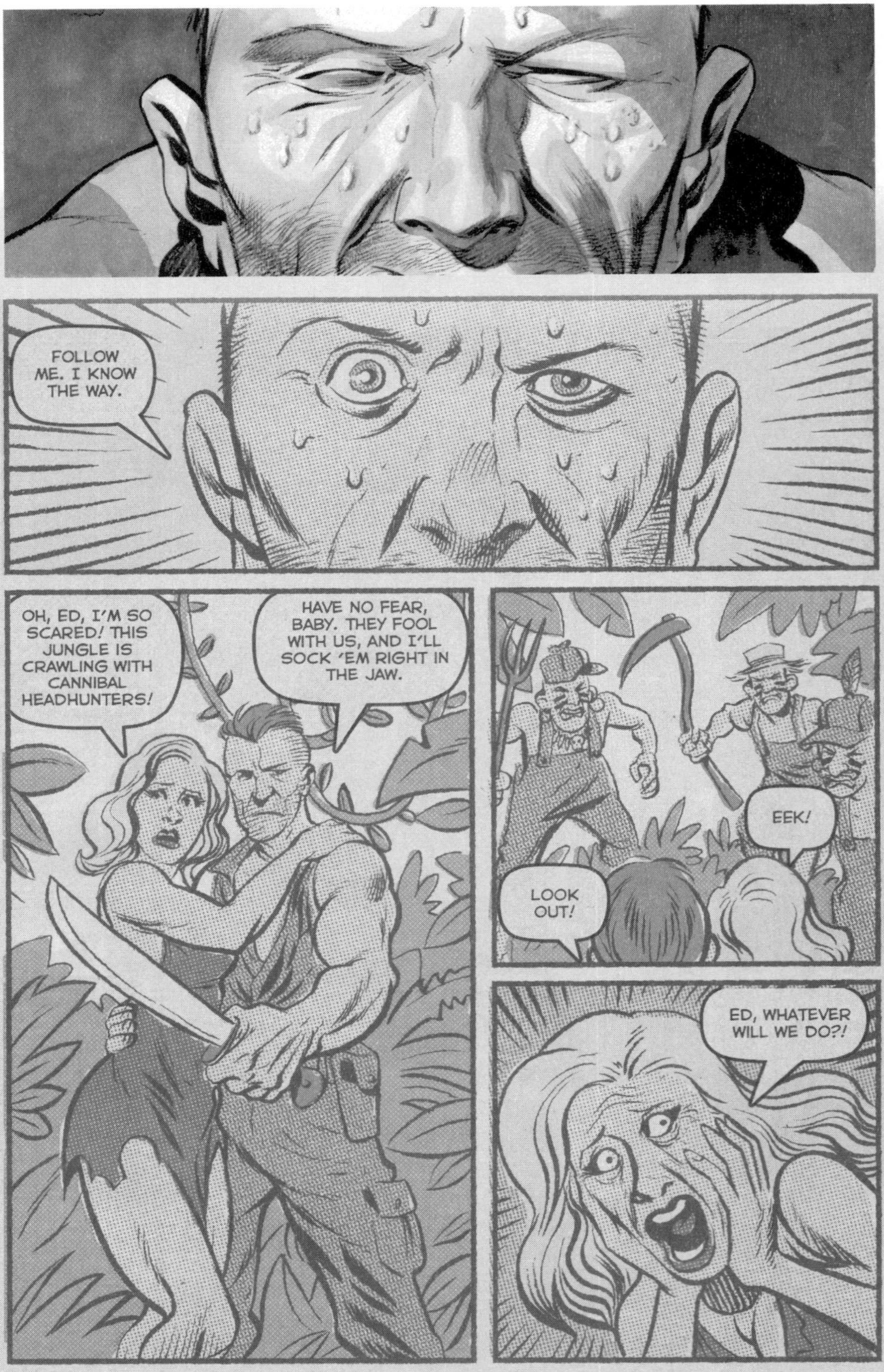
FOLLOW ME. I KNOW THE WAY.
OH, ED, I'M SO SCARED! THIS JUNGLE IS CRAWLING WITH CANNIBAL HEADHUNTERS!
HAVE NO FEAR, BABY. THEY FOOL WITH US, AND I'LL SOCK 'EM RIGHT IN THE JAW.
EEK!
LOOK OUT!
ED, WHATEVER WILL WE DO?!

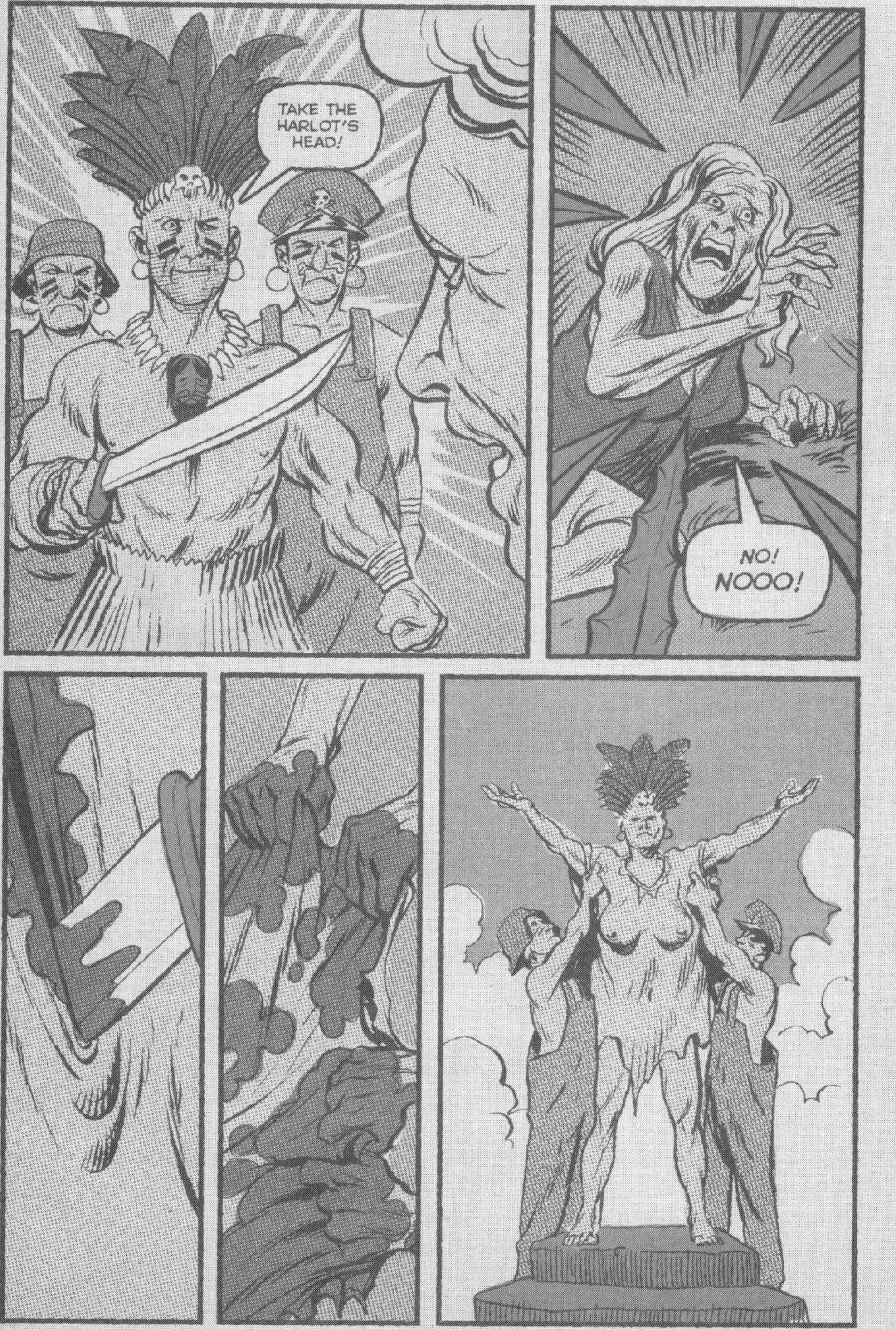
TAKE THE HARLOT'S HEAD!
NO! NOOO!

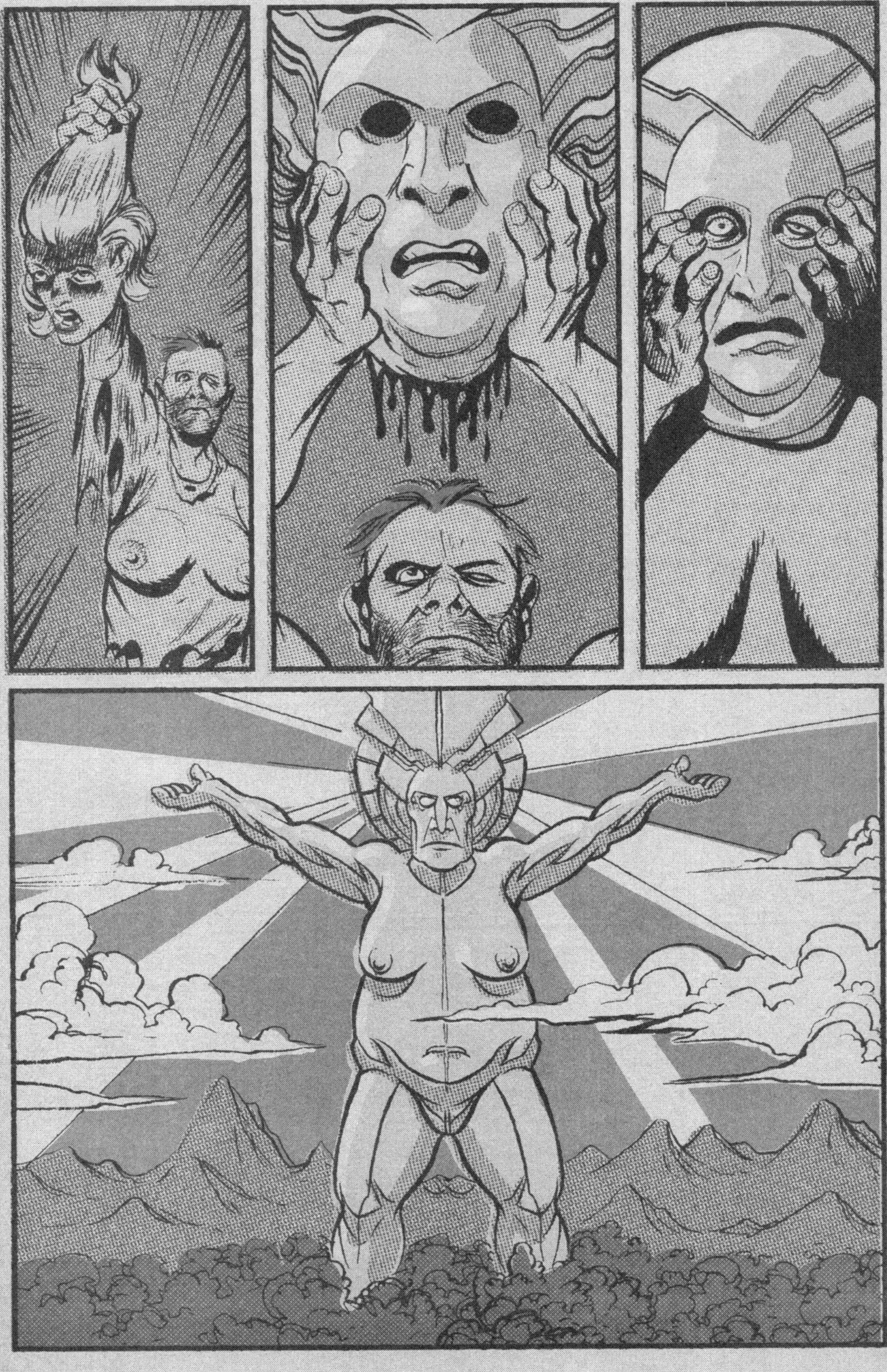

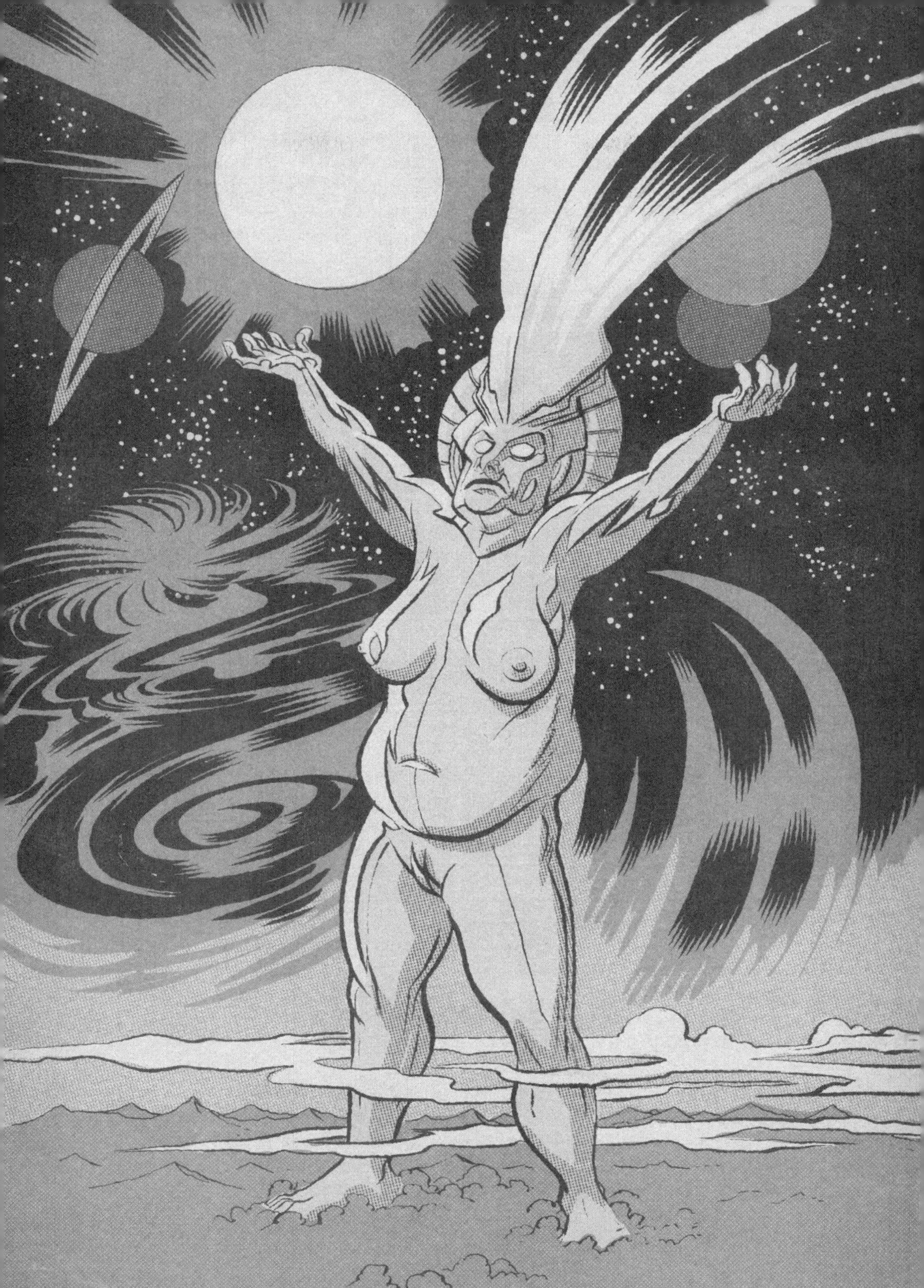

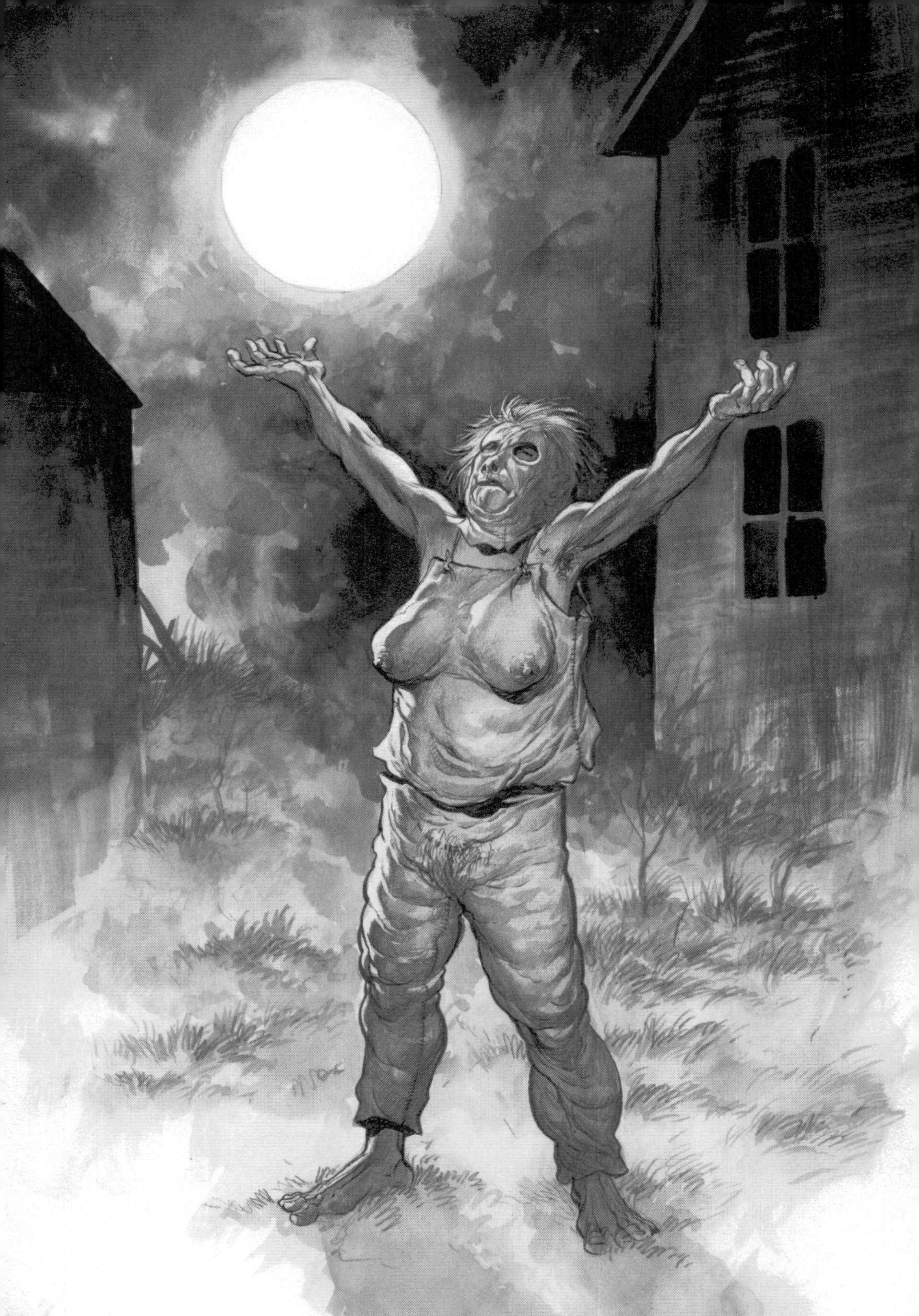

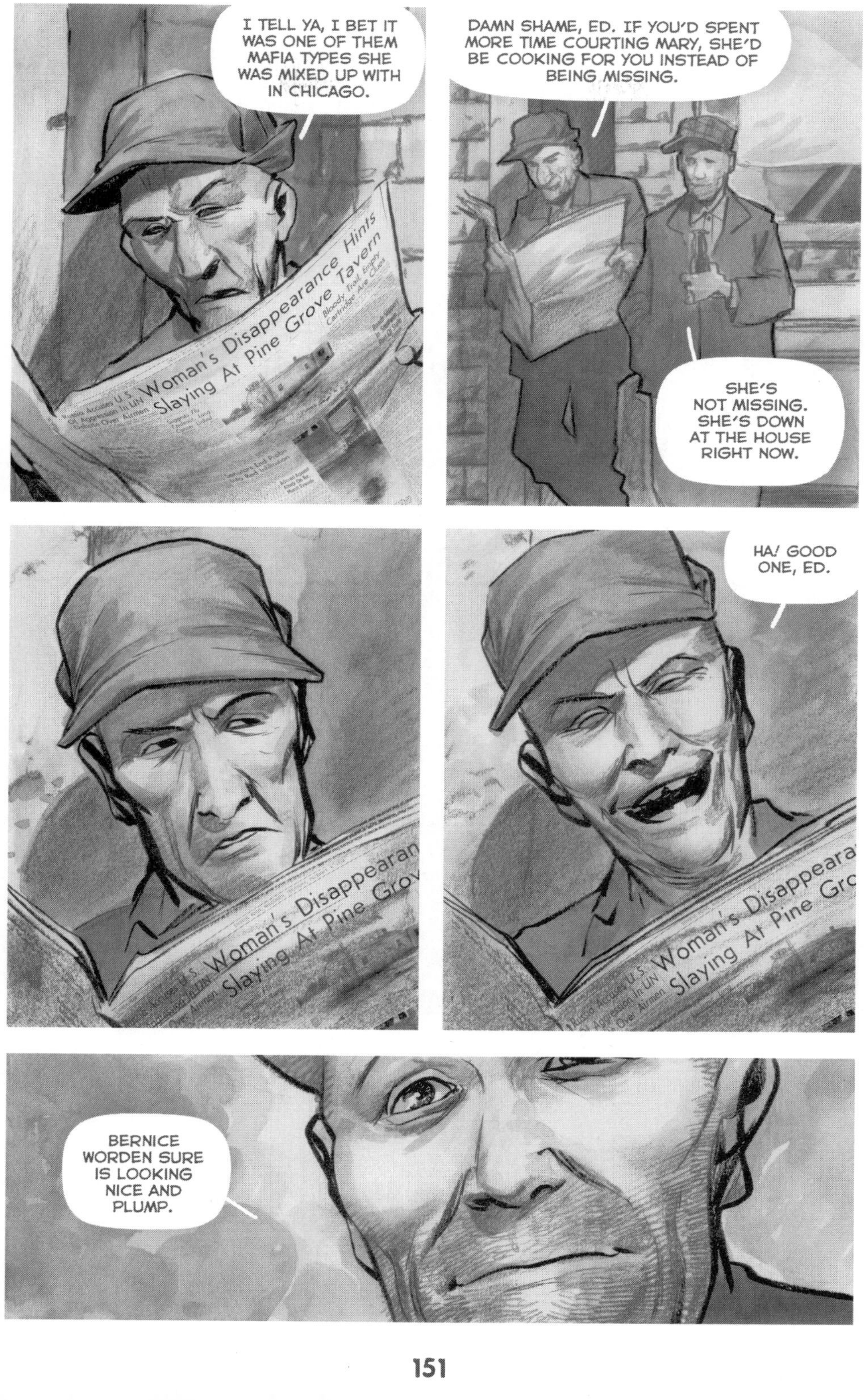
I TELL YA, I BET IT WAS ONE OF THEM MAFIA TYPES SHE WAS MIXED UP WITH IN CHICAGO.
Woman's Disappearance Hints Slaying At Pine Grove Tavern
Bloody Trail, Empty Cartridge Are Clues
Russia Accuses U.S. Of Aggression In UN
DAMN SHAME, ED. IF YOU'D SPENT MORE TIME COURTING MARY, SHE'D BE COOKING FOR YOU INSTEAD OF BEING MISSING.
SHE'S NOT MISSING. SHE'S DOWN AT THE HOUSE RIGHT NOW.
HA! GOOD ONE, ED.
BERNICE WORDEN SURE IS LOOKING NICE AND PLUMP.

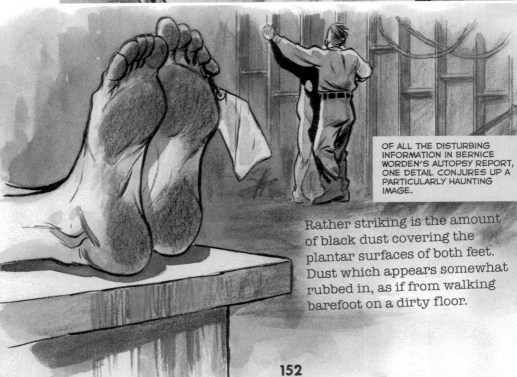
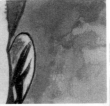

OF ALL THE DISTURBING INFORMATION IN BERNICE WORDEN'S AUTOPSY REPORT, ONE DETAIL CONJURES UP A PARTICULARLY HAUNTING IMAGE.

Rather striking is the amount of black dust covering the plantar surfaces of both feet. Dust which appears somewhat rubbed in, as if from walking barefoot on a dirty floor.

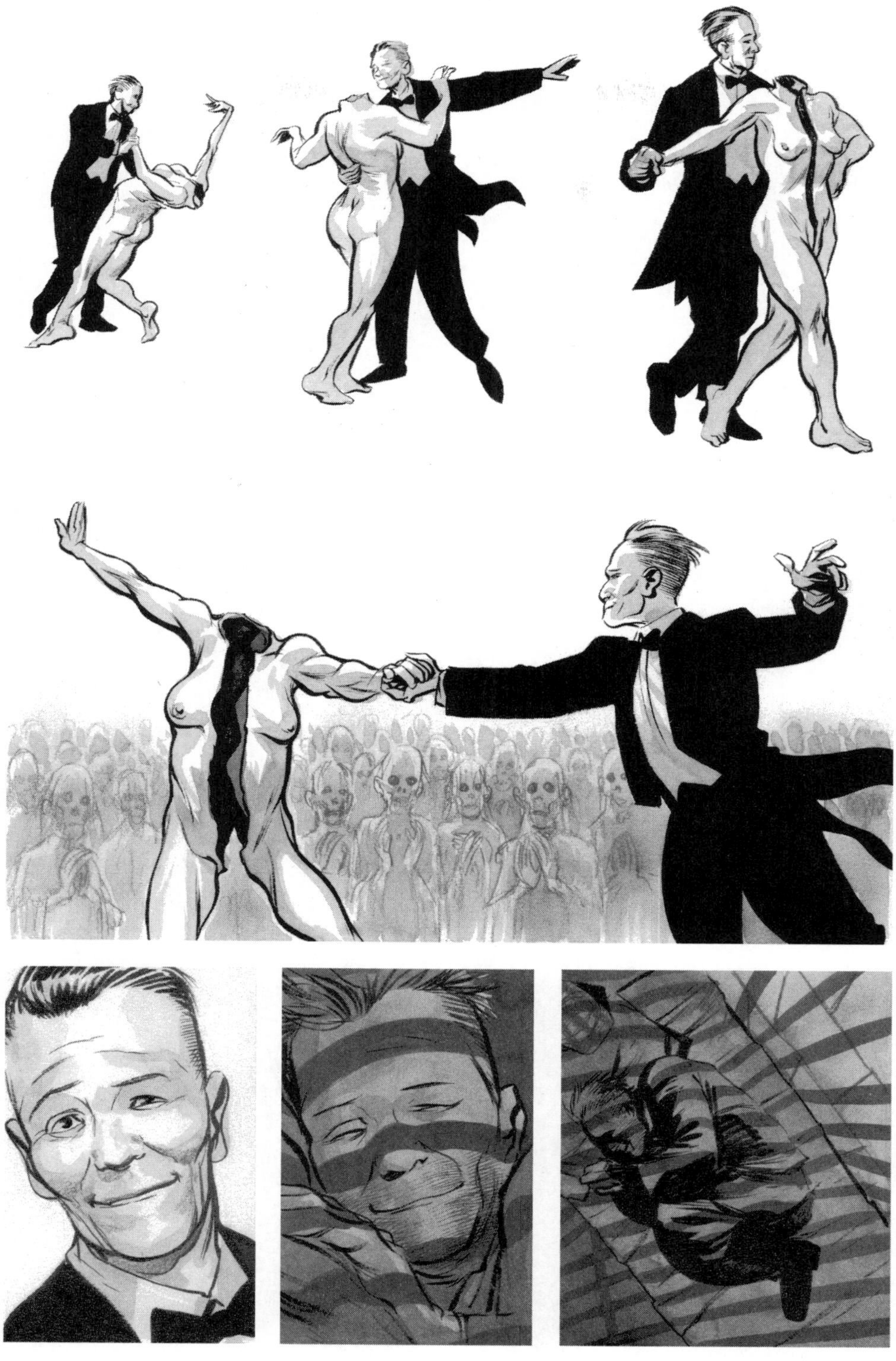

EXTRA	# CHAPTER 9	SPECIAL SECTION

10¢ ★★★

★★★ Wednesday, January 6th, 1958

THE PLIGHT OF PLAINFIELD

By Roger Camden
Guest Editorial

The entire arraignment lasted little more than five minutes. After listening to the recommendation of the prosecutor and the defense attorney, Judge Bunde made a statement. "It seems advisable under the circumstances as related by both the counsel for the state and the counsel for the defendant," he said, "that a report determination be had whether he is whether he was sane at the time of Mrs. Worden's murder.

Then Bunde signed an order committing Eddie to the Central State Hospital for the Criminally Insane at Waupun for a thirty-day examination period and remanded him to the custody of Sheriff Schley who led Eddie back to the jailhouse to await transportation to the mental institution.

Though Gein was a very tedious, it seemed impossible that he could have had the strength to dig up a grave by himself, haul open the casket, remove the corpse and perform his grisly operations on it. Over and over they puzzled over the sandy soil on that ten acres of his a few condemned—all in the space of months murder.

techniques for identifying the victims from their remains. By comparing dirt particles gathered at the crime scene with soil samples from local cemeteries, the technicians hoped to determine the validity of Gein's claim.

But the sheer quantity of evidence—by far, the largest amount ever handled by the ten-year-old Wilson to promise a quick

Gein May Have Slain At Least 2 Women, Crime Lab Reports

Believe Head Of Spinster In Collection

By Kent Blake
Staff Reporter, City desk

When a reporter asked Kileen if Augusta Gein was one of the women on the list, the

The entire arraignment lasted little more than five minutes. After listening to the recommendations of the prosecutor and the defense attorney, Judge Bunde made a statement.

"It now seems advisable under the circumstances as related by both the counsel for the state and the counsel
—CONTINUED ON FOLLOWING

Gein was one of the women on the list, the DA shook his head. According to Kileen, Gein had denied opening his mother's coffin. Of course, his mother's coffin, added Kileen, was encased in a concrete vault. Whether Eddie had tried—and failed—to reach Augusta's body was something that the district attorney could not, or would not, say.

Though its citizens were doing their best to get back to the ordinary business of life, Plainfield remained a community in the still reeling from the sheer monstrousness of the Gein revolutions, mortified by the media attention that had turned it into a backcountry sideshow and deeply riven by conflict over Kileen's plan to dig up the graves, for, while most of the townspeople were eager to see the gnaw-ridding question settled once and for all, others remained fiercely opposed to the idea of violating the hallowed soil of their little cemetery.

Added to this tension were the unabating rumors that continued to send shocks through the town. Stories had spread, for example, that the grisly artifacts found in Gein's bedroom and kitchen weren't the least of what the farmhouse contained, that his basement was full of horrors so dreadful that the police had deemed it best to conceal them from the public. There were also reports, which accounted more than a few sleepless nights for the natives of Plainfield, that investigators had turned up a "death

"excellent in the home of murder-ghoul Ed Gein.

Elsewhere in Wisconsin, the reaction to the Gein atrocities was markedly different, if no less intense. In fact, the statewide response to the Plainfield horrors was so striking that it immediately attracted the interest of various psychologists, who had never witnessed a mass phenomenon quite like it. Besides the extreme fascination with every detail of the case, from the precise number of masks found inside Eddie's house to the menus of his jailhouse dinners, the crimes had generated an unprecedented outbreak of black humor, a craze for Gein-related sick jokes (dubbed "Geiners") that quickly swept the state.

Within days of the discovery of the crimes, every youngster in Wisconsin, it seemed, was swapping "Geiners," not only with schoolmates but with parents as well. Grim jokes became the latest rage, repeated with near-obsessive frequency wherever people gathered. As early as Friday, November 22, Dr. Rudolf Mathieu, chief psychologist at the Wisconsin Diagnostic Center in Madison, was theorizing about the significance of Gein humor, which he likened to "the jokes exchanged among soldiers who are going into battle."

The entire arraignment lasted little more than five minutes. After listening to the recommendations of the prosecutor and the defense attorney, Judge Bunde made

hara County's DA Open More Graves

their remains. By comparing dirt particles gathered at the crime scene with soil samples from local cemeteries, the technicians hoped to determine the validity of Gein's claim.

But the sheer quantity of evidence—by far, the largest amount ever handled by the ten-year-old Crime Lab

...lls Found in House of Horror

INDEX	

★★★

WEATHER
HIGH 28 LOW 4

"I always took him as
perfectly harmless."

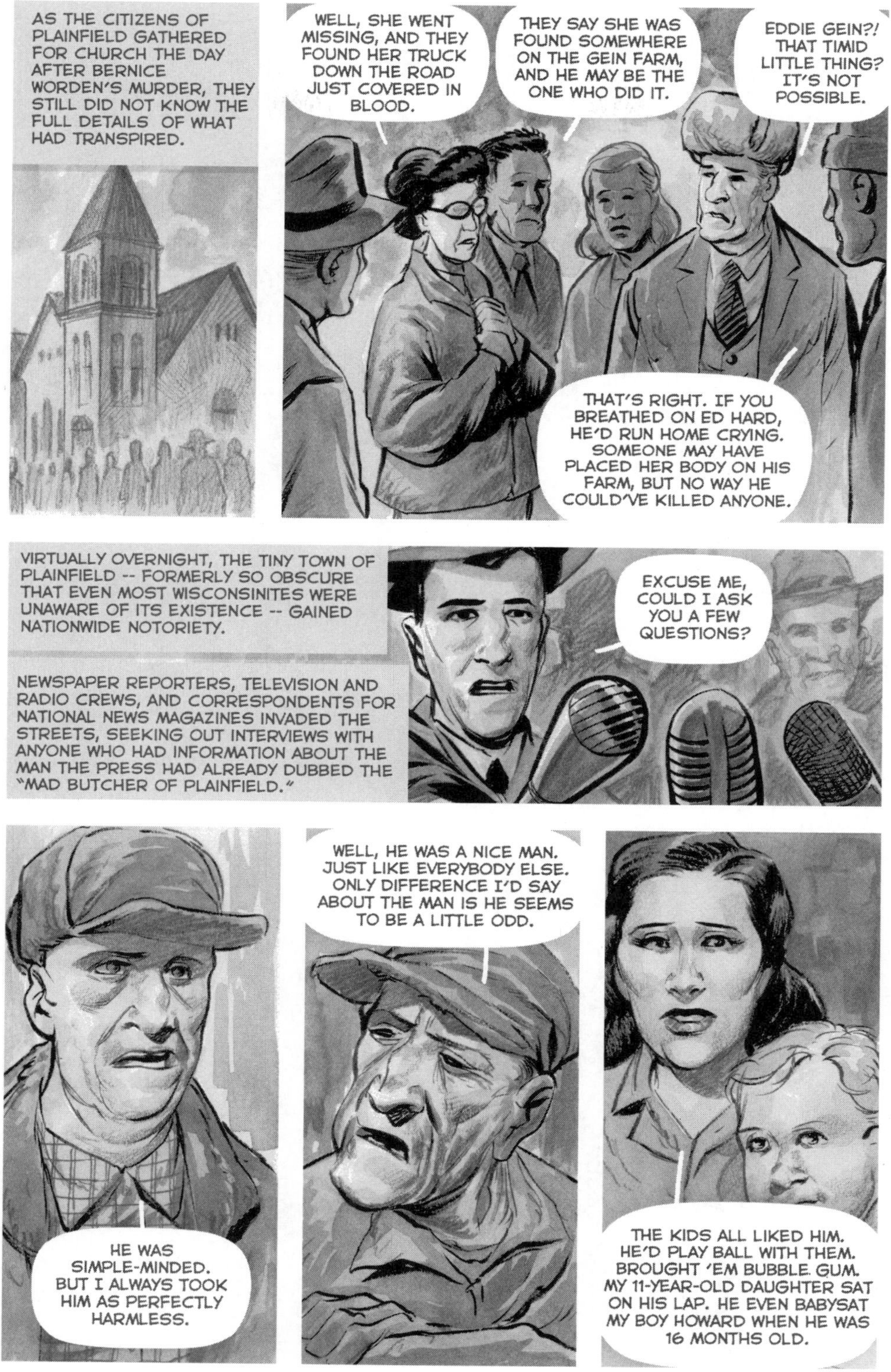
AS THE CITIZENS OF PLAINFIELD GATHERED FOR CHURCH THE DAY AFTER BERNICE WORDEN'S MURDER, THEY STILL DID NOT KNOW THE FULL DETAILS OF WHAT HAD TRANSPIRED.
WELL, SHE WENT MISSING, AND THEY FOUND HER TRUCK DOWN THE ROAD JUST COVERED IN BLOOD.
THEY SAY SHE WAS FOUND SOMEWHERE ON THE GEIN FARM, AND HE MAY BE THE ONE WHO DID IT.
EDDIE GEIN?! THAT TIMID LITTLE THING? IT'S NOT POSSIBLE.
THAT'S RIGHT. IF YOU BREATHED ON ED HARD, HE'D RUN HOME CRYING. SOMEONE MAY HAVE PLACED HER BODY ON HIS FARM, BUT NO WAY HE COULD'VE KILLED ANYONE.
VIRTUALLY OVERNIGHT, THE TINY TOWN OF PLAINFIELD -- FORMERLY SO OBSCURE THAT EVEN MOST WISCONSINITES WERE UNAWARE OF ITS EXISTENCE -- GAINED NATIONWIDE NOTORIETY.
NEWSPAPER REPORTERS, TELEVISION AND RADIO CREWS, AND CORRESPONDENTS FOR NATIONAL NEWS MAGAZINES INVADED THE STREETS, SEEKING OUT INTERVIEWS WITH ANYONE WHO HAD INFORMATION ABOUT THE MAN THE PRESS HAD ALREADY DUBBED THE "MAD BUTCHER OF PLAINFIELD."
EXCUSE ME, COULD I ASK YOU A FEW QUESTIONS?
HE WAS SIMPLE-MINDED. BUT I ALWAYS TOOK HIM AS PERFECTLY HARMLESS.
WELL, HE WAS A NICE MAN. JUST LIKE EVERYBODY ELSE. ONLY DIFFERENCE I'D SAY ABOUT THE MAN IS HE SEEMS TO BE A LITTLE ODD.
THE KIDS ALL LIKED HIM. HE'D PLAY BALL WITH THEM. BROUGHT 'EM BUBBLE GUM. MY 11-YEAR-OLD DAUGHTER SAT ON HIS LAP. HE EVEN BABYSAT MY BOY HOWARD WHEN HE WAS 16 MONTHS OLD.

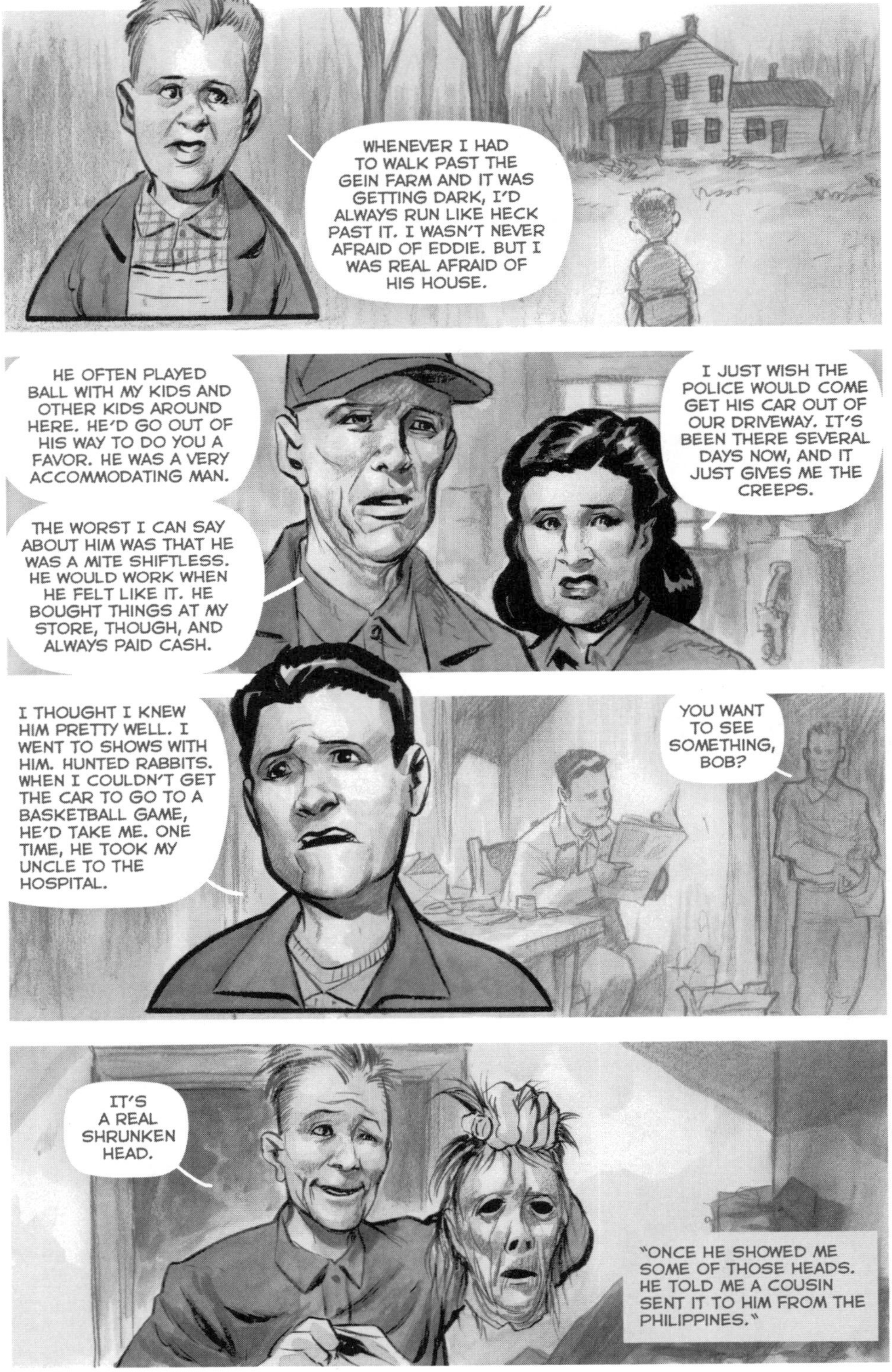
WHENEVER I HAD TO WALK PAST THE GEIN FARM AND IT WAS GETTING DARK, I'D ALWAYS RUN LIKE HECK PAST IT. I WASN'T NEVER AFRAID OF EDDIE. BUT I WAS REAL AFRAID OF HIS HOUSE.
HE OFTEN PLAYED BALL WITH MY KIDS AND OTHER KIDS AROUND HERE. HE'D GO OUT OF HIS WAY TO DO YOU A FAVOR. HE WAS A VERY ACCOMMODATING MAN.
THE WORST I CAN SAY ABOUT HIM WAS THAT HE WAS A MITE SHIFTLESS. HE WOULD WORK WHEN HE FELT LIKE IT. HE BOUGHT THINGS AT MY STORE, THOUGH, AND ALWAYS PAID CASH.
I JUST WISH THE POLICE WOULD COME GET HIS CAR OUT OF OUR DRIVEWAY. IT'S BEEN THERE SEVERAL DAYS NOW, AND IT JUST GIVES ME THE CREEPS.
I THOUGHT I KNEW HIM PRETTY WELL. I WENT TO SHOWS WITH HIM. HUNTED RABBITS. WHEN I COULDN'T GET THE CAR TO GO TO A BASKETBALL GAME, HE'D TAKE ME. ONE TIME, HE TOOK MY UNCLE TO THE HOSPITAL.
YOU WANT TO SEE SOMETHING, BOB?
IT'S A REAL SHRUNKEN HEAD.
"ONCE HE SHOWED ME SOME OF THOSE HEADS. HE TOLD ME A COUSIN SENT IT TO HIM FROM THE PHILIPPINES."

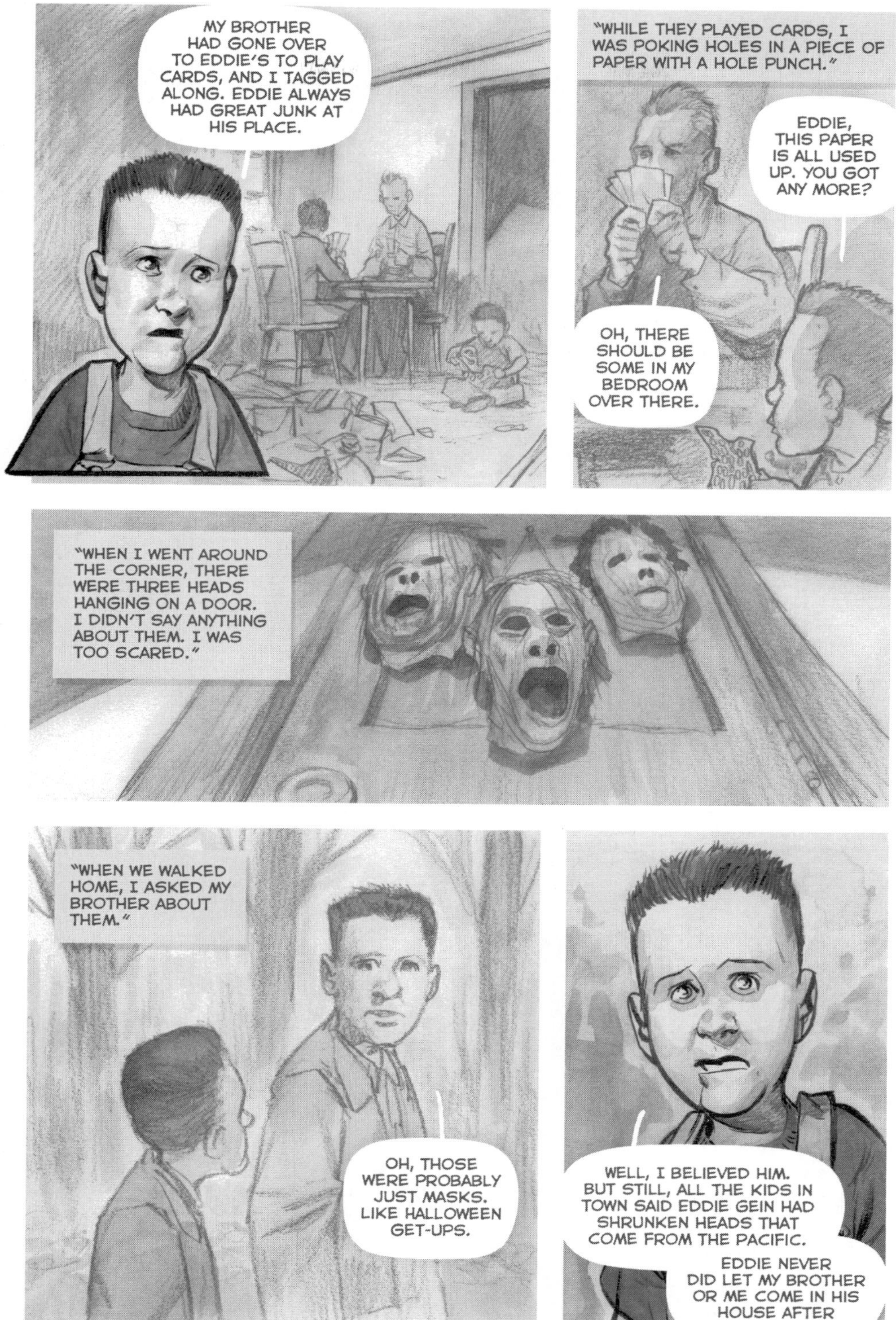

MY BROTHER HAD GONE OVER TO EDDIE'S TO PLAY CARDS, AND I TAGGED ALONG. EDDIE ALWAYS HAD GREAT JUNK AT HIS PLACE.
"WHILE THEY PLAYED CARDS, I WAS POKING HOLES IN A PIECE OF PAPER WITH A HOLE PUNCH."
EDDIE, THIS PAPER IS ALL USED UP. YOU GOT ANY MORE?
OH, THERE SHOULD BE SOME IN MY BEDROOM OVER THERE.
"WHEN I WENT AROUND THE CORNER, THERE WERE THREE HEADS HANGING ON A DOOR. I DIDN'T SAY ANYTHING ABOUT THEM. I WAS TOO SCARED."
"WHEN WE WALKED HOME, I ASKED MY BROTHER ABOUT THEM."
OH, THOSE WERE PROBABLY JUST MASKS. LIKE HALLOWEEN GET-UPS.
WELL, I BELIEVED HIM. BUT STILL, ALL THE KIDS IN TOWN SAID EDDIE GEIN HAD SHRUNKEN HEADS THAT COME FROM THE PACIFIC.
EDDIE NEVER DID LET MY BROTHER OR ME COME IN HIS HOUSE AFTER THAT DAY.

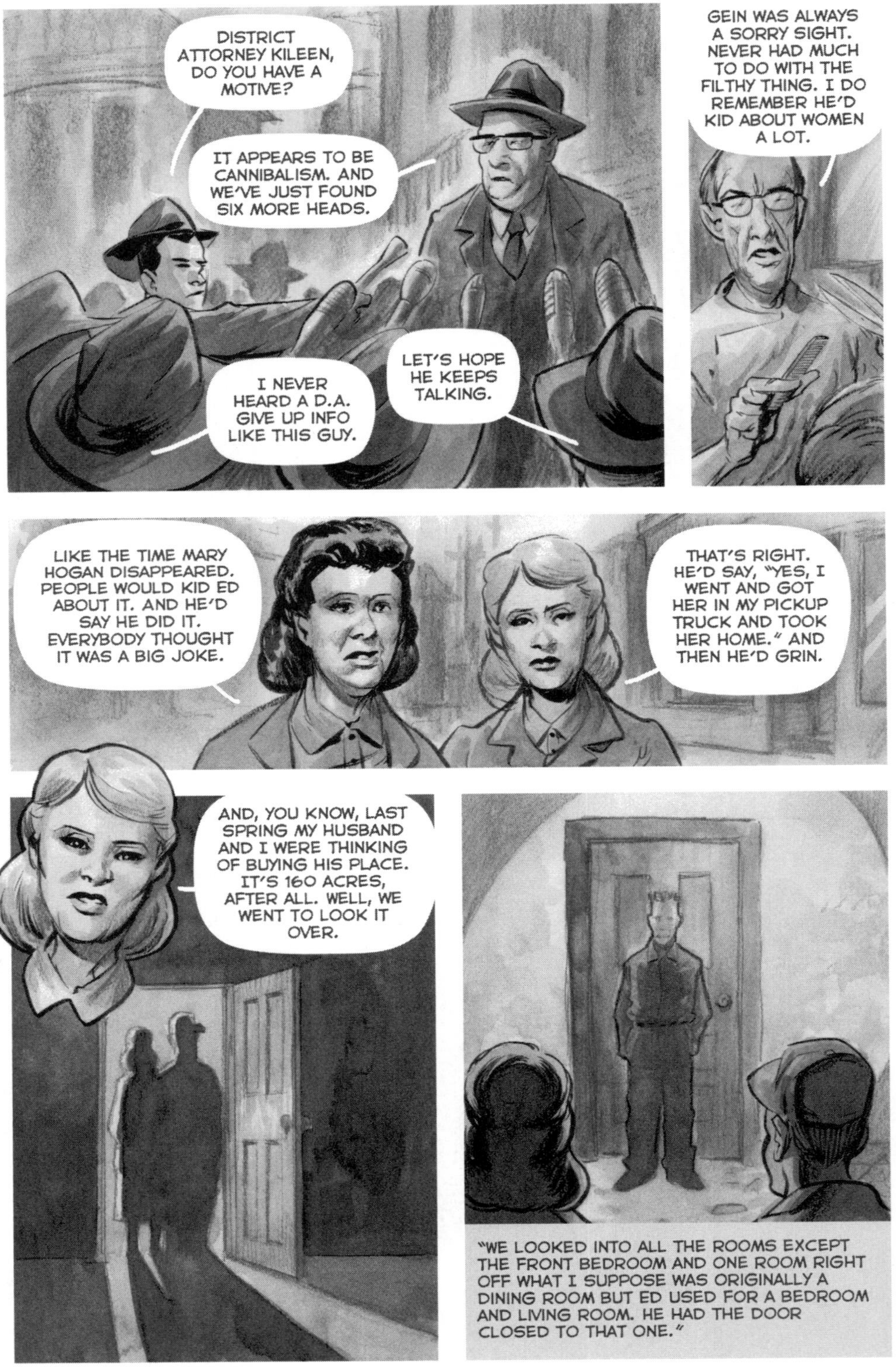
DISTRICT ATTORNEY KILEEN, DO YOU HAVE A MOTIVE?
IT APPEARS TO BE CANNIBALISM. AND WE'VE JUST FOUND SIX MORE HEADS.
I NEVER HEARD A D.A. GIVE UP INFO LIKE THIS GUY.
LET'S HOPE HE KEEPS TALKING.
GEIN WAS ALWAYS A SORRY SIGHT. NEVER HAD MUCH TO DO WITH THE FILTHY THING. I DO REMEMBER HE'D KID ABOUT WOMEN A LOT.
LIKE THE TIME MARY HOGAN DISAPPEARED. PEOPLE WOULD KID ED ABOUT IT. AND HE'D SAY HE DID IT. EVERYBODY THOUGHT IT WAS A BIG JOKE.
THAT'S RIGHT. HE'D SAY, "YES, I WENT AND GOT HER IN MY PICKUP TRUCK AND TOOK HER HOME." AND THEN HE'D GRIN.
AND, YOU KNOW, LAST SPRING MY HUSBAND AND I WERE THINKING OF BUYING HIS PLACE. IT'S 160 ACRES, AFTER ALL. WELL, WE WENT TO LOOK IT OVER.
"WE LOOKED INTO ALL THE ROOMS EXCEPT THE FRONT BEDROOM AND ONE ROOM RIGHT OFF WHAT I SUPPOSE WAS ORIGINALLY A DINING ROOM BUT ED USED FOR A BEDROOM AND LIVING ROOM. HE HAD THE DOOR CLOSED TO THAT ONE."

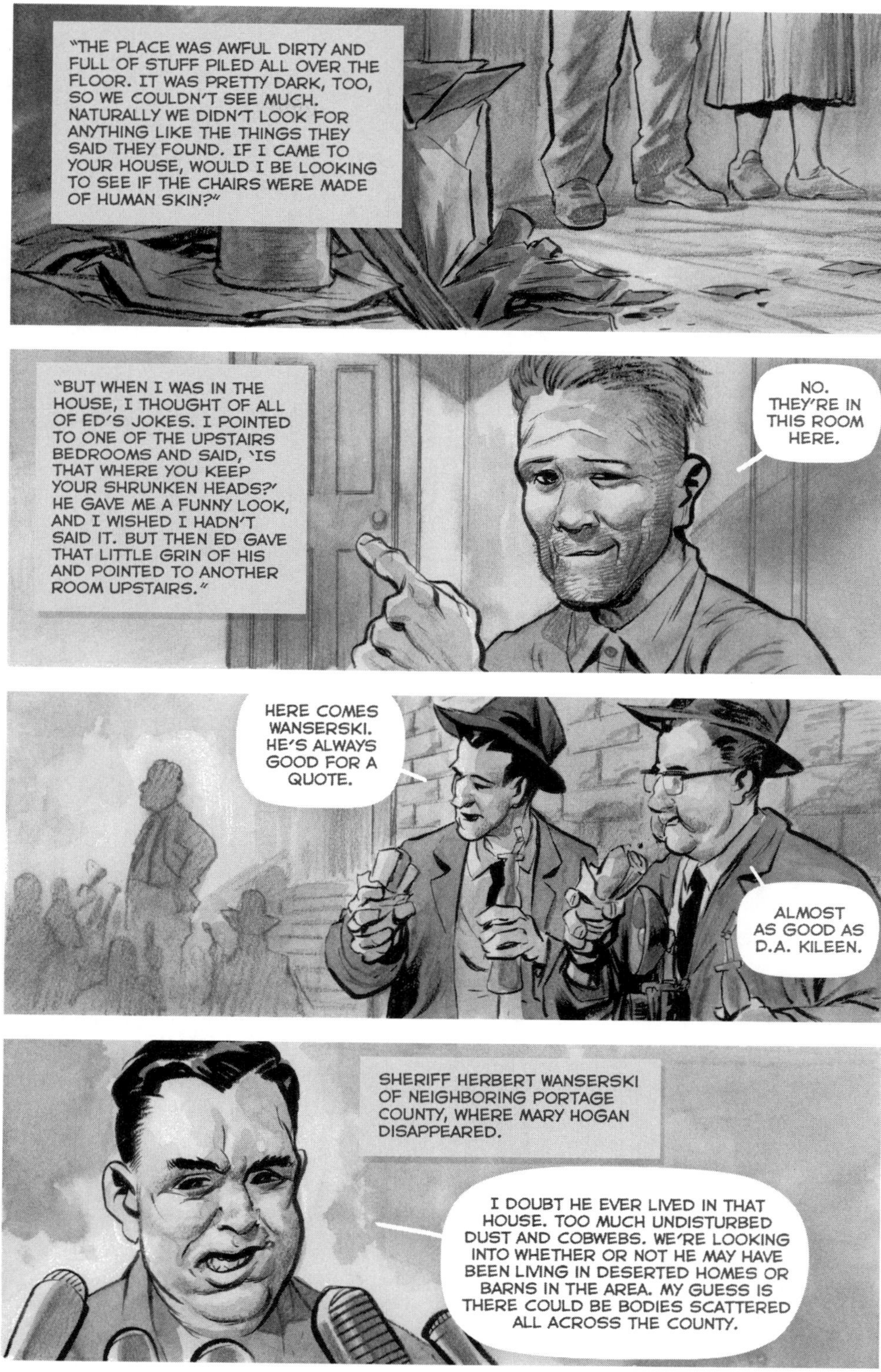
"THE PLACE WAS AWFUL DIRTY AND FULL OF STUFF PILED ALL OVER THE FLOOR. IT WAS PRETTY DARK, TOO, SO WE COULDN'T SEE MUCH. NATURALLY WE DIDN'T LOOK FOR ANYTHING LIKE THE THINGS THEY SAID THEY FOUND. IF I CAME TO YOUR HOUSE, WOULD I BE LOOKING TO SEE IF THE CHAIRS WERE MADE OF HUMAN SKIN?"
"BUT WHEN I WAS IN THE HOUSE, I THOUGHT OF ALL OF ED'S JOKES. I POINTED TO ONE OF THE UPSTAIRS BEDROOMS AND SAID, 'IS THAT WHERE YOU KEEP YOUR SHRUNKEN HEADS?' HE GAVE ME A FUNNY LOOK, AND I WISHED I HADN'T SAID IT. BUT THEN ED GAVE THAT LITTLE GRIN OF HIS AND POINTED TO ANOTHER ROOM UPSTAIRS."
NO. THEY'RE IN THIS ROOM HERE.
HERE COMES WANSERSKI. HE'S ALWAYS GOOD FOR A QUOTE.
ALMOST AS GOOD AS D.A. KILEEN.
SHERIFF HERBERT WANSERSKI OF NEIGHBORING PORTAGE COUNTY, WHERE MARY HOGAN DISAPPEARED.
I DOUBT HE EVER LIVED IN THAT HOUSE. TOO MUCH UNDISTURBED DUST AND COBWEBS. WE'RE LOOKING INTO WHETHER OR NOT HE MAY HAVE BEEN LIVING IN DESERTED HOMES OR BARNS IN THE AREA. MY GUESS IS THERE COULD BE BODIES SCATTERED ALL ACROSS THE COUNTY.

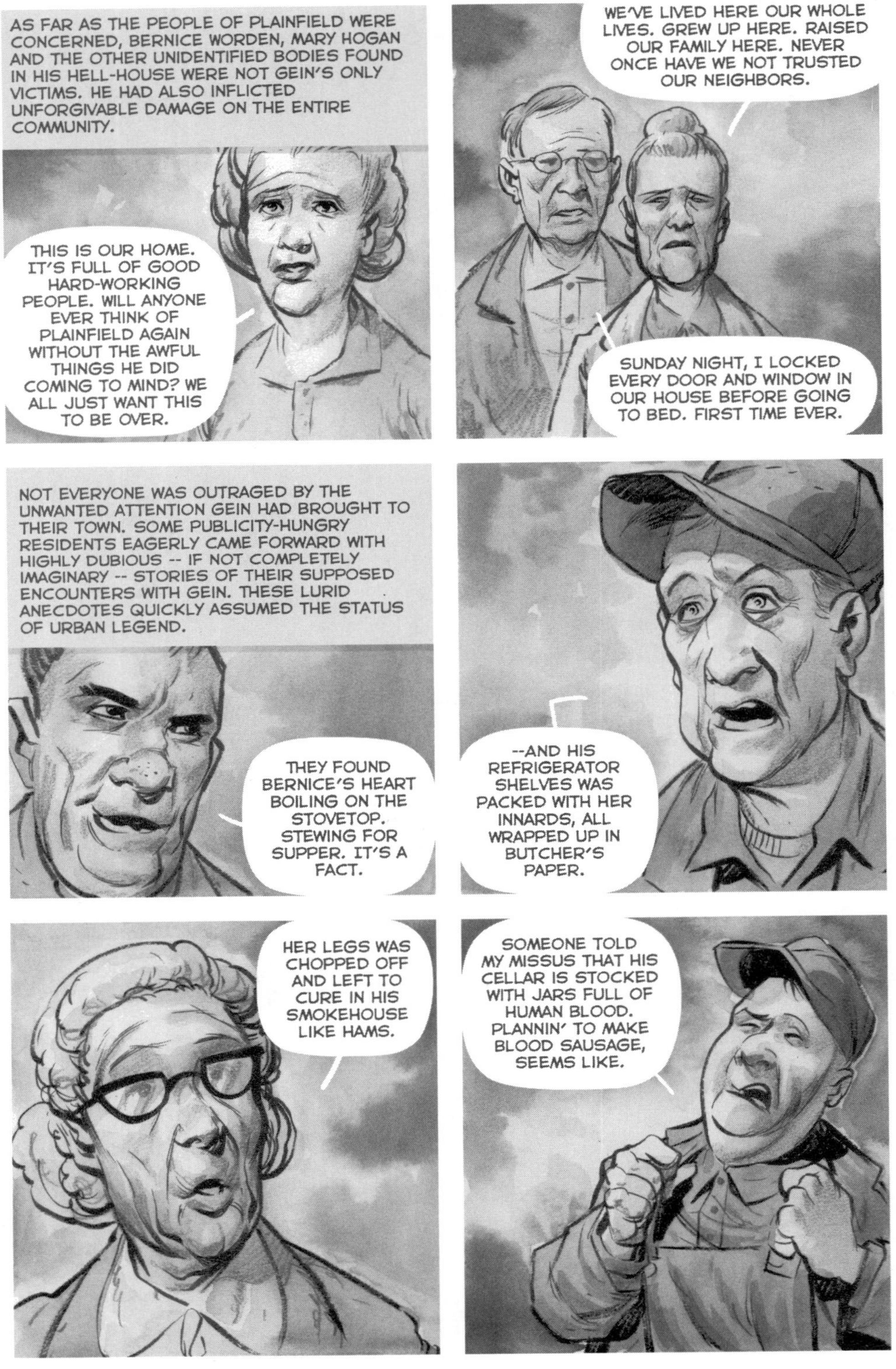
AS FAR AS THE PEOPLE OF PLAINFIELD WERE CONCERNED, BERNICE WORDEN, MARY HOGAN AND THE OTHER UNIDENTIFIED BODIES FOUND IN HIS HELL-HOUSE WERE NOT GEIN'S ONLY VICTIMS. HE HAD ALSO INFLICTED UNFORGIVABLE DAMAGE ON THE ENTIRE COMMUNITY.
THIS IS OUR HOME. IT'S FULL OF GOOD HARD-WORKING PEOPLE. WILL ANYONE EVER THINK OF PLAINFIELD AGAIN WITHOUT THE AWFUL THINGS HE DID COMING TO MIND? WE ALL JUST WANT THIS TO BE OVER.
WE'VE LIVED HERE OUR WHOLE LIVES. GREW UP HERE. RAISED OUR FAMILY HERE. NEVER ONCE HAVE WE NOT TRUSTED OUR NEIGHBORS.
SUNDAY NIGHT, I LOCKED EVERY DOOR AND WINDOW IN OUR HOUSE BEFORE GOING TO BED. FIRST TIME EVER.
NOT EVERYONE WAS OUTRAGED BY THE UNWANTED ATTENTION GEIN HAD BROUGHT TO THEIR TOWN. SOME PUBLICITY-HUNGRY RESIDENTS EAGERLY CAME FORWARD WITH HIGHLY DUBIOUS -- IF NOT COMPLETELY IMAGINARY -- STORIES OF THEIR SUPPOSED ENCOUNTERS WITH GEIN. THESE LURID ANECDOTES QUICKLY ASSUMED THE STATUS OF URBAN LEGEND.
THEY FOUND BERNICE'S HEART BOILING ON THE STOVETOP. STEWING FOR SUPPER. IT'S A FACT.
--AND HIS REFRIGERATOR SHELVES WAS PACKED WITH HER INNARDS, ALL WRAPPED UP IN BUTCHER'S PAPER.
HER LEGS WAS CHOPPED OFF AND LEFT TO CURE IN HIS SMOKEHOUSE LIKE HAMS.
SOMEONE TOLD MY MISSUS THAT HIS CELLAR IS STOCKED WITH JARS FULL OF HUMAN BLOOD. PLANNIN' TO MAKE BLOOD SAUSAGE, SEEMS LIKE.

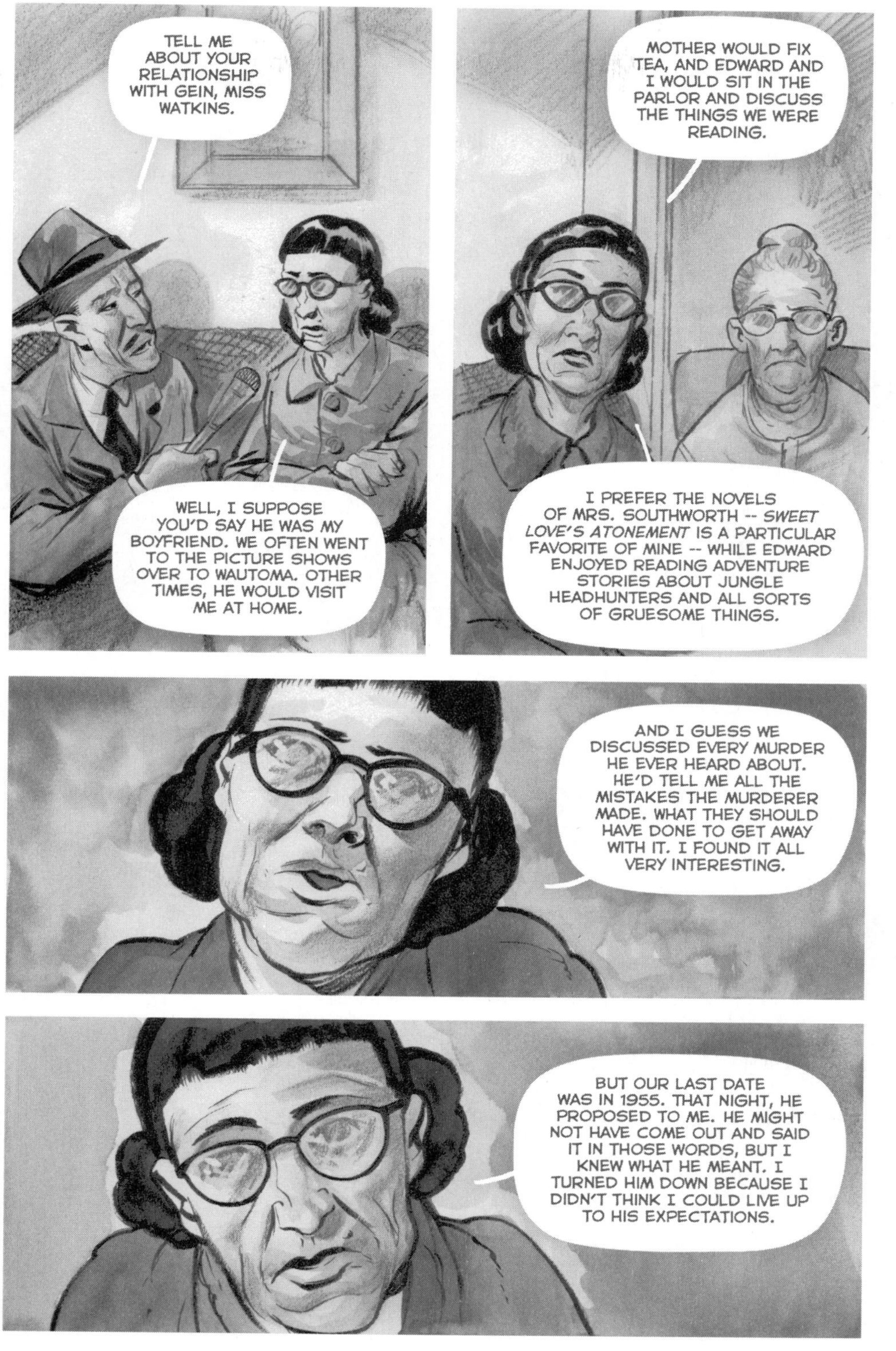
TELL ME ABOUT YOUR RELATIONSHIP WITH GEIN, MISS WATKINS.
WELL, I SUPPOSE YOU'D SAY HE WAS MY BOYFRIEND. WE OFTEN WENT TO THE PICTURE SHOWS OVER TO WAUTOMA. OTHER TIMES, HE WOULD VISIT ME AT HOME.
MOTHER WOULD FIX TEA, AND EDWARD AND I WOULD SIT IN THE PARLOR AND DISCUSS THE THINGS WE WERE READING.
I PREFER THE NOVELS OF MRS. SOUTHWORTH -- *SWEET LOVE'S ATONEMENT* IS A PARTICULAR FAVORITE OF MINE -- WHILE EDWARD ENJOYED READING ADVENTURE STORIES ABOUT JUNGLE HEADHUNTERS AND ALL SORTS OF GRUESOME THINGS.
AND I GUESS WE DISCUSSED EVERY MURDER HE EVER HEARD ABOUT. HE'D TELL ME ALL THE MISTAKES THE MURDERER MADE. WHAT THEY SHOULD HAVE DONE TO GET AWAY WITH IT. I FOUND IT ALL VERY INTERESTING.
BUT OUR LAST DATE WAS IN 1955. THAT NIGHT, HE PROPOSED TO ME. HE MIGHT NOT HAVE COME OUT AND SAID IT IN THOSE WORDS, BUT I KNEW WHAT HE MEANT. I TURNED HIM DOWN BECAUSE I DIDN'T THINK I COULD LIVE UP TO HIS EXPECTATIONS.

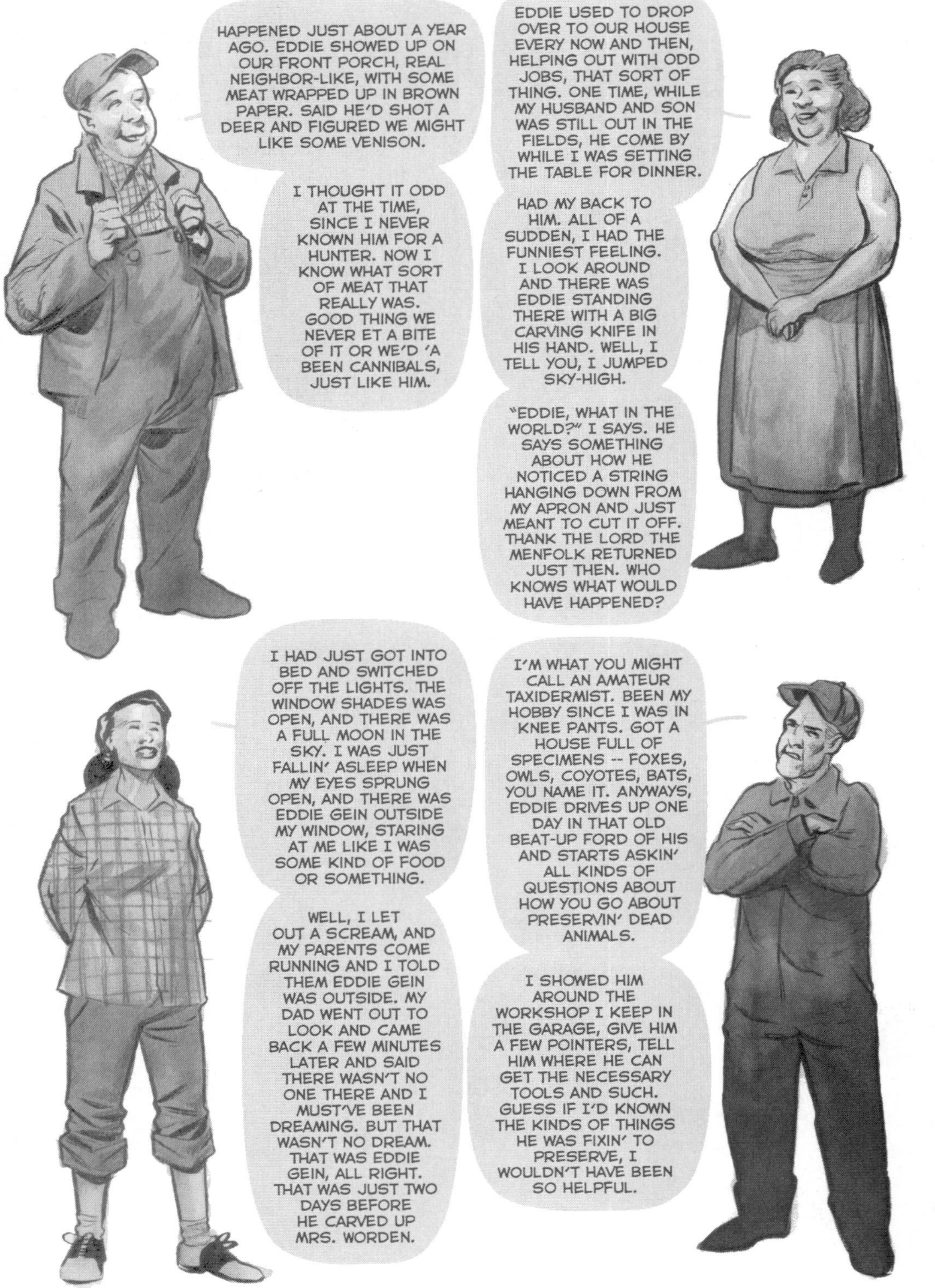
HAPPENED JUST ABOUT A YEAR AGO. EDDIE SHOWED UP ON OUR FRONT PORCH, REAL NEIGHBOR-LIKE, WITH SOME MEAT WRAPPED UP IN BROWN PAPER. SAID HE'D SHOT A DEER AND FIGURED WE MIGHT LIKE SOME VENISON.
I THOUGHT IT ODD AT THE TIME, SINCE I NEVER KNOWN HIM FOR A HUNTER. NOW I KNOW WHAT SORT OF MEAT THAT REALLY WAS. GOOD THING WE NEVER ET A BITE OF IT OR WE'D 'A BEEN CANNIBALS, JUST LIKE HIM.
EDDIE USED TO DROP OVER TO OUR HOUSE EVERY NOW AND THEN, HELPING OUT WITH ODD JOBS, THAT SORT OF THING. ONE TIME, WHILE MY HUSBAND AND SON WAS STILL OUT IN THE FIELDS, HE COME BY WHILE I WAS SETTING THE TABLE FOR DINNER.
HAD MY BACK TO HIM. ALL OF A SUDDEN, I HAD THE FUNNIEST FEELING. I LOOK AROUND AND THERE WAS EDDIE STANDING THERE WITH A BIG CARVING KNIFE IN HIS HAND. WELL, I TELL YOU, I JUMPED SKY-HIGH.
"EDDIE, WHAT IN THE WORLD?" I SAYS. HE SAYS SOMETHING ABOUT HOW HE NOTICED A STRING HANGING DOWN FROM MY APRON AND JUST MEANT TO CUT IT OFF. THANK THE LORD THE MENFOLK RETURNED JUST THEN. WHO KNOWS WHAT WOULD HAVE HAPPENED?
I HAD JUST GOT INTO BED AND SWITCHED OFF THE LIGHTS. THE WINDOW SHADES WAS OPEN, AND THERE WAS A FULL MOON IN THE SKY. I WAS JUST FALLIN' ASLEEP WHEN MY EYES SPRUNG OPEN, AND THERE WAS EDDIE GEIN OUTSIDE MY WINDOW, STARING AT ME LIKE I WAS SOME KIND OF FOOD OR SOMETHING.
WELL, I LET OUT A SCREAM, AND MY PARENTS COME RUNNING AND I TOLD THEM EDDIE GEIN WAS OUTSIDE. MY DAD WENT OUT TO LOOK AND CAME BACK A FEW MINUTES LATER AND SAID THERE WASN'T NO ONE THERE AND I MUST'VE BEEN DREAMING. BUT THAT WASN'T NO DREAM. THAT WAS EDDIE GEIN, ALL RIGHT. THAT WAS JUST TWO DAYS BEFORE HE CARVED UP MRS. WORDEN.
I'M WHAT YOU MIGHT CALL AN AMATEUR TAXIDERMIST. BEEN MY HOBBY SINCE I WAS IN KNEE PANTS. GOT A HOUSE FULL OF SPECIMENS -- FOXES, OWLS, COYOTES, BATS, YOU NAME IT. ANYWAYS, EDDIE DRIVES UP ONE DAY IN THAT OLD BEAT-UP FORD OF HIS AND STARTS ASKIN' ALL KINDS OF QUESTIONS ABOUT HOW YOU GO ABOUT PRESERVIN' DEAD ANIMALS.
I SHOWED HIM AROUND THE WORKSHOP I KEEP IN THE GARAGE, GIVE HIM A FEW POINTERS, TELL HIM WHERE HE CAN GET THE NECESSARY TOOLS AND SUCH. GUESS IF I'D KNOWN THE KINDS OF THINGS HE WAS FIXIN' TO PRESERVE, I WOULDN'T HAVE BEEN SO HELPFUL.

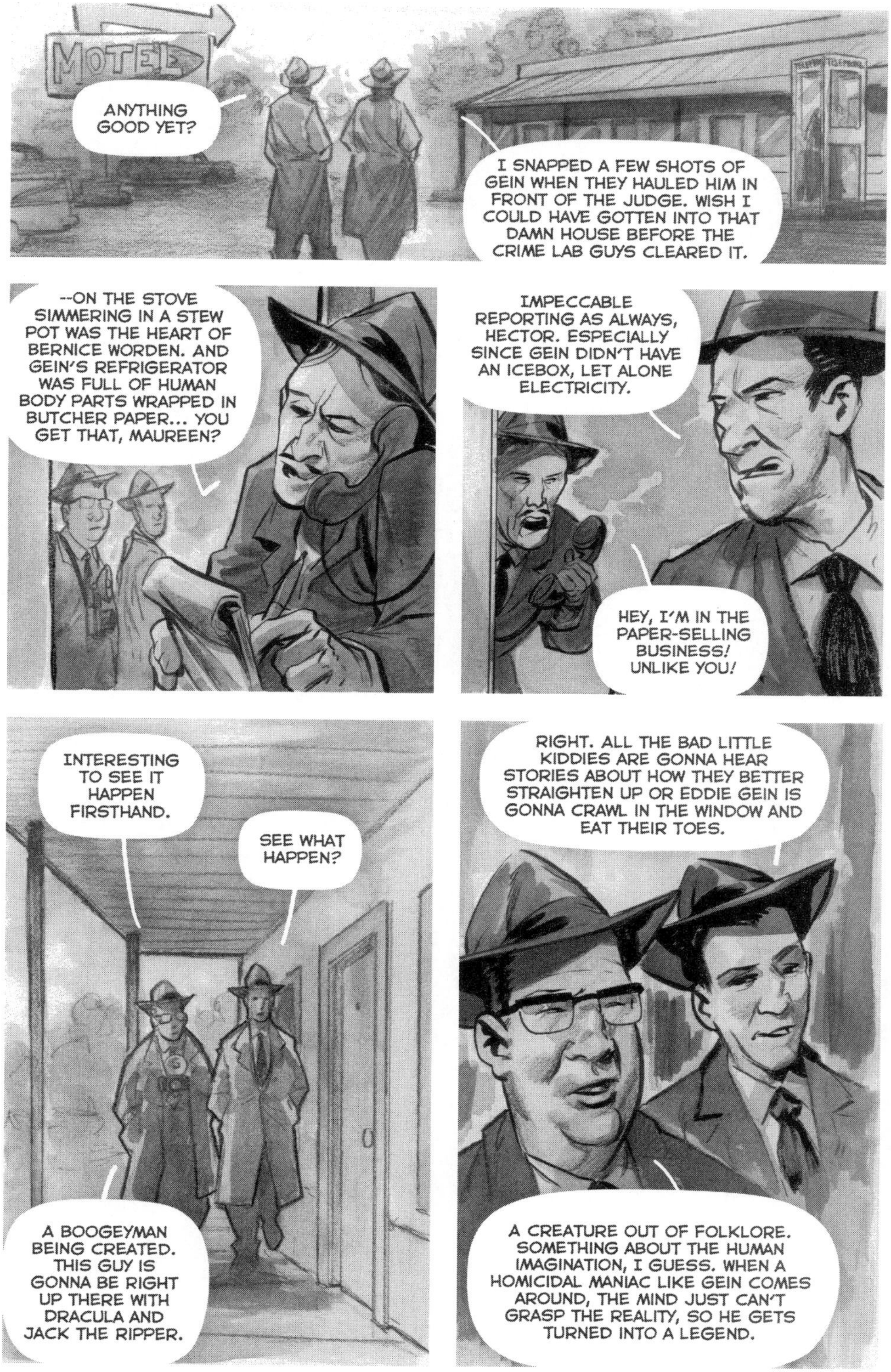
MOTEL
ANYTHING GOOD YET?
I SNAPPED A FEW SHOTS OF GEIN WHEN THEY HAULED HIM IN FRONT OF THE JUDGE. WISH I COULD HAVE GOTTEN INTO THAT DAMN HOUSE BEFORE THE CRIME LAB GUYS CLEARED IT.
--ON THE STOVE SIMMERING IN A STEW POT WAS THE HEART OF BERNICE WORDEN. AND GEIN'S REFRIGERATOR WAS FULL OF HUMAN BODY PARTS WRAPPED IN BUTCHER PAPER... YOU GET THAT, MAUREEN?
IMPECCABLE REPORTING AS ALWAYS, HECTOR. ESPECIALLY SINCE GEIN DIDN'T HAVE AN ICEBOX, LET ALONE ELECTRICITY.
HEY, I'M IN THE PAPER-SELLING BUSINESS! UNLIKE YOU!
INTERESTING TO SEE IT HAPPEN FIRSTHAND.
SEE WHAT HAPPEN?
A BOOGEYMAN BEING CREATED. THIS GUY IS GONNA BE RIGHT UP THERE WITH DRACULA AND JACK THE RIPPER.
RIGHT. ALL THE BAD LITTLE KIDDIES ARE GONNA HEAR STORIES ABOUT HOW THEY BETTER STRAIGHTEN UP OR EDDIE GEIN IS GONNA CRAWL IN THE WINDOW AND EAT THEIR TOES.
A CREATURE OUT OF FOLKLORE. SOMETHING ABOUT THE HUMAN IMAGINATION, I GUESS. WHEN A HOMICIDAL MANIAC LIKE GEIN COMES AROUND, THE MIND JUST CAN'T GRASP THE REALITY, SO HE GETS TURNED INTO A LEGEND.

DAILY

CHAPTER 10

WEATHER
Section 10a
HIGH 12 LOW -2

★★★ Monday, January 13th, 1958

A LITTLE MAD SOMETIMES

10c ★★★

By Leland Bynquist
Lead reporter, City desk

The entire arraignment lasted little more than five minutes. After listening to the recommendations of the prosecutor and the defense attorney, Judge Bundie made a statement. "It seems advisable under the circumstances as related by both the counsel for the state and the counsel for the defendant," he said, "that expert determination be had whether he is now competent to stand trial," as well as whether he was sane at the time of Mrs. Worden's murder. Then Bundie signed an order committing Eddie to the Central State Hospital for the Criminally Insane at Waupun for a thirty-day examination period and remanded him to the custody of Sheriff Schley who led Eddie back to the jailhouse to await transportation to the mental institution.

Though Gein was a wily fellow, it seemed impossible that he could have had the strength to dig up a grave by himself, break open the casket, remove the corpse and perform its grisly operations on it, then rebury the coffin and smooth the earth so that no trace of his crime remained—all in the space of a few hours. Moreover, the townspeople didn't see how such an activity could possibly have gone undetected, particularly over the course of several years. Gein, they argued...

techniques for identifying the victims from their remains. By comparing dirt particles gathered at the crime scene with soil samples from local cemeteries, the technicians hoped to determine the validity of Gein's claim.

But the sheer quantity of evidence—by far the largest amount ever handled by the ten-year-old Crime Lab—made it hard for Wilson to promise a quick resolution. Though Kileen urged the director to give the soil analysis top priority, it was clear that a final analysis might take weeks, even months.

In the meantime, Kileen was under growing pressure from the Plainfield citizenry to determine the truth of Gein's assertion. It was becoming increasingly obvious that the townsfolk would never be able to rest without knowing whether their loved ones had, in fact, been ravaged in their graves. On Friday afternoon, therefore, following his meeting with Judge Bundie and the other officials, Kileen called a press conference to make an electrifying announcement.

Early the next week, he told the reporters, and contingent on the permission of the next-of-kin, two graves would be opened in the Plainfield cemetery. Kileen's hope was that such prying would not only settle the question once and for all but also prove that the strange little incubus was up to... Gein was not seem to have become suddenly dubious about the whole proceeding. When asked by one of the reporters why this should be so, Gein said, "I never did it at all. I'm not even sure it happened. You know... it seems like something I dreamed." "Do you?" his initial enthusiasm, Kileen now appeared in a hesitant mood. When he, too, was asked by one of the assembled newsmen to explain his change of heart, he gave a small shrug and admitted that, now that the moment had come, he wasn't so sure he wanted to know the truth...

Lawyer Urges Early Sanity Test for Gein

By Kent Blake
Staff Reporter, Circular

Though Gein was a wily fellow it seemed impossible that he could have had the strength to dig up a grave by himself break open the casket, remove the corpse and perform its grisly operations on it, then rebury the coffin and smooth over the sandy soil so that no trace of his crime remained—all in the space of a few hours. Moreover, the townspeople didn't see how such an activity could possibly have gone undetected, particularly over the course of several years. Gein, they argued, would have had to perform his nocturnal pilgrimages by furtive light, and even in his area as isolated and lonely as Plainfield, it hardly seemed credible that he one would have ever operated a single free digging session from the cemetery to reclaim Gein's pickup truck parked there in the night and wandered after the strange little incubus was up to, this operation severely spasified to comment on the situation was the various of Gein's claim. But the sheer quantity of evidence—by far, the largest amount ever handled by the ten-year-old Crime Lab—made it hard for Wilson to promise a quick resolution. Though Kileen urged the director to give the soil analysis top priority, it was clear that a final answer might take weeks, even months.

In the meantime, Kileen was under growing pressure from the Plainfield citizenry to determine the truth of Gein's assertion. It was becoming increasingly obvious that the townsfolk would never be able to rest without knowing whether their loved ones had, in fact, been ravaged in their graves. On Friday afternoon, therefore, following his meeting with Judge Bundie and the other officials, Kileen called a press conference to make an electrifying announcement. Early the next week, he told the reporters, and contingent on the permission of the next-of-kin, two graves would be opened in the Plainfield cemetery. Kileen's hope was only absent have, to this amount equaled so.

...us DA
...Graves

...comparing dirt particles ...crime scene with soil ...local cemetery, the ...hoped to determine the validity of Gein's claim.

But the sheer quantity of evidence—by far, the largest amount ever handled by the ten-year-old Crime Lab—made it hard for Wilson to promise a quick resolution. Though Kileen urged the director to give the soil analysis top priority, it was clear that a final answer might take weeks, even months, even months.

...marriage and have soon ...graves ...crossed from the ...Gein's pickup, truck ...the night and wandered ...little incubus was up to, ...gruesome beyond ...what the strange little ...rudely gratified to comment ...person narrowly gratified to comment on ...situation was the justice of the Plainfield ...cemetery, Pat Danna, who reported ...directly Pat Danna even though ...that this strange little had been ...even though this strange little had ...been...

...according to Kileen, Gein...

"I've never killed anyone
to my knowledge."

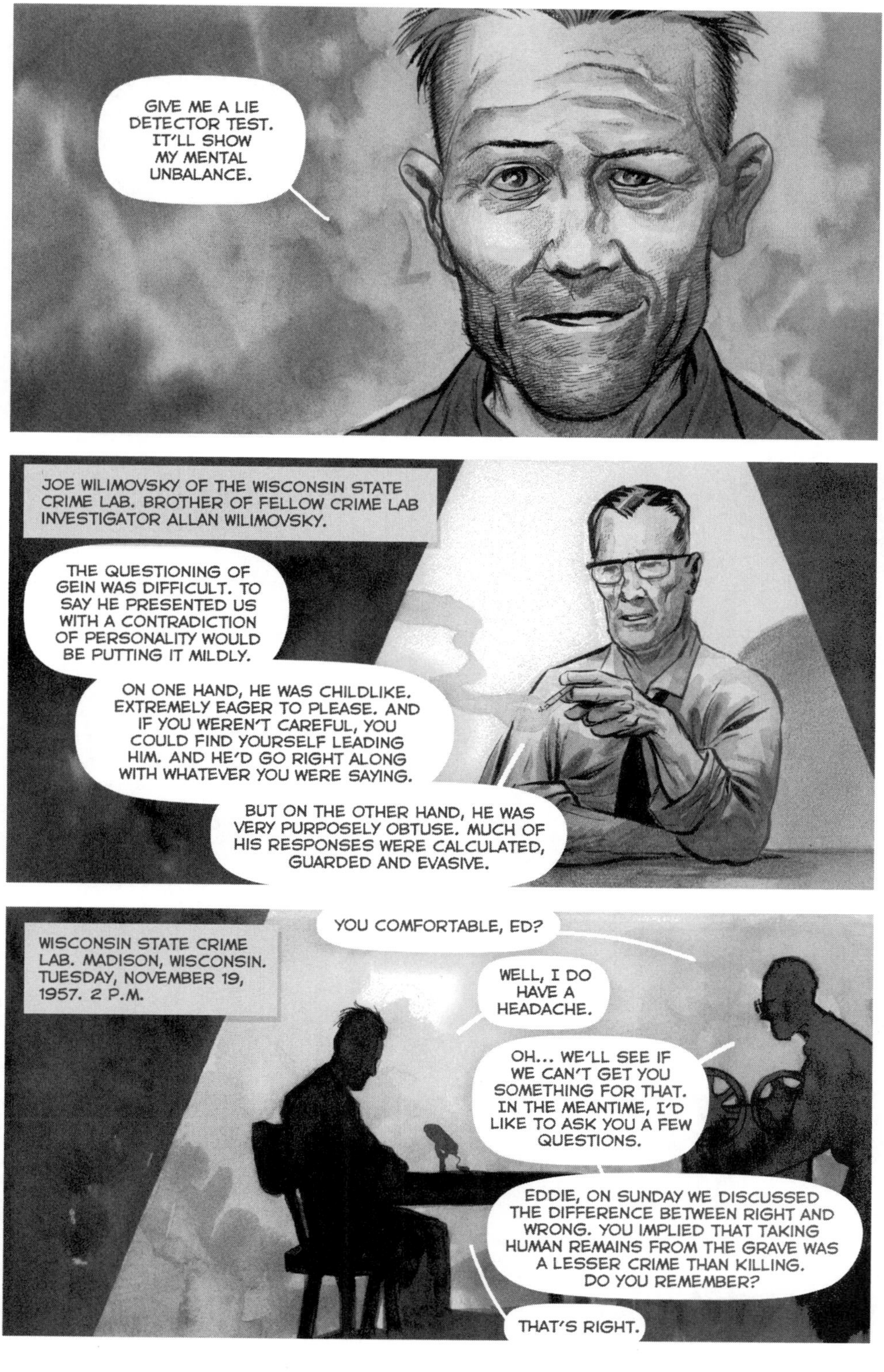
GIVE ME A LIE DETECTOR TEST. IT'LL SHOW MY MENTAL UNBALANCE.
JOE WILIMOVSKY OF THE WISCONSIN STATE CRIME LAB. BROTHER OF FELLOW CRIME LAB INVESTIGATOR ALLAN WILIMOVSKY.
THE QUESTIONING OF GEIN WAS DIFFICULT. TO SAY HE PRESENTED US WITH A CONTRADICTION OF PERSONALITY WOULD BE PUTTING IT MILDLY.
ON ONE HAND, HE WAS CHILDLIKE. EXTREMELY EAGER TO PLEASE. AND IF YOU WEREN'T CAREFUL, YOU COULD FIND YOURSELF LEADING HIM. AND HE'D GO RIGHT ALONG WITH WHATEVER YOU WERE SAYING.
BUT ON THE OTHER HAND, HE WAS VERY PURPOSELY OBTUSE. MUCH OF HIS RESPONSES WERE CALCULATED, GUARDED AND EVASIVE.
WISCONSIN STATE CRIME LAB. MADISON, WISCONSIN. TUESDAY, NOVEMBER 19, 1957. 2 P.M.
YOU COMFORTABLE, ED?
WELL, I DO HAVE A HEADACHE.
OH... WE'LL SEE IF WE CAN'T GET YOU SOMETHING FOR THAT. IN THE MEANTIME, I'D LIKE TO ASK YOU A FEW QUESTIONS.
EDDIE, ON SUNDAY WE DISCUSSED THE DIFFERENCE BETWEEN RIGHT AND WRONG. YOU IMPLIED THAT TAKING HUMAN REMAINS FROM THE GRAVE WAS A LESSER CRIME THAN KILLING. DO YOU REMEMBER?
THAT'S RIGHT.

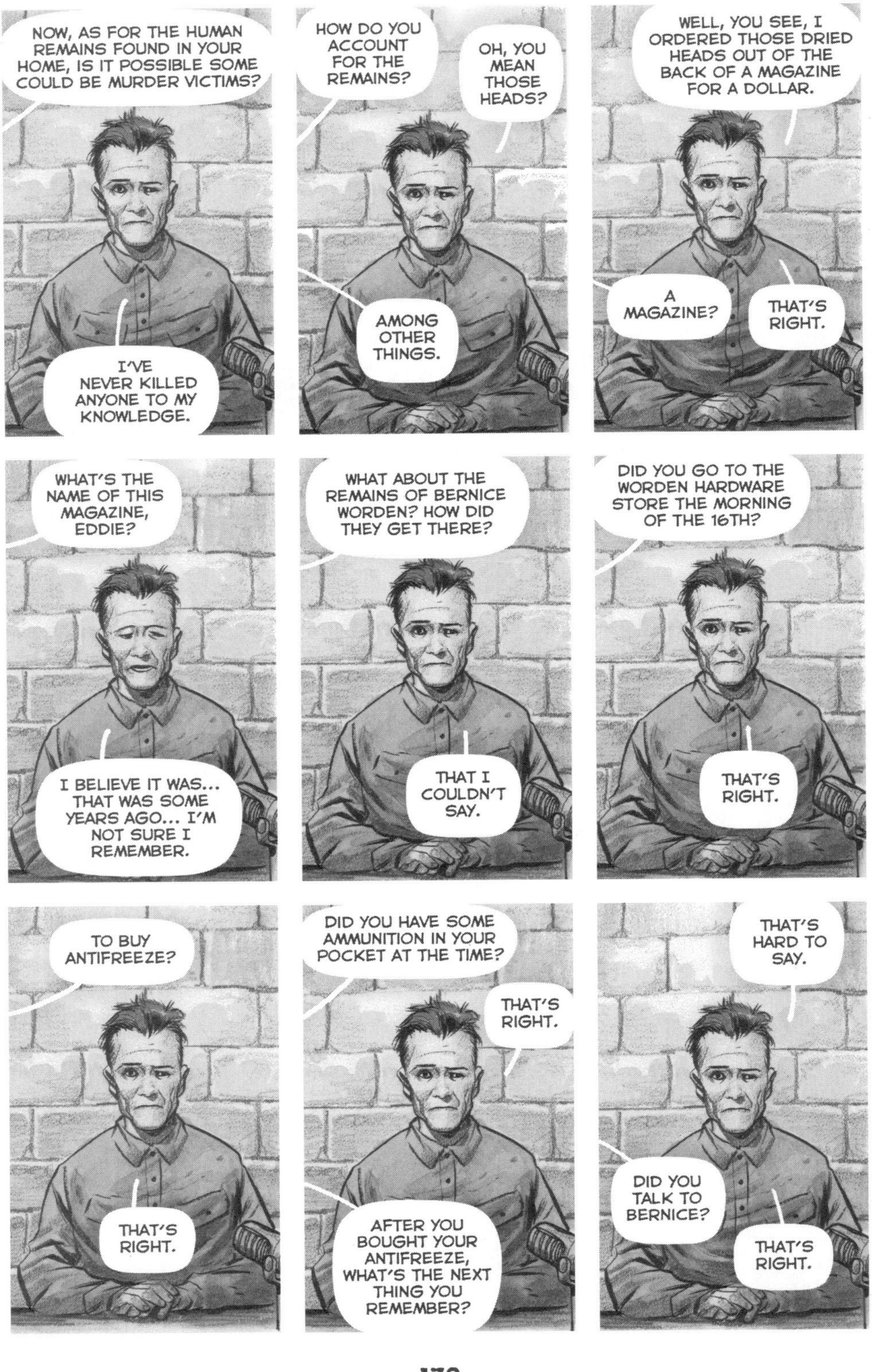
NOW, AS FOR THE HUMAN REMAINS FOUND IN YOUR HOME, IS IT POSSIBLE SOME COULD BE MURDER VICTIMS?
I'VE NEVER KILLED ANYONE TO MY KNOWLEDGE.
HOW DO YOU ACCOUNT FOR THE REMAINS?
OH, YOU MEAN THOSE HEADS?
AMONG OTHER THINGS.
WELL, YOU SEE, I ORDERED THOSE DRIED HEADS OUT OF THE BACK OF A MAGAZINE FOR A DOLLAR.
A MAGAZINE?
THAT'S RIGHT.
WHAT'S THE NAME OF THIS MAGAZINE, EDDIE?
I BELIEVE IT WAS... THAT WAS SOME YEARS AGO... I'M NOT SURE I REMEMBER.
WHAT ABOUT THE REMAINS OF BERNICE WORDEN? HOW DID THEY GET THERE?
THAT I COULDN'T SAY.
DID YOU GO TO THE WORDEN HARDWARE STORE THE MORNING OF THE 16TH?
THAT'S RIGHT.
TO BUY ANTIFREEZE?
THAT'S RIGHT.
DID YOU HAVE SOME AMMUNITION IN YOUR POCKET AT THE TIME?
THAT'S RIGHT.
AFTER YOU BOUGHT YOUR ANTIFREEZE, WHAT'S THE NEXT THING YOU REMEMBER?
THAT'S HARD TO SAY.
DID YOU TALK TO BERNICE?
THAT'S RIGHT.

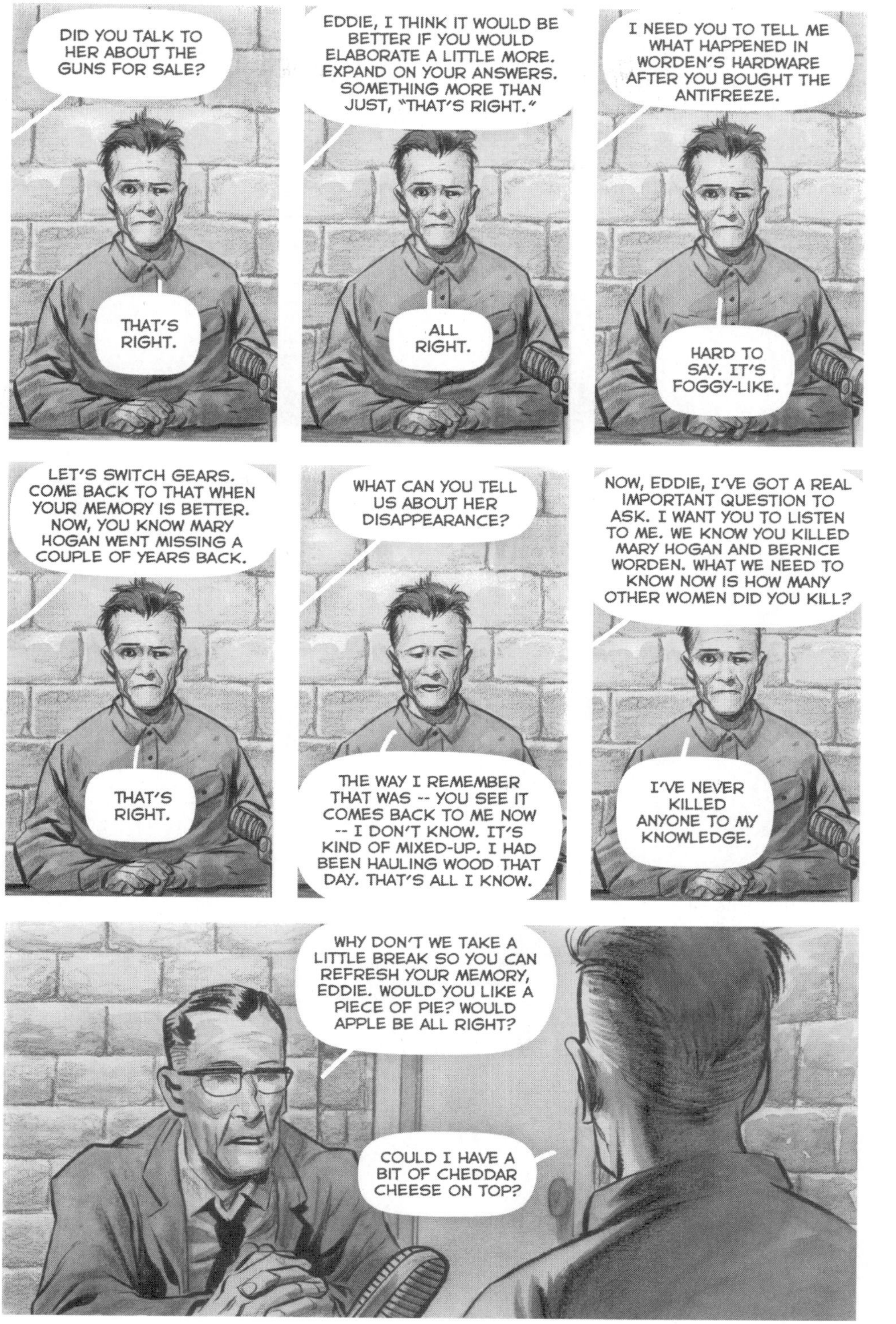
DID YOU TALK TO HER ABOUT THE GUNS FOR SALE?
THAT'S RIGHT.
EDDIE, I THINK IT WOULD BE BETTER IF YOU WOULD ELABORATE A LITTLE MORE. EXPAND ON YOUR ANSWERS. SOMETHING MORE THAN JUST, "THAT'S RIGHT."
ALL RIGHT.
I NEED YOU TO TELL ME WHAT HAPPENED IN WORDEN'S HARDWARE AFTER YOU BOUGHT THE ANTIFREEZE.
HARD TO SAY. IT'S FOGGY-LIKE.
LET'S SWITCH GEARS. COME BACK TO THAT WHEN YOUR MEMORY IS BETTER. NOW, YOU KNOW MARY HOGAN WENT MISSING A COUPLE OF YEARS BACK.
THAT'S RIGHT.
WHAT CAN YOU TELL US ABOUT HER DISAPPEARANCE?
THE WAY I REMEMBER THAT WAS -- YOU SEE IT COMES BACK TO ME NOW -- I DON'T KNOW. IT'S KIND OF MIXED-UP. I HAD BEEN HAULING WOOD THAT DAY. THAT'S ALL I KNOW.
NOW, EDDIE, I'VE GOT A REAL IMPORTANT QUESTION TO ASK. I WANT YOU TO LISTEN TO ME. WE KNOW YOU KILLED MARY HOGAN AND BERNICE WORDEN. WHAT WE NEED TO KNOW NOW IS HOW MANY OTHER WOMEN DID YOU KILL?
I'VE NEVER KILLED ANYONE TO MY KNOWLEDGE.
WHY DON'T WE TAKE A LITTLE BREAK SO YOU CAN REFRESH YOUR MEMORY, EDDIE. WOULD YOU LIKE A PIECE OF PIE? WOULD APPLE BE ALL RIGHT?
COULD I HAVE A BIT OF CHEDDAR CHEESE ON TOP?

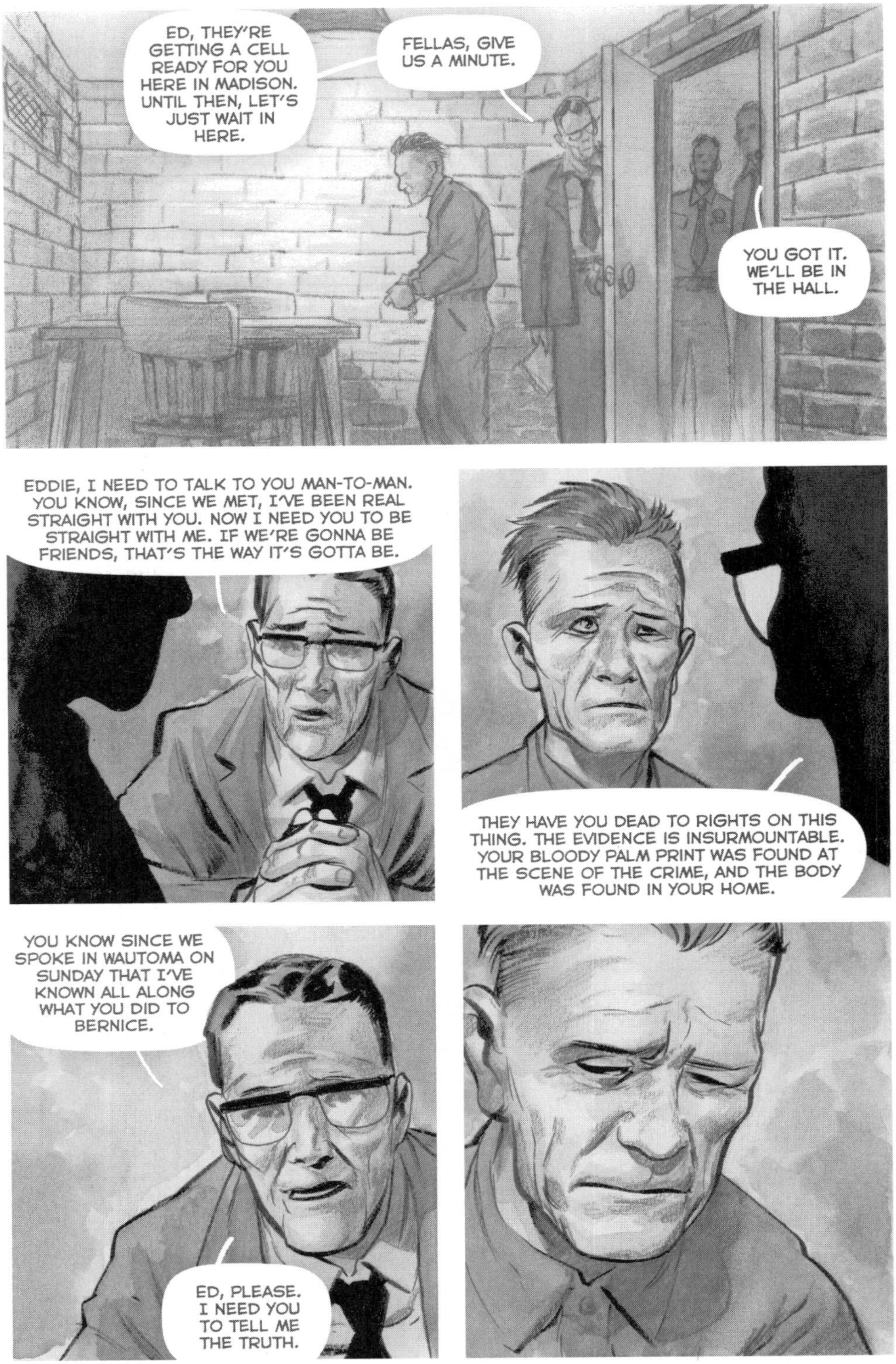
ED, THEY'RE GETTING A CELL READY FOR YOU HERE IN MADISON. UNTIL THEN, LET'S JUST WAIT IN HERE.
FELLAS, GIVE US A MINUTE.
YOU GOT IT. WE'LL BE IN THE HALL.
EDDIE, I NEED TO TALK TO YOU MAN-TO-MAN. YOU KNOW, SINCE WE MET, I'VE BEEN REAL STRAIGHT WITH YOU. NOW I NEED YOU TO BE STRAIGHT WITH ME. IF WE'RE GONNA BE FRIENDS, THAT'S THE WAY IT'S GOTTA BE.
THEY HAVE YOU DEAD TO RIGHTS ON THIS THING. THE EVIDENCE IS INSURMOUNTABLE. YOUR BLOODY PALM PRINT WAS FOUND AT THE SCENE OF THE CRIME, AND THE BODY WAS FOUND IN YOUR HOME.
YOU KNOW SINCE WE SPOKE IN WAUTOMA ON SUNDAY THAT I'VE KNOWN ALL ALONG WHAT YOU DID TO BERNICE.
ED, PLEASE. I NEED YOU TO TELL ME THE TRUTH.

WELL, I GUESS I MUST HAVE SHOT HER.

OFFICER, COULD YOU GET SHERIFF SCHLEY AND SUPERINTENDENT WILSON IN HERE?

AND WE'RE RECORDING AGAIN. OK, ED, WE'LL PICK UP WHERE WE LEFT OFF.

YOU KNOW, NONE OF THE THINGS THAT BROUGHT ME HERE WOULD HAVE HAPPENED HAD MY NEIGHBORS BEEN KINDER TO ME.

IS THAT SO?

THEY'RE DIRTY DEALERS.

ED, LET'S STAY ON POINT.

THIS CHEESE IS DRY.

ED, IT'S VERY IMPORTANT THAT WE KNOW HOW MANY PEOPLE YOU KILLED.

TO MY KNOWLEDGE, I DON'T REMEMBER KILLING ANYONE.

NOW, ED, THAT'S NOT WHAT WE JUST DISCUSSED, REMEMBER? BE STRAIGHT WITH ME. WE KNOW ABOUT MARY AND BERNICE. HOW MANY OTHERS?

IN A WAY, I CAN'T REMEMBER IT. I MIGHT HAVE DONE SOMETHING. THE EVIDENCE POINTS TO IT, BUT IT'S HARD FOR ME TO BELIEVE I DONE IT.

WHAT DOES THE EVIDENCE TELL YOU, ED?

I DON'T SEE HOW, BUT I MUST'VE KILLED BERNICE.

AND WHAT ABOUT THE REST OF THE REMAINS?

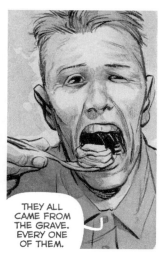

THEY ALL CAME FROM THE GRAVE. EVERY ONE OF THEM.

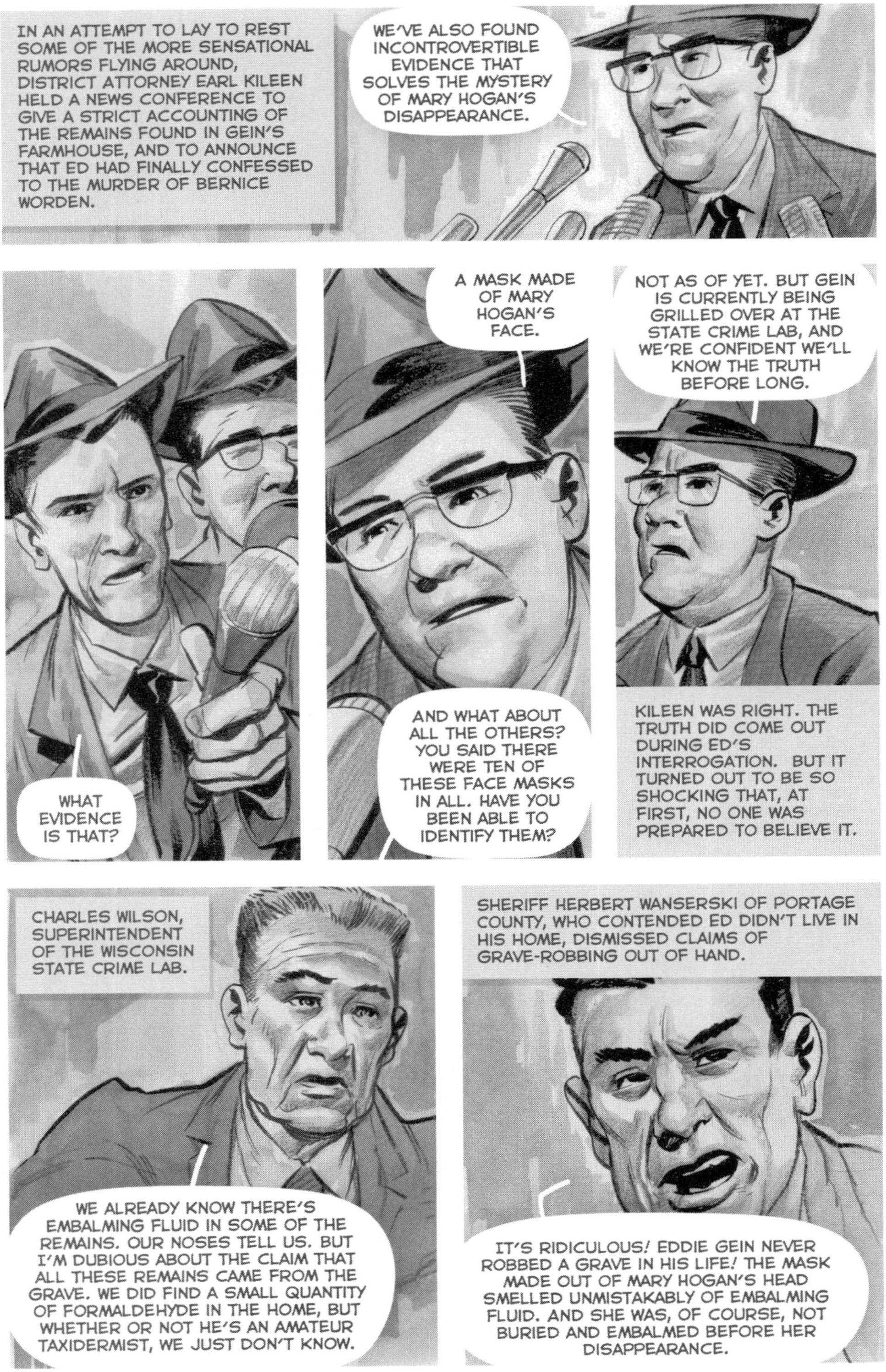
IN AN ATTEMPT TO LAY TO REST SOME OF THE MORE SENSATIONAL RUMORS FLYING AROUND, DISTRICT ATTORNEY EARL KILEEN HELD A NEWS CONFERENCE TO GIVE A STRICT ACCOUNTING OF THE REMAINS FOUND IN GEIN'S FARMHOUSE, AND TO ANNOUNCE THAT ED HAD FINALLY CONFESSED TO THE MURDER OF BERNICE WORDEN.
WE'VE ALSO FOUND INCONTROVERTIBLE EVIDENCE THAT SOLVES THE MYSTERY OF MARY HOGAN'S DISAPPEARANCE.
WHAT EVIDENCE IS THAT?
A MASK MADE OF MARY HOGAN'S FACE.
AND WHAT ABOUT ALL THE OTHERS? YOU SAID THERE WERE TEN OF THESE FACE MASKS IN ALL. HAVE YOU BEEN ABLE TO IDENTIFY THEM?
NOT AS OF YET. BUT GEIN IS CURRENTLY BEING GRILLED OVER AT THE STATE CRIME LAB, AND WE'RE CONFIDENT WE'LL KNOW THE TRUTH BEFORE LONG.
KILEEN WAS RIGHT. THE TRUTH DID COME OUT DURING ED'S INTERROGATION. BUT IT TURNED OUT TO BE SO SHOCKING THAT, AT FIRST, NO ONE WAS PREPARED TO BELIEVE IT.
CHARLES WILSON, SUPERINTENDENT OF THE WISCONSIN STATE CRIME LAB.
WE ALREADY KNOW THERE'S EMBALMING FLUID IN SOME OF THE REMAINS. OUR NOSES TELL US. BUT I'M DUBIOUS ABOUT THE CLAIM THAT ALL THESE REMAINS CAME FROM THE GRAVE. WE DID FIND A SMALL QUANTITY OF FORMALDEHYDE IN THE HOME, BUT WHETHER OR NOT HE'S AN AMATEUR TAXIDERMIST, WE JUST DON'T KNOW.
SHERIFF HERBERT WANSERSKI OF PORTAGE COUNTY, WHO CONTENDED ED DIDN'T LIVE IN HIS HOME, DISMISSED CLAIMS OF GRAVE-ROBBING OUT OF HAND.
IT'S RIDICULOUS! EDDIE GEIN NEVER ROBBED A GRAVE IN HIS LIFE! THE MASK MADE OUT OF MARY HOGAN'S HEAD SMELLED UNMISTAKABLY OF EMBALMING FLUID. AND SHE WAS, OF COURSE, NOT BURIED AND EMBALMED BEFORE HER DISAPPEARANCE.

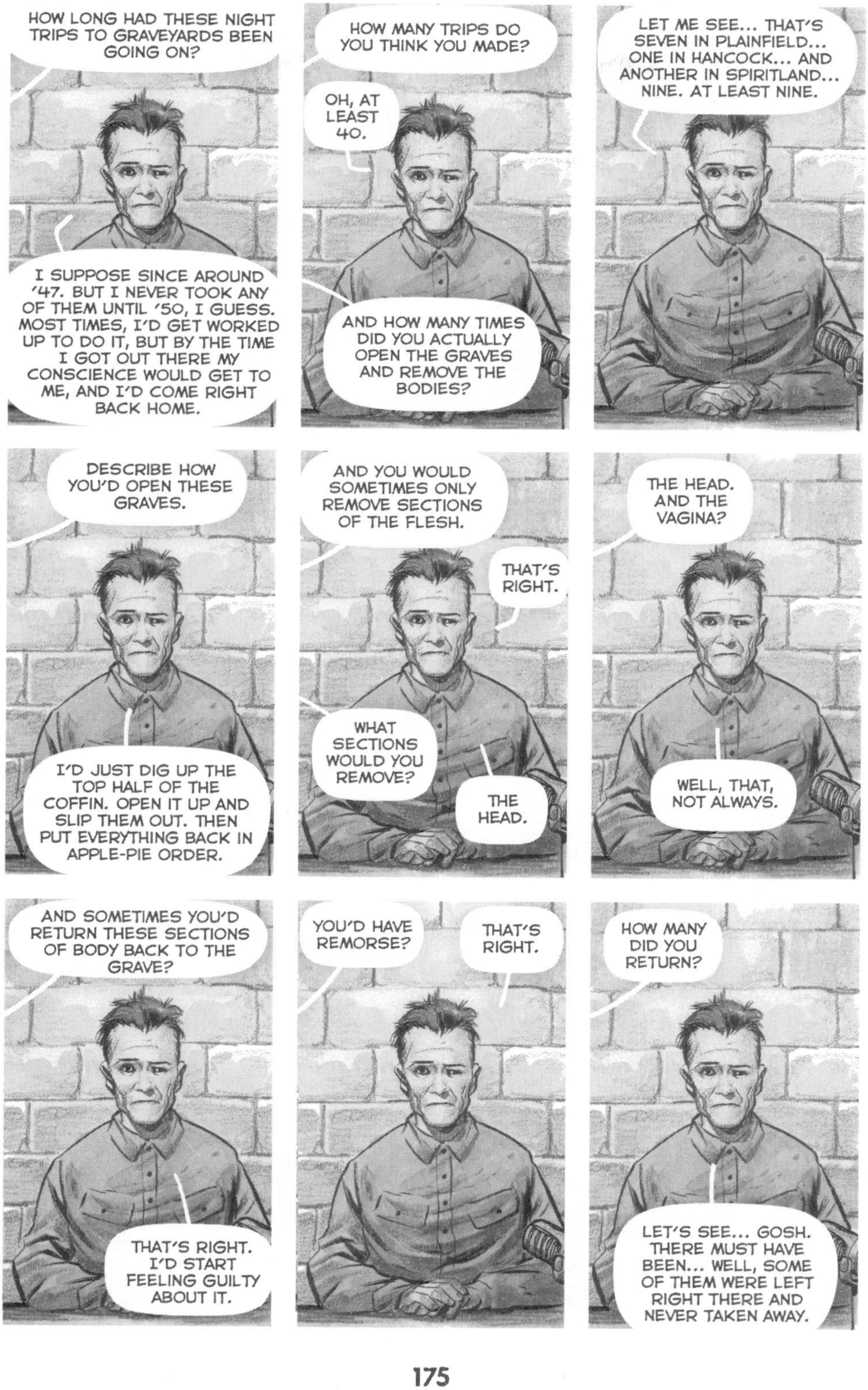
HOW LONG HAD THESE NIGHT TRIPS TO GRAVEYARDS BEEN GOING ON?
I SUPPOSE SINCE AROUND '47. BUT I NEVER TOOK ANY OF THEM UNTIL '50, I GUESS. MOST TIMES, I'D GET WORKED UP TO DO IT, BUT BY THE TIME I GOT OUT THERE MY CONSCIENCE WOULD GET TO ME, AND I'D COME RIGHT BACK HOME.
HOW MANY TRIPS DO YOU THINK YOU MADE?
OH, AT LEAST 40.
AND HOW MANY TIMES DID YOU ACTUALLY OPEN THE GRAVES AND REMOVE THE BODIES?
LET ME SEE... THAT'S SEVEN IN PLAINFIELD... ONE IN HANCOCK... AND ANOTHER IN SPIRITLAND... NINE. AT LEAST NINE.
DESCRIBE HOW YOU'D OPEN THESE GRAVES.
I'D JUST DIG UP THE TOP HALF OF THE COFFIN. OPEN IT UP AND SLIP THEM OUT. THEN PUT EVERYTHING BACK IN APPLE-PIE ORDER.
AND YOU WOULD SOMETIMES ONLY REMOVE SECTIONS OF THE FLESH.
THAT'S RIGHT.
WHAT SECTIONS WOULD YOU REMOVE?
THE HEAD.
THE HEAD. AND THE VAGINA?
WELL, THAT, NOT ALWAYS.
AND SOMETIMES YOU'D RETURN THESE SECTIONS OF BODY BACK TO THE GRAVE?
THAT'S RIGHT. I'D START FEELING GUILTY ABOUT IT.
YOU'D HAVE REMORSE?
THAT'S RIGHT.
HOW MANY DID YOU RETURN?
LET'S SEE... GOSH. THERE MUST HAVE BEEN... WELL, SOME OF THEM WERE LEFT RIGHT THERE AND NEVER TAKEN AWAY.

DO YOU RECALL TAKING ANY OF THOSE FEMALE PARTS, THE VAGINA SPECIFICALLY, AND HOLDING IT OVER YOUR PENIS TO COVER IT?

I BELIEVE THAT'S TRUE.

WOULD YOU EVER PUT ON A PAIR OF WOMEN'S PANTIES OVER YOUR BODY, AND THEN PUT SOME OF THESE VAGINAS OVER YOUR PENIS?

THAT COULD BE.

HAVE YOU EVER WANTED TO REMOVE YOUR PENIS? TO BECOME A WOMAN?

YES, THAT DID COME INTO MY MIND WHEN I WAS YOUNGER.

AND THESE MASKS THAT YOU MADE, HOW LONG WOULD YOU WEAR THEM?

OH, NOT LONG. MAYBE AN HOUR. I HAD OTHER THINGS TO DO.

AND WEARING THESE SCALPS AND VAGINAS, DID IT GIVE YOU SOME FORM OF SEXUAL GRATIFICATION?

I WILL ADMIT TO FEELING THAT.

AND THESE WOMEN THAT YOU CHOSE, THEY WERE ELDERLY WOMEN? MANY OF THEM YOU KNEW?

YES.

WOULD YOU SAY THEY RESEMBLED YOUR MOTHER?

I BELIEVE THAT'S TRUE.

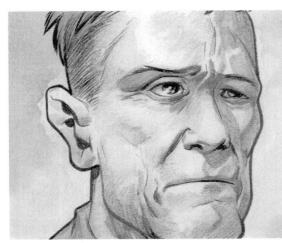

DO YOU THINK YOU WERE WEARING THESE MASKS AND OTHER PARTS OF THESE WOMEN TO REMEMBER YOUR MOTHER? THAT YOU WANTED TO BE YOUR MOTHER?

THAT COULD BE.

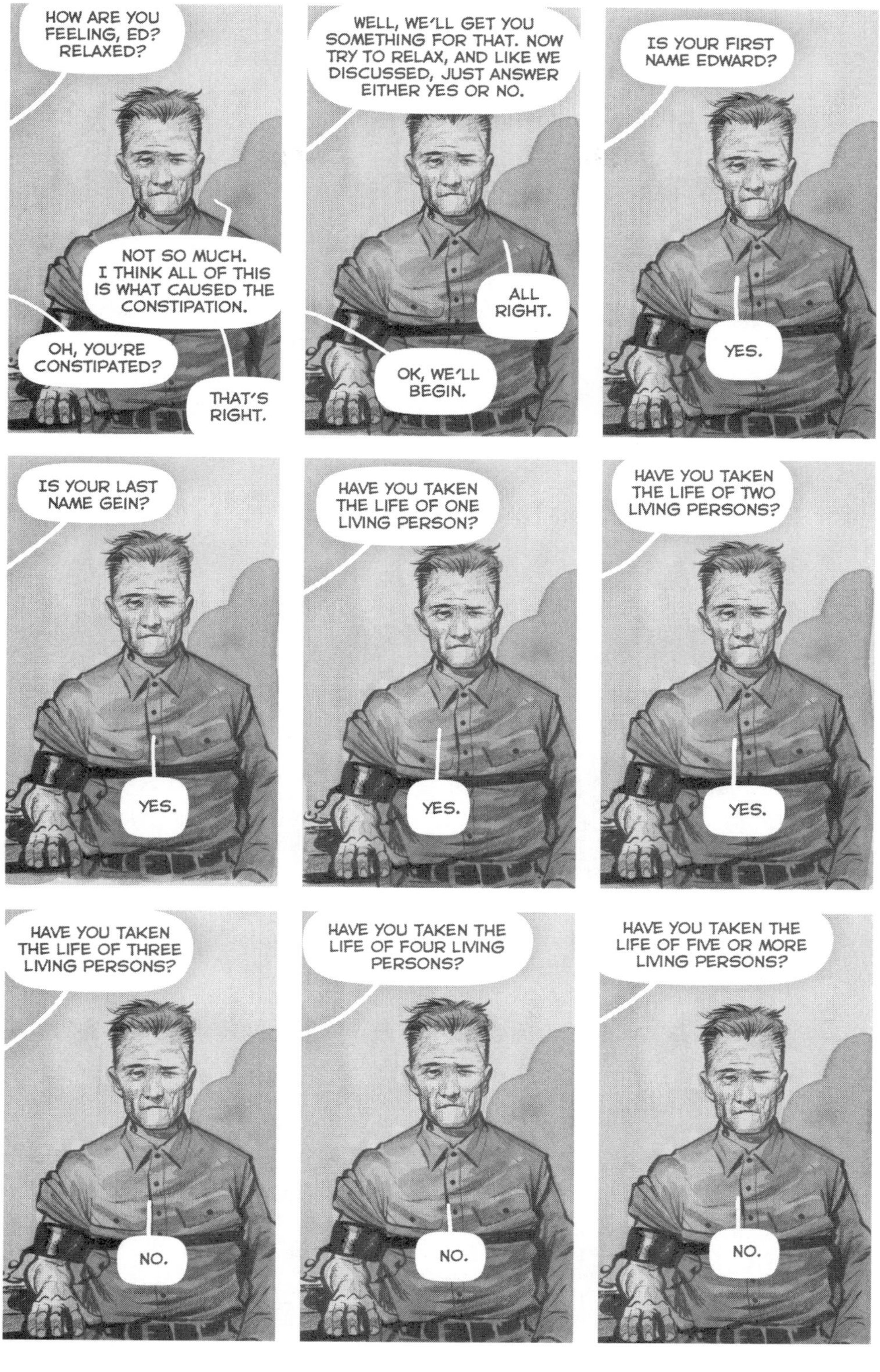
HOW ARE YOU FEELING, ED? RELAXED?
NOT SO MUCH. I THINK ALL OF THIS IS WHAT CAUSED THE CONSTIPATION.
OH, YOU'RE CONSTIPATED?
THAT'S RIGHT.
WELL, WE'LL GET YOU SOMETHING FOR THAT. NOW TRY TO RELAX, AND LIKE WE DISCUSSED, JUST ANSWER EITHER YES OR NO.
ALL RIGHT.
OK, WE'LL BEGIN.
IS YOUR FIRST NAME EDWARD?
YES.
IS YOUR LAST NAME GEIN?
YES.
HAVE YOU TAKEN THE LIFE OF ONE LIVING PERSON?
YES.
HAVE YOU TAKEN THE LIFE OF TWO LIVING PERSONS?
YES.
HAVE YOU TAKEN THE LIFE OF THREE LIVING PERSONS?
NO.
HAVE YOU TAKEN THE LIFE OF FOUR LIVING PERSONS?
NO.
HAVE YOU TAKEN THE LIFE OF FIVE OR MORE LIVING PERSONS?
NO.

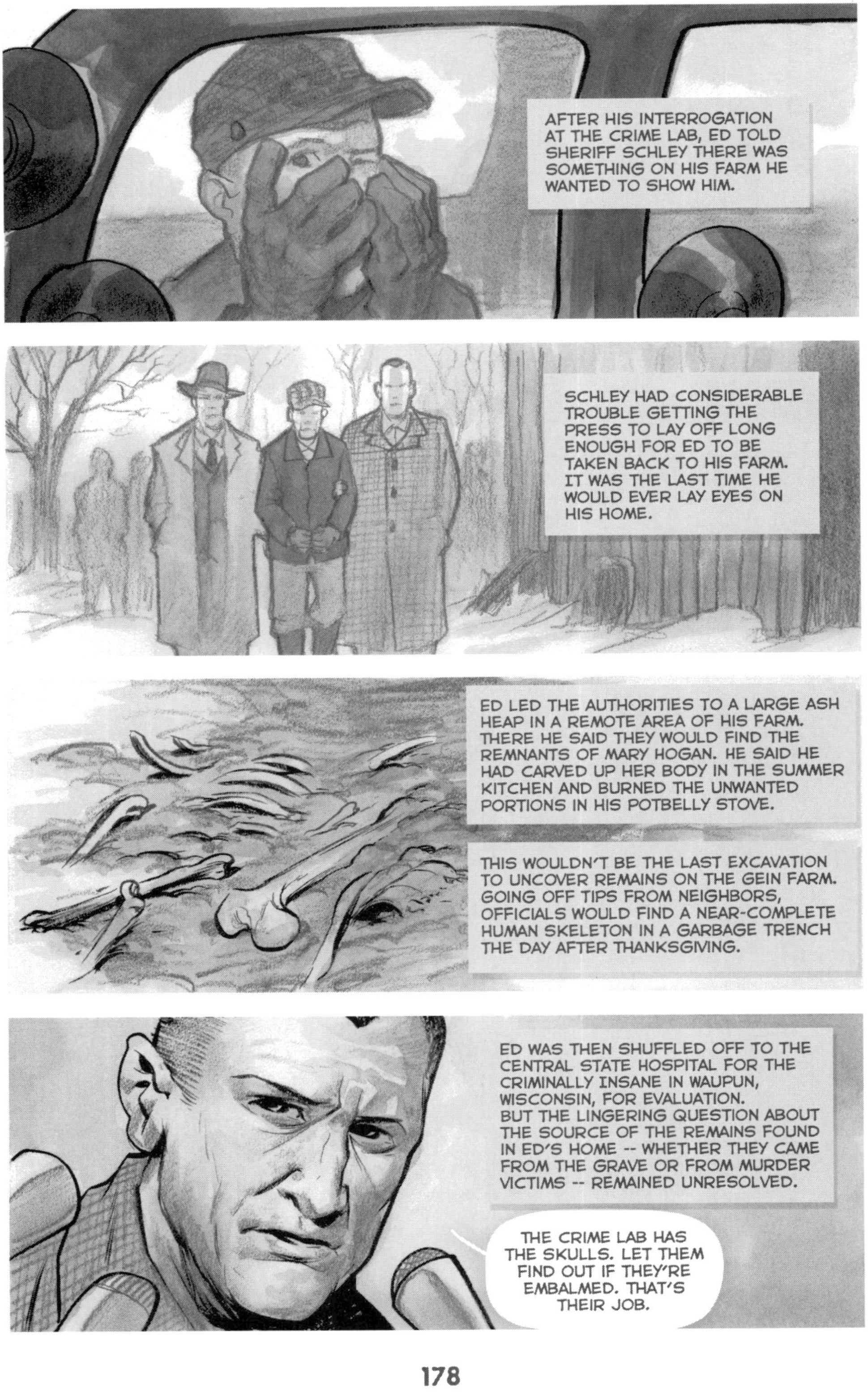
AFTER HIS INTERROGATION AT THE CRIME LAB, ED TOLD SHERIFF SCHLEY THERE WAS SOMETHING ON HIS FARM HE WANTED TO SHOW HIM.
SCHLEY HAD CONSIDERABLE TROUBLE GETTING THE PRESS TO LAY OFF LONG ENOUGH FOR ED TO BE TAKEN BACK TO HIS FARM. IT WAS THE LAST TIME HE WOULD EVER LAY EYES ON HIS HOME.
ED LED THE AUTHORITIES TO A LARGE ASH HEAP IN A REMOTE AREA OF HIS FARM. THERE HE SAID THEY WOULD FIND THE REMNANTS OF MARY HOGAN. HE SAID HE HAD CARVED UP HER BODY IN THE SUMMER KITCHEN AND BURNED THE UNWANTED PORTIONS IN HIS POTBELLY STOVE.
THIS WOULDN'T BE THE LAST EXCAVATION TO UNCOVER REMAINS ON THE GEIN FARM. GOING OFF TIPS FROM NEIGHBORS, OFFICIALS WOULD FIND A NEAR-COMPLETE HUMAN SKELETON IN A GARBAGE TRENCH THE DAY AFTER THANKSGIVING.
ED WAS THEN SHUFFLED OFF TO THE CENTRAL STATE HOSPITAL FOR THE CRIMINALLY INSANE IN WAUPUN, WISCONSIN, FOR EVALUATION. BUT THE LINGERING QUESTION ABOUT THE SOURCE OF THE REMAINS FOUND IN ED'S HOME -- WHETHER THEY CAME FROM THE GRAVE OR FROM MURDER VICTIMS -- REMAINED UNRESOLVED.
THE CRIME LAB HAS THE SKULLS. LET THEM FIND OUT IF THEY'RE EMBALMED. THAT'S THEIR JOB.

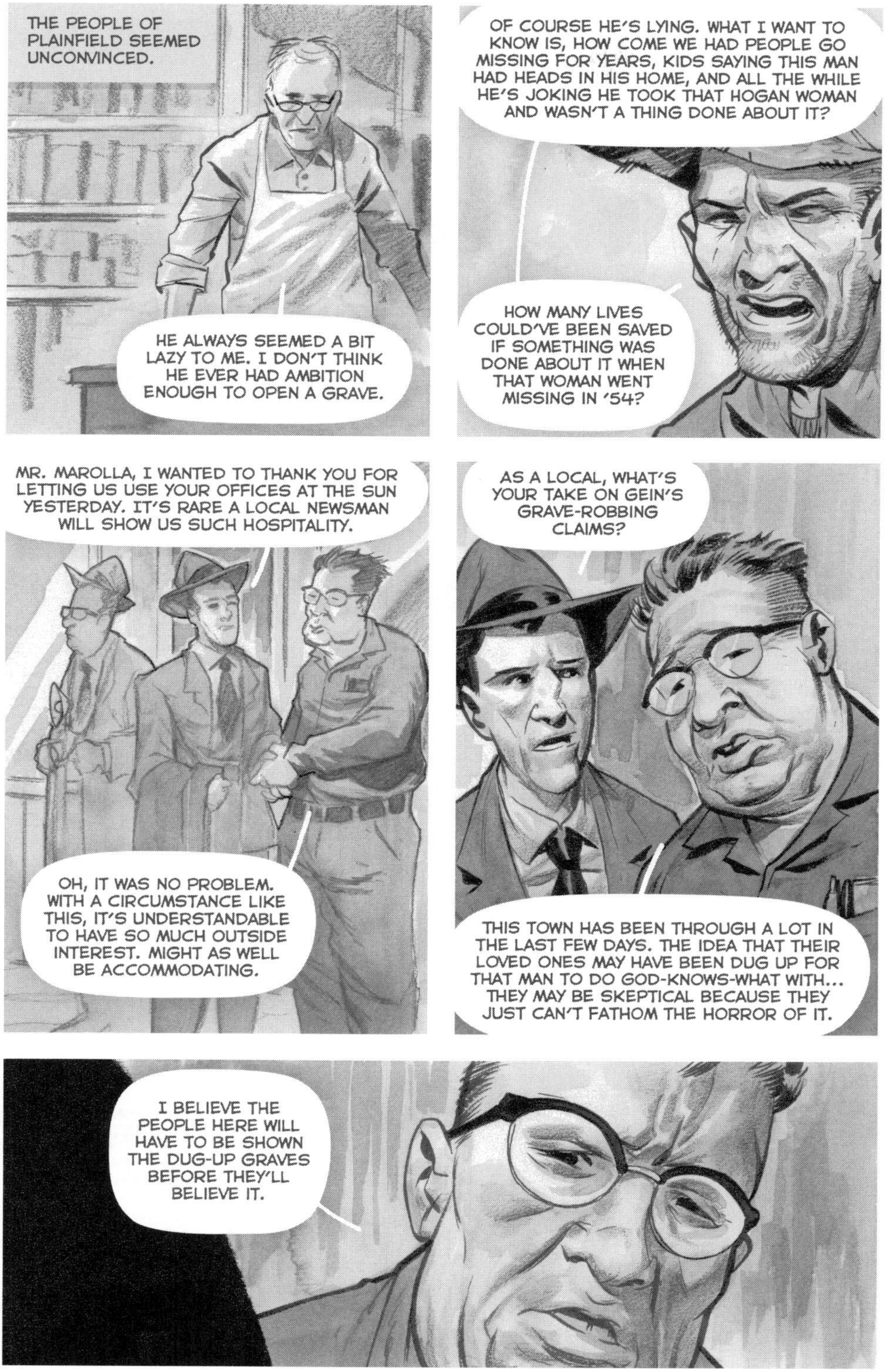
THE PEOPLE OF PLAINFIELD SEEMED UNCONVINCED.
HE ALWAYS SEEMED A BIT LAZY TO ME. I DON'T THINK HE EVER HAD AMBITION ENOUGH TO OPEN A GRAVE.
OF COURSE HE'S LYING. WHAT I WANT TO KNOW IS, HOW COME WE HAD PEOPLE GO MISSING FOR YEARS, KIDS SAYING THIS MAN HAD HEADS IN HIS HOME, AND ALL THE WHILE HE'S JOKING HE TOOK THAT HOGAN WOMAN AND WASN'T A THING DONE ABOUT IT?
HOW MANY LIVES COULD'VE BEEN SAVED IF SOMETHING WAS DONE ABOUT IT WHEN THAT WOMAN WENT MISSING IN '54?
MR. MAROLLA, I WANTED TO THANK YOU FOR LETTING US USE YOUR OFFICES AT THE SUN YESTERDAY. IT'S RARE A LOCAL NEWSMAN WILL SHOW US SUCH HOSPITALITY.
OH, IT WAS NO PROBLEM. WITH A CIRCUMSTANCE LIKE THIS, IT'S UNDERSTANDABLE TO HAVE SO MUCH OUTSIDE INTEREST. MIGHT AS WELL BE ACCOMMODATING.
AS A LOCAL, WHAT'S YOUR TAKE ON GEIN'S GRAVE-ROBBING CLAIMS?
THIS TOWN HAS BEEN THROUGH A LOT IN THE LAST FEW DAYS. THE IDEA THAT THEIR LOVED ONES MAY HAVE BEEN DUG UP FOR THAT MAN TO DO GOD-KNOWS-WHAT WITH... THEY MAY BE SKEPTICAL BECAUSE THEY JUST CAN'T FATHOM THE HORROR OF IT.
I BELIEVE THE PEOPLE HERE WILL HAVE TO BE SHOWN THE DUG-UP GRAVES BEFORE THEY'LL BELIEVE IT.

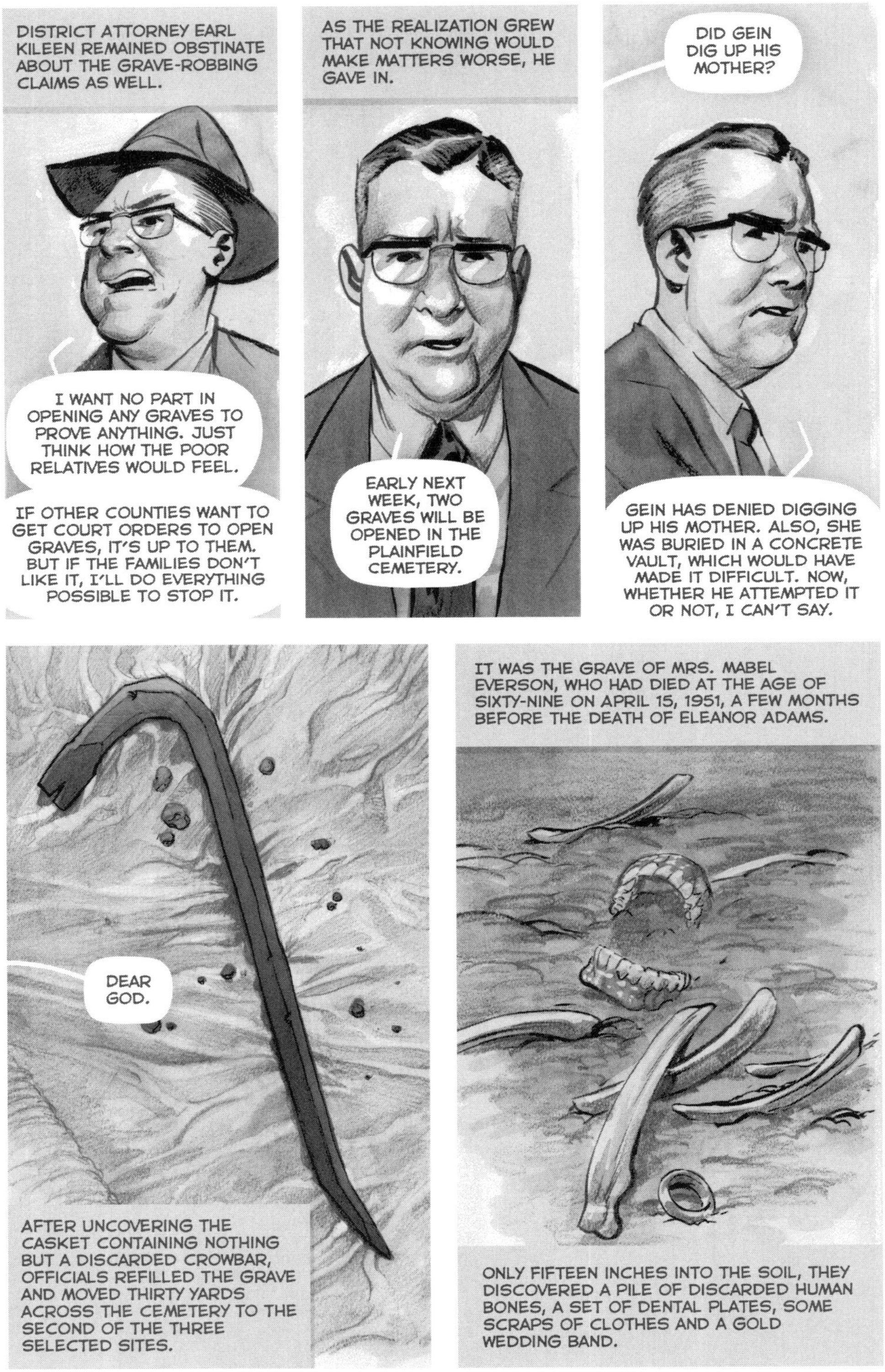
DISTRICT ATTORNEY EARL KILEEN REMAINED OBSTINATE ABOUT THE GRAVE-ROBBING CLAIMS AS WELL.
I WANT NO PART IN OPENING ANY GRAVES TO PROVE ANYTHING. JUST THINK HOW THE POOR RELATIVES WOULD FEEL.
IF OTHER COUNTIES WANT TO GET COURT ORDERS TO OPEN GRAVES, IT'S UP TO THEM. BUT IF THE FAMILIES DON'T LIKE IT, I'LL DO EVERYTHING POSSIBLE TO STOP IT.
AS THE REALIZATION GREW THAT NOT KNOWING WOULD MAKE MATTERS WORSE, HE GAVE IN.
EARLY NEXT WEEK, TWO GRAVES WILL BE OPENED IN THE PLAINFIELD CEMETERY.
DID GEIN DIG UP HIS MOTHER?
GEIN HAS DENIED DIGGING UP HIS MOTHER. ALSO, SHE WAS BURIED IN A CONCRETE VAULT, WHICH WOULD HAVE MADE IT DIFFICULT. NOW, WHETHER HE ATTEMPTED IT OR NOT, I CAN'T SAY.
DEAR GOD.
AFTER UNCOVERING THE CASKET CONTAINING NOTHING BUT A DISCARDED CROWBAR, OFFICIALS REFILLED THE GRAVE AND MOVED THIRTY YARDS ACROSS THE CEMETERY TO THE SECOND OF THE THREE SELECTED SITES.
IT WAS THE GRAVE OF MRS. MABEL EVERSON, WHO HAD DIED AT THE AGE OF SIXTY-NINE ON APRIL 15, 1951, A FEW MONTHS BEFORE THE DEATH OF ELEANOR ADAMS.
ONLY FIFTEEN INCHES INTO THE SOIL, THEY DISCOVERED A PILE OF DISCARDED HUMAN BONES, A SET OF DENTAL PLATES, SOME SCRAPS OF CLOTHES AND A GOLD WEDDING BAND.

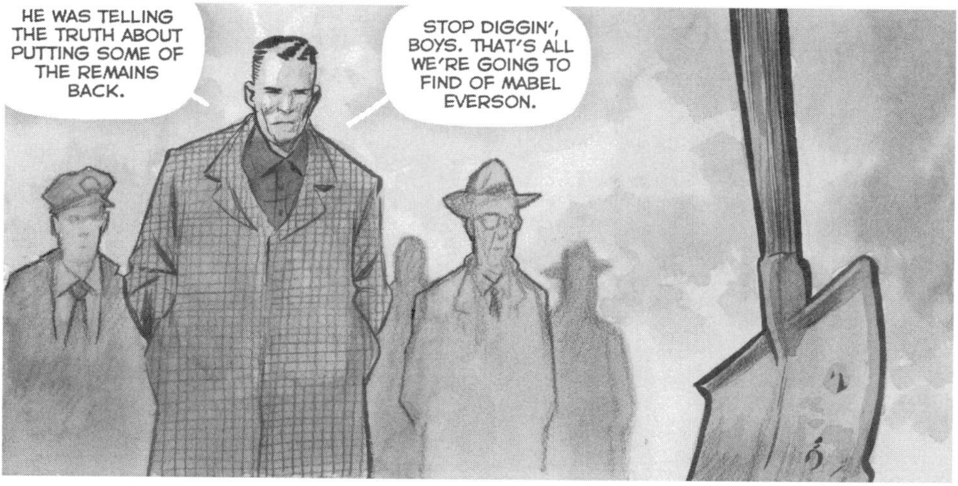
HE WAS TELLING THE TRUTH ABOUT PUTTING SOME OF THE REMAINS BACK.
STOP DIGGIN', BOYS. THAT'S ALL WE'RE GOING TO FIND OF MABEL EVERSON.

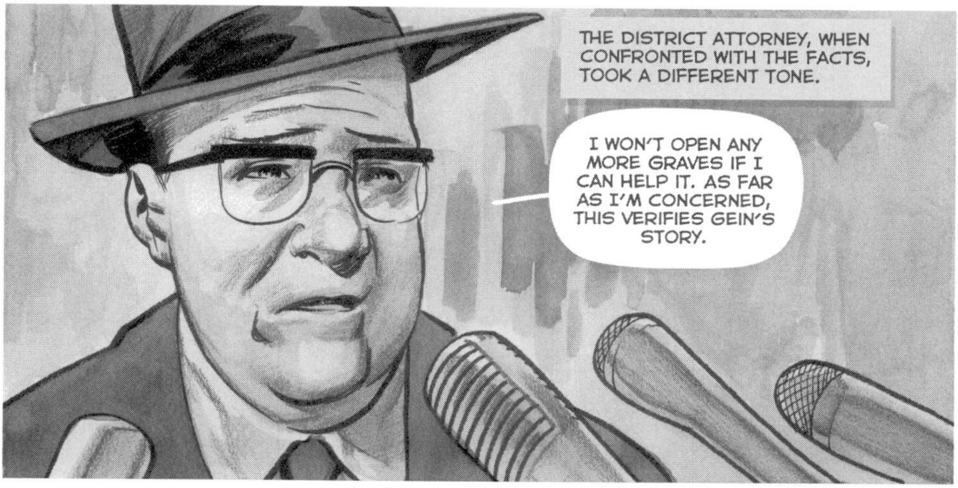
THE DISTRICT ATTORNEY, WHEN CONFRONTED WITH THE FACTS, TOOK A DIFFERENT TONE.
I WON'T OPEN ANY MORE GRAVES IF I CAN HELP IT. AS FAR AS I'M CONCERNED, THIS VERIFIES GEIN'S STORY.

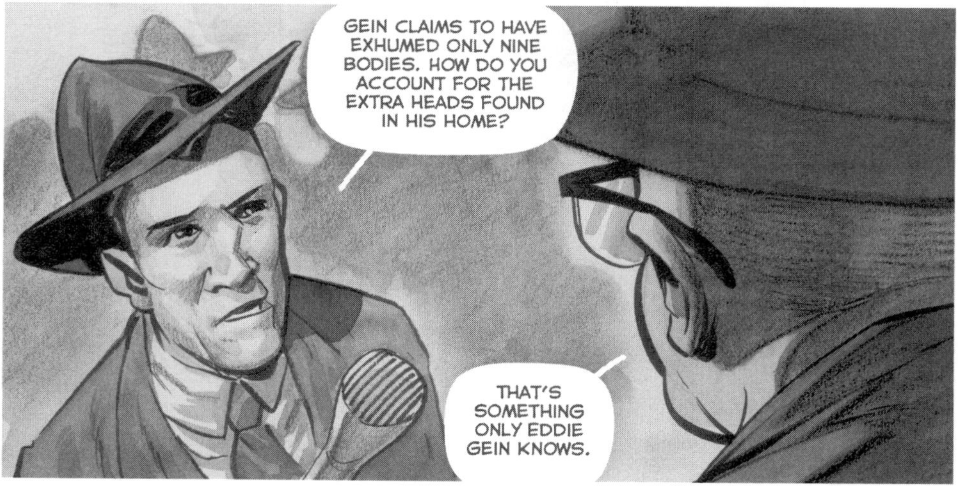
GEIN CLAIMS TO HAVE EXHUMED ONLY NINE BODIES. HOW DO YOU ACCOUNT FOR THE EXTRA HEADS FOUND IN HIS HOME?
THAT'S SOMETHING ONLY EDDIE GEIN KNOWS.

CENTRAL STATE HOSPITAL FOR THE CRIMINALLY INSANE. WAUPUN, WISCONSIN. NOVEMBER 25, 1957.

I'M GOING TO SHOW YOU SOME PICTURES. YOU TELL ME WHAT YOU THINK IS GOING ON IN THEM.

OH, EVEN GHOSTS?

UH, SURE.

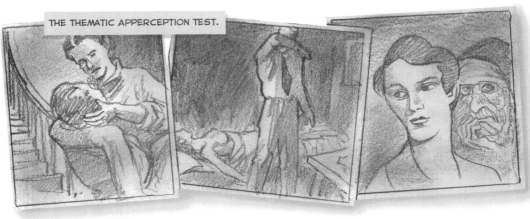

THE THEMATIC APPERCEPTION TEST.

WELL, I'D SAY THAT'S A WOMAN, A MOTHER, I GUESS, ABOUT TO KISS HER SON.

LOOKS TO ME LIKE THERE'S A WOMAN LYING DEAD IN HER BED AND SOME MAN, HER HUSBAND MAYBE, OR HER SON, IS CRYING, MAYBE BECAUSE HE FEELS BAD ABOUT KILLING HER.

THAT'S AN OLD LADY WHISPERING SOMETHING TO HER SON, MAYBE WARNING HIM ABOUT BAD PEOPLE.

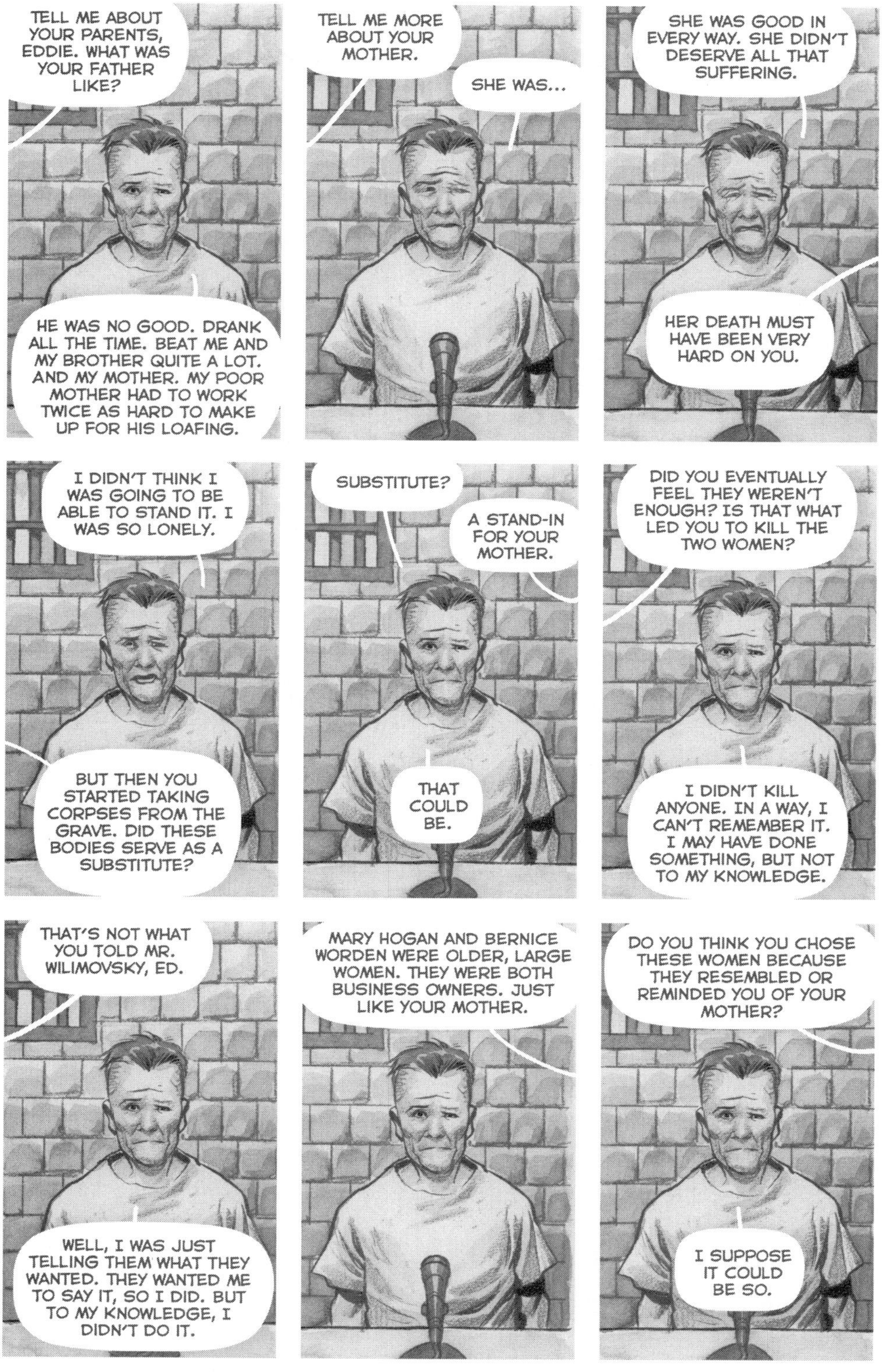
TELL ME ABOUT YOUR PARENTS, EDDIE. WHAT WAS YOUR FATHER LIKE?
HE WAS NO GOOD. DRANK ALL THE TIME. BEAT ME AND MY BROTHER QUITE A LOT. AND MY MOTHER. MY POOR MOTHER HAD TO WORK TWICE AS HARD TO MAKE UP FOR HIS LOAFING.
TELL ME MORE ABOUT YOUR MOTHER.
SHE WAS...
SHE WAS GOOD IN EVERY WAY. SHE DIDN'T DESERVE ALL THAT SUFFERING.
HER DEATH MUST HAVE BEEN VERY HARD ON YOU.
I DIDN'T THINK I WAS GOING TO BE ABLE TO STAND IT. I WAS SO LONELY.
BUT THEN YOU STARTED TAKING CORPSES FROM THE GRAVE. DID THESE BODIES SERVE AS A SUBSTITUTE?
SUBSTITUTE?
A STAND-IN FOR YOUR MOTHER.
THAT COULD BE.
DID YOU EVENTUALLY FEEL THEY WEREN'T ENOUGH? IS THAT WHAT LED YOU TO KILL THE TWO WOMEN?
I DIDN'T KILL ANYONE. IN A WAY, I CAN'T REMEMBER IT. I MAY HAVE DONE SOMETHING, BUT NOT TO MY KNOWLEDGE.
THAT'S NOT WHAT YOU TOLD MR. WILIMOVSKY, ED.
WELL, I WAS JUST TELLING THEM WHAT THEY WANTED. THEY WANTED ME TO SAY IT, SO I DID. BUT TO MY KNOWLEDGE, I DIDN'T DO IT.
MARY HOGAN AND BERNICE WORDEN WERE OLDER, LARGE WOMEN. THEY WERE BOTH BUSINESS OWNERS. JUST LIKE YOUR MOTHER.
DO YOU THINK YOU CHOSE THESE WOMEN BECAUSE THEY RESEMBLED OR REMINDED YOU OF YOUR MOTHER?
I SUPPOSE IT COULD BE SO.

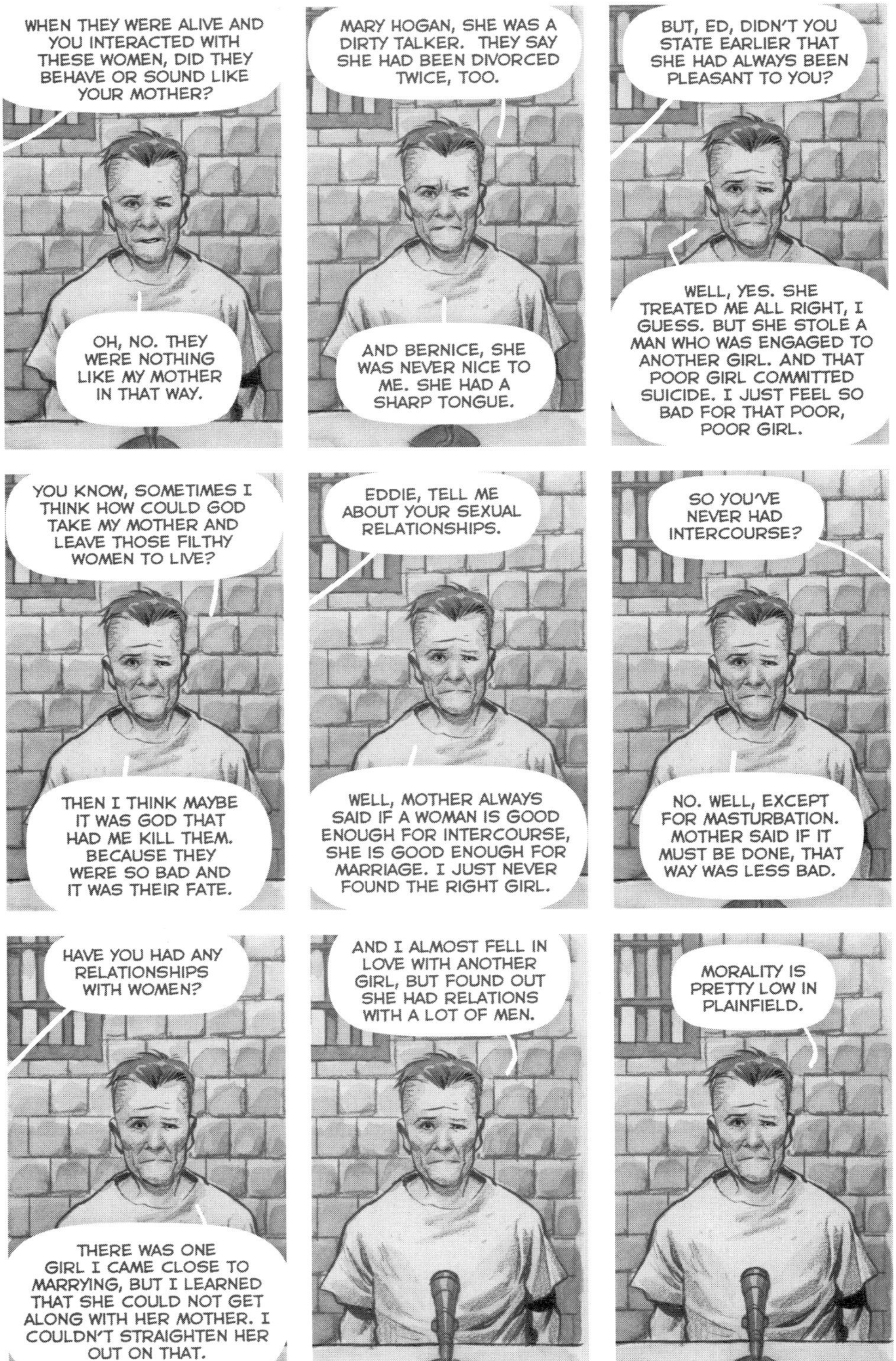
WHEN THEY WERE ALIVE AND YOU INTERACTED WITH THESE WOMEN, DID THEY BEHAVE OR SOUND LIKE YOUR MOTHER?
OH, NO. THEY WERE NOTHING LIKE MY MOTHER IN THAT WAY.
MARY HOGAN, SHE WAS A DIRTY TALKER. THEY SAY SHE HAD BEEN DIVORCED TWICE, TOO.
AND BERNICE, SHE WAS NEVER NICE TO ME. SHE HAD A SHARP TONGUE.
BUT, ED, DIDN'T YOU STATE EARLIER THAT SHE HAD ALWAYS BEEN PLEASANT TO YOU?
WELL, YES. SHE TREATED ME ALL RIGHT, I GUESS. BUT SHE STOLE A MAN WHO WAS ENGAGED TO ANOTHER GIRL. AND THAT POOR GIRL COMMITTED SUICIDE. I JUST FEEL SO BAD FOR THAT POOR, POOR GIRL.
YOU KNOW, SOMETIMES I THINK HOW COULD GOD TAKE MY MOTHER AND LEAVE THOSE FILTHY WOMEN TO LIVE?
THEN I THINK MAYBE IT WAS GOD THAT HAD ME KILL THEM. BECAUSE THEY WERE SO BAD AND IT WAS THEIR FATE.
EDDIE, TELL ME ABOUT YOUR SEXUAL RELATIONSHIPS.
WELL, MOTHER ALWAYS SAID IF A WOMAN IS GOOD ENOUGH FOR INTERCOURSE, SHE IS GOOD ENOUGH FOR MARRIAGE. I JUST NEVER FOUND THE RIGHT GIRL.
SO YOU'VE NEVER HAD INTERCOURSE?
NO. WELL, EXCEPT FOR MASTURBATION. MOTHER SAID IF IT MUST BE DONE, THAT WAY WAS LESS BAD.
HAVE YOU HAD ANY RELATIONSHIPS WITH WOMEN?
THERE WAS ONE GIRL I CAME CLOSE TO MARRYING, BUT I LEARNED THAT SHE COULD NOT GET ALONG WITH HER MOTHER. I COULDN'T STRAIGHTEN HER OUT ON THAT.
AND I ALMOST FELL IN LOVE WITH ANOTHER GIRL, BUT FOUND OUT SHE HAD RELATIONS WITH A LOT OF MEN.
MORALITY IS PRETTY LOW IN PLAINFIELD.

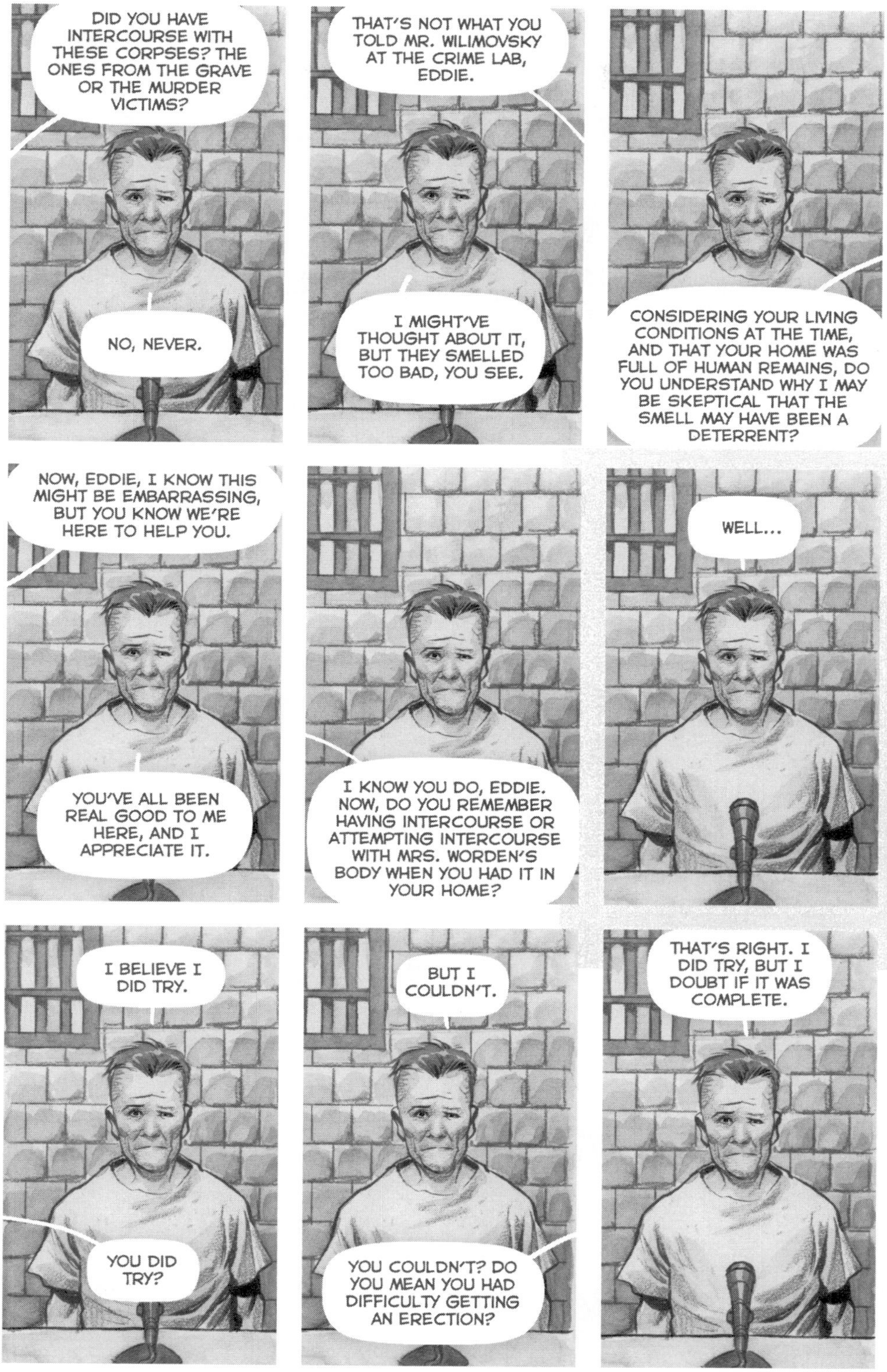
DID YOU HAVE INTERCOURSE WITH THESE CORPSES? THE ONES FROM THE GRAVE OR THE MURDER VICTIMS?
NO, NEVER.
THAT'S NOT WHAT YOU TOLD MR. WILIMOVSKY AT THE CRIME LAB, EDDIE.
I MIGHT'VE THOUGHT ABOUT IT, BUT THEY SMELLED TOO BAD, YOU SEE.
CONSIDERING YOUR LIVING CONDITIONS AT THE TIME, AND THAT YOUR HOME WAS FULL OF HUMAN REMAINS, DO YOU UNDERSTAND WHY I MAY BE SKEPTICAL THAT THE SMELL MAY HAVE BEEN A DETERRENT?
NOW, EDDIE, I KNOW THIS MIGHT BE EMBARRASSING, BUT YOU KNOW WE'RE HERE TO HELP YOU.
YOU'VE ALL BEEN REAL GOOD TO ME HERE, AND I APPRECIATE IT.
I KNOW YOU DO, EDDIE. NOW, DO YOU REMEMBER HAVING INTERCOURSE OR ATTEMPTING INTERCOURSE WITH MRS. WORDEN'S BODY WHEN YOU HAD IT IN YOUR HOME?
WELL...
I BELIEVE I DID TRY.
YOU DID TRY?
BUT I COULDN'T.
YOU COULDN'T? DO YOU MEAN YOU HAD DIFFICULTY GETTING AN ERECTION?
THAT'S RIGHT. I DID TRY, BUT I DOUBT IF IT WAS COMPLETE.

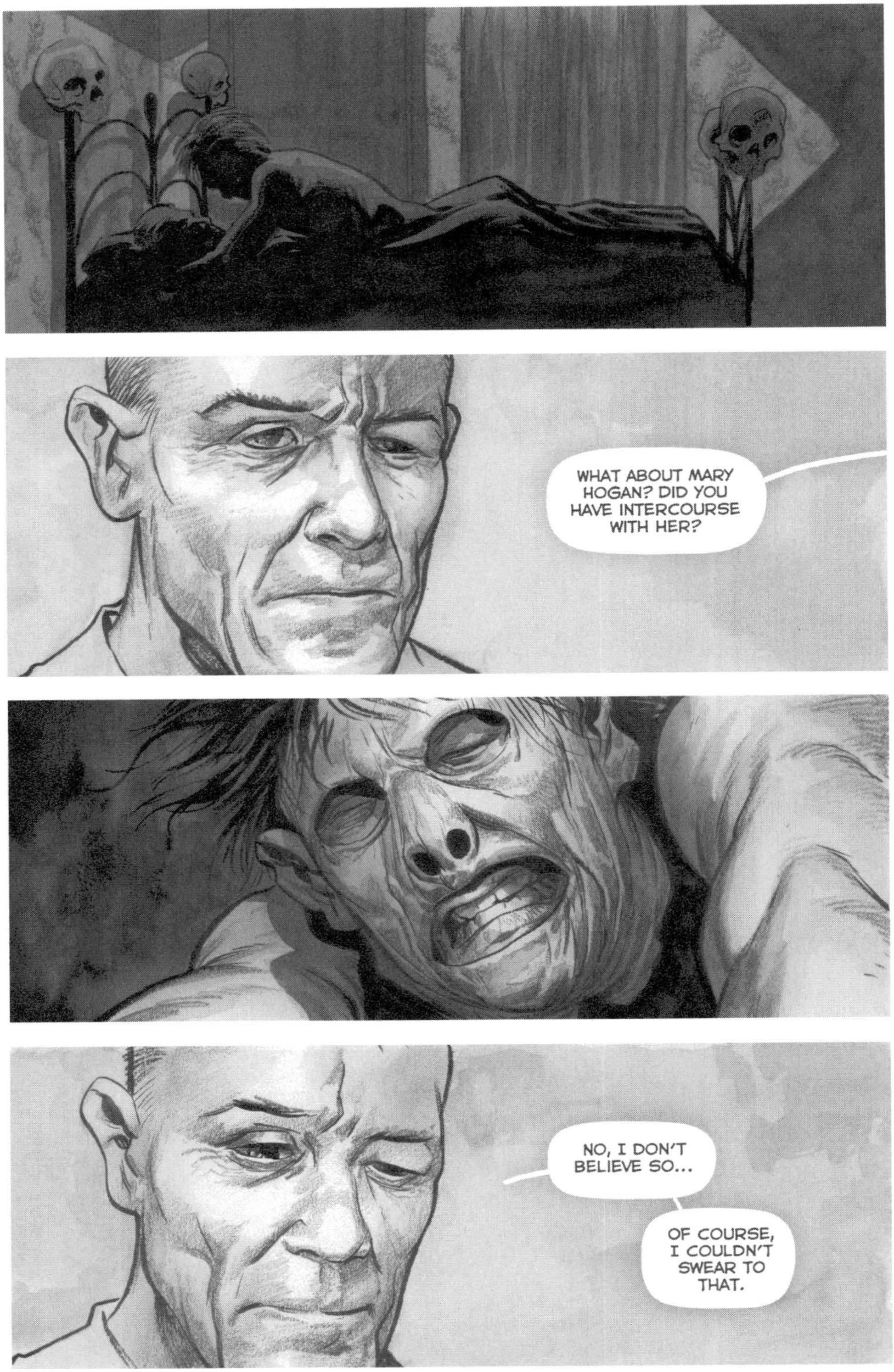
WHAT ABOUT MARY HOGAN? DID YOU HAVE INTERCOURSE WITH HER?
NO, I DON'T BELIEVE SO...
OF COURSE, I COULDN'T SWEAR TO THAT.

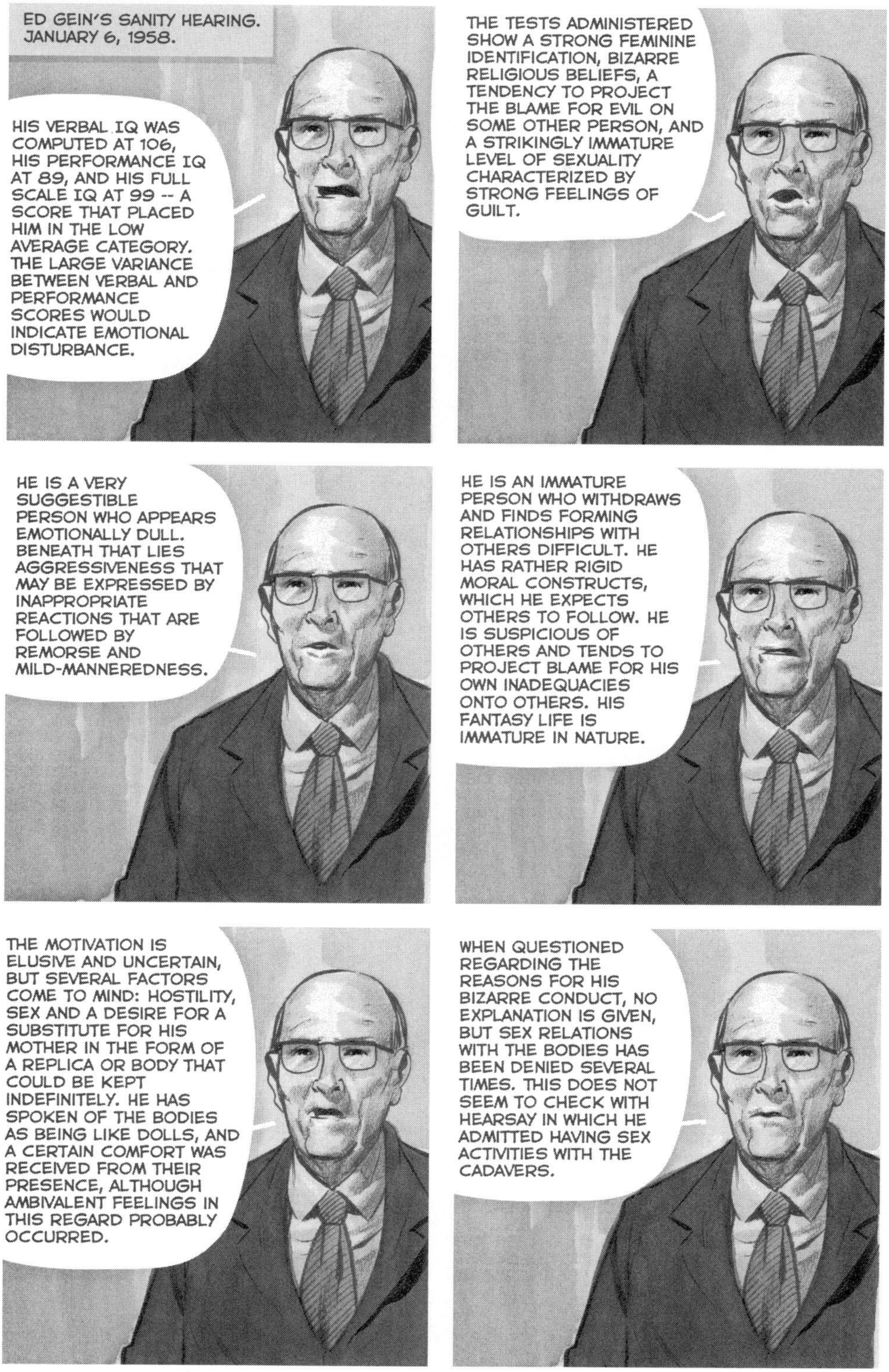
ED GEIN'S SANITY HEARING. JANUARY 6, 1958.
HIS VERBAL IQ WAS COMPUTED AT 106, HIS PERFORMANCE IQ AT 89, AND HIS FULL SCALE IQ AT 99 -- A SCORE THAT PLACED HIM IN THE LOW AVERAGE CATEGORY. THE LARGE VARIANCE BETWEEN VERBAL AND PERFORMANCE SCORES WOULD INDICATE EMOTIONAL DISTURBANCE.
THE TESTS ADMINISTERED SHOW A STRONG FEMININE IDENTIFICATION, BIZARRE RELIGIOUS BELIEFS, A TENDENCY TO PROJECT THE BLAME FOR EVIL ON SOME OTHER PERSON, AND A STRIKINGLY IMMATURE LEVEL OF SEXUALITY CHARACTERIZED BY STRONG FEELINGS OF GUILT.
HE IS A VERY SUGGESTIBLE PERSON WHO APPEARS EMOTIONALLY DULL. BENEATH THAT LIES AGGRESSIVENESS THAT MAY BE EXPRESSED BY INAPPROPRIATE REACTIONS THAT ARE FOLLOWED BY REMORSE AND MILD-MANNEREDNESS.
HE IS AN IMMATURE PERSON WHO WITHDRAWS AND FINDS FORMING RELATIONSHIPS WITH OTHERS DIFFICULT. HE HAS RATHER RIGID MORAL CONSTRUCTS, WHICH HE EXPECTS OTHERS TO FOLLOW. HE IS SUSPICIOUS OF OTHERS AND TENDS TO PROJECT BLAME FOR HIS OWN INADEQUACIES ONTO OTHERS. HIS FANTASY LIFE IS IMMATURE IN NATURE.
THE MOTIVATION IS ELUSIVE AND UNCERTAIN, BUT SEVERAL FACTORS COME TO MIND: HOSTILITY, SEX AND A DESIRE FOR A SUBSTITUTE FOR HIS MOTHER IN THE FORM OF A REPLICA OR BODY THAT COULD BE KEPT INDEFINITELY. HE HAS SPOKEN OF THE BODIES AS BEING LIKE DOLLS, AND A CERTAIN COMFORT WAS RECEIVED FROM THEIR PRESENCE, ALTHOUGH AMBIVALENT FEELINGS IN THIS REGARD PROBABLY OCCURRED.
WHEN QUESTIONED REGARDING THE REASONS FOR HIS BIZARRE CONDUCT, NO EXPLANATION IS GIVEN, BUT SEX RELATIONS WITH THE BODIES HAS BEEN DENIED SEVERAL TIMES. THIS DOES NOT SEEM TO CHECK WITH HEARSAY IN WHICH HE ADMITTED HAVING SEX ACTIVITIES WITH THE CADAVERS.

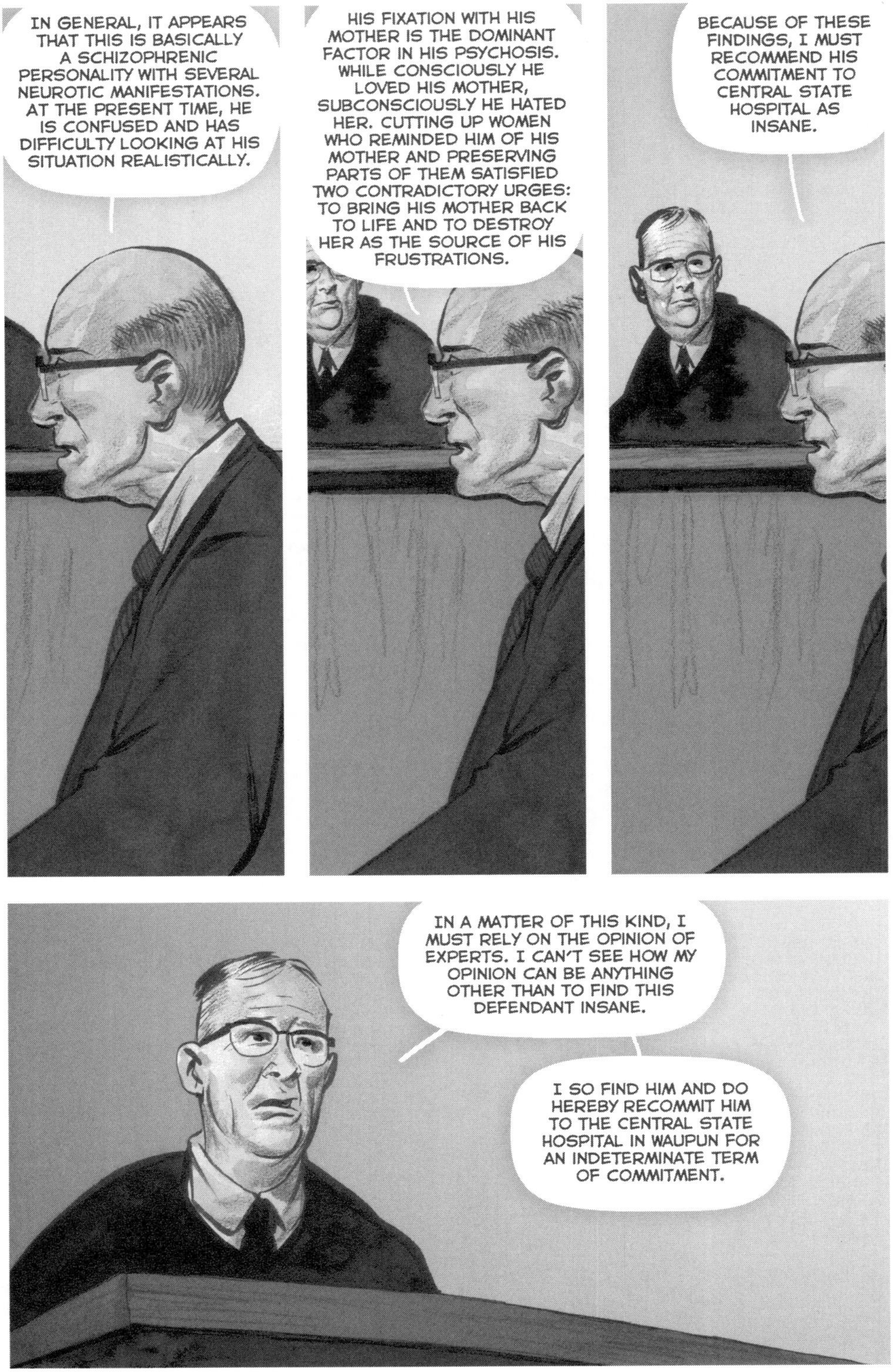
IN GENERAL, IT APPEARS THAT THIS IS BASICALLY A SCHIZOPHRENIC PERSONALITY WITH SEVERAL NEUROTIC MANIFESTATIONS. AT THE PRESENT TIME, HE IS CONFUSED AND HAS DIFFICULTY LOOKING AT HIS SITUATION REALISTICALLY.
HIS FIXATION WITH HIS MOTHER IS THE DOMINANT FACTOR IN HIS PSYCHOSIS. WHILE CONSCIOUSLY HE LOVED HIS MOTHER, SUBCONSCIOUSLY HE HATED HER. CUTTING UP WOMEN WHO REMINDED HIM OF HIS MOTHER AND PRESERVING PARTS OF THEM SATISFIED TWO CONTRADICTORY URGES: TO BRING HIS MOTHER BACK TO LIFE AND TO DESTROY HER AS THE SOURCE OF HIS FRUSTRATIONS.
BECAUSE OF THESE FINDINGS, I MUST RECOMMEND HIS COMMITMENT TO CENTRAL STATE HOSPITAL AS INSANE.
IN A MATTER OF THIS KIND, I MUST RELY ON THE OPINION OF EXPERTS. I CAN'T SEE HOW MY OPINION CAN BE ANYTHING OTHER THAN TO FIND THIS DEFENDANT INSANE.
I SO FIND HIM AND DO HEREBY RECOMMIT HIM TO THE CENTRAL STATE HOSPITAL IN WAUPUN FOR AN INDETERMINATE TERM OF COMMITMENT.

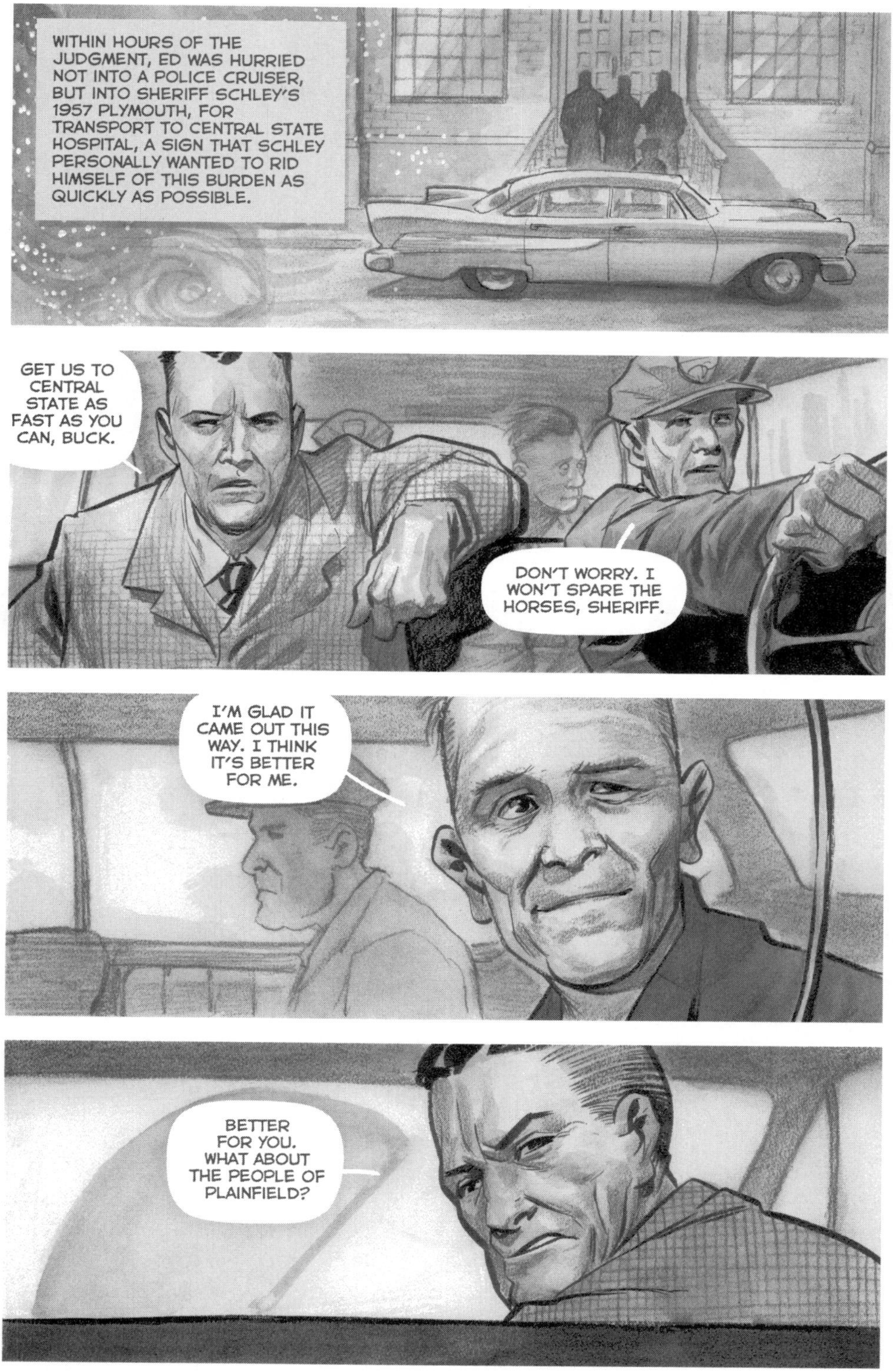
WITHIN HOURS OF THE JUDGMENT, ED WAS HURRIED NOT INTO A POLICE CRUISER, BUT INTO SHERIFF SCHLEY'S 1957 PLYMOUTH, FOR TRANSPORT TO CENTRAL STATE HOSPITAL, A SIGN THAT SCHLEY PERSONALLY WANTED TO RID HIMSELF OF THIS BURDEN AS QUICKLY AS POSSIBLE.
GET US TO CENTRAL STATE AS FAST AS YOU CAN, BUCK.
DON'T WORRY. I WON'T SPARE THE HORSES, SHERIFF.
I'M GLAD IT CAME OUT THIS WAY. I THINK IT'S BETTER FOR ME.
BETTER FOR YOU. WHAT ABOUT THE PEOPLE OF PLAINFIELD?

AUCTION SALE CANCELED | Section 2c

INDEX Politics   2
        Television   6
        Celebrity   5
        Unusual   7
        Personal   9
        Finance   13
        Sport   15
        Cinema   18

DAILY CHAPTER 11

10¢ ★★★

★★★ Friday, March 21st, 1958

IN THE END...

By Kent Blake
Staff Reporter, City desk

The entire arraignment lasted little more than five minutes. After listening to the recommendation of the prosecutor and the defense attorney, Judge Bundie made a statement. "It seems advisable under the circumstances as related by both the counsel for the state and the counsel for the defendant," he said, "that expert determination be made whether he is competent to stand trial," as well as whether he was sane at the time of Mrs. Worden's murder. Then Bundie signed an order committing Eddie to the Central State Hospital for the Criminally Insane at Waupun for a thirty-day examination period and remanded him to the custody of Sheriff Schley, who led Eddie back to the jailhouse to await transportation to the mental institution.

Through Gein was a wily fellow, it seemed impossible that he could have had the strength to dig up a grave by himself, break open the casket, remove the corpse and perform his grisly operations on it, then rebury the coffin and smooth over the sandy soil so that no trace of his crime remained—all in the space of a few hours. Moreover, the townspeople didn't see how such an activity could possibly have gone undetected, particularly over the course of several years. Gein, they argued, would have had to perform his necHuma

techniques for identifying the victims from their remains. By comparing dirt particles gathered at the crime scene with soil samples from local cemeteries, the technicians hoped to determine the validity of Gein's claim.

But the sheer quantity of evidence—by far the largest amount ever handled by the ten-year-old Crime Lab—made it hard for Wilson to promise a quick resolution. Though Kileen urged the director to give the task top priority, it was clear that a final answer might take weeks, even months.

In the meantime, Kileen was under growing pressure from the Plainfield citizenry to get back to the ordinary business of life.

PHOTO / Sally Corben

When a reporter asked Kileen if Augusta Gein was one of the women on the list, the DA shook his head. According to Kileen, Gein had denied opening his mother's coffin. Of course, his mother's coffin, added Kileen, was encased in a concrete vault. Whether Eddie had tried—and failed—to reach Augusta's body was something that the district attorney could not, or would not, say. Though its citizens were doing their best to get back to the ordinary business of life, Plainfield remained a community in crisis, still reeling from the sheer monstrousness of the Gein revelations, mortified by the media attention that had turned it into a generating some positive feelings for his hometown was the printing of a commemorative postage stamp honoring the prairie chicken, which would be "introduced on its first day of issue" through the Plainfield post office. By designating Plainfield as the place of issue for the prairie chicken stamp, the government would create favorable publicity for the town, not only among the country's millions of philatelists but also in the national press.

Just how seriously Walker's proposal was taken is a matter of conjecture. In any event, nothing ever came of it. Walker and his neighbors had no choice but to learn to live with their hometown's new (and, as it would turn out, permanent) reputation—to resign themselves to seeing the "fair name of Plainfield" (as one observer put it) forever "modified as the home of murder-ghoul Ed Gein. Elsewhere in Wisconsin, the reaction to the Gein atrocities was markedly different. It no less intense. In fact, the statewide response to the Plainfield horrors was so striking that it immediately attracted the interest of various psychologists, who had never witnessed a mass phenomenon quite like it. Realize the extreme fascination with every detail of the case, from the precise number of masks found inside Eddie's house to the menus of his jailhouse dinner, the crime had generated an unprecedented outbreak of black humor, a craze for Gein-related sick jokes (dubbed "Geiners") that quickly swept the state. Within days of the

Gein's House of Horrors Is Destroyed by Morning Fire

Was One Way to "Clean Up Case"

By Leland Bynquist
Local reporter, City desk

though he added that if the survivors "don't like it, I'll do everything possible to stop it. For a while, it seemed as if the Crime Lab might offer the best solution to the problem. Charles Wilson had nine of his men working full-time on the case, analyzing the evidence and employing the most up-to-date techniques for identifying the victims from their remains. By comparing dirt particles gathered at the crime scene with soil samples from local cemeteries, the technicians hoped to determine the validity of Gein's claim. But like the sheer quantity of evidence—by far, the largest amount ever handled by the ten-year-old Crime Lab—made it hard for Wilson to promise a quick resolution. Though Kileen urged the director to give the task top priority, it was clear that a final answer might take weeks, even months.

In the meantime, Kileen was under growing pressure from the Plainfield citizenry to determine the truth of Gein's assertion. It

Of course, his mother's coffin, added Kileen, was encased in a concrete vault. Whether Eddie had tried—and failed—to reach Augusta's body was something that the district attorney could not, or would not, say.

Though its citizens were doing their best to get back to the ordinary business of life, Plainfield remained a community in crisis, still reeling from the sheer monstrousness of the Gein revelations, mortified by the media attention that had turned it into a

PHOTO / Sally Corben

Lawyer Urg
Sanity Test for Gein

By Kent Blake
Staff Reporter, City desk

Though Gein was a wily fellow, it seemed impossible to dig up... corpse the only his rebury... upon the grisly openside so... rebury the coffin and so... soil so that no trace of... hours. Moreover, the townspe... how such an activity could poss... gone undetected, particularly ove... course of several years. Gein, they... have had to perform his nec

of Gein's claim. But the sheer quantity of evidence—by far, the largest amount ever handled by the ten-year-old Crime Lab—made it hard for Wilson to promise a quick resolution. Through Kileen urged the director to give the task top priority, it was clear that a final answer might take weeks, even months.

In the meantime, Kileen was under growing pressure from the Plainfield citizenry to get back to the ordinary business of life, Plainfield remained a community in crisis, still reeling from the sheer monstrousness of the Gein revelations, mortified by the media attention that had turned it into a

ng Woman,
Kileen Reveals

By Dale Simone
Local reporter, City desk

...Gein didn't want to do the only way the...never could not, ever, be definitively... to find Kileen answered only as deputy... the about it answered only as deputy... attorney of Adams County. con-... movement and crisis, Adams County, con-...

Plai
Bloc

"Every man to his
own tastes."

DESPITE THE JUDGE'S ASSURANCES THAT ED WOULD NEVER WALK THE STREETS OF PLAINFIELD AGAIN, THE CITIZENS WERE ANGERED BY THE DECISION. MOST FELT ED HAD GOTTEN OFF LIGHTLY.

IT WAS QUICKLY POINTED OUT THAT THE JUDGE'S ORDER MERELY STATED THAT GEIN WAS NOT COMPETENT TO STAND TRIAL AT THAT TIME.

IF THE DOCTORS AT CENTRAL STATE HOSPITAL WERE TO FIND HIM SANE ONE DAY, ED COULD STILL BE TRIED. AND, TO THE PEOPLE OF PLAINFIELD, THE MOST HORRIFYING ASPECT OF THAT SCENARIO WAS THAT GEIN MIGHT BE FOUND NOT GUILTY BY REASON OF INSANITY AND GO FREE.

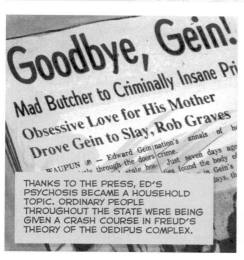

Goodbye, Gein!
Mad Butcher to Criminally Insane Pri
Obsessive Love for His Mother
Drove Gein to Slay, Rob Graves

WAUPUN (R) — Edward Gein nation's annals of h

THANKS TO THE PRESS, ED'S PSYCHOSIS BECAME A HOUSEHOLD TOPIC. ORDINARY PEOPLE THROUGHOUT THE STATE WERE BEING GIVEN A CRASH COURSE IN FREUD'S THEORY OF THE OEDIPUS COMPLEX.

I'LL BE DAMNED. ALWAYS KNEW HE WAS A MAMA'S BOY BUT NEVER FIGURED ON THIS.

NEVER DID COTTON TO THAT AUGUSTA GEIN. ACTING LIKE SHE WAS BETTER THAN EVERYONE ELSE. POOR EDDIE. SHUT UP IN THAT HOUSE WITH THAT WOMAN ALL THOSE YEARS.

POOR EDDIE?! HE BUTCHERED TWO WOMEN AND DUG UP DEAD FOLKS!

I KNOW, BUT WHO MADE HIM THAT WAY?

I DON'T CARE IF HIS MOTHER WAS HITLER IN A SKIRT! HE AIN'T GETTIN' ANY SYMPATHY OUTTA ME!

WELL, YOU KNOW EDDIE LOST HIS MOTHER AROUND CHRISTMASTIME. THEN HE TOOK MARY HOGAN AROUND CHRISTMAS OF '54, AND BERNICE RIGHT BEFORE THANKSGIVING.

IF YOU ASK ME, HE WAS MISSING HIS MOTHER AROUND THE HOLIDAYS.

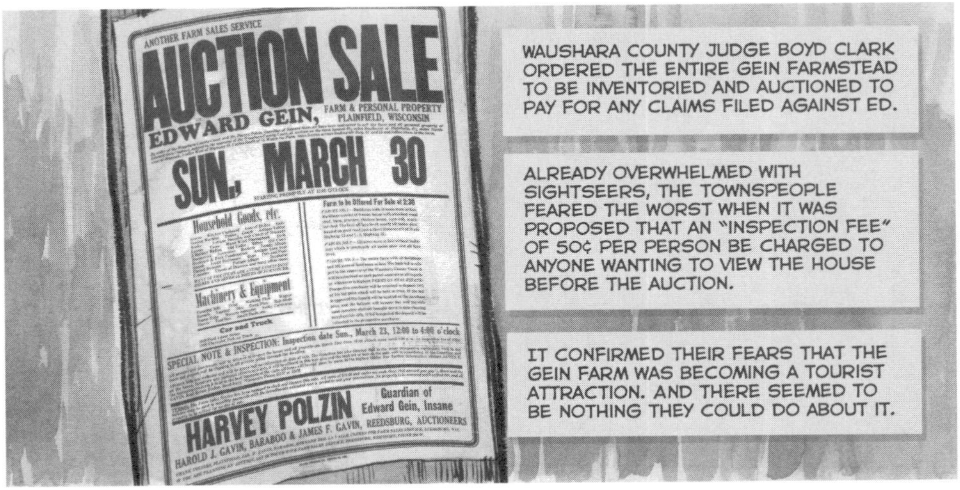
ANOTHER FARM SALES SERVICE
AUCTION SALE
EDWARD GEIN,
FARM & PERSONAL PROPERTY
PLAINFIELD, WISCONSIN
SUN., MARCH 30
Household Goods, etc.
Machinery & Equipment
Car and Truck
SPECIAL NOTE & INSPECTION: Inspection date Sun., March 23, 12:00 to 4:00 o'clock
HARVEY POLZIN
Guardian of Edward Gein, Insane
HAROLD J. GAVIN, BARABOO & JAMES F. GAVIN, REEDSBURG, AUCTIONEERS
WAUSHARA COUNTY JUDGE BOYD CLARK ORDERED THE ENTIRE GEIN FARMSTEAD TO BE INVENTORIED AND AUCTIONED TO PAY FOR ANY CLAIMS FILED AGAINST ED.
ALREADY OVERWHELMED WITH SIGHTSEERS, THE TOWNSPEOPLE FEARED THE WORST WHEN IT WAS PROPOSED THAT AN "INSPECTION FEE" OF 50¢ PER PERSON BE CHARGED TO ANYONE WANTING TO VIEW THE HOUSE BEFORE THE AUCTION.
IT CONFIRMED THEIR FEARS THAT THE GEIN FARM WAS BECOMING A TOURIST ATTRACTION. AND THERE SEEMED TO BE NOTHING THEY COULD DO ABOUT IT.

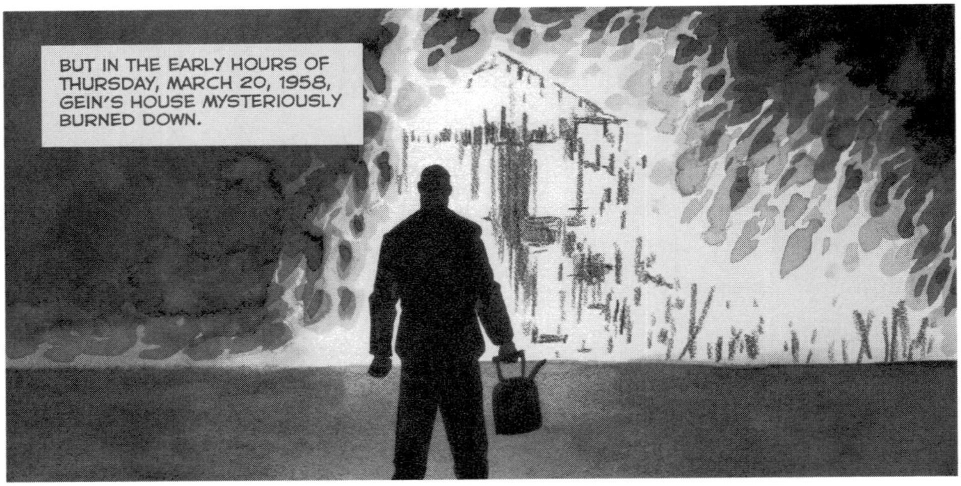
BUT IN THE EARLY HOURS OF THURSDAY, MARCH 20, 1958, GEIN'S HOUSE MYSTERIOUSLY BURNED DOWN.

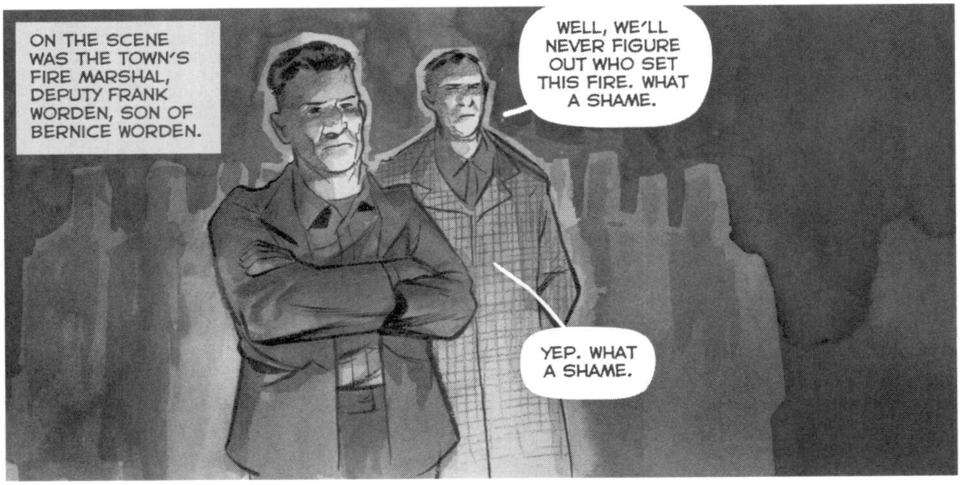
ON THE SCENE WAS THE TOWN'S FIRE MARSHAL, DEPUTY FRANK WORDEN, SON OF BERNICE WORDEN.
WELL, WE'LL NEVER FIGURE OUT WHO SET THIS FIRE. WHAT A SHAME.
YEP. WHAT A SHAME.

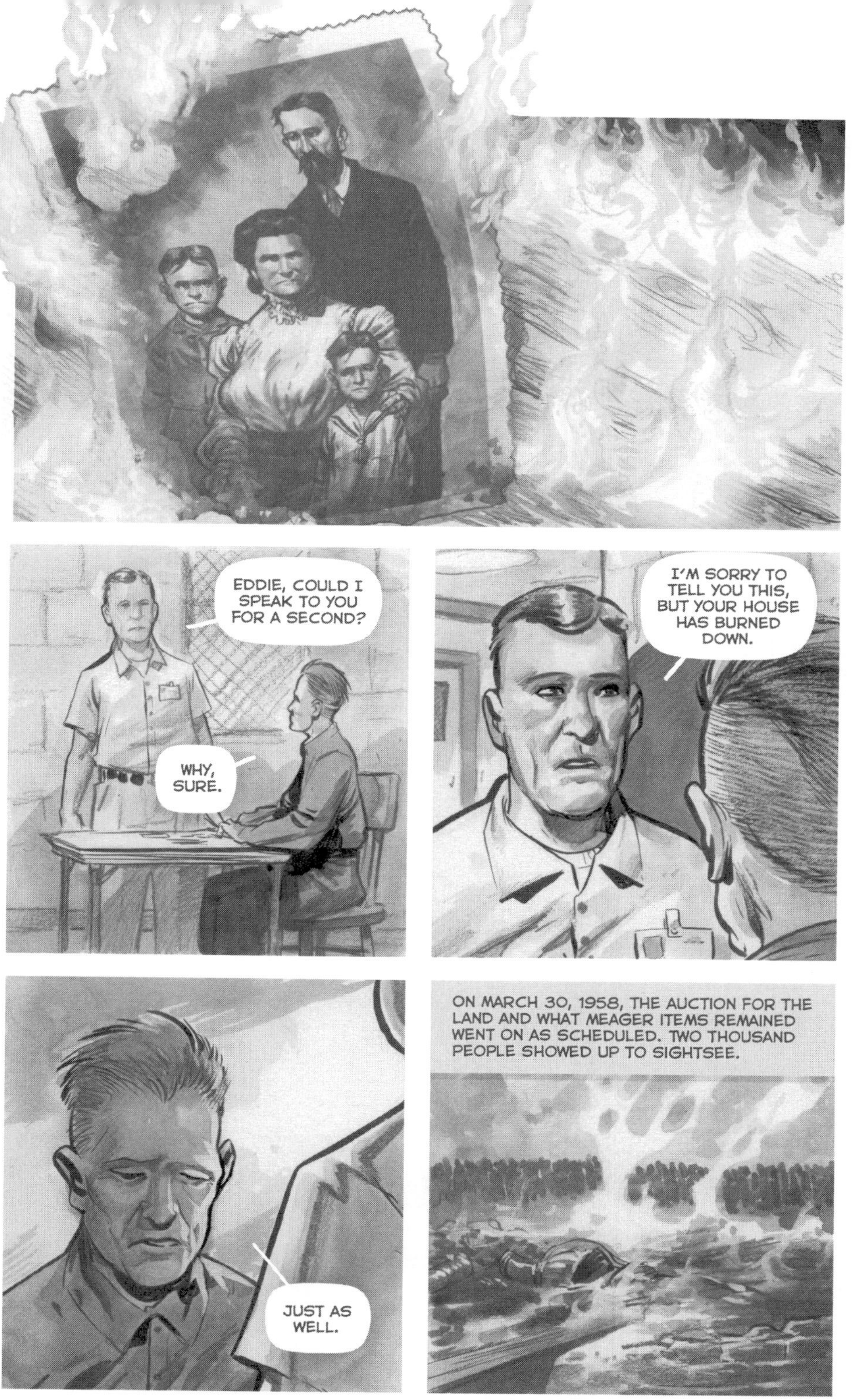
EDDIE, COULD I SPEAK TO YOU FOR A SECOND?
WHY, SURE.
I'M SORRY TO TELL YOU THIS, BUT YOUR HOUSE HAS BURNED DOWN.
JUST AS WELL.
ON MARCH 30, 1958, THE AUCTION FOR THE LAND AND WHAT MEAGER ITEMS REMAINED WENT ON AS SCHEDULED. TWO THOUSAND PEOPLE SHOWED UP TO SIGHTSEE.

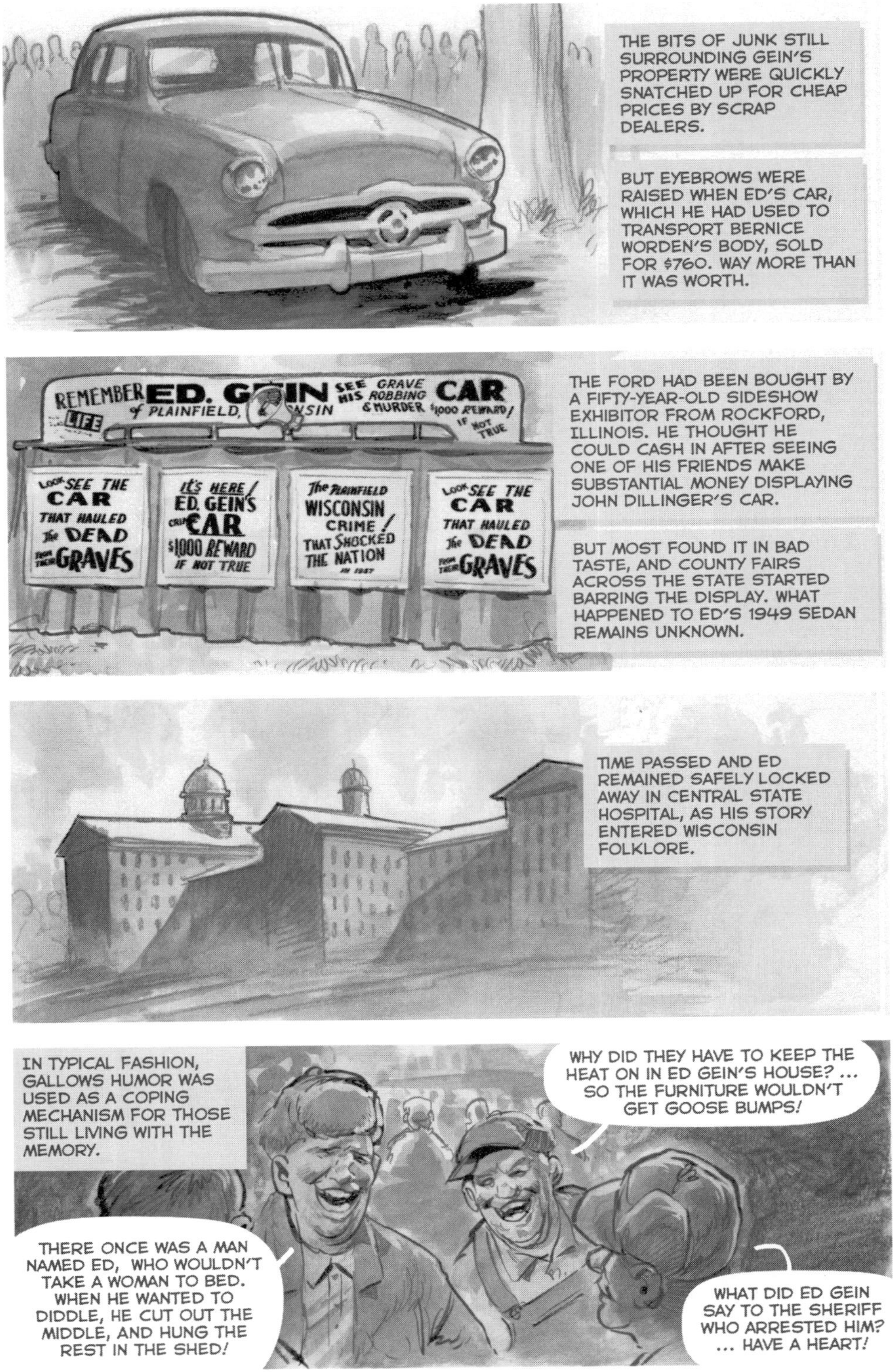
THE BITS OF JUNK STILL SURROUNDING GEIN'S PROPERTY WERE QUICKLY SNATCHED UP FOR CHEAP PRICES BY SCRAP DEALERS.
BUT EYEBROWS WERE RAISED WHEN ED'S CAR, WHICH HE HAD USED TO TRANSPORT BERNICE WORDEN'S BODY, SOLD FOR $760. WAY MORE THAN IT WAS WORTH.
REMEMBER
SEE HIS GRAVE ROBBING & MURDER CAR
$1000 REWARD! IF NOT TRUE
LIFE
LOOK SEE THE CAR THAT HAULED THE DEAD GRAVES
IT'S HERE! ED. GEIN'S CAR $1000 REWARD IF NOT TRUE
THE PLAINFIELD WISCONSIN CRIME! THAT SHOCKED THE NATION
LOOK SEE THE CAR THAT HAULED THE DEAD GRAVES
THE FORD HAD BEEN BOUGHT BY A FIFTY-YEAR-OLD SIDESHOW EXHIBITOR FROM ROCKFORD, ILLINOIS. HE THOUGHT HE COULD CASH IN AFTER SEEING ONE OF HIS FRIENDS MAKE SUBSTANTIAL MONEY DISPLAYING JOHN DILLINGER'S CAR.
BUT MOST FOUND IT IN BAD TASTE, AND COUNTY FAIRS ACROSS THE STATE STARTED BARRING THE DISPLAY. WHAT HAPPENED TO ED'S 1949 SEDAN REMAINS UNKNOWN.
TIME PASSED AND ED REMAINED SAFELY LOCKED AWAY IN CENTRAL STATE HOSPITAL, AS HIS STORY ENTERED WISCONSIN FOLKLORE.
IN TYPICAL FASHION, GALLOWS HUMOR WAS USED AS A COPING MECHANISM FOR THOSE STILL LIVING WITH THE MEMORY.
WHY DID THEY HAVE TO KEEP THE HEAT ON IN ED GEIN'S HOUSE? ... SO THE FURNITURE WOULDN'T GET GOOSE BUMPS!
THERE ONCE WAS A MAN NAMED ED, WHO WOULDN'T TAKE A WOMAN TO BED. WHEN HE WANTED TO DIDDLE, HE CUT OUT THE MIDDLE, AND HUNG THE REST IN THE SHED!
WHAT DID ED GEIN SAY TO THE SHERIFF WHO ARRESTED HIM? ... HAVE A HEART!

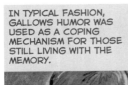

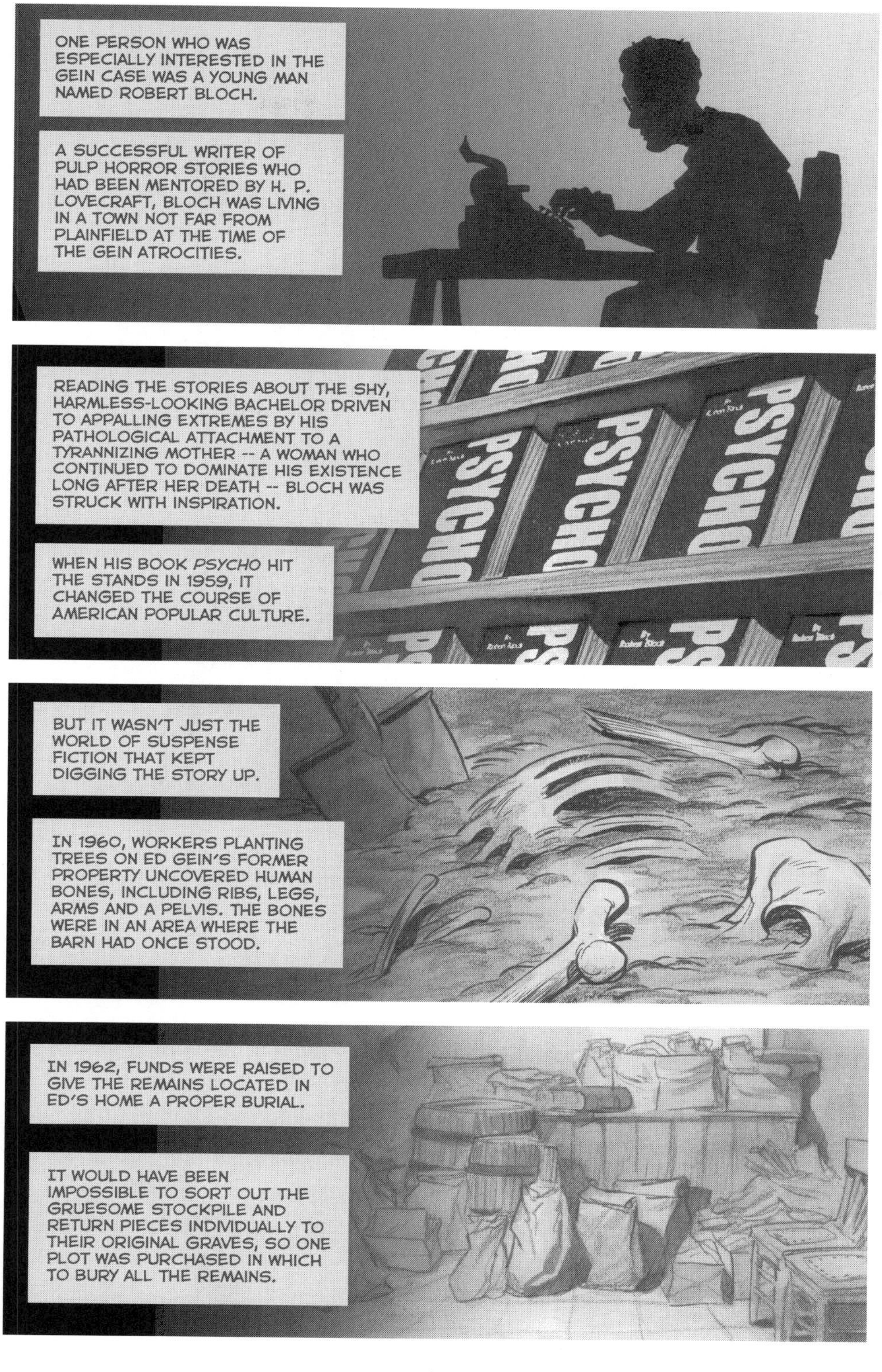
ONE PERSON WHO WAS ESPECIALLY INTERESTED IN THE GEIN CASE WAS A YOUNG MAN NAMED ROBERT BLOCH.
A SUCCESSFUL WRITER OF PULP HORROR STORIES WHO HAD BEEN MENTORED BY H. P. LOVECRAFT, BLOCH WAS LIVING IN A TOWN NOT FAR FROM PLAINFIELD AT THE TIME OF THE GEIN ATROCITIES.
READING THE STORIES ABOUT THE SHY, HARMLESS-LOOKING BACHELOR DRIVEN TO APPALLING EXTREMES BY HIS PATHOLOGICAL ATTACHMENT TO A TYRANNIZING MOTHER -- A WOMAN WHO CONTINUED TO DOMINATE HIS EXISTENCE LONG AFTER HER DEATH -- BLOCH WAS STRUCK WITH INSPIRATION.
PSYCHO
WHEN HIS BOOK *PSYCHO* HIT THE STANDS IN 1959, IT CHANGED THE COURSE OF AMERICAN POPULAR CULTURE.
BUT IT WASN'T JUST THE WORLD OF SUSPENSE FICTION THAT KEPT DIGGING THE STORY UP.
IN 1960, WORKERS PLANTING TREES ON ED GEIN'S FORMER PROPERTY UNCOVERED HUMAN BONES, INCLUDING RIBS, LEGS, ARMS AND A PELVIS. THE BONES WERE IN AN AREA WHERE THE BARN HAD ONCE STOOD.
IN 1962, FUNDS WERE RAISED TO GIVE THE REMAINS LOCATED IN ED'S HOME A PROPER BURIAL.
IT WOULD HAVE BEEN IMPOSSIBLE TO SORT OUT THE GRUESOME STOCKPILE AND RETURN PIECES INDIVIDUALLY TO THEIR ORIGINAL GRAVES, SO ONE PLOT WAS PURCHASED IN WHICH TO BURY ALL THE REMAINS.

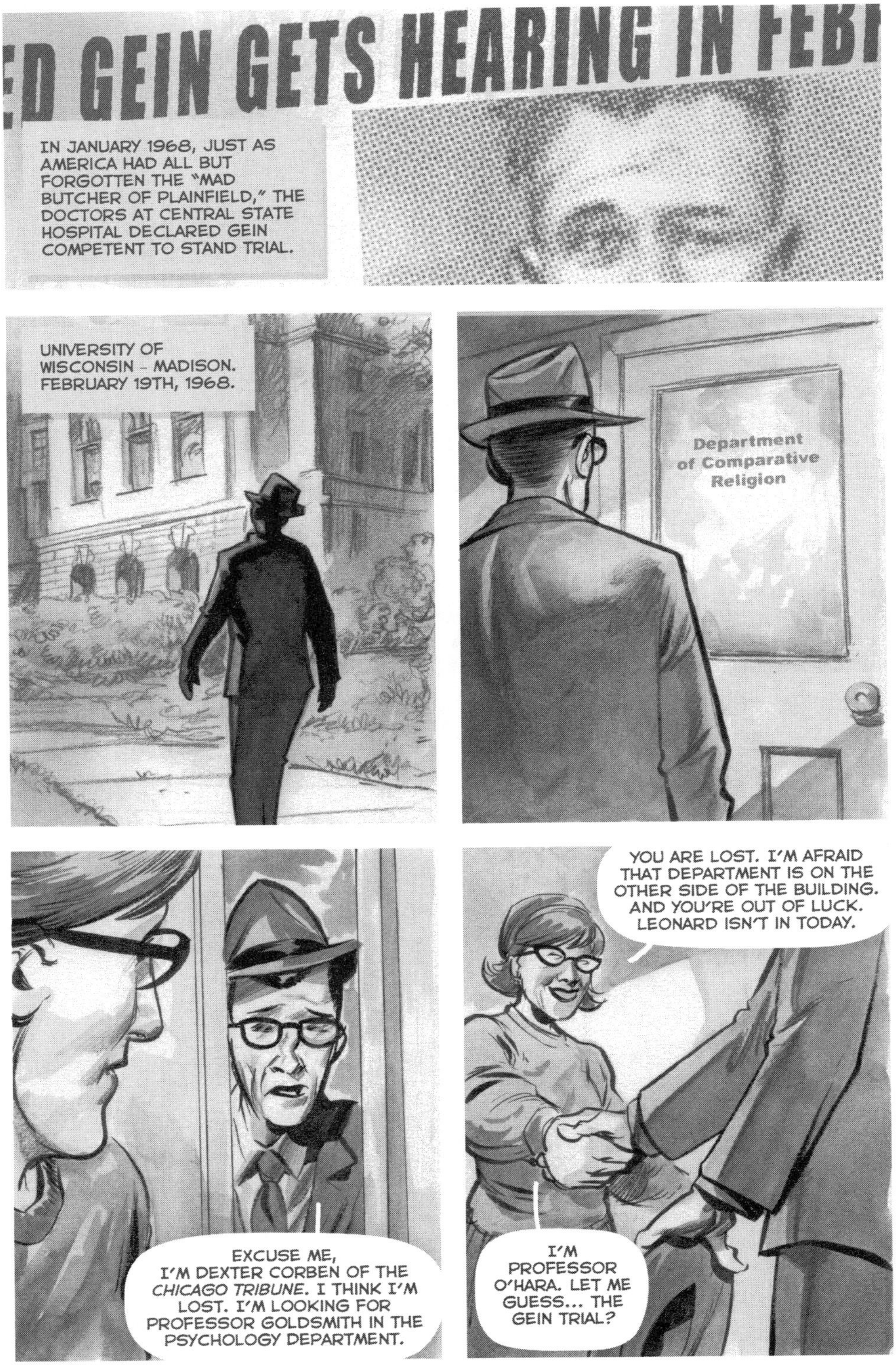
ED GEIN GETS HEARING IN FEB
IN JANUARY 1968, JUST AS AMERICA HAD ALL BUT FORGOTTEN THE "MAD BUTCHER OF PLAINFIELD," THE DOCTORS AT CENTRAL STATE HOSPITAL DECLARED GEIN COMPETENT TO STAND TRIAL.
UNIVERSITY OF WISCONSIN - MADISON. FEBRUARY 19TH, 1968.
Department of Comparative Religion
EXCUSE ME, I'M DEXTER CORBEN OF THE *CHICAGO TRIBUNE*. I THINK I'M LOST. I'M LOOKING FOR PROFESSOR GOLDSMITH IN THE PSYCHOLOGY DEPARTMENT.
YOU ARE LOST. I'M AFRAID THAT DEPARTMENT IS ON THE OTHER SIDE OF THE BUILDING. AND YOU'RE OUT OF LUCK. LEONARD ISN'T IN TODAY.
I'M PROFESSOR O'HARA. LET ME GUESS... THE GEIN TRIAL?

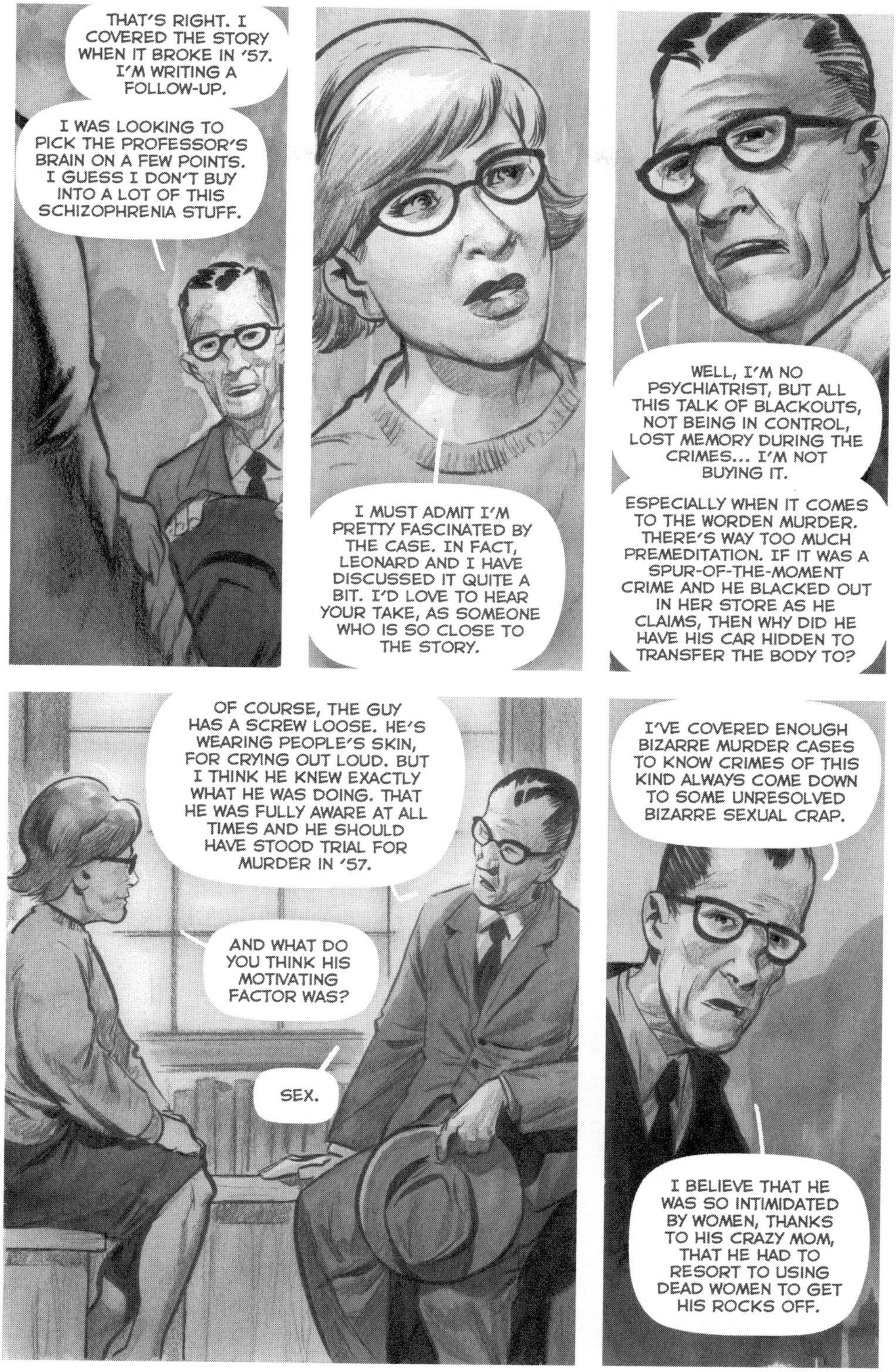
THAT'S RIGHT. I COVERED THE STORY WHEN IT BROKE IN '57. I'M WRITING A FOLLOW-UP.
I WAS LOOKING TO PICK THE PROFESSOR'S BRAIN ON A FEW POINTS. I GUESS I DON'T BUY INTO A LOT OF THIS SCHIZOPHRENIA STUFF.
I MUST ADMIT I'M PRETTY FASCINATED BY THE CASE. IN FACT, LEONARD AND I HAVE DISCUSSED IT QUITE A BIT. I'D LOVE TO HEAR YOUR TAKE, AS SOMEONE WHO IS SO CLOSE TO THE STORY.
WELL, I'M NO PSYCHIATRIST, BUT ALL THIS TALK OF BLACKOUTS, NOT BEING IN CONTROL, LOST MEMORY DURING THE CRIMES... I'M NOT BUYING IT.
ESPECIALLY WHEN IT COMES TO THE WORDEN MURDER. THERE'S WAY TOO MUCH PREMEDITATION. IF IT WAS A SPUR-OF-THE-MOMENT CRIME AND HE BLACKED OUT IN HER STORE AS HE CLAIMS, THEN WHY DID HE HAVE HIS CAR HIDDEN TO TRANSFER THE BODY TO?
OF COURSE, THE GUY HAS A SCREW LOOSE. HE'S WEARING PEOPLE'S SKIN, FOR CRYING OUT LOUD. BUT I THINK HE KNEW EXACTLY WHAT HE WAS DOING. THAT HE WAS FULLY AWARE AT ALL TIMES AND HE SHOULD HAVE STOOD TRIAL FOR MURDER IN '57.
AND WHAT DO YOU THINK HIS MOTIVATING FACTOR WAS?
SEX.
I'VE COVERED ENOUGH BIZARRE MURDER CASES TO KNOW CRIMES OF THIS KIND ALWAYS COME DOWN TO SOME UNRESOLVED BIZARRE SEXUAL CRAP.
I BELIEVE THAT HE WAS SO INTIMIDATED BY WOMEN, THANKS TO HIS CRAZY MOM, THAT HE HAD TO RESORT TO USING DEAD WOMEN TO GET HIS ROCKS OFF.

IT IS A SHAME LEONARD ISN'T HERE. I THINK YOU WOULD HAVE HAD AN INTERESTING CONVERSATION. HE DEFINITELY WOULD HAVE AGREED WITH YOU ON GEIN'S MOMMY ISSUES. HE IS A BEYOND-HOPELESS FREUDIAN.

SO YOU DON'T BUY THAT OEDIPUS COMPLEX STUFF?

FREUD HAD A FEW DECENT INSIGHTS. I JUST DON'T THINK YOU CAN ACCOUNT FOR SOME OF THIS STUFF BY SAYING THAT GEIN WAS OVERLY ATTACHED TO HIS MOTHER.

I DON'T KNOW. SHE MUST HAVE DONE SOME NUMBER ON HIM AS A KID TO MAKE HIM GO DIG UP DEAD WOMEN FOR A DATE.

POSSIBLY. BUT A BIZARRE ATTACHMENT TO CORPSES ISN'T NEW. IT HAPPENS IN SOME RELIGIOUS RITUALS. EVER HEAR OF THE TORAJA PEOPLE?

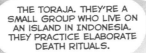

THE WHAT?

THE TORAJA. THEY'RE A SMALL GROUP WHO LIVE ON AN ISLAND IN INDONESIA. THEY PRACTICE ELABORATE DEATH RITUALS.

THEY PRESERVE THEIR DEAD LOVED ONES AND KEEP THEM AT HOME FOR A LONG TIME BEFORE BURYING THEM. AFTERWARDS, THEY DIG UP THE CORPSES EVERY FEW YEARS, DRESS THEM IN NEW CLOTHES, EVEN TAKE PICTURES WITH THEM BEFORE REBURYING THEM.

TAKES ALL KINDS, I GUESS. BUT THESE PEOPLE AREN'T DIGGING UP THEIR LOVED ONES TO HAVE SEX WITH THEM.

WELL, AS I THINK LEONARD WOULD TELL YOU, GEIN WAS A CLASSIC NECROPHILE. WHETHER OR NOT HE ACTUALLY HAD INTERCOURSE WITH THE BODIES, HE CLEARLY HAD AN EROTIC INTEREST IN THEM.

WHEN YOU SAY "CLASSIC"...?

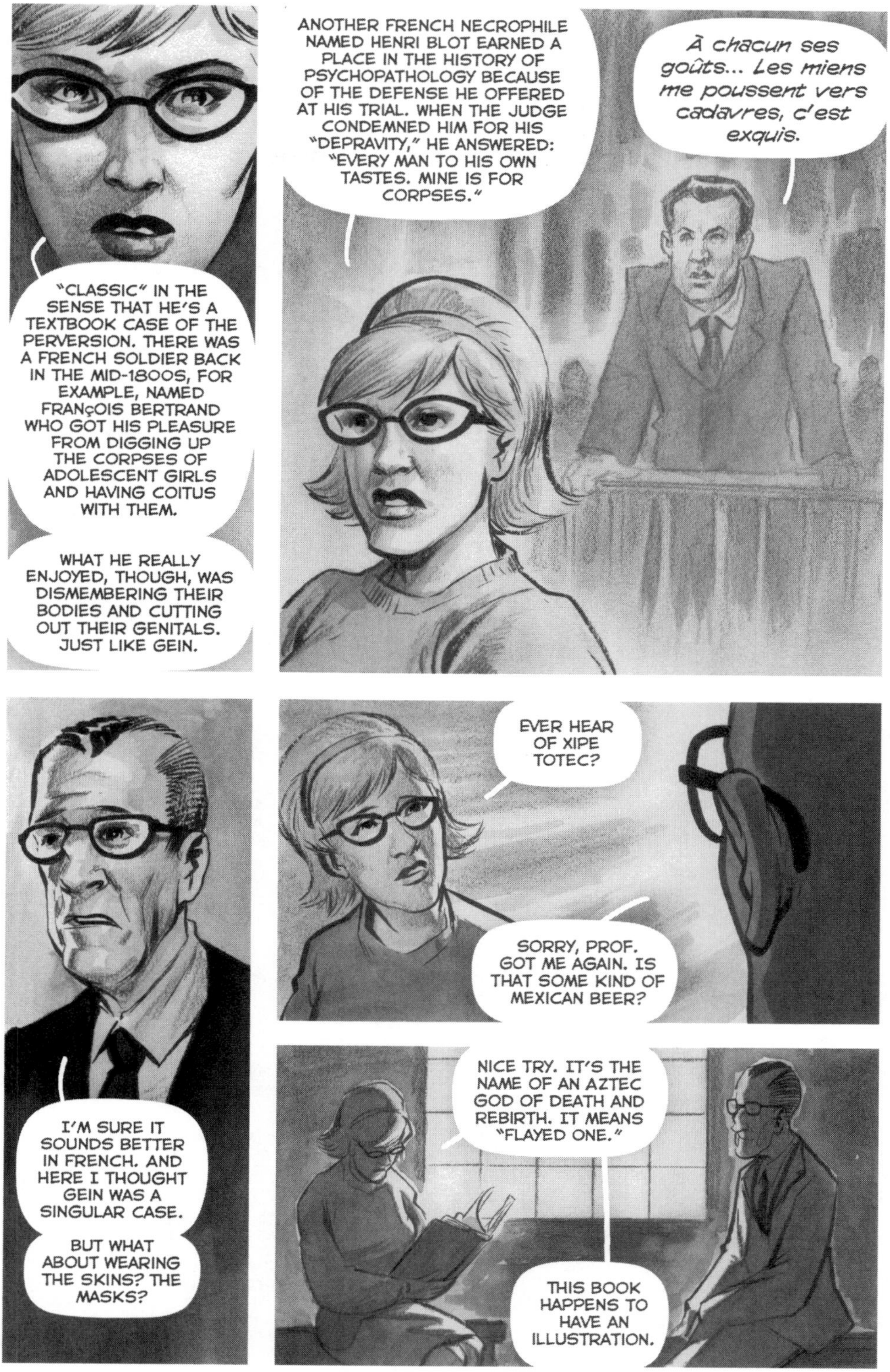
"CLASSIC" IN THE SENSE THAT HE'S A TEXTBOOK CASE OF THE PERVERSION. THERE WAS A FRENCH SOLDIER BACK IN THE MID-1800S, FOR EXAMPLE, NAMED FRANçOIS BERTRAND WHO GOT HIS PLEASURE FROM DIGGING UP THE CORPSES OF ADOLESCENT GIRLS AND HAVING COITUS WITH THEM.
WHAT HE REALLY ENJOYED, THOUGH, WAS DISMEMBERING THEIR BODIES AND CUTTING OUT THEIR GENITALS. JUST LIKE GEIN.
ANOTHER FRENCH NECROPHILE NAMED HENRI BLOT EARNED A PLACE IN THE HISTORY OF PSYCHOPATHOLOGY BECAUSE OF THE DEFENSE HE OFFERED AT HIS TRIAL. WHEN THE JUDGE CONDEMNED HIM FOR HIS "DEPRAVITY," HE ANSWERED: "EVERY MAN TO HIS OWN TASTES. MINE IS FOR CORPSES."
À chacun ses goûts... Les miens me poussent vers cadavres, c'est exquis.
I'M SURE IT SOUNDS BETTER IN FRENCH. AND HERE I THOUGHT GEIN WAS A SINGULAR CASE.
BUT WHAT ABOUT WEARING THE SKINS? THE MASKS?
EVER HEAR OF XIPE TOTEC?
SORRY, PROF. GOT ME AGAIN. IS THAT SOME KIND OF MEXICAN BEER?
NICE TRY. IT'S THE NAME OF AN AZTEC GOD OF DEATH AND REBIRTH. IT MEANS "FLAYED ONE."
THIS BOOK HAPPENS TO HAVE AN ILLUSTRATION.

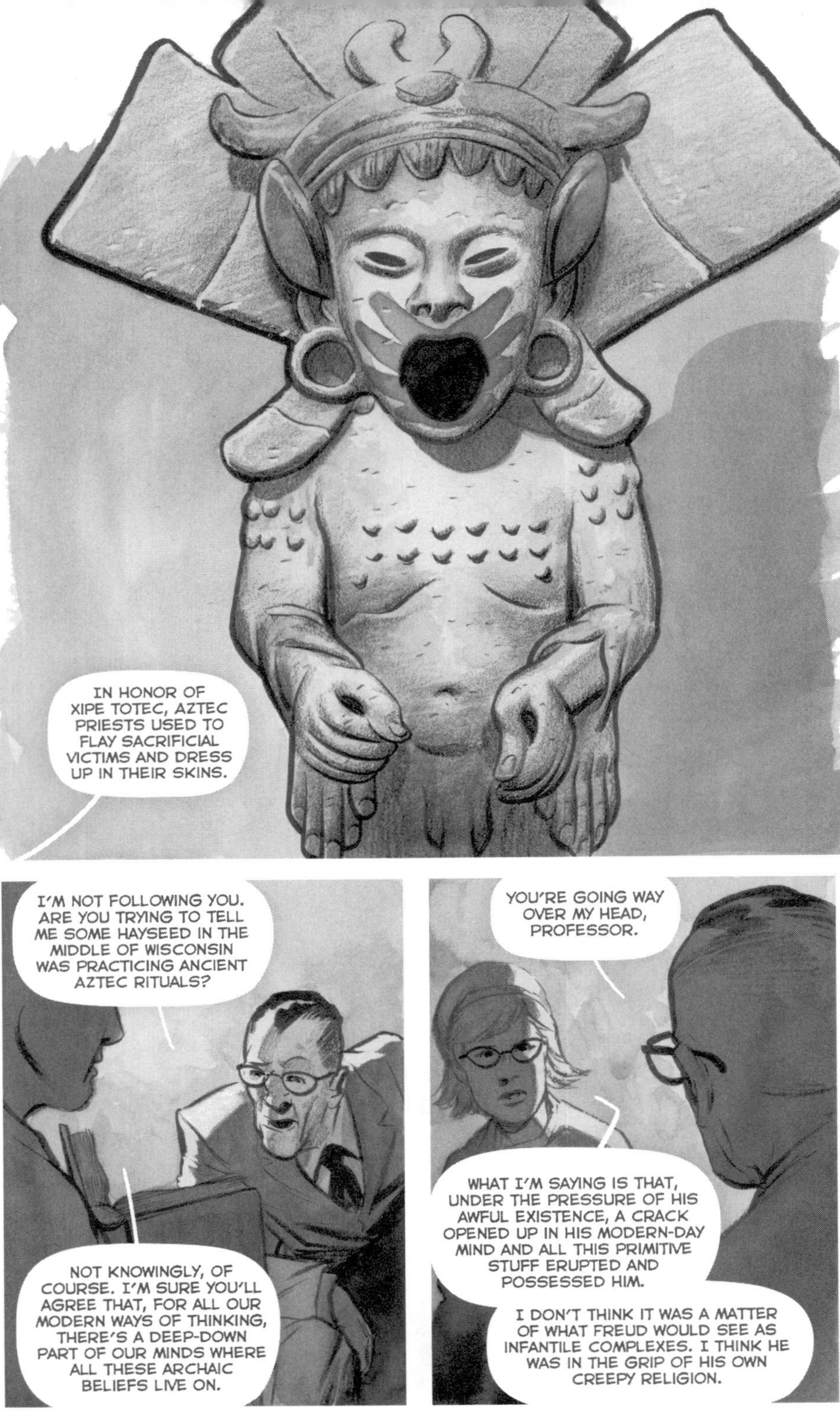
IN HONOR OF XIPE TOTEC, AZTEC PRIESTS USED TO FLAY SACRIFICIAL VICTIMS AND DRESS UP IN THEIR SKINS.
I'M NOT FOLLOWING YOU. ARE YOU TRYING TO TELL ME SOME HAYSEED IN THE MIDDLE OF WISCONSIN WAS PRACTICING ANCIENT AZTEC RITUALS?
NOT KNOWINGLY, OF COURSE. I'M SURE YOU'LL AGREE THAT, FOR ALL OUR MODERN WAYS OF THINKING, THERE'S A DEEP-DOWN PART OF OUR MINDS WHERE ALL THESE ARCHAIC BELIEFS LIVE ON.
YOU'RE GOING WAY OVER MY HEAD, PROFESSOR.
WHAT I'M SAYING IS THAT, UNDER THE PRESSURE OF HIS AWFUL EXISTENCE, A CRACK OPENED UP IN HIS MODERN-DAY MIND AND ALL THIS PRIMITIVE STUFF ERUPTED AND POSSESSED HIM.
I DON'T THINK IT WAS A MATTER OF WHAT FREUD WOULD SEE AS INFANTILE COMPLEXES. I THINK HE WAS IN THE GRIP OF HIS OWN CREEPY RELIGION.

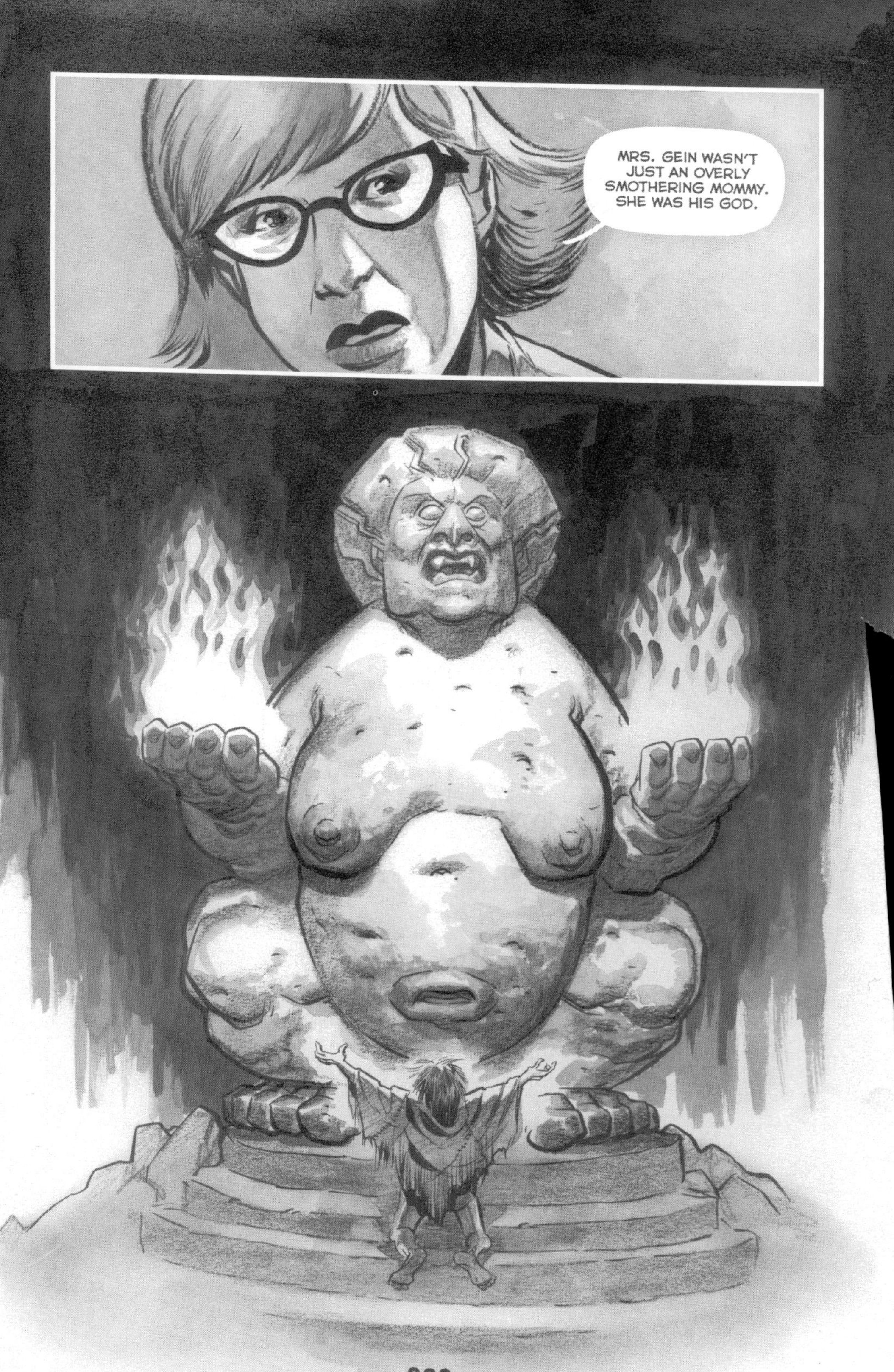
MRS. GEIN WASN'T JUST AN OVERLY SMOTHERING MOMMY. SHE WAS HIS GOD.

GEIN'S TRIAL BEGINS. WAUTOMA, WISCONSIN. THURSDAY, NOVEMBER 7, 1968.

BETWEEN THE TIME SPUTNIK, THE FIRST MAN-MADE OBJECT TO ORBIT EARTH, WAS CIRCLING OUR GLOBE AND THE CREW OF APOLLO 8 WERE PREPARING TO BECOME THE FIRST HUMANS TO ORBIT THE MOON, ED GEIN WAS QUIETLY LOCKED AWAY AS WORLD EVENTS PASSED BY.

THOSE IN ATTENDANCE AT HIS TRIAL WERE SHOCKED BY THE TRANSFORMATION OF HIS APPEARANCE.

LOOKS LIKE MY UNCLE CARL.

I DON'T BELIEVE IT. I ALMOST FEEL SORRY FOR THAT LONELY LITTLE OLD GUY. BUT THEN I START TO THINK ABOUT WHAT HE DID...

THE DEFENSE, WHICH ENTERED A PLEA OF NOT GUILTY BY REASON OF INSANITY, REQUESTED A BENCH TRIAL. THAT MEANT THERE WOULD BE NO JURY, AND THE JUDGE WOULD HAVE THE FINAL SAY.

THE TRIAL WOULD BE CONDUCTED IN TWO PARTS. FIRST, GEIN WOULD BE TRIED FOR THE MURDER OF BERNICE WORDEN. THEN, IF FOUND GUILTY, THE SECOND PHASE OF THE TRIAL WOULD IMMEDIATELY BEGIN TO DECIDE IF HE HAD BEEN SANE DURING THE MURDER.

PROSECUTION, YOU MAY CALL YOUR FIRST WITNESS.

JUDGE, WE WISH TO CALL FRANK WORDEN. HOWEVER, THERE IS AN ISSUE: MR. WORDEN HAS INFORMED ME THAT THERE COULD BE VIOLENCE IF HE IS IN THE SAME ROOM WITH MR. GEIN.

WELL, WE CAN'T HAVE THAT. WHAT IF MR. GEIN SITS IN THE HALL LEADING TO THE HOLDING CELLS WHEN MR. WORDEN TESTIFIES?

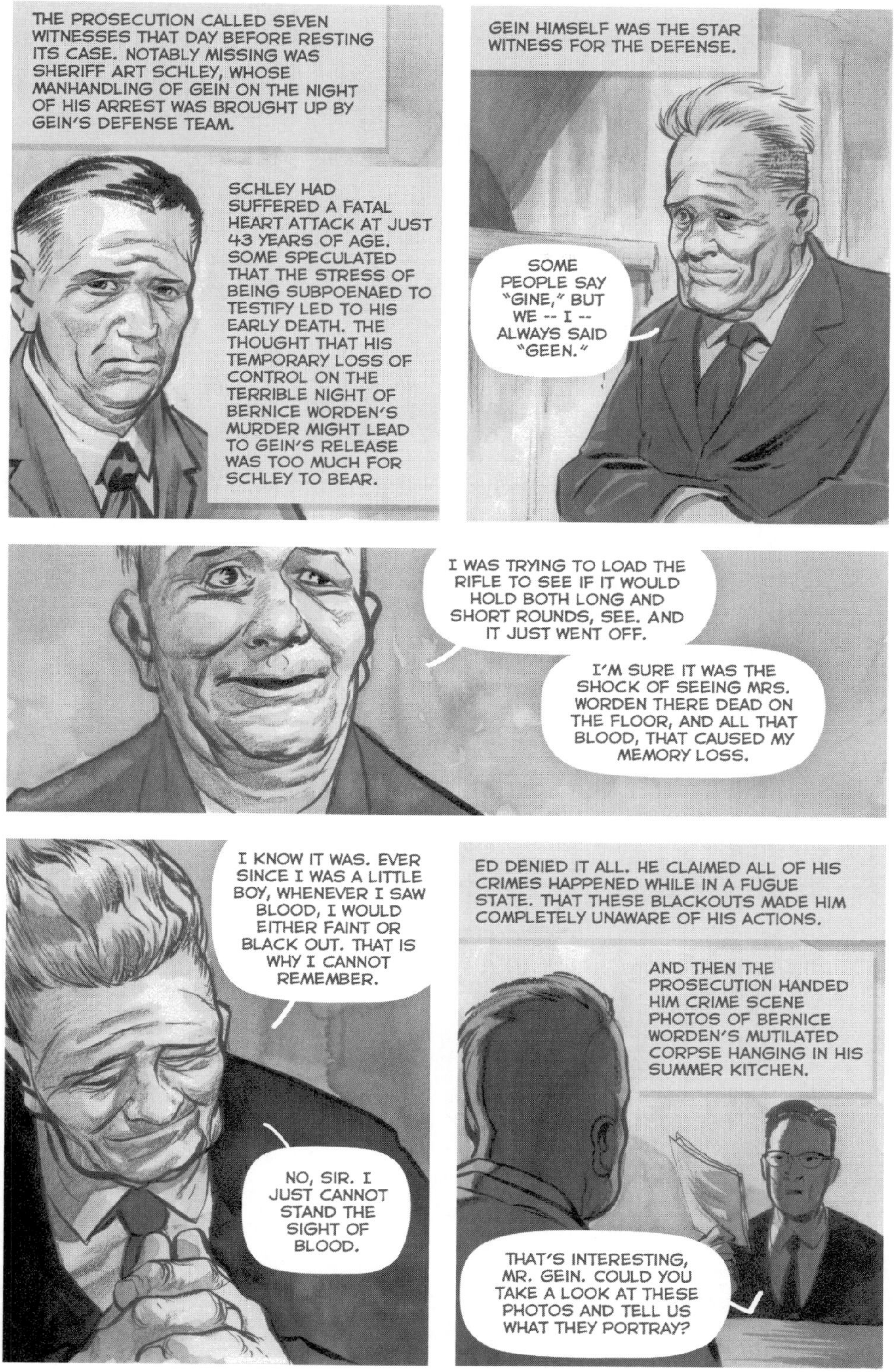
THE PROSECUTION CALLED SEVEN WITNESSES THAT DAY BEFORE RESTING ITS CASE. NOTABLY MISSING WAS SHERIFF ART SCHLEY, WHOSE MANHANDLING OF GEIN ON THE NIGHT OF HIS ARREST WAS BROUGHT UP BY GEIN'S DEFENSE TEAM.
SCHLEY HAD SUFFERED A FATAL HEART ATTACK AT JUST 43 YEARS OF AGE. SOME SPECULATED THAT THE STRESS OF BEING SUBPOENAED TO TESTIFY LED TO HIS EARLY DEATH. THE THOUGHT THAT HIS TEMPORARY LOSS OF CONTROL ON THE TERRIBLE NIGHT OF BERNICE WORDEN'S MURDER MIGHT LEAD TO GEIN'S RELEASE WAS TOO MUCH FOR SCHLEY TO BEAR.
GEIN HIMSELF WAS THE STAR WITNESS FOR THE DEFENSE.
SOME PEOPLE SAY "GINE," BUT WE -- I -- ALWAYS SAID "GEEN."
I WAS TRYING TO LOAD THE RIFLE TO SEE IF IT WOULD HOLD BOTH LONG AND SHORT ROUNDS, SEE. AND IT JUST WENT OFF.
I'M SURE IT WAS THE SHOCK OF SEEING MRS. WORDEN THERE DEAD ON THE FLOOR, AND ALL THAT BLOOD, THAT CAUSED MY MEMORY LOSS.
I KNOW IT WAS. EVER SINCE I WAS A LITTLE BOY, WHENEVER I SAW BLOOD, I WOULD EITHER FAINT OR BLACK OUT. THAT IS WHY I CANNOT REMEMBER.
NO, SIR. I JUST CANNOT STAND THE SIGHT OF BLOOD.
ED DENIED IT ALL. HE CLAIMED ALL OF HIS CRIMES HAPPENED WHILE IN A FUGUE STATE. THAT THESE BLACKOUTS MADE HIM COMPLETELY UNAWARE OF HIS ACTIONS.
AND THEN THE PROSECUTION HANDED HIM CRIME SCENE PHOTOS OF BERNICE WORDEN'S MUTILATED CORPSE HANGING IN HIS SUMMER KITCHEN.
THAT'S INTERESTING, MR. GEIN. COULD YOU TAKE A LOOK AT THESE PHOTOS AND TELL US WHAT THEY PORTRAY?

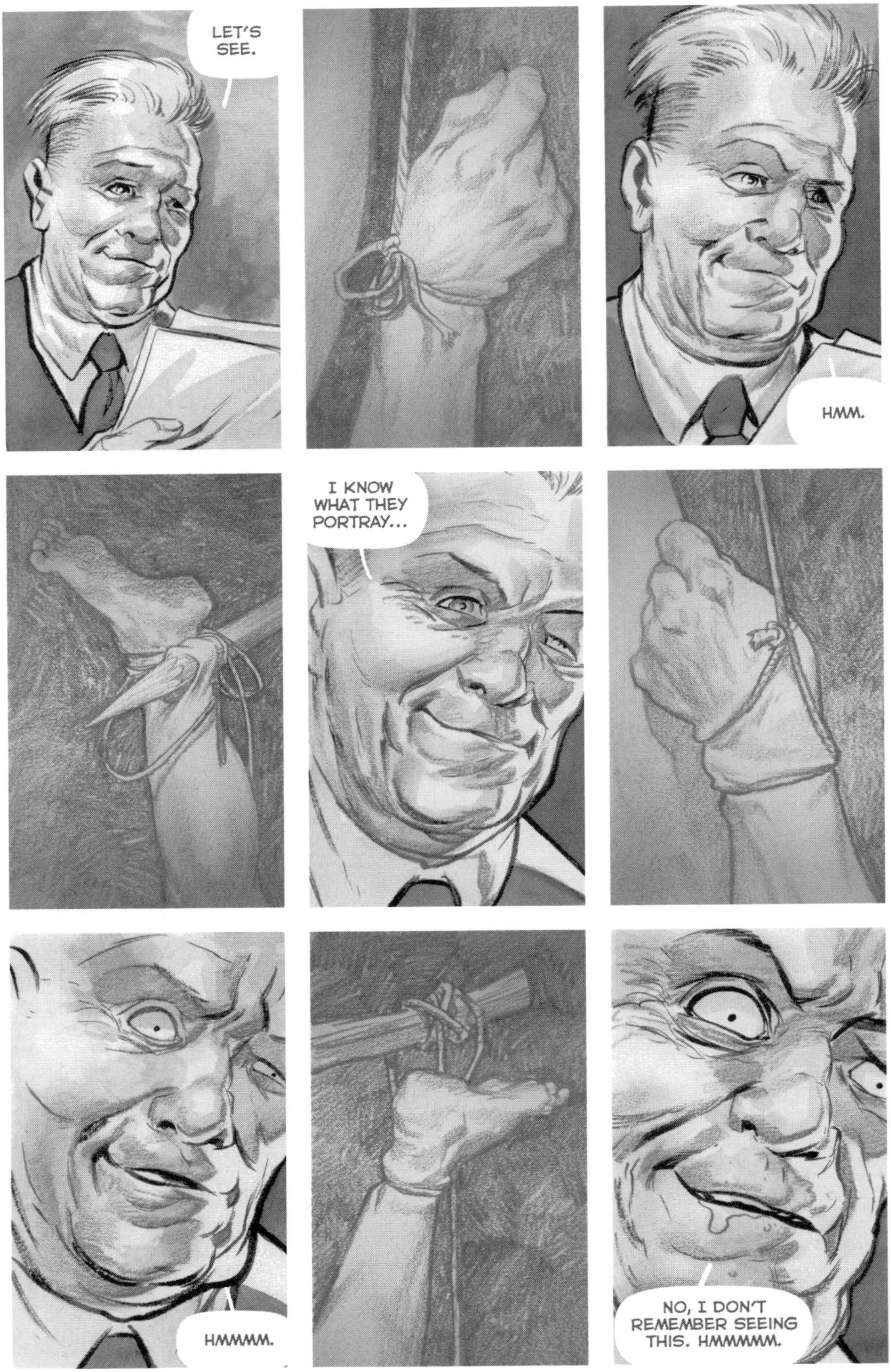
LET'S SEE.
HMM.
I KNOW WHAT THEY PORTRAY...
HMMMM.
NO, I DON'T REMEMBER SEEING THIS. HMMMMM.

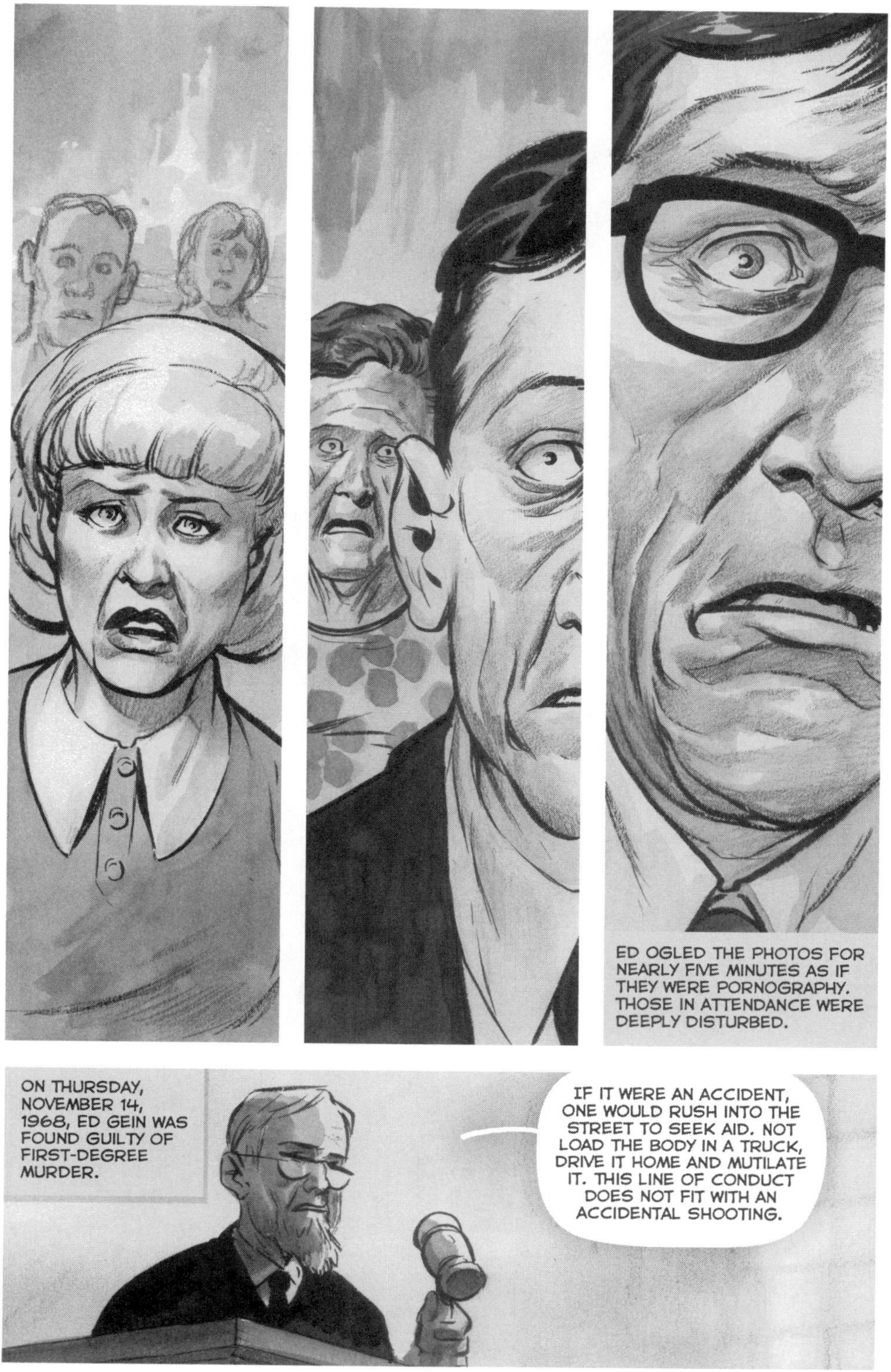
ED OGLED THE PHOTOS FOR NEARLY FIVE MINUTES AS IF THEY WERE PORNOGRAPHY. THOSE IN ATTENDANCE WERE DEEPLY DISTURBED.
ON THURSDAY, NOVEMBER 14, 1968, ED GEIN WAS FOUND GUILTY OF FIRST-DEGREE MURDER.
IF IT WERE AN ACCIDENT, ONE WOULD RUSH INTO THE STREET TO SEEK AID. NOT LOAD THE BODY IN A TRUCK, DRIVE IT HOME AND MUTILATE IT. THIS LINE OF CONDUCT DOES NOT FIT WITH AN ACCIDENTAL SHOOTING.

IMMEDIATELY AFTER THE VERDICT, THE SECOND PART OF THE TRIAL BEGAN. IT TOOK ONLY A FEW HOURS FOR ED TO BE FOUND INSANE AND ORDERED BACK TO THE MAXIMUM-SECURITY HOSPITAL.

HOW DO YOU FEEL ABOUT THE VERDICT?

OH, I'M LOOKING FORWARD TO GETTING BACK TO THE HOSPITAL. THEY TREAT YOU PRETTY GOOD THERE.

BUT AS HIS LIFE BEGAN TO WANE, ED BECAME RESTLESS IN THE HOSPITAL. TO EVERYONE'S SURPRISE, ED PETITIONED FOR HIS RELEASE IN 1974.

I'VE FULLY RECOVERED MY MENTAL HEALTH, AND THERE IS NO REASON I SHOULD REMAIN HERE.

I DOUBT THAT ANYBODY WOULD BE HAPPY LOCKED UP. IT'S HUMAN NATURE TO WANT TO GO SOMEPLACE.

ED, LET'S TALK ABOUT YOUR CRIMES...

I DON'T WANT TO RAKE UP THE PAST!

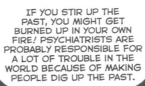

IF YOU STIR UP THE PAST, YOU MIGHT GET BURNED UP IN YOUR OWN FIRE! PSYCHIATRISTS ARE PROBABLY RESPONSIBLE FOR A LOT OF TROUBLE IN THE WORLD BECAUSE OF MAKING PEOPLE DIG UP THE PAST.

I THINK A LOT OF THE PRISONERS FROM HERE MIGHT GO OUT AND KILL 'EM, ROB 'EM, CLUB 'EM BECAUSE OF DIGGING UP THE PAST.

OK, ED, WE DON'T HAVE TO TALK ABOUT YOUR PAST. LET'S TRY SOMETHING ELSE. I'M GOING TO STATE A FEW COMMON PROVERBS AND YOU TELL ME WHAT THEY MEAN.

OK, THEN.

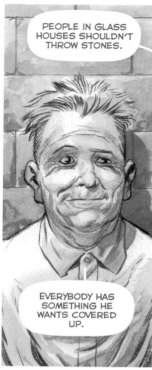

PEOPLE IN GLASS HOUSES SHOULDN'T THROW STONES.

EVERYBODY HAS SOMETHING HE WANTS COVERED UP.

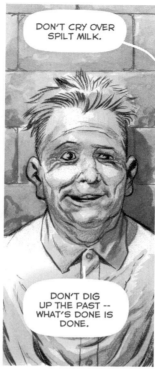

DON'T CRY OVER SPILT MILK.

DON'T DIG UP THE PAST -- WHAT'S DONE IS DONE.

STILL WATERS RUN DEEP.

SOME PEOPLE ARE CALM ON THE SURFACE AND HOTHEADS UNDERNEATH.

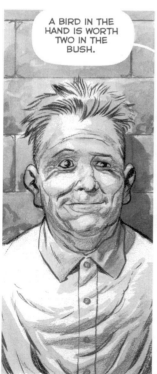

A BIRD IN THE HAND IS WORTH TWO IN THE BUSH.

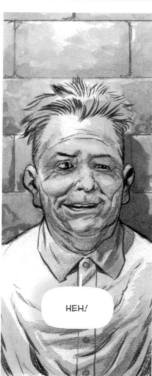

HEH!

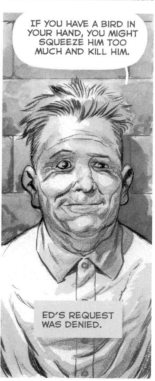

IF YOU HAVE A BIRD IN YOUR HAND, YOU MIGHT SQUEEZE HIM TOO MUCH AND KILL HIM.

ED'S REQUEST WAS DENIED.

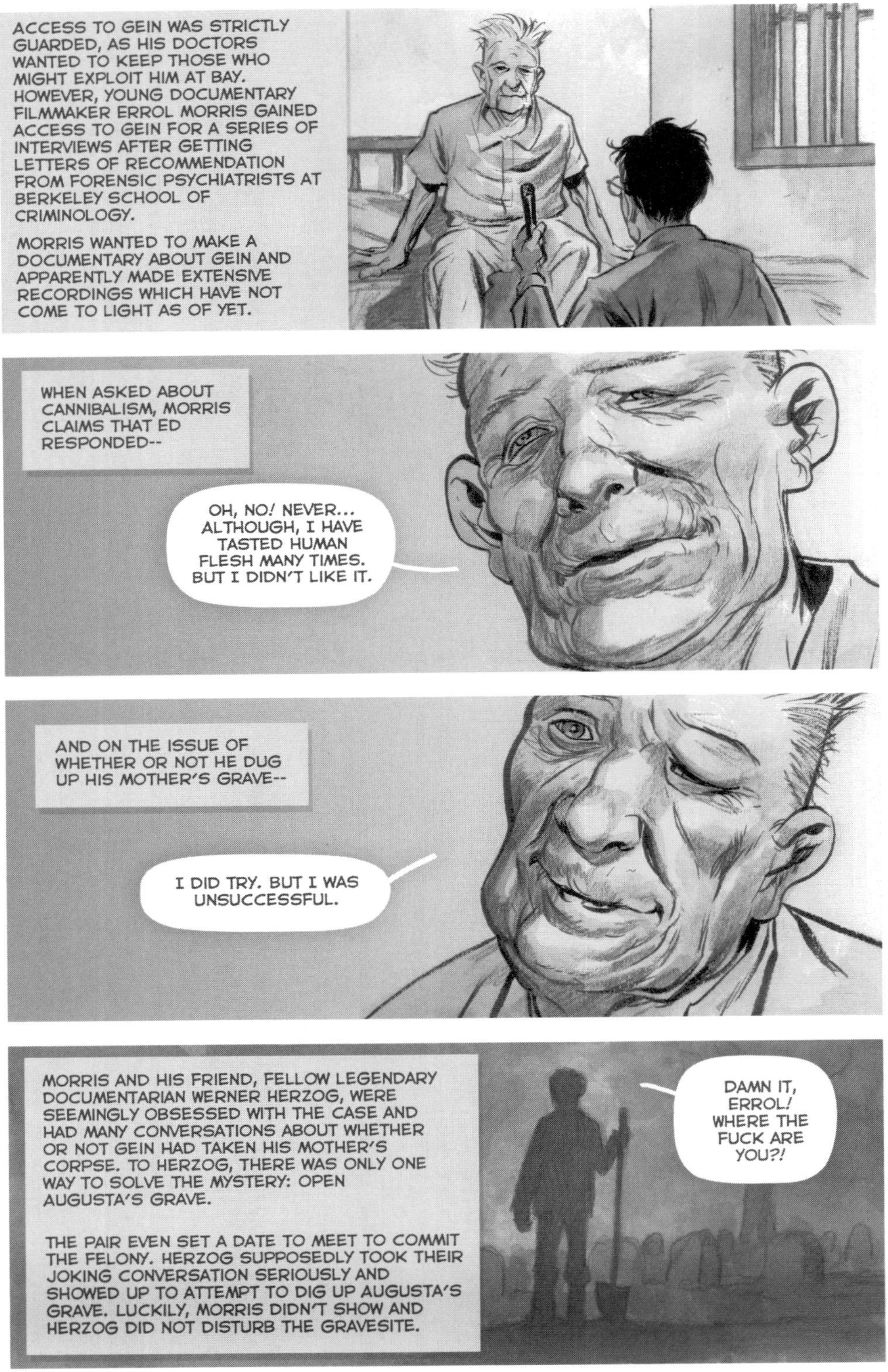
ACCESS TO GEIN WAS STRICTLY GUARDED, AS HIS DOCTORS WANTED TO KEEP THOSE WHO MIGHT EXPLOIT HIM AT BAY. HOWEVER, YOUNG DOCUMENTARY FILMMAKER ERROL MORRIS GAINED ACCESS TO GEIN FOR A SERIES OF INTERVIEWS AFTER GETTING LETTERS OF RECOMMENDATION FROM FORENSIC PSYCHIATRISTS AT BERKELEY SCHOOL OF CRIMINOLOGY.
MORRIS WANTED TO MAKE A DOCUMENTARY ABOUT GEIN AND APPARENTLY MADE EXTENSIVE RECORDINGS WHICH HAVE NOT COME TO LIGHT AS OF YET.
WHEN ASKED ABOUT CANNIBALISM, MORRIS CLAIMS THAT ED RESPONDED--
OH, NO! NEVER... ALTHOUGH, I HAVE TASTED HUMAN FLESH MANY TIMES. BUT I DIDN'T LIKE IT.
AND ON THE ISSUE OF WHETHER OR NOT HE DUG UP HIS MOTHER'S GRAVE--
I DID TRY. BUT I WAS UNSUCCESSFUL.
MORRIS AND HIS FRIEND, FELLOW LEGENDARY DOCUMENTARIAN WERNER HERZOG, WERE SEEMINGLY OBSESSED WITH THE CASE AND HAD MANY CONVERSATIONS ABOUT WHETHER OR NOT GEIN HAD TAKEN HIS MOTHER'S CORPSE. TO HERZOG, THERE WAS ONLY ONE WAY TO SOLVE THE MYSTERY: OPEN AUGUSTA'S GRAVE.
THE PAIR EVEN SET A DATE TO MEET TO COMMIT THE FELONY. HERZOG SUPPOSEDLY TOOK THEIR JOKING CONVERSATION SERIOUSLY AND SHOWED UP TO ATTEMPT TO DIG UP AUGUSTA'S GRAVE. LUCKILY, MORRIS DIDN'T SHOW AND HERZOG DID NOT DISTURB THE GRAVESITE.
DAMN IT, ERROL! WHERE THE FUCK ARE YOU?!

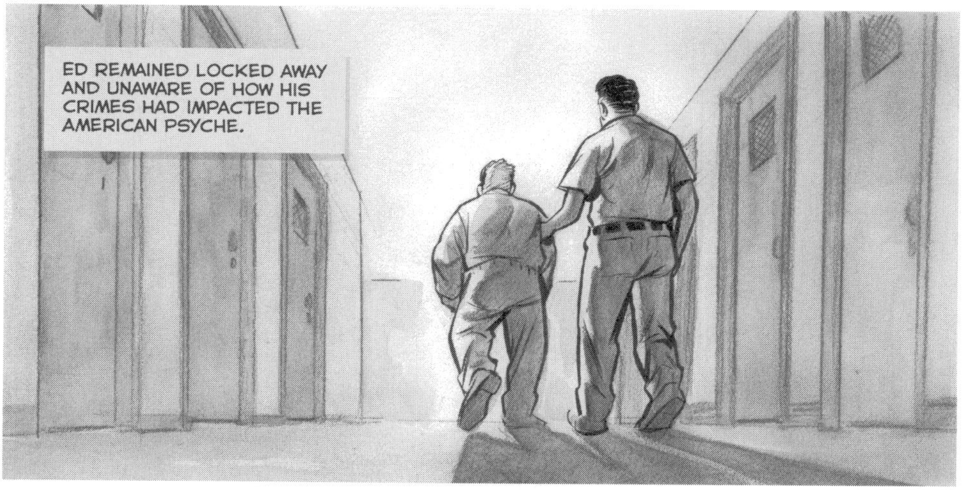
ED REMAINED LOCKED AWAY AND UNAWARE OF HOW HIS CRIMES HAD IMPACTED THE AMERICAN PSYCHE.

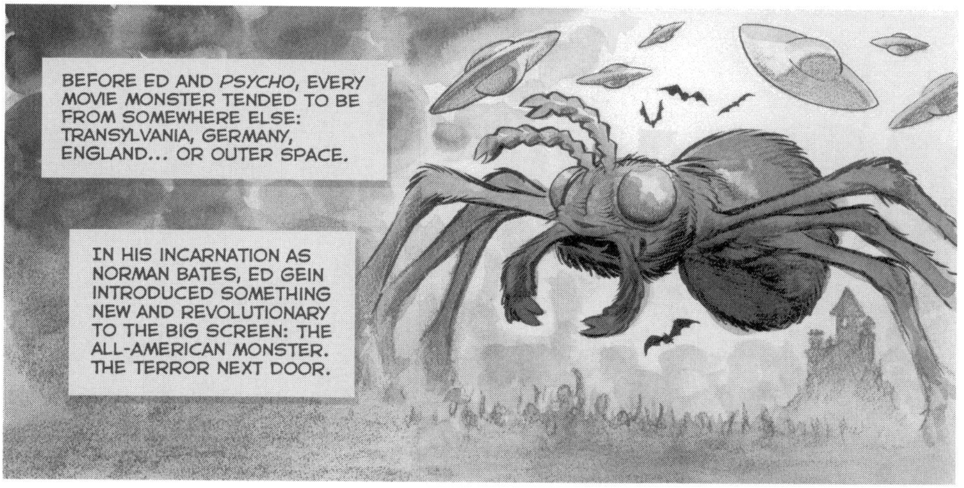
BEFORE ED AND *PSYCHO*, EVERY MOVIE MONSTER TENDED TO BE FROM SOMEWHERE ELSE: TRANSYLVANIA, GERMANY, ENGLAND... OR OUTER SPACE.
IN HIS INCARNATION AS NORMAN BATES, ED GEIN INTRODUCED SOMETHING NEW AND REVOLUTIONARY TO THE BIG SCREEN: THE ALL-AMERICAN MONSTER. THE TERROR NEXT DOOR.

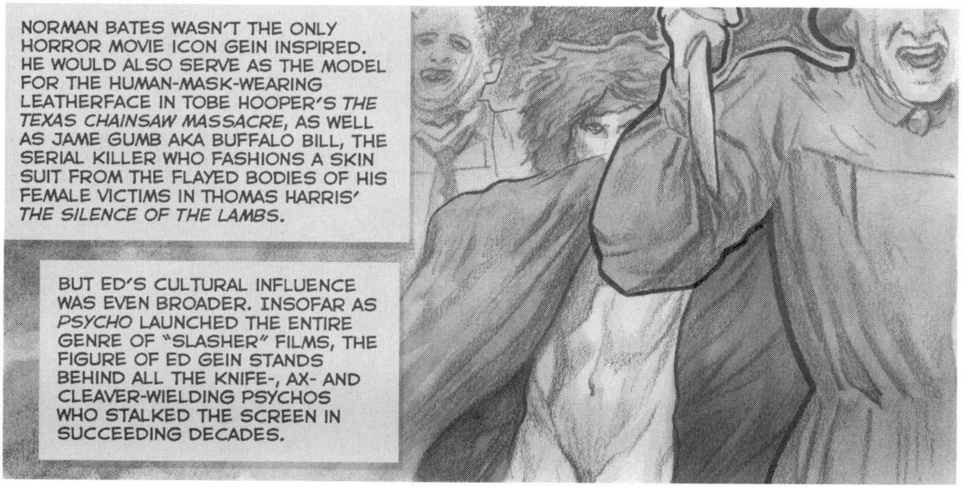
NORMAN BATES WASN'T THE ONLY HORROR MOVIE ICON GEIN INSPIRED. HE WOULD ALSO SERVE AS THE MODEL FOR THE HUMAN-MASK-WEARING LEATHERFACE IN TOBE HOOPER'S *THE TEXAS CHAINSAW MASSACRE*, AS WELL AS JAME GUMB AKA BUFFALO BILL, THE SERIAL KILLER WHO FASHIONS A SKIN SUIT FROM THE FLAYED BODIES OF HIS FEMALE VICTIMS IN THOMAS HARRIS' *THE SILENCE OF THE LAMBS*.
BUT ED'S CULTURAL INFLUENCE WAS EVEN BROADER. INSOFAR AS *PSYCHO* LAUNCHED THE ENTIRE GENRE OF "SLASHER" FILMS, THE FIGURE OF ED GEIN STANDS BEHIND ALL THE KNIFE-, AX- AND CLEAVER-WIELDING PSYCHOS WHO STALKED THE SCREEN IN SUCCEEDING DECADES.

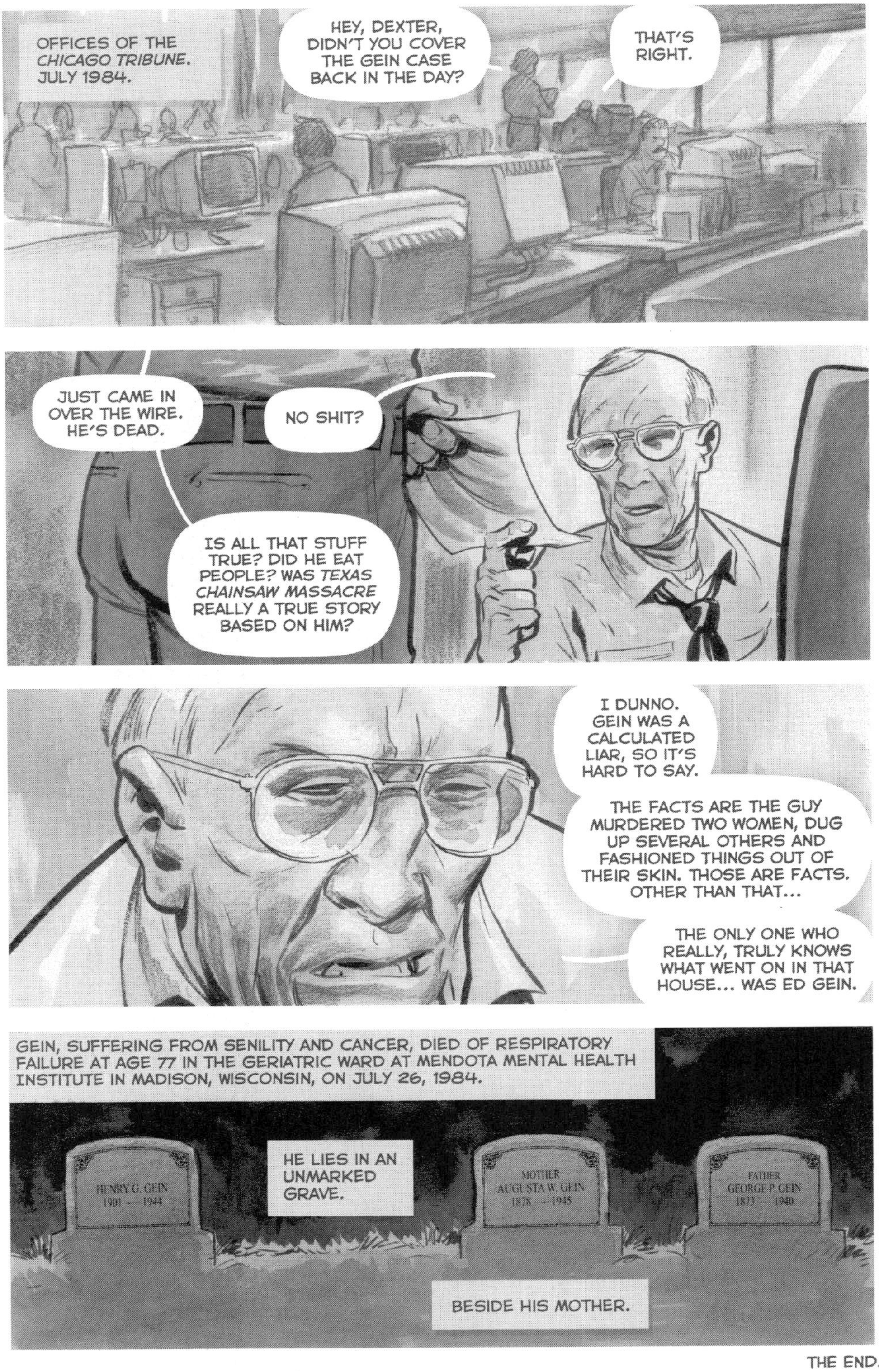
OFFICES OF THE *CHICAGO TRIBUNE*. JULY 1984.
HEY, DEXTER, DIDN'T YOU COVER THE GEIN CASE BACK IN THE DAY?
THAT'S RIGHT.
JUST CAME IN OVER THE WIRE. HE'S DEAD.
NO SHIT?
IS ALL THAT STUFF TRUE? DID HE EAT PEOPLE? WAS *TEXAS CHAINSAW MASSACRE* REALLY A TRUE STORY BASED ON HIM?
I DUNNO. GEIN WAS A CALCULATED LIAR, SO IT'S HARD TO SAY.
THE FACTS ARE THE GUY MURDERED TWO WOMEN, DUG UP SEVERAL OTHERS AND FASHIONED THINGS OUT OF THEIR SKIN. THOSE ARE FACTS. OTHER THAN THAT...
THE ONLY ONE WHO REALLY, TRULY KNOWS WHAT WENT ON IN THAT HOUSE... WAS ED GEIN.
GEIN, SUFFERING FROM SENILITY AND CANCER, DIED OF RESPIRATORY FAILURE AT AGE 77 IN THE GERIATRIC WARD AT MENDOTA MENTAL HEALTH INSTITUTE IN MADISON, WISCONSIN, ON JULY 26, 1984.
HENRY G. GEIN 1901 — 1944
HE LIES IN AN UNMARKED GRAVE.
MOTHER AUGUSTA W. GEIN 1878 — 1945
FATHER GEORGE P. GEIN 1873 — 1940
BESIDE HIS MOTHER.

THE END.

"DID YOU
HEAR WHAT
EDDIE GEIN
DONE?"

NOTES:
"JUST THE FACTS"

This graphic dramatization of the Ed Gein case is based almost entirely on primary source material: contemporary accounts from Wisconsin newspapers, forensic documents, psychiatric reports and more. In our depictions of Gein's early life and in a number of other places, we have created scenarios and characters based on his own confessions. Though the incident of childhood sexual assault has not been corroborated, it was rumored to have occurred. For the sake of narrative clarity, we have created two journalists — Jack Humple and Dexter Corben — as composite characters, representative of the scores of reporters who descended on Plainfield following the discovery of Gein's crimes. One character is wholly fictitious: the professor of ancient religions, Professor O'Hara, who serves as a spokesperson for our theory (itself based on deep research) about the ritualistic nature of Gein's grotesque practices.

Below are some facts that might be of interest to readers:

PAGE 10-11: Alfred Hitchcock's remarks are quoted from a famous interview conducted by renowned French movie director and critic François Truffaut.

PAGE 22: The Geins' store did take part in a Palmolive giveaway.

PAGE 27: We know from newspaper items that George Gein took subsidies of $14 for provisions, though the circumstances and purpose of these subsidies is unclear.

PAGE 29: The vaudeville superstar Eva Tanguay performed in La Crosse, Wis., months after the Geins had left the town. But the racy (for the time) image of the curvy entertainer surely would have sparked fury in the puritanical Augusta Gein.

PAGE 40: The staircase incident actually happened in La Crosse. We moved it to Plainfield for the purpose of narrative.

PAGE 104: The look of fictitious photographer Jack Humple was modeled after that of William Gaines as a tribute to the late EC Comics publisher. The character of Dexter Corben was given a broken nose to make him easily distinguishable throughout the passage of time in the book.

PAGE 141: In one of his interrogations, Ed Gein stated that, on the day he murdered Mary Hogan, he was at Pine Grove Cemetery looking for information about a girl who had been thrown from a horse. He then volunteered to help fill in a grave. Though we searched extensively, we were unable to find any information on the death of a girl thrown from a horse, or any record of a child being buried in that cemetery on December 9, 1954. The only burial in Pine Gove that day was that of an elderly woman who also happened to be named Mary. For dramatic purposes, we speculated that Gein was scoping out this grave to rob and was inspired to commit the murder of Mary Hogan upon seeing the name Mary on the gravestone. While this is conjecture, when asked if assisting in the burial inspired him to kill Mary Hogan, Gein replied, "I never thought of that. That could be."

PAGE 148: The severed head in Panel 1 is another EC Comics homage. It is meant to resemble the severed head on the cover of *Crime Suspen-Stories #22,* the issue used in the infamous Senate Subcommittee on Juvenile Delinquency that brought about the unjust end of EC Comics.

PAGE 197: Toward the end of the novel *Psycho,* after Norman Bates' arrest, Robert Bloch writes of the Bates case: "Some [newspaper] write-ups compared it to the Gein affair up north, a few years back."

PAGE 202: A statue of a human skin–wearing Aztec god called Xipe Totec — whose name means "our lord, the flayed one" — is part of the collection at the Kimbell Art Museum in Fort Worth, Texas. It can be viewed at: https://kimbellart.org/collection/ap-197939

PAGE 211: Thomas Harris' Buffalo Bill (*The Silence of the Lambs*) combines Ed Gein's skin suit obsession with the serial killer Ted Bundy's method of snaring young female victims by wearing an arm cast and asking them for help loading heavy objects into his car.

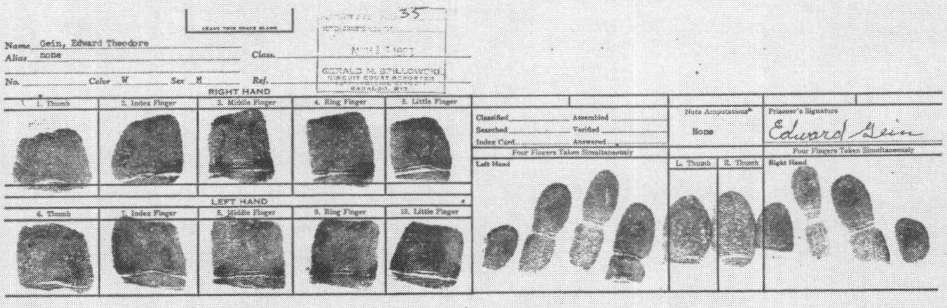
Name Gein, Edward Theodore
Alias none
Color W
Sex M
RIGHT HAND
1. Thumb
2. Index Finger
3. Middle Finger
4. Ring Finger
5. Little Finger
LEFT HAND
6. Thumb
7. Index Finger
8. Middle Finger
9. Ring Finger
10. Little Finger
None
Prisoner's Signature
Edward Gein
Four Fingers Taken Simultaneously
Left Hand
L. Thumb
R. Thumb
Right Hand

Edward Gein's fingerprints

APPENDIX I

The following appendix contains excerpts from an interview of Dr. George Arndt conducted in 1987 by Harold Schechter for his book *Deviant: The Shocking True Story of Ed Gein, the Original "Psycho."* Dr. Arndt was a psychiatrist who studied Gein extensively and published a seminal article on the case, *Community Reactions to a Horrifying Event.* Also present during the interview was Judge Robert Gollmar.

INTERVIEW: GEORGE ARNDT / ELKHORN, WI / MAY 30, 1987

HS: As you got to know Gein, what emerged?

GA: The other thing that came out was the personality problem, schizoidal personality.

HS: Very specifically, when you say schizoidal personality ...

GA: Lonely, isolated bachelor recluse. Withdrawn individual who does just his own thing. Comes in literally out of the cold now and then when he needs some supplies at a store or something like this, or needs to earn some cash to do something. But remember, this was before the days of medical assistance, and general relief was not easy to get in central Wisconsin because there were so many people who needed it.

HS: Would his schizoidal personality have been consistent with his functioning within a community for so many years?

GA: Yes.

HS: But he was subject to delusions.

GA: Yes, but that would have been the schizophrenia that could come and go.

HS: So, the schizophrenia and the schizoidal personality are distinct?

GA: Yes. One's more personality. It's a fixed way of coping and doing things all the way through one's life, whereas with schizophrenic reaction, you may have a man who's extremely upset, delusional, paranoid, suspicious temporarily. It can become permanent, or it can wax and wane.

HS: What was the nature of Gein's treatment?

GA: Remember he went in almost pre-tranquilizer. At least, tranquilizers hadn't found their way into forensic hospitals. The main thing was just allowing him to be there without pressure, stabilized, which was the old standard treatment for people who were in hospitals. And many of them did respond after a few months of that. Gein's behaviors were such that it wasn't safe to let him out. Because he was not one who could recognize that this was an illness and that this had to be prevented from recurring.

HS: Would he have received some kind of psychotherapy?

GA: People would meet and talk with him and he'd be involved in some of the assignments there. I know before my time there he was working in the lapidary shop.

GOLLMAR: I always wanted some of that jewelry, but I never could get it.

GA: When I was there in the 70's, people were still writing and asking for a lock of his hair and things like that (laughs).

HS: Would there have been a time when he was put on tranquilizers?

GA: He was not grossly disturbed in that sense.

HS: Did Gein ever tell you the details of his crime?

GA: Remember, I got involved with him later, when he had sealed over a great deal, and he did not want to go back over those things. It was not easy for him when he petitioned to get out. When the judge got him in the late '60s, that was a situation where he had improved — already a decade had gone by. And then he petitioned to get out in the '70s, when I got involved. I said, "Look, you're petitioning to get out. You're going to have to share with me and the other psychiatrists." And even then, he was reluctant. As time went by, the other psychiatrists and I did a report, and I kept saying, "He's gotten sicker in the last few months." Later, he got even sicker. It was a case of Gein decompensating as he got closer to getting out. I think one of the reasons for that he was wondering, *How am I going to take care of myself? I'm going to have to face the world again. I can't stay withdrawn like I have been here in the mental hospital, where I get three hots and a cot.*

APPENDIX II

The following appendix contains excerpts from an interview of Irene Hill Bailey conducted in 1987 by Harold Schechter for his book *Deviant: The Shocking True Story of Ed Gein, the Original "Psycho."*

INTERVIEW: IRENE HILL BAILEY / HANCOCK, WI / JUNE 4, 1987

HS: I've come across your name in a lot of the accounts. Gein knew your family pretty well?

IB: Well, yes. We used to have him come over and do odd jobs for us, you know. We were, at the time, in a little country store, and pretty much tied up. So, whenever we had something to do that we couldn't handle right then, we'd ask him to help out.

HS: What sort of jobs would Gein do for you?

IB: Oh, he'd run errands for us, like that mostly. At that time, we bought groceries from a warehouse in Wisconsin Rapids and you had to pick them up — they did not deliver — and sometimes we had him go and pick up a few things for us. And certain times, just personal things that we had him go get for us.

HS: How was he as a kid?

IB: Well, I didn't really know him much at that time, but he was always a guy with a big smile on his face, you know, and sort of, well, a little different.

HS: One question that comes up is, were people ever in his house? Did anyone know ... have any sense at that point?

IB: Well, no. Only he had shown different people these masks that he had made, and he told them that he had a cousin that had gotten these from, you know, these magazines or one thing or another. At that time, they had all this weird stuff they hung on the walls. And that's what he had told them.

HS: Everyone I've spoken to that knew him said he was very odd.
IB: Yeah, well, the thing I didn't like was just the way he seemed to want

to be accepted but didn't know how. He was always looking at all the young girls going by, and he'd have this little silly grin on his face that I didn't quite appreciate. [laughs].

HS: How'd you feel when they discovered the murders?

IB: Shocked, absolutely shocked. From that night until Monday morning, my family never ate a thing. We drank coffee, that's all. We were just in deep shock. Because he was there that night at our house.

My son, Bob, wanted to use the car, and the battery was dead. So, my husband said, "Well, why don't you get Ed Gein? Go get [Irene's daughter] Darlene's car and go over there and get Ed Gein to come over and go down and get a new battery for you." So that's what he did. He was going to take the truck, but Darlene said no because her husband had been out in the woods with it, and he'd taken off the running lights. She said she didn't want him on the road in the traffic — this was deer-hunting time — with that truck. So, she said, "You take the car and go over there." So that's what he did.

And he got Ed to come over and he took him down and they got a new battery and put it in the car. By that time, it was dinnertime, and he'd come over to the house, so I said, "Well, you might as well eat with us." So he did. And in the meantime, my son-in-law had come home. He'd been into the village and had heard what happened down there at the store. He come home and he told us about it. And Ed sat there, listening to it all, and he says, "Well, there must have been somebody pretty cold-blooded."

And we talked about it, and he seemed to me like he felt cold or something all the time. We had this space heater in the house at the time, and he kept hovering around that stove all night, all the time there, until it was time to eat. After a while, we heard that the state crime lab was coming in, and my son said, "I'd kind of like to go downtown and just see, you know, the activity around town." So Ed says, "Well, I'll take you down." And so he was going to take him downtown, and they had just got into the car when the officers come. They come over to the store. I had gone over there so my husband could come home and eat. I told my husband about it and he went home, and I'd been there maybe five minutes more when the officers come in there and wanted to know if I knew Ed Gein. And I said, "Yes, I know him. I've known him for years." They said, "Do you know where I can find him?" I said, "He's sitting right over there in my yard, right there in the car, unless he's taken off." I says, "They were going to go downtown to see what was going on."

So the sheriff walked over to the car. The car was running, Bob said, and they was just ready to take off. And the sheriff asked Ed if he would come over to the sheriff's car. He said sure, and he got in the car and that was the last I saw of him until they had the hearing.

HS: One thing I read said Gein claimed he couldn't stand the sight of blood, and he would never like to see animals dressed out and that sort of thing.

IB: I would think that would be false with the assumption that if he was going hunting all the time for rabbits and such, he was bound to see some blood there.

HS: Was he nice to you?

IB: He was very nice to me. There was only one time in my life that I've thought about afterwards. I know my neighbor there, Roselle, she used to worry because he'd park his car right up behind the store like that. And I'd go to the house for one thing or another, and he'd be left alone in there for sometimes three, four minutes. But one time, he was over there, and he was standing up at the counter, and I was on the other side of the counter, and he picked up this butcher knife and he run his finger along the top of the thing and looked at me kind of strange, and I said, "Ed, put that darn thing down! That's sharp! Before you get cut!" And he dropped it, just like that. But, what he had in mind, I don't know. I thought about that afterwards. At the time, I didn't think nothing of it. I was just thinking, put it down, because that thing had a real edge on it. My husband always kept the knives sharp there in the saw. But never in my life did I think he would hurt anybody, because he was just such an easygoing person and willing to help, except for one night..

My husband's uncle lived in a trailer house right outside, and he was not well at all. He had to go to the hospital, and my husband asked Bob to take the car and go over to Ed to see if he would take him. Bob went over there, and he said Ed was actually ugly that night. He didn't care about going at all. What it was all about, I don't know. But he did go, he took him.

Ed was always joking, you know, *I did this and I did that.* And he actually did do it! And he would just come right out and say it. That's why nobody took him seriously.

BIOS

Harold Schechter is an American writer who specializes in historical true crime. Twice nominated for the Edgar Award, he is the author of the nonfiction books *Fatal, Fiend, Bestial, Deviant, Deranged, Depraved, The Serial Killer Files, The Mad Sculptor,* and *Man-Eater;* the Amazon Charts and *Washington Post* bestseller *Hell's Princess: The Mystery of Belle Gunness, Butcher of Men;* the Amazon Original Stories collection *Bloodlands, Ripped from the Headlines;* and *Maniac: The Bath School Disaster And The Birth Of The Modern Mass Killer.* Schechter received his PhD in American literature from the State University of New York in Buffalo. A professor emeritus at Queens College, he is married to the poet Kimiko Hahn. For more information, visit www.haroldschechter.com.

Eric Powell is a multiple Eisner Award-winning comics writer, artist and publisher who has worked for every major comics company on such characters as *Superman, The Hulk, Hellboy, Judge Dredd, Star Wars* and *The Simpsons.* But he is mostly recognized for his critically acclaimed dark comedy series *The Goon.*

Phil Balsman is a graduate of the Kubert School, and in 2003 began his career as one of the founding members of the in-house lettering department at DC Comics. In 2007 he started doing design work for manga publisher Kodansha, and in 2010 he formed Odin Star Industries, where he and his wife (fellow Kubie Paige Pumphrey) work together in Brooklyn, New York. In 2018 he received the Eisner Awards for Best Publication Design and Best Archival Collection for his work on the *AKIRA 35th Anniversary Edition* box set. See his work at odinstarindustries.com.